IN SEARCH OF MIND

Books by Jerome Bruner

The Process of Education (1960)
Toward a Theory of Instruction (1966)
Processes of Cognitive Growth: Infancy (1968)
The Relevance of Education (1971)
Beyond the Information Given: Studies
    in the Psychology of Knowing (1973)
On Knowing: Essays for the Left Hand (1979)
Under Fire in Britain (1980)
In Search of Mind: Essays in Autobiography (1983)

BOOKS IN THE ALFRED P. SLOAN FOUNDATION SERIES

Disturbing the Universe, *by Freeman Dyson*
Advice to a Young Scientist, *by Peter Medawar*
The Youngest Science, *by Lewis Thomas*
Haphazard Reality, *by Hendrik B. G. Casimir*
In Search of Mind, *by Jerome Bruner*

THIS BOOK IS PUBLISHED AS PART
OF AN ALFRED P. SLOAN FOUNDATION PROGRAM.

JEROME BRUNER

IN SEARCH
OF MIND

Essays in Autobiography

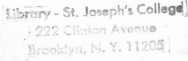

HARPER & ROW, PUBLISHERS, New York
Cambridge, Philadelphia, San Francisco, London
1817   Mexico City, São Paulo, Sydney

Grateful acknowledgment is made for permission to reprint:

Lines from "The Circus Animal's Desertion" and "The Municipal Gallery Revisited" from *Collected Poems of William Butler Yeats*. Copyright 1940 by Georgie Yeats, renewed 1968 by Bertha Georgie Yeats, Michael Butler Yeats and Anne Yeats. Reprinted by permission of Macmillan Publishing Co., Inc. and Macmillan, London, Limited.

Lines from "Renascence" from *Collected Poems*, by Edna St. Vincent Millay (Harper & Row, Publishers, Inc.). Copyright 1917, renewed 1945 by Edna St. Vincent Millay. Reprinted by permission of Norma Millay Ellis.

FIRST EDITION

Designer: Sidney Feinberg

Library of Congress Cataloging in Publication Data

Bruner, Jerome Seymour.
  In search of mind.
  (Alfred P. Sloan Foundation series)
  Includes index.
  1. Bruner, Jerome Seymour. 2. Psychologists—United States—Biography. I. Title. II. Series.
BF109.B78A35 1983   153'.092'4 [B]   83-47526
ISBN 0-06-015191-9 (U.S.A. and Canada)   83 84 85 86 87 10 9 8 7 6 5 4 3 2 1
ISBN 0-06-337035-2 (except U.S.A. and Canada)   83 84 85 86 87 10 9 8 7 6 5 4 3 2 1

In Memory of My Father
at last

Contents

Preface to the Series : xi

IN THE BEGINNING

1. Childhood Lost and Found : 3
2. Into the Academy : 22
3. Graduate School at Harvard : 32
4. The War Years—and Coming Home : 41

IN THE MIDDLE

5. Living in World Three : 55
6. The Judas Eye : 65
7. The Turn to Mind : 105
8. How Mind Begins : 131
9. The World and Words : 157
10. The New Curriculum : 177

IN THE END

11. Ornaments of Consciousness : 201
12. Extravagant People : 218
13. Living in Universities : 242
14. Da Capo : 274

Index : 295

Preface to the Series

The Alfred P. Sloan Foundation has for many years included in its areas of interest the encouragement of a public understanding of science. It is an area in which it is most difficult to spend money effectively. Science in this century has become a complex endeavor. Scientific statements are embedded in a context that may look back over as many as four centuries of cunning experiment and elaborate theory; they are as likely as not to be expressible only in the language of advanced mathematics. The goal of a general public understanding of science, which may have been reasonable a hundred years ago, is perhaps by now chimerical.

Yet an understanding of the scientific enterprise, as distinct from the data and concepts and theories of science itself, is certainly within the grasp of us all. It is, after all, an enterprise conducted by men and women who might be our neighbors, going to and from their workplaces day by day, stimulated by hopes and purposes that are common to all of us, rewarded as most of us are by occasional successes and distressed by occasional setbacks. It is an enterprise with its own rules and customs, but an understanding of that enterprise is accessible to any of us, for it is quintessentially human. And an understanding of the enterprise inevitably brings with it some insights into the nature of its products.

Accordingly, the Sloan Foundation has set out to encourage a representative selection of accomplished and articulate scientists to set down their own accounts of their lives in science. The form those accounts will take has been left in each instance to the author: one may choose an autobiographical approach, another may produce a coherent series of essays, a third may tell the tale of a scientific community of which he was a member. Each author is a man or woman of outstanding accomplishment in his or her field. The word "science" is not construed narrowly: it includes activities in the neighborhood of science such as technology and engineering as well as such disciplines as economics and anthropology as much as it includes physics and chemistry and biology.

The Foundation wishes to express its appreciation of the great and continuing contribution made to the program by its Advisory Committee. The Committee has been chaired since the program's inception by Robert Sinsheimer, Chancellor of the University of California—Santa Cruz. Present members of the Committee are Howard Hiatt, Dean, Harvard School of Public Health; Mark Kac, Professor of Mathematics, University of Southern California; Daniel Kevles, Professor of History, California Institute of Technology; Robert Merton, University Professor Emeritus and Special Service Professor, Columbia University; George A. Miller, Professor of Psychology, Princeton University. Earlier, Daniel McFadden, Professor of Economics, and Philip Morrison, Professor of Physics, both of the Massachusetts Institute of Technology, and Frederick E. Terman, Provost Emeritus, Stanford University, had been members. The Foundation has been represented throughout by Arthur L. Singer, Jr., and Stephen White; and Harper & Row, principal publishers for the program, by Winthrop Knowlton, Simon Michael Bessie and Edward L. Burlingame.

ALBERT REES
President, Alfred P. Sloan Foundation

IN THE BEGINNING

1

Childhood Lost and Found

It was Karl Marx, I think, who once proposed that evolution be studied in reverse, with an eye firmly fixed on the evolved species while glancing backward for hints. Common sense (and scientific puritanism) warns against: Better not know too clearly at the start what you are looking for lest you find it. Yet there are some peculiar reasons why looking back in just that way is what one had better do in exploring the course of an individual life. For while species develop in an extraordinarily chancy way from the bottom of the tree upward, human lives, even when haphazard, "reek with purpose." We ask of man but not of species whether they reached their goal— and whether they thought they did, whether they overreached, whether they persevered, even whether (in Auden's perspicuous phrase) we "preferred some going round to going straight to where we are." It is not that the existence of intention lessens the role of chance in human life, but rather that the meaning of chance changes once we intend. Any thirteen cards from a deck are equally probable or improbable, but once we decide to play bridge with them, a set that contains cards that are all one suit is seen not as chance but as providence. That we happen to have particular intentions or goals may, of course, be the result of strict determinism—inner or outer —but once they come into being, they create their own fate and their own drama.

And there is one other peculiar matter. Once we "intend," once we set a course for ourselves, we no longer go it alone. We commit ourselves to institutions and traditions and "tool kits" which, if our stars read right, will both amplify our powers and lock us in our path. The French say that if a life is to be interesting it must be a one-way street with no return.

All of which, while it may be obvious to common sense, creates peculiar problems for a psychologist, which I am and have been for nearly half a century. For if all of this is true, then when does a life "begin"? How shall we look at childhood before the years when intentions are formed and before we start the march down one-way streets? It is not that it is uninteresting, childhood, as part of a total life. But it surely does not account for a greater part of the passions and purposes of an adult. There was Churchill, indolent and incompetent as a schoolboy. Or Thomas Merton, the sensitive Trappist monk who wrote *The Seven Storey Mountain,* a shallow playboy as an undergraduate. What happened that gave them a second chance, or were their childhoods irrelevant save in some general developmental way that made it possible for them to grasp the instruments that then shaped their later lives? For them it is a little like the *New Yorker* cartoon of the two caterpillars contemplating a gorgeous butterfly above them. One says to the other, "You'll never catch me up in one of *those* things." But then there are those whose lives are as startling in their continuity: Sartre was destined to be a man of letters from the moment he could speak or put pen to paper as a "word child." Of course, we say, he was born into a literary culture and there he remained until the end of his days. So was Lord Russell. But was not Churchill from the start born and bred to wear the purple? When *does* a life start? Or is it a pedant's question, a spinoff from the futile effort to see life as one whole involving a single cast of characters acting out one play from start to closing curtain?

My childhood, as I look back, seems extraordinarily discontinuous with the rest of my life. I can find little in it that would lead anybody to predict that I would become an intellectual or an academic, even less a psychologist. I "happened on" what I became and I recreated my childhood as I became what I did. It was a childhood that was lacking neither in significant "models" nor in traumas of the kind that are popularly thought to produce deep and lasting scars. Yet those significant figures of childhood did not provide the models for my life—save perhaps in some stylistic way. And even the trauma of being born blind, sight not given until after two, seems not to have crippled me in any obvious way, although doubtless it shaped me somehow. The "meaning" of my own childhood history seems to me now to be dependent less upon the context in which events actually happened then, and more upon the context that was created by events afterward. The significance of early events seems to be like time running backward. It is much like Sir Frederic Bartlett's account of memory: The past is a reconstruction rather than a recovery, each reconstruction also containing the mark of what had been reconstructed before. The secret of history is forever lost.

My childhood took place in a prosperous middle-class suburb of New York, I the youngest of four in a nominally observant Jewish family, born in 1915 into the era that was to produce in those years *The Great Gatsby*, Rudolph Valentino, Charles Lindbergh and American Prosperity. It all has the feeling of a completed play, recalled from a distant shore beyond adolescence. I "left" my childhood in some substantive way—at least its place and its connections. The play was finished. But there is some way in which I have, like Peter Pan, remained a child—or rather, there is always a child in the cast ready to speak more lines than it seems were allotted to him.

Perhaps my adolescence was too sudden in its transformation: Everything changed, collapsed, after my father died when I was twelve, or so it seemed to me. My mother, restless to taste the world as a still youngish widow, moved each year and I with her, shifting schools but failing in confusion to shift allegiances, brooding over a lost world but not quite finding a new one. It seemed to extend limitlessly, quite unlike the *rite de passage*, the hullaballoo ceremonies by which the aboriginals of Australia try by every ritual means to compress and dramatize the difference between what went before and what comes after puberty. In any case, I came out on the other shore a proud swimmer, more than a survivor. And I became a man of intentions, oddly old-fashioned though that may sound. At least one side of me did. What much later on I came to think of as the "right-handed me."

But curiously, the less purposeful, more left-handed part of me is no more continuous with childhood than the first. For it too, however impulsive it may be, uses a medium of exchange that I did not encounter until later. Puzzling the relation of impulse and intention when I was in my thirties, right after the war, my good friend the novelist and critic Albert Guérard and I speculated a good deal—rather darkly in the main—about impulse and intention in literature. I think it was that he himself was torn between the two parts of his own talent: a writer of almost Gothic novels, and at the same time a lucid demystifier of Conrad, Gide and Hardy. Talking with him, reading him and "his" novelists, made me aware of how much one's irrational impulses and ideas are changed as they become translated into the myth and art of one's "culture." Or perhaps it is not that they change so much as that they then take on a new guise and, often, a new power. In psychoanalysis, my analyst once remarked that the successive crises in a life were not so much repetitions of the same theme as later editions incorporating what had transpired since. But as later editions became more "institutional" and came increasingly to be framed and phrased in the coin of the culture, they also became the coin by which one enters into the wider society. And then we begin our travel down one-way streets created by our culture.

When I was sixteen, two years before Adolf Hitler came to power, he became for me an apotheosis of Evil—not badness, but Evil intent on destroying those against whom it is directed. The existence of Hitler as a symbol and "text" for my emotions was a fact of contemporary history and not a product of my childhood. He was what the culture had on offer for a sixteen-year-old in 1931. The present, so to speak, was using the past, selecting and shaping and accentuating it in ways in which the past can never use the present. Hitler, in some way, preempted or incorporated the symbols that preceded him. Who knows what past bogeymen were channeled into the symbol of Hitler. It suffices that he was the mythic figure that turned the past into the present. Eventually I went to war against him of "my own free will."

Or, another instance, I read Herman Hesse's *Death and the Lover* when I was fifteen or sixteen. It is a sensuous tale laid in the fearful atmosphere of the Black Death. I "discovered" parts of myself in the novel—or rather, created a vehicle for my past, plagiarized Hesse's story to give a new shape to my "unconscious." Jung once had a patient, a young archaeologist, who dreamed in the coin of the vanished civilization he was studying. Like me, he was altering his history to fit the fabric of his life as he was living it. I do not think that this is merely "displacement" or some sort of repetition compulsion. It is in some unspecifiable way what growth is about: turning around on one's past and remaking it. It is the remaking that matters.

So when one launches on an autobiography, and especially an "intellectual autobiography," one is honestly perplexed about what to make of childhood as actually lived. There are some obvious things to relate that do little more than establish what one's temperament and intelligence were like "then." I was, for example, a bright child. School was at first more puzzling and boring than it was difficult. I was, according to family accounts, both indefatigable and single-tracked in my interests to the point of being considered absent-minded. I was cheerful and buoyant enough to be called "Sonny" (or was it "Sunny"?) until I was twelve. I suppose I continued to be "bright" and buoyant and relatively cheerful. I have certainly remained absentminded. And it is critical to what came after that I was a Jew rather than a Wasp or a Catholic or a Christian Scientist. There have been many times when, like most Jews, I have found being Jewish a burden—something that seemed irrelevant to matters at hand. But curiously, it has taken a lifetime to appreciate fully all that being a Jew entailed for me. An English friend of mine, a novelist, asked me once whether I felt more a Jew than an American, and I realized how difficult it is to define the facets of one's identity even to oneself, let alone to another. Certainly being a Jew has been as constant a feature of my life as, say, being "bright."

But what has all this to do with becoming a psychologist, or a particular kind of psychologist? Why, for example, having happened into psychology, did I get caught up in riddles about the nature of knowing? Reflecting on knowing is, after all, a rather strange activity, and even if it can be said to be an ancient and honorable one, surely one does not study it "just because it is there" any more than Mallory really climbed Everest for that. Was it because I was born blind? Do all redeemed victims of early blindness go my way? Or was it being raised as a skeptical Jew in a tradition devoted, long before Descartes, to the Principle of Doubt? I scared my sister Alice out of her wits one day, having concluded there was no God on the grounds that I could always think of other causes, by opening the window in our "sun parlor" during a fierce lightning storm and asking God to strike me dead if he existed. Was a butterfly lurking in the caterpillar? (It certainly pointed to an empirical career rather than a philosophical one!) Or is there some hidden secret in all this—knowing perhaps symbolizing a wish to spy on the primal scene, as Freud's more fanciful followers would have had us believe? Could any of these reasons make sense without one's taking into account the fact that the problem of knowledge was a central one in the society into which I moved, becoming an academic in my late teens? In any case, we had better put the matter of knowing on the retrospective agenda.

Or where did I pick up my faith in the power of the possible? I am not an optimist (my fear of the inevitability of loss is too great for that comfort), but I believe profoundly in the power of an existence theorem to change our way of doing things, thinking of things, even feeling. A great deal of what I have done in educational "reform" and in working for the better care of the young reflects the conviction that showing what is possible will alter what one will do. I recall the surge of admiration I experienced when for the first time I heard my father say, "Better to light a single candle than to curse the darkness." I think that the existence of a possibility sustains hope and that hope is as essential an ingredient of our life as a species as are our tools. Goethe's cry, *"Mehr licht!"* as he was dying brought tears to my eyes when I first read it. What had all this to do with? Did I in childhood fear being trapped, "the possible" symbolizing escape? Trapped by what or by whom?

Or why am I a fox rather than a hedgehog, preferring to know many things rather than one big thing? Was it my skeptical father who predisposed me against large and coherent systems of thinking by his taking such amused delight in recounting the myriad sources of human folly? I have often marveled at (admired and mocked, that is) men like McDougall, Parsons and Piaget, who believed in singular systems of thought. Curious that I should except Freud, but I have always thought of him more as a great dramatist than as a great theorist.

And finally, for these queries can become endless, what drew me into the way of the wandering intellectual rather than, to sharpen the contrast, an academic disciplinary specialist? There have been times when I thought I would have been better off in the seventeenth century, when it was more usual to follow one's curiosity than the straighter arrow of specialized study. I am not a good "discipline" man and do not like boundaries. Studying perception, becoming convinced that the true story lay in our powers of inference, I shifted to the study of thinking. When I sensed that the way we psychologists studied thinking was too square, too lacking in opportunity for the expression of intuition by our "subjects," I was drawn off to a season of studying an inventors' group and of reading mythology. And then, because the processes of thought are so swift, I retreated to the study of cognitive development, hoping to find my quarry in simpler surroundings moving at a slower pace, until I was finally studying infants. And then back I came from that venture, studying language because it seemed to be what was shaping the primitive processes of early cognition.

Perhaps this is part of being a fox rather than a hedgehog, of having a syntagmatic rather than a paradigmatic mind. Or perhaps it comes out of the early pleasure I took in "looking things up" in my father's beloved Eleventh Edition of the *Encyclopaedia Britannica,* where one thing naturally led to another. But then it might be the insatiable curiosity of the child who, at the end of his second year, is suddenly given the gift of sight. Yet really, I find all these "explanations" superfluous: I was only following my nose and if it looked from outside as if I were "shifting" fields, then it was plainly that the outside was not a good vantage point.

One final point, one that my late friend Henri Tajfel forced on me. He said that I was "prolific": "half-dozen articles a year for thirty-five years and ten books, how come?" To this query, I haven't a clue of an answer. I have never felt that I drive myself particularly hard, nor that I particularly cut myself off from other pleasures. I am neither hermit nor monk. I like research; so do most of my friends. "Writing it up" is for me an extension both of thinking and of dialogue. I find my thinking gets livelier when I have a chance to interact with it on paper. I bat out first drafts and revise, and reanalyze, often with a sense of what rubbish I wrote first time through. And more often than not, the process of committing to paper is conducted bearing in mind an imagined comrade—of whom there have been a treasured small company. Indeed, a very high proportion of my papers and books (with exception of "left-handed essays") have been researched and written in collaboration. That too makes for dialogue. It seems to me that there is nothing remarkable or prolific about it. Or might it be, simply, that like youngest children who have a passion for getting in the last word, committing to paper assures that it will be the last word—at least for a while!

We lived during my childhood in what was then a rather remote suburb of New York—Far Rockaway, where my family moved after my sight had been restored. Good luck and progress in ophthalmology combined to make for a pair of successful operations—the first eye shortly after age two. I have no memories connected either with early blindness or with my newly found sight, none whatsoever. My earliest memories are of a comfortable, large house in Merrill Road, a quiet suburban street. A gate through the fence at the end of the garden let on to a vacant field of meadow grass, across which a path led to the much grander house of my cousins.

There were three tiers of close family. At the top were remote grownups—my father and mother and even more distant Uncle Simon and Aunt Sarah. Next in age to my parents, uncle and aunt came a "middle" group—my older sister Min, my half-brother Adolf, and two cousins who were of an age—ten or fifteen years older than we were. "We" were the four of us. We were the center of my world: until I was six or seven, my sister Alice, not quite two years older than I, hot-tempered and affectionate, and my cousins Marvin and Julia. Alice, born when Min was already fourteen, was an "accident." I was conceived out of my mother's conviction that it is better to raise children in pairs—the child of a theory. I suspect it may have had to do also with my mother's deference to my father's wish for a son. My brother Adolf was from her first marriage.

Julia was my first love; I tagged after her like a puppy. I was the baby and I trailed along. I did not realize it then, but my sister Alice thought me "handicapped" by the heavy glasses required after my cataract operation.

My parents, as I have related, were remote figures, though they were physically present. My father traveled a great deal for business. He seemed an adventurous figure to me. My mother regulated the details of every day, principally health and nourishment. She was a woman with little fantasy or playfulness. I did not take my troubles to her and she did not confide hers to me. I do not recall her ever telling me a story—save a few glimpses from her childhood of Cossacks charging into the ghetto of Cszenstokowa, where she had grown up as a girl, images of houses being set afire and people fleeing: my first consciousness of being a Jew. She rarely read and was little interested in the world. She did her duty: an obedient wife and a routinely caring mother, yet a reserved and private person. I do not know to this day what annoyed her, angered her, delighted her. She loved animals, particularly strays, and we had a succession of cats and dogs, our own and visitors, which she would nurse back to health and to further wandering. With her children, and I was no exception, she virtually never showed any affection directly—by kisses or hugs or, for that matter, even by direct expression. My oldest sister told me years later that Mother had the theory that a show of affection or too much praise would cause her children to respect her less. I think that her theory perhaps fitted her temperament. She was never a demonstrative person and, oddly, I cannot remember her ever kissing me save to greet me after I or she had been away, and it was a rather ritual kiss. I do not remember my mother ever hugging me. I was puzzled, I recall, at the affectionate greetings my friends received from their mothers. It must have been a shock to my mother to find she had given birth to a blind baby. She never talked about it with me until she was an old lady and I a dutiful visiting grown-up son, and then she said very little. Her emotional commitment centered on ill health, and I was closest to her when being nursed through childhood illnesses—always marked by being fed a delicious concoction of "beef tea." I was, in her eyes, an "easy" child but a "delicate" one; Alice the difficult and robust one. Alice was matter-of-fact and worldly as a child, I head-in-clouds and enthusiastic. My mother distrusted enthusiasm and did not respond to mine. Ours was a truce between styles, affectionate enough, and it remained that throughout childhood and after. I do not recall ever quarreling with her. Nor do I recall her ever punishing me. She did not know me well nor I her.

My sister Min was my functional mother, the classic "oldest sister." She worked for my father, commuting with him most days into "the city." She was my confidante. It was to her that I turned with my enthusiasms and with tales about playmates. I was extraordinarily insensitive to the family crises of those years (or I have repressed them), for I have no memory at all of the hubbub precipitated by my father's business setback when I was six. His lawyer, it seems, had counseled him to invest in stocks of several grain and malt companies on the firm tip that Prohibition was about to be repealed. It was 1922.

My father had been born of a poor family in Poland, in an industrial town near Cracow. My mother came from a more prosperous family of merchants and professionals, and on her mother's death had gone to live with an aunt and uncle. When Father finished school in his teens, he took to selling woolens for a textile mill. My mother had married young before she met my father. She was carrying Adolf when her husband died suddenly and unexpectedly on a business trip to Berlin. Shortly after Adolf's birth my parents were married, and within a year Min was born. It was the turn of the century; the Czar was involved in the Eastern adventures that led to the Russo-Japanese War and was expanding his armies. My father and his brother Simon were in danger of being drafted, and raised money enough to get out. They came to America, to New York, planning to bring families later, when they had made some money.

There was room for my father's kind of energy and drive in the New World. Starting again as a woolen salesman, attending night school to learn the language, going to lectures at Cooper Union, within a few years he owned his own woolen business. He prospered and by the end of the war was a mover in local causes. He was a founder of Maimonides Hospital, worked for the Jewish Board of Guardians and for Masonic charities. He spent a good deal of time at it. By the time we had moved out to Far Rockaway, we had a car and a part-time chauffeur. By then he had gone into manufacturing watches. His brother Simon manufactured watch cases, but their business dealings were not happy.

My father's convictions were strong. Once, when he failed to find his usual paper at the station, the old *New York Sun,* I was sent off to the village to fetch a copy. Failing to find one, I returned with Hearst's *Journal.* He told me that I must never bring "that paper" into the house again, that Hearst was a wicked man who would stir up a war to sell his papers. It was not a scolding, but a tutorial. I was nine at the time. He had the gift of bringing his world to life in his talk. Mayor Hylan of New York was involved in a political scandal, or Galli-Curci was the finest voice at the Metropolitan Opera, or Houdini had brought off another of his miraculous escapes.

I cannot ever remember my father in shirtsleeves. Nor did we "do" things together. There were occasional visits to friends or relatives and "rides" in the car into the country on fine Sundays. And we occasionally had weekend guests. He had no interest whatsoever in sports and not much in young children. He was a reader, a music listener, a conversationalist, an autodidact with his own circle of friends whose families were friends of our family—mostly prospering businessmen who, like him, were immigrants to America making their way. He was a conservative in politics, an individualist in social philosophy who so admired Theodore Roosevelt that he named my sister for Roosevelt's daughter. He was patriotic, disliked "complainers" and "knockers" and "hypocrites." He was, I think, a snob and a climber, but a kindly one. He doubtless lived above his means, but in those heady days of the 1920s one's means were likely to be inflated by optimism.

In any event, he was my founding image of a man of the world. Seeing him off in midwinter on the *Leviathan* fueled my first fantasies about Europe. He also had taste for lovely things. I recall a Dürer engraving on the wall of his library, *The Expulsion from the Garden,* and odd little "treasures" from a dealer, "Mr. Magnificent," from whom he would buy a bronze head of an Arab boy or an Italianate Sheba descending a marble staircase.

We moved when I was six or seven to another neighborhood and I began "real" school and made new friends. Our cousins were less a part of us. It was an "open plan" neighborhood, adjoining back gardens and lawns running into each other, over and through which we would play our games, conduct Indian raids and pass on the news. For six years, until my father died, I led a blissfully happy child's life with a half-dozen or so close friends nearby. We were all Catholics and Jews, I suppose all upwardly mobile.

I don't recall feeling particularly or distinctly Jewish. Far Rocka-way was a "mixed" community. My father had left the local syna-gogue when I was ten—he did not like the rabbi and thought "heavy" ceremony was hypocrisy—and had joined the Reform tem-ple, a rather Protestantized expression of Judaism. The "temple" was presided over by a worldly and scholarly rabbi who was an admired friend of my father's. I think the shift from Orthodox to Reform may have been a form of climbing as well. I missed the ritual of religious holidays, the tent at Succoth, the celebration of Judas Maccabeus at Hanukkah, the fasting for Yom Kippur and the blast of the ram's horn at the new year. The Reform temple played down such emotionalism. The only spiritual religious feeling I can recall was for the mystery of the great scrolls of the Torah in the Ark behind the pulpit, a dark-red light flickering in the hanging lamp above. Where had they come from? When I first encountered the intensely ritualistic, "heavy" Orthodox praying at the Wailing Wall of Jerusalem nearly a half century later, I was my father's son. Had it to be *that* ritual?

Sundays had a special quality. My father was usually home, there were guests, and best of all, there was the romance of the Sunday *Times.* Radio was a new toy, and the newsreels were primitive. The rotogravure section of the *Times,* with its rich smell of brown sepia ink, never failed to thrill. The Kaiser chopping wood at Doorn, Royal Navy reviews at Spithead, President Harding with his cabinet round the great table, or the unsmiling Calvin Coolidge. In some curious way, the *Times* fitted in with the world of the "series" adventure books we all read in those days—the Rover Boys, Tom Swift, the Boy Allies. When I graduated to "crime books," to Nick Carter, my father told me they were "cheap sensationalism." He was dying at home.

I was closer to him than I had been when he was active. I never read another Nick Carter.

My brother Adolf lived at home in the new house in his rooms next to the attic, with a magnifying shaving mirror on a scissors extension in his bathroom that never ceased fascinating me. He and my father did not get on well, though I was only dimly aware of it. My brother was a rather scattered dilettante who never quite committed himself to any particular profession. My father, I think, regarded his dilettantism as a moral failing. It was my omnivorously interested older brother who was my companion on outings. His was the first bicycle on which I rode. It was he with whom I first fished. He it was who took me for my first airplane ride—in a Waco biplane in Harrisburg, Pennsylvania, where he had taken me on one of his rare trips (he was an agoraphobe) promoting Rolex Oyster watches, newly introduced into America. It was with him that I first visited the Akeley habitat rooms at the Museum of Natural History. After each expedition, I was obliged to write an essay. Adolf (a good golfer) let me caddy for him. Never once did he make anything of my vision. And I rarely let him down.

With the help of heavy glasses my central vision was corrected almost to normal. What removal of the lenses produces, if a cataract operation is a good one, is a narrowing of the effective visual field just by dint of putting the lens outside the eye, in a spectacle frame in front, rather than in the eye. When one moves the eye off center in ordinary ocular movement, the line of regard then passes through an inefficiently formed part of the spectacle lens and vision is distorted. In consequence, an aphakic viewer with spectacles must move his head rather than his eyes in order to keep a visual target both centered and optically undistorted. Nor can you change the shape of the lens if you have none in order to accommodate for distance. But that is a fairly trivial matter, for the pupil can focus the eye as a *camera obscura* by changing size. It was not until I was fitted with contact lenses as an adult that I realized what I had missed by way of peripheral vision as a child. But one can, after all, take in the world by successive positioning of a quite small cone of clear vision, even if one has to do so by moving one's head rather than one's eyes. I am sure that during childhood and after, the requirement of moving my head to see clearly gave me a specious air of great alertness! Indeed, if there is anything to the James-Lange theory (with its reverse-twist argument that we are frightened because we flee, sad because we cry, etc.), then perhaps I *was* more alert because I had to move my head about to keep up with the passing scene!

I started at school, the local public school, within easy walking distance of home, when I was six. My friends were there and we walked to and from school together. It was a rather dull and puzzling place. I had no particular intellectual curiosity where school was concerned. I tried to do what I was told, but that was not always easy, for much of the time it was not quite clear to me what it was that was wanted. I must have seemed a dreamy child to my teachers in those early years. My family took little interest in what school was about and, for that matter, so did I. There is nothing about my "academic record" before my teens to suggest that I would choose an academic career.

The only early "intellectual" experience I can remember (with the exception of sampling my father's *Encyclopaedia Britannica* in a rather random way) was my encounter with "light-years." I learned somewhere—perhaps from the *Book of Knowledge,* a children's encyclopedia—that some stars were so many million light-years away —light-years gripped me!—that their light would travel for millions of years *after* they were extinguished. This was so overwhelming to me that it produced a prick of tears and awe as I looked into the night sky. I was eleven at the time. I thought, could you travel out to the end of the light pencil and know when you'd passed it by the stars' disappearing? Then I found that *sound* traveled. It was dead of winter. I was at Lord's Pond, where we skated. A man was chopping down a tree on the other side of the pond. He raised his ax, struck the tree . . . pause . . . then *thud.* But *what* was traveling?

The one teacher at school who had impressed me (I had settled down to a medium-level truce by then) was Miss Orcutt. Just after the Sound Experience she confided to me in the schoolyard one very cold morning that the molecules were moving too slowly for her, and then told me about Brownian movement and molecules and that the faster the molecules went, the warmer it became. I decided later that day that the skin must be sensitive to molecules bouncing off it and that we felt cold when there were not many bounces.

It was just about this time that my father fell ill. It was a terminal cancer, though I did not know it. Perhaps that was the secret, the invisible and puzzling thing that I was searching to understand in the night sky. My father was home now, steadily home for the first time, in bed longer each week. I enjoyed his being at home, though I knew there was something terribly wrong that nobody would mention. The house was made strange by visitors. During his last months I had two dreadful nightmares.

In one of them, everybody in the world dies save me, and then a new generation appears. How do I tell them everything that was known before? (Perhaps that is why I still have his morocco-bound Eleventh Edition of the *Encyclopaedia!*) In another, I find myself in the midst of a trackless waste. I am in some sort of wheeled vehicle; I can go any way I wish. Which way shall I go? The choice was appalling and would wake me, terrified.

Loss filled that final year of childhood. My sister Min was married (I learned years later that the wedding was set ahead in recognition of my father's failing health), and it was only when she went off to Bermuda for a honeymoon that I grasped she had gone for good. The house grew darker. Then my cousins. One evening, behind the closed doors of my father's sickroom, there was angry talk, my uncle coming darkly from the stairs, departing without a goodbye to anybody. They had had a bitter business quarrel, something long-festering. Watches. They parted enemies. My father died a few months later. The last time I visited my cousins' house was the February afternoon of my father's death. I was sent to tell them. After the funeral, I did not see them again for thirty years.

In the months following I had two recurrent nightmares. In one, an egg in a plain white egg cup cracks as I look at it, and I wake in terror. In the other, I hold the secret knowledge of where I have hidden my father's body and I am in imminent danger of being found out. When I wake I am unsure whether it is a dream.

Looking back now as a psychologist and an adult, I know how very ambivalent I was toward my father, and how much that ambivalence provided fertile soil for later values. I loved his worldliness and his wit. His travels brought the world near, and particularly brought Europe near. His wit made the world an exciting and manageable place. Unlike the classic case of the American child of a European immigrant father, I did not reject him, and the idea of being "ashamed" of him never crossed my mind. He was too powerful and vivid a presence in any setting he chose to enter. But I can recall episodes in the year or two before his death that speak to my silent rebellion—besides the one in which I stood at the window in the thunderstorm daring God, if there was one, to strike me with lightning! One had to do with being sent home from a neighbor's for misbehaving. My father was furious—not at me but at the neighbor, whom he said that he could buy and sell ten times over. I loved having him on my side, but I hated what he said. And on another occasion, he forbade me to bring a black school friend home, the unspoken implication being that he was not a proper playmate.

And so I became a European in spirit, my father's son, a post-adolescent Communist and "premature antifascist" who denounced the world of business and the measure of money, though I never dreamed of renouncing the trust fund my father left to see me through college. In some puzzling way I remained in love with my father's style and at war with his aims (or what I created and re-created as his aims while I was finding my way to my own).

After my father's death in 1927, my mother began to move. She had, curiously, come to life. Before, she had always dressed rather somberly. Now her wardrobe brightened. She had no plans save, I think, to break a little with the past and start a new life. We moved the year after, just as I was about to finish school with my "gang" in Far Rockaway. We kept moving. Before we were done with it, I was to attend six different high schools in four years. What *I* found was the water. I took to it first with three friends: Lenny, Justin and Whitey. We were summer water rats; we lived constantly in each other's company my fourteenth and fifteenth summers, always by or in the water. And in Florida, where we went winters, I explored the canals and the harbor, fishing for amberjack and jacklighting for shrimp in an old skiff. Later there was an outboard motor.

My formal "secondary" schooling was appalling, though my scholastic record was satisfactory enough. I never stayed anywhere long enough to get really involved with teachers, or indeed with the continuity of school subjects per se. I was not particularly "popular," nor was I disliked. It was a time spent mostly with one or two friends or, simply, alone. I tried to conform to teenage norms in dress and talk, but I was not very good at it. I think I was considered a rather queer kid—"nice enough, you know, but funny." At my high school in Florida, I "went out" for track. I even became captain of the team, such as it was. It seemed a little silly to me, although I was proud of it. I was not a *bad* quarter-miler. I had been at the school the winter before—my mother's first Southern wandering. When I returned the next winter, the teacher who "coached" track asked me if I would come out again, and when I did, he told me I was to be captain. That in turn earned me a "letter," a high school sweater with two stripes and a star on its left arm. Wearing it, I felt like a fraud.

It was a period of becoming self-conscious and ashamed of being a Jew. I was the perennial stranger needing entry. Even coming home to my friends, I needed to be reaccredited. I developed a few ingratiative skills, but my heart was not in it. I settled for the company of a few other kids who were shy, or waterborne, or more likely both.

I *did* pick up some intellectual tricks, though. I had a French teacher, a South Carolinian lady, whom we all adored. I turned my mind to learning French and learned it. I liked mathematics and was good at it. I enjoyed history and read it with pleasure. But in all my years of high school, I had no serious course in science save, of all things, one in physical geography taught by a blind and elderly teacher at the prep school to which I was sent in my last year because my sister and brother-in-law felt that I should take more Regents' Examinations in the State of New York in order to get admitted to college. It was a year spent mostly alone. The school was a "tutoring school" and I lived by myself in a rooming house on the edge of the Cornell campus—walking miles into the country, reading, studying, utterly out of time and place. I fitted no categories. Interestingly, I did rather enjoy the time alone, particularly time studying. And it was good luck too, for I did take a rash of Regents' Examinations and did well enough at them to be able to get into college the next year.

What a curious adolescence! I longed for something but did not know what. I read a good deal, quite undirected—Sinclair Lewis's novels, Richard Halliburton's travel books, Raphael Sabatini, that Herman Hesse novel. I read poetry and found Edna St. Vincent Millay. There was something for the sixteen-year-old in lines like

> Deep in the earth I rested now.
> Cool is its hand upon the brow
> And soft its breast beneath the head
> Of one who is so gladly dead.

My mother wandered on—in search of health and company, back and forth to Florida, to California, to "the country." I admired her pluck. In Florida, she went for her swim every day, rain or shine.

Girls were rather remote. They were mostly at parties, at which I was not very good. I was shy, ill at ease, and thought of myself as rather ugly—bad complexion, heavy glasses, not much small talk. My sweetheart at sixteen was the sister of one of my water rat friends.

We necked lightly. I was not much for girls. That was part of a later waking up.

Her brother was a gifted and eccentric boy and one of my closest friends. It was he who got us interested in racing outboards. His father bought him a sliver of a racing shell, duly named *Demon,* and the water rats became the "Demon crew." It was our first venture into expertise—real expertise. We would Simonize her upturned bottom and rub in graphite to form a surface so smooth that one could blow a penny along it. And we ran a mix of Bon Ami powder and light oil through the engine to polish the inner surfaces. The propeller in the underbody, detached from the shaft, would spin like a top. We were at it endlessly as soon as we reassembled for the summer. Weekdays we tinkered. Weekends we raced. Lenny was a daring and clever boat handler. He got better; we all got better, our "Demon crew." We shared. We read manuals as religious novices read the lives of saints, tested weird fuel mixtures, tested weight distributions. It was heady stuff for sixteen-year-olds. The payoff came the second summer, in the Round Manhattan race in 1932, the "big" race. *Demon* took first honors on corrected time. Lenny received a huge cup and there he was that winter in a full-page ad in *Motor Boating,* sponsoring Mobiloil Marine! That was our last summer. We went our ways to college. I know now that the "Demon crew" was my first taste of collaboration, indeed collaborative research. The four of us were a team in that intense way that adolescents form teams—and research workers!

That fall I left home, or, better, left my mother and went off to Durham, North Carolina, to become a freshman at Duke. It was in September of 1933. I was seventeen. Hitler had come to power the preceding January. Roosevelt had just been elected to office. The country was deep into the Depression. My life was about to change drastically to another script.

There is an essay or a letter of Arnold Bennett's, written in reaction to a visit to France. He remarks on Frenchwomen and Englishwomen. The French, he says, sacrifice the girl to the woman, the English the woman to the girl. It is a fatuous remark, perhaps, but it set me thinking, when I read it, about the functions of immaturity. Little question that in some fashion a culture "uses" the immaturity of its children to shape them, to "socialize" them, and there have been times in the history of the social sciences when this "socialization process" has been a major preoccupation of scholars. But there is one feature of socialization that has rarely been written about. It has to do with the degree of commitment and the kind of commitment that a home or a community or, indeed, a culture imposes on the young who grow up in it. Perhaps it is what one means in the psychoanalytic sense by identification—the process of modeling oneself on others or on roles that are defined by one's group.

I suppose one of the distinctive things about play in childhood is that it buffers the player against too literal a commitment to whatever it is one is playing at, while at the same time giving the player a chance to explore possibilities. Many societies, indeed, are said to be highly permissive about play (and commitment?) in childhood and then mark by strict ceremony the "passing out" into adulthood, at which point the child becomes a man or woman with strict limitations on what remains possible. It is a gripping theme, the transition from the one estate to the other, and I have rarely enjoyed an intellectual task more than the one that led to a paper I presented on it as the keynote address to the International Congress of Psychology in Tokyo in 1972. I shall come back to it in a later chapter, "How Mind Begins," but I need to say a few things about it here, looking back at my own childhood, and particularly on the matter of early commitment or its lack.

I doubt my family had any firm ideas about what they wanted me to do. I think my father vaguely harbored the idea that I should be a lawyer and I suspect this was based both on the Jewish immigrant's wish to "better" his children by steering them into the professions and on his admiration and friendship for his own lawyer—a rather stiff gentleman always referred to before us as Mr. Neckritz. I do not recall anybody in my family ever trying to "interest" me in any particular profession or indeed any way of life save that of being "respectable middle class," which had to do with standing on your own feet, not cheating or lying, and earning a decent living—and much more tacitly, being loyal to family, friends, community; and even more implicitly, being a Jew. That was never defined. It did not mean being religious (my family was certainly not that) or even being a *good* Jew. It meant something about being compassionate, in any case about not being cold toward the human condition, and it meant not so much being intelligent as being diligent about using your head —your *Kopf*. I think too there was a hidden agenda in my father's Judaism: It was antiritual.

That was not a very heavy heritage from childhood and it did not impose any sense of binding commitment on me. There were no economic pressures to create the kind of anxiety that makes an adolescent tense about occupational choices. I know we were "comfortable" and money was not discussed; indeed, I don't think my father even discussed it with my mother, which may have been why she later let my brother, with no outside advice, invest and lose a very large sum of her money in the stock market. Fortunately, it was not all lost. In any case, all through childhood I was like an unhatched chick living rather dreamily off a yolk whose constancy was such that I was hardly aware of it.

When I was hatched, it was into a world I did not understand: My father was dead, my family scattered, the rate of change too great for me to latch onto anything very concrete. The six high schools were, of course, a storm to live through. The experience kept me uncommitted yet, oddly, longing. I suppose I was lucky in temperament. I went my way cheerfully enough, and from those years I retain flash-bulb memories of enormous beauty, many of them, curiously, connected with water, as for example looking down through a glass box at tropical fish swimming around an old wreck a friend and I had rowed out to in Biscayne Bay, or the skip rise around me of a school of amberjack reflecting the late-afternoon sun. In some way, I was in storage all those years—either in the closed egg of childhood or behind the defenses I had built to cope with an uprooted adolescence.

Going off to college, then, was going to my first home after childhood (and, as it turned out, my permanent one). I went with a confused longing. It never occurred to me that I was escaping, and it surely was not that. My son Whitley once complained to me in jest about *his* search for discontinuity in his school experience—going from Shady Hill to Phillips Exeter to Harvard, each slightly more of the same, indeed perhaps too much so. Mine was not like that at all. For me, going to college (after I discovered what it meant to be there for four years, in a kind of paradise) was the caterpillar finally getting "up in one of *those* things." I think that the curiously light commitment of my childhood is what made the decade that was to come so intense, so committing and (in certain respects) so full of delayed aches and pains.

But let me turn to that now.

2

Into the Academy

I was surprised when I was accepted at Duke. My record was so confused after all those schools that I thought perhaps nobody would accept me. I had no idea what to expect. I took a sleeper to Durham, North Carolina, in September 1933. When I woke early in the morning and raised the blind, the train was racing across red clay country, rednecks and blacks with tin lizzies and mule carts at the crossings. I flinched. But in a few hours, I was "on campus," a Gothic extravaganza in the midst of a great pine forest. It was the custom to greet whomever one met on the paths and walks, and I was charmed by the "Hey, ha you" of my Southern fellow students. In a few days I was installed in my room in Kilgo Quad, with a delightful Philadelphia Quaker for a roommate and a lively gang on our "entry," as the subdivisions of the quadrangle were called. We felt "at home together" almost at once—ate together at the Union, had bull sessions late into the night. There was the son of a trainer of trotting horses from Goshen, New York, a gentle and spare lad we all felt protective toward. And a serious, slightly older classmate from Pittsburgh, who was full of cheerful industry and into all manner of enterprises. The mix was remarkable, as I think about it now. A redheaded New Yorker, a Jew, was the most courteous among us. He had been sent to Duke by his father—a banker, a "cotton factor"—to learn more about the South. And there was the son of an immigrant Italian postal clerk from a New Jersey bedroom suburb of New York. There were two or three Southerners, but they had their own friends. That first year, we were our own community.

We were freshmen, and in no time we had fallen into the under-graduate pattern. The psychologist Roger Barker comments in one of his papers that the best predictor of human behavior is *where* the somebody is. In the post office, we behave post office, no matter what else we may have on our agenda. We were Duke freshmen: we went to football games, wore our "beanies," dated freshman girls, gossiped at the Union, went to classes, gambled for small stakes, behaved "Duke freshmen." Bull sessions were about sports, our professors, girls, campus personalities—and just a few tentative ideas ("Is beauty all in the eye of the beholder?"). It was about as tribal as one can get in a modern society. And it was perfect—an easy entry into the anteroom of grown-up society. It was not difficult to become what in those days was "Joe College," a way of talking, thinking, relating. It was the year of Garbo's *Queen Christina*, of the musical *Roberta* on Broadway, of "Smoke Gets in Your Eyes." In the Men's Union after dinner each evening, student jazz bands played for a crowded hour. Hitler and the Reichstag fire, the Depression, and the darkening world were more in the occasionally read *New York Times* than in everyday consciousness.

It lasted until Christmas and it was a period of camaraderie, toler-ance and fellowship that was new and delicious for the dozen or so sixteen-to-nineteen-year-olds on that entry in Kilgo. The "sorting" started when we returned. It was Rush Week; the college fraternities began "looking us over" as possible "pledges" who would become full members the following year. I must have been exceptionally naive: It had not crossed my mind that Jews were not acceptable—which I learned late in the week, when one of my fraternity hosts, upon my mentioning that I was Jewish, told me apologetically that *his* fraternity was not permitted to elect Jews. I felt as if a great gate had been lowered. On one side was a world in which fraternities and philistines did their brainless divisive thing, and if that was their world, they could have it. Rush Week ended the idyll of freshman year, and by the end of the year we had sorted out into groups that mirrored the wider world. Without quite realizing it, I drifted or was siphoned into the "brainy" set, somewhat apart and out of the spirit of undergraduate "pep." We thought of ourselves as more worldly, more intellectual, more detached, less "childish"—but it was all rather tentative.

Just before that first Christmas, before the end of the idyll, I went to a performance of Handel's *Messiah* in Duke chapel. The classic lines from Matthew rang out: "The trumpets shall sound and the dead shall be raised, be raised incorruptible." The image of my dying father and the guilty dream of hiding him in secret burial leaped to mind. I did not weep; the tears simply flowed, as if unstopped. I walked the twilit, winter-chilled, alien North Carolina town for two hours afterward. I cannot remember anything except loneliness and relief. My war with my mother's detachment was over, my yearning for my father temporarily done. I had found a new home. As my train moved back toward New York across the Jersey meadows, I vowed I must never again be hassled by my family. I had declared my independence, or so I thought.

Eventually I landed in psychology. That it happened to be psychology was partly the place, partly the people, partly the times. I had gone to Duke, vaguely expecting I would go into the law (with that image of our much respected family lawyer in mind) yet vaguely thinking I would shop around. My introduction to psychology was through William McDougall—worldly, rather plodding in lecture style, with bursts of wit, an impeccable and alien figure one could see walking the college paths in heavy tweeds even as winter turned into summerly spring. It did not "grab" me, his introduction to psychology: too patly argued and not enough questions left.

It was what followed that was to engage me, lectures given the next year in comparative psychology by Donald Keith Adams, and in neuropsychology by Karl Zener. I was caught by the idea of the evolution of mind. Adams and Zener were fresh from Berlin, where they had worked with Köhler and the budding young Kurt Lewin, apostles of the still "new" Gestalt psychology. Indeed, the first "battle" within psychology of which I was aware was between Thorndike (who interpreted his cats' behavior in puzzle boxes as blind trial-and-error shaped by rewards and punishment from outside) and Adams (whose proposal was that adaptive behavior in puzzle boxes grew out of the hypotheses generated by the organism in response to the available cues in the environment). If the environment contained relevant and combinable cues, animals would respond with "insightful" hypotheses. But you could also design blind environments that would make their inhabitants look stupid. The difference between Thorndike's cat's world and Adams's was that in the former there was a bare cage, a string hanging down isolated from the middle of the ceiling (which, if pulled, miraculously caused a gate to open or a bit of food to enter). In the world of Adams's cat, the string was visibly connected across the ceiling of the cage to the latch that held the door. Thorndike's animals were sampling their world for loose ends, hoping to hit on something, anything. Adams's were scanning a perceptually connected environment. What else for Thorndike's cats but to move, seeking by random trial and error?

It is a curious thing about those early-encountered "paradigms" or "metaphors." One never knows where they will lead. Yet echoes of the Thorndike-Adams controversy led me years later to a "hypothesis theory" of perception, that the perception of events was governed by hypotheses generated by available cues and by programs for putting them together. That in turn and even more years later led Noam Chomsky (as he once reported) to the notion of a Language Acquisition Device that generated hypotheses about the grammar of well-formed utterances. And still later, for there is no stop to it, the same metaphor led me to a theory of thinking and then of education.

Duke in the 1930s mixed the high intellectual endeavor of the minority with fraternity life, gala football Saturdays and big-band "proms" for the majority. The spanking new Gothic campus, laid out as a hollow cross, with a bronze statue at the intersect (James Buchanan Duke, erect with cigar in hand), was the home of a very mixed faculty, distinguished newcomers side by side with holdover hacks. The "course offering" for freshmen was dreary. It was still the era of "compulsory" courses—a particularly dull one in English composition, full of banalities about "good communication," taught by one of the hacks, and even a required year-long one on the Bible in deference to Duke's Methodism, my section taught by an ex-preacher in homiletic style. (Were I forced to teach such a course, I think I would organize it around the Devil, as in parts of Milton's *Paradise Lost*.) But I was sustained by a "fast" math course on the calculus and by Pierre Loti's *Pêcheur d'Islande*, taught by a lively young instructor, my first encounter with symbolism as an idea.

Whatever happened after Christmas of freshman year? Was it the narrowing circle of friends? Something turned. I have never seriously been bored since. Stephen Spender told me that after his first term at Oxford, *he* was never bored again. Is there some strange intellectual chemistry in late adolescence?

The year ended. I came home. It no longer felt like home. After a few weeks, I signed on as a porter in the Steward's Department of a cruise liner doing a Central American tour. It was grinding, dull work, cleaning, setting up "horse races," loading cases of rum in

Jamaica and off-loading baggage in New York. It was a rough world, working the ships. A riffraff gang made up the porters' crews in those days—surprisingly sentimental, always on the edge of rackets and petty crime, yet helpful to each other. I was egged on by my mates into a fight with another porter, who was ribbing me too hard as a "college boy." To my relief, he backed down with the classic "What's the matter, can't you take a joke?"

How curious. I date my "continuous" adult life from that summer. Return to college was picking up a thread. I roomed with a mathematician-athlete, a Jew, the son of immigrant parents in Chicago. Lee Arnold had come to Duke on an athletic scholarship as a schoolboy football star. *His* freshman year had ended with the discovery that he liked mathematics better than football and that he was good at it. It was from him that I first heard of Riemann, Lobachevsky and alternative geometries. He was the first I ever heard to express the view that the foundations of mathematics stemmed from the nature of mind and not from "nature." We shared that adolescent intoxication of thinking and talking about our own thoughts. Eventually the Athletic Department took us on to tutor "athletes" in academic trouble—our first taste of teaching. Lee eventually became a professor of aeronautical engineering at New York University. We must have been a pair of incipient little professors even then—though it would never have occurred to us.

I finished the undergraduate requirements on the double and started graduate work a year early. A lively group of graduate students had been drawn to Duke by the academic "stars" it had lured away from other universities. Our cigar-smoking donor, James Duke, had left the university a forty-million-dollar endowment. The graduate school was small, the Psychology Department distinguished. The philistinism of Durham, North Carolina, strengthened our in-group bonds. We were our own little academy, we graduate students. We drank beer with corned beef sandwiches at Levy Brothers in the heart of Durham, talking of Sigmund Freud, Malinowski, Bernard Berenson, Aldous Huxley.

Wealth helps! There was a rich flow of visitors come to lecture at Duke. They sharpened intellectual debate. Aldous Huxley (himself!) talked on scientific utopias; Margaret Mead on cultural relativism; Edna Millay read her poems and flirted with young men. Psychology had its own weekly colloquium, glittering with what seemed to me "great names." We did not want for worldliness.

Those late 1930s created something of a pressure cooker in that isolated faculty of newcomers. Intellectual and political debate was intense. The New Deal, a new wave of labor organization in the South, the Japanese invasion of Manchuria, Mussolini's attack on Ethiopia, Hitler's patently evil intentions—all these made for a spiritual restlessness in that smug setting. We cast about for ways of expressing this discontent.

I refused to attend the compulsory weekly chapel and wrote bitterly (too bitterly) to the dean about compulsion at a time when dictators were rising in the world. I was suspended. The dean was appalling! The magisterial McDougall, champion of lost causes, heir of dissenting Mancunian Whigs, came to my rescue. I was reinstated, to work as a volunteer in his laboratory—on his brave but futile experiments to prove that Lamarckian inheritance worked in the genetic transmission of intelligence. The next year I had another seizure of conscience. Some seniors, disturbed by reports of widespread cheating in the College, had banded themselves together as an anonymous "honor society" and announced they would report any cheating they observed to the dean. This time I wrote a long (and surprisingly cool) letter to the college paper, condemning vigilantes and informers. No cause could justify them. Better teaching and a more serious intellectual atmosphere were the only answers. The letter produced a flurry. The dean (it was the same one who had suspended me over the chapel issue) was forced to call off the "honor society." I had made an enemy. From then on, I was a "troublemaker." I found I liked the role. I was a bumptious and self-important young man.

Psychology was almost as intense a subject for our little group as politics. It too had become a little "politicized." There was a "debate" in those days as to whether learning was passive, incremental and a mirror, or whether it was stepwise, discontinuous and driven by hypotheses. For us, the continuity view made man too tamely a creature of his environment, behaviorism at its worst. The chief protagonist of behaviorism was Kenneth Spence at Yale. He was its rising star. The opposing view, that learning was driven by internally generated hypotheses confirmed or disconfirmed by events, was set forth with great fire by I. Krechevsky (later a close friend and collaborator, but then my hero). There is every reason to suppose, let me admit, that *both* forms of learning can and do occur, under appropriate circumstances. But we wanted it one way *or* the other.

Psychology feeds political and moral convictions all too easily. It never occurred to us that we were taking a political stance. Just look at the evidence!

There has been a good deal written about what lures students into a career in science. I fit one of the categories often discussed—early involvement in research with a respected teacher. In my last undergraduate year at Duke, my imprinting became irreversible. I began on hormonal control of sexual behavior in the female rat, my first published paper. If it was unsophisticated biochemically, it nonetheless hooked me on research. Hooking, I think, is partly the pleasure of mastering techniques to test ideas. But there was also the pleasure of sharing the joys of night hours around a lab with the young zoologists doing *their* things. As I'd ride my bike back from the biology laboratories to my room over those midnight-empty two miles, my head spun with half-baked speculations. Does the thymus, in fact, secrete a substance that blocks the emergence of adult sexual *behavior?* Or does it work by tuning the nervous system of my female rats to "see" the males in an unsexy way? I hankered after the latter explanation. Oh, to prove it!

Then a research project with our resident behaviorist, Tom McCulloch, fresh from Yale and Spence! I'm told it was the earliest study of conditioned helplessness in the literature, though that was not its point. I was out to show Tom (and his behaviorist friends) that reward and punishment, like experience itself, did not have an automatic effect, "stamping in" or "stamping out" behavior that preceded them. You could change the "attitude" of animals to reward and punishment and change their effect on behavior. Tom mocked me gently. "Show me." I concocted a little experiment (on rats, of course)—and I still think it was one of the neatest I've ever done, though its publication created not the slightest ripple. I trained one group of rats just to "take it" when they encountered shock. There was nothing for them to do but bear it. They couldn't get off the grid. Then we put them and their unshocked litter mates into a new task, where they had to choose one of two runways out of a water tank where they were swimming: one lighted, the other dark. A wrong choice led to shock, the very same shock that the exposed animals had learned they had to live with. The "resigned" rats took many more trials to learn the unpunished way out of the task. And they went in for much less VTE (Vicarious Trial and Error, as it was then called)—looking back and forth inquisitively between the two runways. They behaved, it seemed to me, as if they never thought they had a chance of solving the simple little problem we had set them. Shock for them was an inevitable part of the landscape. I had overturned the behaviorist's reinforcement applecart—so it seemed to me. I guess I was being "prematurely" cognitive!

Being a psychologist in those days of the late 1930s was a curious occupation. What was *I* doing (given my biases) working with rats? Well, rats were the canonical medium of the day for settling issues in learning and motivation. Even Edward Chace Tolman, my hero in learning theory, had dedicated his monumental *Purposive Behavior in Animals and Men* to "M.N.A.," *Mus norvegicus albinus.* (He was among the distinguished parade of visitors to the Psychology Colloquium.) For reasons that now seem bizarre, you *had* to convert contested issues into rat terms in order to enter the "in" debates— even over psychoanalysis. I doubt anybody would have denied that the evolution of the nervous system mattered. It was the belief, rather, that the underlying *processes* were simple and could *even* be demonstrated in the rat. Culture and language? That was not part of the debate. The greatest gift the department at Duke could give me —which they did—was my own little animal lab and my own rats.

I even enrolled in 1937 in a summer course in animal surgery at Cold Spring Harbor, Long Island. Did I ever enjoy any technical triumph more than transplanting ovarian tissue into the white of a rabbit's eye so that I could *see* the estrous cycle running its course by the change in color of the transplant?

Talk about the divided self! After those six weeks at Cold Spring Harbor, I went off to help my anthropologist friend Leonard Broom. He was studying change in dance forms among the Cherokee Indians produced by contact with their white neighbors. It never occurred to me that there was any *conflict* between what anthropologists did and what I had been doing. "We psychologists" (I was twenty-one) knew that whatever the anthropologists found would have to be explained by the very same elementary processes we studied. The idea of the autonomy of cultural forms (one of Broom's great passions) never quite percolated into my psychologist's consciousness.

That last year at Duke was 1938, the bitter winding down of the Spanish Civil War. My roommate, Irv Dunston, and I were invited to become members of a Marxist "study group" held at the home of a gifted young mathematics professor. Each week we would prepare by reading something of Marx or Lenin. I liked the slogans—that production was for use and not for profit, to each according to his effort, and so on—but the turgid arguments of Marxist "thinkers" repelled me. What weird psychological ideas.

My fondness for the slogans must have been enough, for we were asked eventually to join a "cell" of the Communist Party in Durham, "with real working-class people." After a late-into-the-night discussion, we decided that this was our duty. Was not the Abraham Lincoln Brigade doing its duty beside the Loyalists in Spain? Had not Léon Blum shown that the Communists could work in a Popular Front?

The half-dozen meetings of the "cell" I attended were appalling! Gabriel Almond in a classic book on the appeals of communism draws a distinction between the extrinsic and the intrinsic lure of the Party. The extrinsic appeal was what had drawn me—the appeal of a political party that fought for the "underdog" against the "oppressors." The cell meetings, in that dingy apartment near the railroad station in Durham, were the intrinsic, the conspiratorial appeal—our code names included. Long, tedious discussions of "democratic centralism" boiled down to the doctrine that you could discuss but not disagree with the platform of the Central Committee. The "working-class people" in our cell had that cheerless dogmatism that set them so apart from those they would have liked to lead to salvation. My "duties" were to take an active part on campus in the American Student Union, to get the "right" candidates into office. I was already doing that. Doing it under those imposed conditions made me feel like a sneak thief. I guess I wasn't very good Party material. I find myself altogether too attracted to clever and witty people, even when they hold outrageous views.

The year ended; I departed Durham. I never even had to resign from the Party. I was given no names or contacts, but told simply that I would soon know who and how. I guess I didn't make it.

The happy time at Duke was at an end. Friends were leaving; my teachers encouraged my wish for a change. But where? Go to Yale to work with the great Robert Yerkes on animal behavior: that was Donald Adams's advice. Karl Zener, a Harvard man, whom I had helped in his Pavlovian experiments with dogs, urged Cambridge. Would either place have me? Two books I read that spring—Kurt Koffka's *Principles of Gestalt Psychology* and Gordon Allport's *Personality*—shook my faith in the finality of research on animals. That favored Harvard. I applied to both places and was accepted by both.

Imagery, I think, decided. Harvard was not only William but Henry James; its was the intellectual purity of Santayana (I had read his *The Last Puritan* that same spring). At Harvard too were Walter Cannon, Karl Lashley and other prima ballerinas. Yale was adolescence: Frank Merriwell and golden youths with "Y" on their sweaters. I went to see Yerkes; there was little intellectual resonance. I dared ask McDougall for his advice. He graciously had me to tea in his garden, where he warned me that Harvard was implacably antimentalist and reductionist. Only Oxford was worse, he said.

To the young man on his way to Harvard in 1938, there was no question that it was in the universities that the New World would be made. And I wanted in.

3

Graduate School at Harvard

Early in the autumn of 1938, I arrived in Cambridge and enrolled as a graduate student at Harvard. I had spent the summer in a tiny French Canadian village, reading and walking and canoeing, spending evenings talking with a militant railroad shop steward from Montreal, a man of enormous integrity named Cory Kilcupp. I had landed there by ordained chance. Wanting a summer to collect myself, I had started from New York with two suitcases—one with clothes, the other with books: books on psychology, on the nervous system, and a few novels, including my beloved *Portrait of the Artist as a Young Man*. I went to the end of the spur line into the Laurentians, got off and found a family who would take in a boarder for a month or so, Kilcupp's aging parents.

One book I particularly remember. It fascinated me with its crude simplicity: Bechterev's *Principles of Reflexology*. I struggled against it. It had a fierce finality about it, a reductionism that I found detestable: much the same reaction I had had when, the autumn before, I had attended my first American Psychological Association meeting at Dartmouth College and heard Clark Hull deliver a paper on "Mind, Mechanism, and Behavior." When I arrived in Cambridge, I was full of psychology, yet not quite knowing what to expect.

I walked about Harvard Square and the Yard and felt in the presence of the great. The towering elms, the oddly pleasing mix of architectural styles, the to me "pure" scholars walking the crisscross paths under the trees. This was Athens and I was walking the Agora!

It appealed greatly to the intellectual snob in me. I lived in a bed-sitter on Prescott Street, right off the Yard, and the bells of Memorial Hall tolled my hours. I bought my card for the Harvard Coop, wandered through the back shelves of Schoenhof's bookstore looking for secondhand bargains, shifted to a Leavitt & Peirce tobacco, and became a "regular" at the Robbins Library of Philosophy and Psychology in Emerson Hall, where I also had an office that had (I was told) once been occupied by Edward Lee Thorndike. Emerson Hall became my home.

The graduate students—how could I know then that several of them were to become lifelong friends?—were all I could ask for. They had come from Köhler at Swarthmore and knew the latest wrinkles on Gestalt theory, or from places like Minnesota that specialized in large-scale testing and "number crunching" by statistical techniques. We were a proper mix.

We lunched together every day in our own "enlisted men's mess" in Emerson Hall, much as the faculty, in the big Seminar Room, lunched on sandwiches of cheese and tinned meat, and vile coffee—a custom that had become established when Professor Boring had developed ulcers some years before and could not (why not?) lunch at the Faculty Club. The "junior officers," the younger faculty, would drift into our lunchroom to argue with us, having left the senior officers' mess a little early. At a distance of polite reserve were the "greats" who sequestered themselves in the Seminar Room: Gordon Allport, Professor Boring, Jack Beebe-Center, Robert White. There were more "remote" members, like Henry Murray and K. S. Lashley, who appeared only occasionally at the lunch.

The "teaching" of graduate students, for all the courses and seminars, was very much a master-student relationship. You "worked with" Lashley or Allport or whomever. Debate was incessant and remarkably good-natured among the graduate students, and the sharing of interests was cordial and genuine. Whatever we were to turn into later, we were "psychologists" first. We went together to Kurt Goldstein's seminar on brain and behavior, to Bob White's on "lives in progress," to Gordon Allport's on the life history, to Smitty Stevens's on operationism, to Köhler's William James lectures, to Professor Boring's on sensation and perception, to Kurt Lewin's on topological psychology, whether we were intending eventually to be animal psychologists, social psychologists, psychophysicists, whatever. After hours, we argued about Lashley's notion that there was in the cerebral cortex much less specialization of function than had previously been supposed, about Allport's controversial doctrine that habits eventually become motives, about Boring's flamboyant idea that a *Zeitgeist* dominated historical periods of scientific thought, about Bill Sheldon's wild claims about the relation between physique and temperament, about any going idea. We even organized our own private seminars, to which faculty were not invited. In the manner of our mentors, we wrote our research up in "papers," and one year were very smug about having published almost as much as the faculty. That, of course, was what they were trying to get us to do—though we did not see it that way. We were dead sure, our little elite group, that we were chosen. The list of past doctorates was posted at the center of the main corridor, as if to goad us: our own Boring, Stevens, Allport, etc., but also Thorndike, Tolman, Skinner, Hoagland, Wever, Bray, and most of the contemporary luminaries about whose work we argued daily. This was the place where the future of psychology was being shaped, as the past had been shaped before. Our teachers took us seriously—substantively and stylistically. Our papers were submitted to awe-inspiring scrutiny. Boring and Allport, particularly, were watchdogs of the written word, the latter's marginal "awk" being particularly dreaded.

Professor Boring early proclaimed the dictum of the "eighty-hour week." We all routinely trotted back to "the lab" after dinner, junior faculty included.

But the third floor of Emerson was as much a club as a workplace. Smitty Stevens was the key figure in this monkish life. We knew that some of the senior members, notably Allport and Murray, found him deplorably "narrow" in his interests; he lavished his crotchety enthusiasm (or peevishness) on any subject anybody would care to raise—whether scientific, political or artistic. His passions were total and maddening. His assaults were always cheerful, often outrageous. Playing pool at Leavitt & Peirce between dinner and the return to the lab, he said, "You like Bach because it's 'second-component music,' just like your physique!" He was totally hooked on Sheldon's ideas about physique and temperament. Nothing was beneath his contempt or above his suspicion. His sneers were *ad rem*, never *ad hominem*. He would bully, bait, even sulk to make his point. He expected the same in return. He was not everybody's dish, but he was a superb model of commitment.

The older faculty, save for Boring, tended to sequester them-

selves with their own circle of students. Harry Murray had his devoted band at the Clinic, dedicated to the ideal of a full and complete
picture of personality based on batteries of clinical and test procedures. Murray was a master at this form of portraiture—fastidious
and daring. But the papers and monographs his students turned out
were pale copies of the master's. Murray's psychological sensitivity,
his genius, did not easily translate into work for journeymen. At his
best, he inspired his brilliant students to subtlety and depth and to
the dark side of human dilemmas. His real teaching instruments
were the myth (particularly the myth of Icarus, fallen into the sea
when his borrowed wings were melted by too close a flight to the sun
—Murray's fable for our times) and the novel (particularly Melville's
Moby Dick). He attracted extraordinary students, for he was a charismatic figure. But the less able students were a bit pathetic: there is
no way of being a pedestrian Harry Murray. To hear Murray diag-
nose the stories that people made up in response to the pictures of
his Thematic Apperception Test was, I thought, like reading Henry
James.

Gordon Allport was another champion of "wholeness" in that
period. His book on *Personality* had predisposed me to Harvard the
year before. If Murray stood for Freud, Jung and the night view of
human nature, Gordon Allport's was the day view. His idols were the
German phenomenologists and characterologists. He had spent a
postdoctoral year in Germany and been smitten by the *Geisteswissenschaft* of Dilthey and Spranger, the idea of values as the organiz-
ers of ways of life, values like power, wealth, service, religious tran-
scendence, beauty, abstract knowledge. He gave short shrift to
Freud's tragic view of childhood and the family drama as forming
adult personality. His was a more optimistic, more "American" view,
for all its German Romantic origins. Interests and habits, whenever
formed in the course of life, developed their own motives, were
"functionally autonomous." Man reformed his life by the act of engagement in new skills, new habits, new interests. But curiously,
Allport was suspicious of the idea that personalities were bent by the
culture, that (in his contemptuous phrase) a personality was only the
subjective mirror of culture. That was too "fixative" a conception.

The two of them, Allport and Murray, were by necessity allies in
the Harvard psychological scene, different as they were in theory
and in personal style—Mozart and Wagner. Murray, trained originally as a physician, was intuitive, almost boyish in enthusiasm

(though rather pessimistic about the human condition), worldly and witty, a Boston Brahmin. He knew little about academic psychology, and could not have cared less about translating his ideas into the coin of contemporary theories of learning or motivation. Allport was controlled, fastidious in style and work habits, optimistic about improving human nature and the human condition. He was an Ohioan. His espousal of *Geisteswissenschaft,* the science of mind, in contrast to *Naturwissenschaft,* natural science, made him as restless with reductionism as Murray was. A superb teacher, Allport was always "prepared," his lectures being exquisitely structured—never waffling. He was a shy man, whom many students "read" as formal and a bit chilly, very different from Murray, with his intuitive impulsiveness, his enthusiastic approach to things. They were a curious pair of respectful allies in that hard-nosed environment.

Allport was a learned man. I liked his broad scholarship, his attempts to link up with contemporary psychological theory. But though I became one of his "students" and we spent much time together talking shop and collaborating on research, he did not have a deep effect on my style of thinking. Neither did Harry Murray. The study of personality per se was not for me. Admiring though I was of "wholeness," of understanding the particulars in the context of the "full person," the *direct* study of personality-as-whole struck me as either too diffuse or (in reaction) too ridden with static classifications of types and values and traits. I wanted something more daring, some penetrating principle that would simplify, would render the surface complexity into something like a crystal.

The dominant tone at Harvard did not come from the Allport-Murray wing, but from "experimental psychology." That was where my principal interests lay. Our little Emerson Hall in-group was interested in the "mainline" topics: in perception, memory, learning, motivation, neuropsychology and animal behavior. These were the specialties of the "main" department. Lunch talk among the graduate students at the "enlisted men's mess" was principally about these mainline topics. And they were the stuff of our sandlot seminars.

Those noisy, quarrelsome weekly sessions, those sandlot seminars, were among the best intellectual experiences I had ever lived through. We graduate students had organized them to prepare for the "prelims," the examination to be passed before launching on a thesis. We each "presented" a topic and then an interpretive free-for-all followed. Not surprisingly, we "seminarians" did well at the "prelims." I, apparently, had done particularly well. Gordon Allport said to me, "You'll never know as much psychology again."

A curious footnote. The "prelims" consisted of four examinations spread over three days, Monday through Wednesday. On Wednesday night we had a party—Mason Haire, Bill Prentice, Dorwin Cartwright, Al Baldwin and some others. I woke early on Thursday morning, lay in bed for fifteen minutes anxiously reviewing that morning's examination. When I came out of my hypnotic state, I realized that what I had been doing was posing to myself all the most impossible questions about psychology I could dredge up. I still suffer occasionally from my "fourth day" neurosis about psychology!

Let me say a bit more about Professor Boring and his effect on us —for it was a powerful one. Edwin Garrigues Boring was a short, square man, deeply serious about psychology, the seriousness relieved by a twinkling eye and a great quaking laugh. He was the historical conscience, the writer of the major works on the history of psychology. His tiny inner office opened off a great file-filled one occupied by his secretary and by a massive collection of reprints in boxes. An Eastern Shore Quaker, he maintained a "plain style" and concern unsullied by Harvard airs and graces. *He* worked an eighty-hour week. There was a frightening directness to his reactions. Appraise an intellectual issue sloppily or fail to carry out your duties and you would get one of his single-spaced letters, meticulously corrected for typos in his crabbed script. After one of his lectures, I raised a few questions about the interpretation he had put on some experiments in memory. He listened fairly and admitted my point—a minor one. I served as a section man in his introductory course, in those days divided by sex: ten o'clock at Harvard and noon at Radcliffe. I had a dental appointment and missed his following ten o'clock lecture, going to the one at noon, the "Radcliffe repeat." He had included my point in his ten o'clock presentation. I found a "Boring letter" in my box when I returned to Emerson Hall a few minutes later. It was a blast—written right after the ten o'clock—for my discourtesy in not coming to his lecture to hear his response to my point. He walked into my room just as I was finishing it—full of apologies and chagrin. You knew immediately where you stood with Boring!

In psychology he stood for the rigorously experimental, the explicit, the psychophysical. How physical events were transformed into sensations, how these were then turned into percepts by the operations of inference, and how these were then turned into representation in memory—these were the skeleton questions for psychology. His mentors were the British Associationists and the succession of German psychophysiologists and psychophysicists, from Helmholtz through Wundt, who had turned the philosophical insights of Locke, Berkeley and Hume into laboratory science. His "sense datum" theory of mental life seemed old-fashioned to me (as I shall have occasion to relate in a later chapter). But I delighted in the elegance of his reasoning. He became a kind of one-man reference group for me. I cared deeply that he appreciate and admire not *what* I was doing but *how* I was doing it. It was a relationship that started in those graduate school days and continued until his death. We differed on many substantive matters, but we never stopped trying to communicate. Long before Karl Popper, Boring was the exponent of the idea that science was a set of procedures for finding out more easily when you are wrong. It was from Boring that I had the hardest time declaring my independence—a demanding, Quaker father impossible to please.

For all our scholarly preoccupation in those days just before the war, we knew the world was coming apart. Hitler was going from conquest to conquest, America was withdrawn in isolation, Europe seemed appeasing and corrupt before the troubles. At Harvard, President Conant and Ralph Barton Perry had established the Committee on the Present Danger, in which I became involved. I was leftist and "interventionist" in my sympathies and was convinced that unless America threw in its weight against Fascism, a long night was in store for us all. I had a passionate and personal hatred of Hitler—a loathing I still feel more than thirty years after his death.

Gordon Allport asked me to assist him in a psychological analysis of essays on "My Life in Germany Before and After January 30, 1933" that had been submitted by émigrés to a "competition" sponsored by the *Atlantic Monthly*. I read the accounts with fascinated horror. So many people had denied the reality of what was happening until, finally, they were engulfed by it. We cocoon ourselves in our ordinariness even as the flames lick at the edges. Those essays were appalling—and pathetic.

By the time I was starting on a thesis, I was so involved in the war, I chose as my topic the nature of propaganda broadcasting of belligerent nations, and spent the summer of 1940 in Princeton, where Hadley Cantril had established (on the model of the BBC unit in London) a foreign-broadcast monitoring service for gathering the output of German, Italian and Japanese shortwave transmitters beamed at North and South America. I began the tedious process of sifting and analyzing. It is strange work. On the one hand, one tries to figure out what the broadcasts are intending to establish as their "picture." On the other, one hopes to get beneath their intentions to plumb their state of mind. You look for trends, like the use of adjectives of "strength/weakness" and of "morality/immorality" in the language of communiqués, a shift from the one to the other usually signaling that estimates of military progress have gone from good to bad. There were lots of little tricks to the trade. Within a week of finishing my thesis, in June 1941, I was on my way to Washington to work for the brand-new Foreign Broadcast Monitoring Service of the FCC.

But it had been growing slowly. In the summer of 1939 I had gone off to Europe with my good friend Leo Hurvich; it was my first visit, in a summer on the edge of war. We did the usual itinerary: London, Paris briefly, the south of France, and then Italy. War was declared. We were in Venice, of all places. We departed there in company with a troupe of charming young lady dancers, the Chester Hale ensemble, and found our way across Switzerland and then to a France in chaos. In a few days we were back in the Paris of the phony war, deep in blackout. There we encountered Isadora Duncan's brother Raymond, who lived in a premature commune in the Rue de Seine, garbed always in Grecian toga, celebrating either the gentle Christ or Henry Ford (whom he had cast in awful verse as a man of peace). We joined his commune for several weeks, awaiting word about passage back to America. It was an odd entourage of weavers, batik makers, mostly ladies. They were very kind. Eventually, with other tardy Americans, we were shipped to Bordeaux and put on board the S.S. *Shawnee,* diverted from the New York–Florida run to save the "American colony" of Paris. As *The New Yorker* put it on our arrival, "Last week the *Shawnee* arrived in New York with the cast of *The Sun Also Rises.*" But it was not all comic. Leaving Bordeaux, steaming out of the Garonne, I felt a little the deserter—a Jew leaving others to their fate, a failed brother's keeper.

That first trip gave me a new sense of connection with Europe. The visit was full of odd emblematic happenings that fixated the mind. Out of perverse curiosity, Leo and I decided to stay in a Fascist youth hostel in Milan, the Arnaldo Mussolini House. We listened to the braggadocio of young reserve officers of a regiment called "The

Wolves of Tuscany." How could the English be expected to fight, they asked, when they had to carry their toasters with them? Next day we walked the roofs of the Duomo, stunned by the skillful pride that could install such glorious sculpture out of view of all save those willing to struggle along catwalks. Did the culture that created the Duomo make Mussolini and those silly braggarts of I Lupi di Toscana?

The "phony war" was soon over. Hitler invaded Poland, then France. The Blitz began. I was deep into my thesis. For me, the war had already started. Franklin Delano Roosevelt was my hero.

It was also my first year of married life. My wife, Katherine Frost, was a gentle Maine Yankee with a genius for order. A skillful editor and as involved in the war as I was, she helped speed things on their way. It was a happy domestic time and within the year we were off together on that Washington assignment.

4

The War Years—and Coming Home

There I was at the Foreign Broadcast Monitoring Service, hired to monitor "enemy" broadcasts (though we were not at war) and to report the results to the State and the War Departments. I toiled over sheaves of paper each day in a ramshackle building near Union Station. My wife and I lived in a red brick box in Falls Church, completed a few weeks before we moved in.

We were a motley crew at the Monitoring Service: academics, journalists, free-lance writers, émigrés, pundits. We were to glean intelligence from the broadcasts of every belligerent or potential belligerent we could monitor. Each morning—and after Pearl Harbor, our mornings started at six sharp—we arrived to find the preceding evening's broadcasts translated and printed in "Ditto" by our émigré translators. The journalists, our realists, would dive like gannets on this "clue" or that "item" about Field Marshal X, General Y or the Battle of Z. We conceptualists totted up our trends on key themes. We were out to read signs of self-doubt or overoptimism or wicked intent in the enemy mind. The realists and the conceptualists did not get on.

I can remember no instance of feedback from War or State or any other customer to whom our midday reports would go. Perhaps there was some at a higher level, but downstairs it felt like sending our daily offering into the void. It was "fun" all right, but in the anxious days after Pearl Harbor I became a bit discouraged. Was this a useful job for a psychologist to be doing in the midst of war?

Late in the gloomy spring of 1942, Rensis Likert blazed on the

Washington scene equipped with a mandate to establish, as part of Roosevelt's new Office of Facts and Figures, a bureau for studying how American morale was holding up, how public opinion was responding to various war appeals, etc. Likert combined charm, intelligence and energy, and I happily shifted jobs. We were the Program Surveys Division of the Bureau of Agricultural Economics—what more innocent! And in a few months Likert had recruited one of the most distinguished staffs of young behavioral scientists ever to work under a single roof. Today they occupy chairs of psychology, sociology and anthropology at Stanford, Chicago and Columbia.

Our "method" was the "open-ended interview," carried out on nationwide samples by a gifted field staff of interviewers. We worked for the Treasury on their war bond campaigns, the War Production Board on worker morale, and the White House on the absorption of women into the labor forces, and kept tabs for our own agency on how well people were informed about war issues and where they were getting their information.

One survey made a particularly deep impression on me. We compared the readers of Colonel McCormick's isolationist *Chicago Tribune* with a matched sample of readers of other Chicago papers on a variety of questions about the war—whether American participation was really "necessary," whether it mattered who won in Europe, and the like. Do readers flock to a paper to confirm their own views or do they get them from their paper? The *Tribune*'s readers, whichever way it went, were an astonishingly alienated lot, their distrust of "the foreign" profound. I could scarcely believe some of the bitter interviews I read. Later in the war, in Paris after the liberation, I dined with Admiral Muselier, the man who, at De Gaulle's instructions, had "liberated" St. Pierre and Miquelon in the Gulf of St. Lawrence, to the huge annoyance of Roosevelt. Animated by his intense dislike of De Gaulle, Roosevelt had used an unforgivable phrase in a public statement: "the so-called Free French have liberated St. Pierre." Muselier had not forgotten it. "Do all Americans despise foreigners?" Those *Chicago Tribune* readers come to mind. I told him about them and tried to assure him that some of them hated Roosevelt even more than they hated foreigners.

General Hershey, head of the wartime draft, asked for a study to find out how the draft would be viewed now that we were calling up married men and the like. The findings were an eye-opener. Dissatisfaction had rarely to do with the *amount* of sacrifice people had to make, so long as others were seen as sacrificing equally. The local draft boards were what assured our respondents that such was the case. Hershey knew his business. That month of working for him was always on target.

The wartime Washington in which I lived—the information services—was riven with competition for power and position. Power struggles so easily became dissociated from function. The relation between research and policy was often problematic. Research was as often used to justify a claim or to shore up a position as to find out useful knowledge. No surprise then that our "shop" was suddenly and drastically cut, and for no clearer reason than had underlain its expansion. Likert had lost favor.

Hadley Cantril offered me a job at Princeton, as associate director of his Office of Public Opinion Research. I was to work directly with the State Department on public understanding and support of our foreign policies. We quit Washington for Princeton—my wife, my year-old son, Whitley, and I. Each week I traveled to Washington to report to John Dickey (later president of Dartmouth College) at State, staying Thursday nights with the Tolmans, hospitable, gifted friends. Ruth Tolman had worked with me at Likert's and Richard (the brother of the psychologist Edward Tolman) was Conant's deputy at the National Defense Research Board. Hadley did not rest content with official connections. He "planted" our survey findings here and there in "backstairs" Washington—with Judge Rosenman, the President's confidant and speechwriter; with the brilliant Oscar Cox, another White House intimate; and with Gerard Lambert, the retired St. Louis pharmaceutical manufacturer who kept a house in Washington and one in Princeton and lobbied tirelessly for his internationalist convictions. Lambert loved being close to power; so did Cantril. Both were men of liberal persuasion, greatly attracted to Roosevelt and his circle, romantically given to a view of events that put too much emphasis on who dined with whom and too little on the sweep of historical and economic forces.

The weekly message to John Dickey at the State Department was not to be deterred by any seeming resistance in mass opinion to postwar plans then being hatched. There was simply not enough substance and not enough stability in mass opinion to have it count as a major factor in decisions about the United Nations or Bretton Woods. I hope the message gave nerve to those gifted men securing the peace. I doubt it made much difference.

A frequent fellow houseguest of the Tolmans' on Thursday nights was Robert Oppenheimer—brilliant, discursive in his interests, lavishly intolerant, ready to pursue any topic anywhere, extraordinarily lovable. I had no idea what he was doing, only that it was war work and in the Southwest. We talked about most anything, but psychology and the philosophy of physics were irresistible. We became close friends. I shall come back to him later.

I usually arrived at the Tolmans' from Princeton early of a Thursday evening and had my own key. One Thursday evening in midwinter 1943–44, two cars were parked outside the house, both occupied. I thought it rather odd. When I let myself in, I found myself face to face with a kindly and rumpled man who introduced himself as Mr. Baker. Ruth and Richard, he told me, had gone to a Ration Board Appeals sitting and had said I was coming. We had a drink together. He had known Köhler, he told me, during the early days of *Gestalttheorie* in Berlin, and in Copenhagen he had known Edgar Rubin, who was famous for his work on visual figure-ground reversals, and whose work had particularly interested him. "You see, there are things in the world where knowing *one* aspect of them precludes knowing others at the same time." His son, he told me, had once stolen a trinket from a shop, and then later, without any prompting, confessed how he had got it. "He had done wrong, yet I was proud of him. Could I look at him at one and the same time both in the light of love and in the light of justice?" Did I think, he asked, that the human mind was particularly subject to such complementarity? There could be no question who my fellow guest was. It *must* be Niels Bohr. But Bohr was in Denmark. Those two occupied cars came back to mind. I decided I would just continue the conversation. Had he ever come across the German philosopher Vaihinger's *The Philosophy of "As If"*? Yes, but it hadn't gone far enough in exploring this precluding feature of knowing. We were considering whether some motives were particularly subject to complementarity when Ruth and Richard returned and it was bedtime. Next morning at breakfast ("Mr. Baker" still rested), I confessed my suspicions to Richard about who their visitor must be. He told me that Bohr had been secretly flown out of Denmark and then across the Atlantic.

Our Princeton office had an archive of all the major public opinion in America—all on IBM cards ready for sorting. Cantril urged me to do a book on it. I spent days on end going over tables and charts in the old Dutch farmhouse outside Princeton we had rented that year—cutting our own wood to supplement our meager coal ration, tending a few chickens, attending the drama of the two spinster neighbors on the neighboring farm caught up in the masculinity of their black farmhand. The contrast between Friday in Washington and our farming crossroads was a special delight.

The book that emerged, my first, left me puzzled. What did it mean to talk about *American* opinion? I collated the extant polling data and wrote what I felt was a naive book, *Mandate from the People,* naive as only we psychologists can be naive about public opinion. Polling data with no reference to the power of institutions or history in political life makes thin gruel. Whatever public opinion is, it is not a sum of the opinions of individuals! I did not know how to go beyond it. Years later, *Mandate* provided fodder for historians working over the war period. How different the data looked in the pages of John Blum's book on Morgenthau! I wondered then whether polls can be used out of the historical context of their times.

The book done, I grew restless. I wanted a more direct part in the war. When I went over to Trenton, trying to enlist, I was turned down for "insufficient vision." At least it reduced the guilt, if not the restlessness. Then I discovered that I could work overseas for the Office of War Information if I waived my insurance rights. An "assimilated" major in the Anglo-American Psychological Warfare Division of Supreme Headquarters Allied Expeditionary Force Europe—PWD-SHAEF—I arrived in London just before D-day, and was greeted by buzz bombs.

Our first job once we got to France was to find out whether there would be "troubles" behind the lines of our advancing troops. We were mixed civilian and military, the former (like myself) put into bastard uniforms and given a week in a British training camp in Northamptonshire to learn how to handle the M1 rifle and the Enfield carbine, neither of which I ever had occasion to fire in earnest. Our gallant little band was out of the theater of the absurd! Our chief was a New York commercial pollster, and the British side included a charming Guards captain, Max Michaelis, gifted watercolorist and wealthy eccentric, who had commanded Moors in Franco's army and fought as a ski trooper with the Finns against the Russians in the Winter War. Max was there, I always thought, to monitor us for MI5. I recall how smartly he saluted nuns and priests—"fellow officers." Our other British officer was a psychiatrist named Pierre Turquet, an RMC major, épée champion of Britain, a delightful and an intelligent man. A third was added as we approached Paris—Major Bryce Gallie, the biographer of the pragmatist C. S. Peirce. We boasted as well an American expatriate sculptor, Cecil Howard, aging and wise. The rest were just as unpredictable. Two were Harvard literary men: Albert Guérard (a PFC), the novelist and critic, and Perry Miller, the literary historian (thinly disguised as a cavalry captain). Two were social scientists: John Riley (with whose wife and children mine were staying outside Princeton; he had studied sociology at Harvard with Parsons and Sorokin) and me.

"Psychological warfare" is full of comic opera. Our job was to report on the state of mind and politics in areas through which Allied troops had just passed. We did little surveys about hopes, worries, plans—all meticulously conducted with technical flourish. You go into a battered town and ask people about next year and discover that their deepest hope is for a resumption of the ordinary: to pick up the pieces, to open the shop, to get your prisoner husbands home alive. Perhaps if it had been otherwise, our superiors would have had reason to worry. As things turned out, the ordinariness of human suffering did not disturb strategic plans.

Along the Brittany coast, a local official told us that the island just offshore, the Ile de Bréhat, had been bypassed. Would we go over and "liberate" it, since the detachment of occupying Germans had pulled out two days before? Over we went on an ancient vedette, the *Cambronne II*. The dock on Bréhat was packed, children singing, flags waving. Mme la Barbue, the *grande dame*, poured us champagne, and the mayor, M. LaJort, toasted America. A sad woman complained to me privately that while her son had delivered stolen German ammunition to the underground, her daughter was now about to have her head shaved for dancing with a German soldier. Mme la Barbue, overhearing, exclaimed, "Better to bring the Germans back to dig up the mines they buried around this place." We all made speeches vowing to ban war forever. And for the week following, we were vicarious conquering heroes, liberating villages that had been spared the fighting. It was a play by Genet or Beckett or Pinter.

There was not much trouble in the newly liberated areas—aside from the Free French. A certain M. Coulet had been appointed by General de Gaulle as High Commissioner for all newly liberated territory. The first trouble was his bitter complaint about SHAEF's failing to bring in General de Lattre de Tassigny's Deuxième Division Blindée. Then he focused on us. Why was an Anglo-American team prying into the internal affairs of French local governments and political movements? (It is just possible that he had seen a highly respectful report from our unit on the Franc-Tireurs Partisans, a Communist group, mostly of slum-tough Parisian teenagers who had stayed there in Brittany and fought the whole war in the active underground.) In any case, our unit was quietly and swiftly disbanded in the interest of Allied harmony!

I was transferred to Office of War Information headquarters, then en route to Paris, which was just on the verge of falling. I was also to find Jean Stoetzel (who had been running an underground poll and was to become France's Gallup). We met one afternoon in an arrondissement where street dancing was in progress while the last of the fascist Milice Française were being rounded up from the roofs. Stoetzel and I became fast friends from the start.

I ended up working for Lewis Galantière and Cass Canfield, two splendid bosses. "Cultural relations with the French university world" was my assignment. My chief assistant was John Brown, literary critic and successively cultural attaché at American embassies in Paris, Brussels, Rome and Mexico City, a man full of the love of life. Our office in Paris swarmed with amateur talent—including Simon Michael Bessie, now a distinguished New York publisher—and in time, even the Washington bureaucrats came. We organized literary fortnights, dined incessantly with "leading figures," and might even have done some small good in convincing French intellectuals that Americans were not all either Hemingways or yahoos. What a slender reed on which to rest *amitié franco-américaine!* I even encountered "educational reform" for the first time. The Commission Langevin was rewriting the charter for French public education. John Brown and I "covered" it and even wrote it up after the war for the *Harvard Educational Review.*

"Doing" cultural relations is an odd job. There was to have been a cultural attaché at the embassy. Indeed, it was to have been Thornton Wilder, but he was a casualty of amoebic dysentery in North Africa and had to return to America. So our U.S. Information Service was called in. I was on the spot. I was "highbrow," had a Harvard Ph.D., had published a book, had passingly good manners, and spoke moderate French.

I was given my own "section" at USIS, housed in a cavernous, poorly heated old building overlooking the Place de l'Opéra. There too was the usual USIS Library, doing a thriving business. The section comprised a Philadelphia publisher, a delightful PR lady from California, two professors of French literature, and two old friends—the incomparable John Brown, with his network of Parisian literary friends, and Albert Guérard, later my Harvard colleague. There were also two young ladies, daughters of an admiral and a New York judge—both *bien élevées* and fluent in French. My office assistant was an idealistic and impeccable young Frenchman, descendant of a great French-Jewish banking family, the Lazards. He had spent the war on the run in Vichy France.

Nobody quite knows what "cultural relations" are. We improvised on an imaginary script. Lunches, dinners, cocktail parties, receptions. Your guest of honor one day might be André Malraux, the next day Paul Eluard the poet, then a dinner for the editors of a radical Catholic monthly. What did we talk about? Mostly about the Parisian literary-intellectual scene, about the philosophical implications of *épuration* of collaborators and the psychology of blame and guilt, about writers.

Sartre came to lunch with John Brown and me. The artist, he said, "works toward a freedom of perception within the limits of history and that is what he contributes to society." The artist transcends but engages himself. Sartre found no discontinuity between writing novels, writing plays, writing philosophy, writing pamphlets. Years later, at an Oxford party, I told Iris Murdoch of the encounter, and she said, "Rubbish! Philosophy and novels have nothing to do with each other. Analyzing knowledge and recreating experience are antithetical ways of life. He is just muddled."

Muddled or not, Sartre dominated the immediate postwar Parisian scene. We hit it off extremely well and stayed a long time over lunch. Sartre and I both wore rather thick spectacles! It was something of an unconscious bond. I had the experience once before when as an undergraduate I had been introduced to Aldous Huxley, then also wearing thick spectacles.

Once, Gertrude Stein came along to an opening of a show of contemporary American painting. I was assigned to look after her. She was in those days a bad-tempered and vain old lady who demanded a great deal of attention. I admired her willingness to stay engaged but I had some difficulty reconstructing her myth from her presence. I had admired her writing and, at the end of the day, wished she had not been dragged into something where she could not be the center of the show. It was a painful day.

There were dubious encounters as well. An elderly, wealthy and titled gentleman with an obscure record during the Occupation, which he was trying to improve retrospectively, insisted on giving dinners in honor of various of our visitors. It seemed awkward to refuse. The dinners were elegant and sumptuous by any standards, leave aside the Paris standard of 1944–45. He was a man of the world, not without charm, obviously currying favor with the Americans. A bit too ready to corrupt but nothing more. His secretary *amie* was a clever and striking young woman. She served as hostess. In fact, she had her own agenda: to arrange a show in New York for her young painter boyfriend. Eventually she succeeded. It was all ordinary enough, if a little grubby.

Somehow, those grand dinners with an alcohol lighter for the cigars managed to come into collision with my more established realities. I took two "grand old men" of French psychology to dinner one night—Henri Pieron and Paul Guillaume, both starved for little luxuries. It was bizarre and delightful to talk about operationism, about theories of perception, about "insight" and other "house" topics. This was Paris right after the war, I had to tell myself.

I was good at "committing cultural relations," as we called it. It was amusing in an ironic way. The living was disgracefully easy. And the work? A fantasy for a twenty-six-year-old. Not just Sartre and the visiting T. S. Eliot, but the film star Madeleine Carroll, nominally with the American Red Cross but eager to help for the few months she was in town. I even had a car and a chauffeur to go with the job. Like a Woody Allen film, I suppose.

But there was always an intruding somber undertone. On a Saturday, you might go to the Gare d'Orsay, to the welcoming of liberated French prisoners of war returning from Germany. Huge posters on the station walls: RESPIRER LIBREMENT or AIMER LIBREMENT. Haggard men taking tear-stained women in their arms, hugging slightly frightened children. Or dinner with schoolteachers struggling to get the schools back to normal and worried about the coarsening effect of black marketing on teenagers. The French mood of that period, full of quest, was appealing, indeed moving, full of jarring contrasts.

As 1945 mellowed into spring after a bitter winter of shortages, the black market flourished and French distemper rose. And with it, business as usual. We distributed a picture magazine, suspiciously like the American *Look* and, not surprisingly, put together in London and New York on transparencies by ex-staffers of *Look* serving in OWI. It was called *Voir* in its French version. It cost virtually nothing to produce by way of accountable overhead, but the French printers and distributors, Messageries Hachette, insisted that it be distributed at a price competitive with comparable French magazines. It sold like ice cream. There was no *Paris Match* to compete. We made a great deal of money.

Money and mass media are two subjects I know little about. A fat profit from the sale of a United States Government–financed publication to our French allies? I convinced Galantière and Canfield to let me go back to Washington to talk our home office and the United States Treasury into using our profits to fund some sort of Franco-American cultural exchange. Elmer Davis at OWI was all for it. He let me have a try at Randolph Paul, then Assistant Secretary of the Treasury. There the road ended. Money earned by an agency of government reverts to general funds. There were to be no exceptions. The United States Treasury has never liked inexpedient exceptions to its rules—even youthful outbursts of magnanimity. The world was returning to normal. The war was over.

Two vivid vignettes marked the end of the war for me. On April 12, 1945, I was with a friend, Gaston Coblentz, in the pressroom where American journalists went for their briefings. Briefings were signaled by a loud bell, the number of rings indicating the importance of the news to be issued. Four bells sounded. The briefing officer, a youngish man with a tortured face, came forward: "I wish to announce that the President died in Warm Springs, Georgia, at four o'clock this afternoon, their local time." We were all stunned. The silence seemed endless. Janet Flanner of *The New Yorker* leaped to her feet and shouted hysterically, "You ring four bells for any damned communiqué. Can't you do better than that when the President dies, goddamn it?" A few weeks later, on V-E day, I took a British Wren to dinner at our billet, after which we went on to the Place de la Concorde to see the lights turned on. She was perhaps twenty, a delightful and intelligent girl, full of the excitement of the occasion. At 9 P.M. sharp, as I recall it, the Place came alive in a warm glow of light. My companion broke into sobs. It was her first time as a grownup seeing a city lit up at night!

I came away from those years more "worldly" than I might have been had I spent them haunting Robbins Library. Wanting back into university life, I turned down a job at four times the salary (in audience research) in favor of one at Harvard. I felt starved for intellectual problems that grow out of curiosity rather than outside necessity.

Just before my departure from Paris, absurdity struck again in that odd way that managed to be lucky. So much of that year in Paris had that flavor. I had lunched with the director of cultural affairs at the Foreign Office, Henri Laugier, a distinguished ex-physiologist who later became Assistant Secretary-General at the United Nations. He lamented the lack of paper for starting up French scientific journals again. That evening I mentioned the problem to an air force friend on leave. *He* had just heard two American officers telling their story about newsprint destined for the GI newspaper, *Stars & Stripes.* Two giant rolls of it had got their ends wetted during off-loading at a "mulberry harbor" in Normandy. The rolls could not be used on a newspaper rotary press. I tracked them down, those two fellows, and even got them to deliver their newsprint (by tank rescue truck!) to the Centre National de la Recherche Scientifique. I became an instant cultural hero. The next week, I was duly presented the first postwar French cultural award, the lowly *Officier de l'instruction publique à titre étranger.* By right, I could thereafter teach French children their lessons. I can wear a purplish rosette in my buttonhole.

A few weeks later I was back with my wife, rediscovering my son, sailing a leaky little sloop around Penobscot Bay. My wife resented the long evening gloves I brought her from Hermès in Paris. I suppose they evidenced an insensitivity to her long, dreary rural life in my absence. My young son (like so many young sons who have had their mothers' undivided attention) had his own reasons for viewing this stranger with suspicion. Reentries are never easy. At the end of summer I was back in Cambridge, Massachusetts. My impression was that *it* had changed more than I had.

I was to stay in that Cambridge (save for brief absences) for the next twenty-seven years. In any case, it was where much of what I recount in the following chapters happened. It was where my daughter was born and where my children went to school, grew up, and went away from.

But before we come to that, there is other business at hand. With my return, the "Beginning" was over, the "Middle" about to begin, to be lived not only in Cambridge but in World Three—amidst intellectual issues and disputations that were in existence before I had arrived on the scene, issues that will continue to yeast away after all of us are gone. So let me turn to that world next.

IN THE MIDDLE

5

Living in World Three

There is a dilemma about autobiography when it comes to the life of the mind. Having read Lord Russell's *Autobiography* with delight, I happened shortly afterward to be visiting at the University of Texas, and was taken through their rich manuscript collections. A young curator told me of a plan for an exhibit of documents in the history of symbolic logic. He showed me a discarded manuscript page of Russell's draft of *Principia Mathematica.* "How did you come by it?" I asked. It had been included, it seems, in a letter that Russell had written to Lady Ottoline Morrell, almost a love letter telling of his delight in visiting her flat in London the day before, reading poetry by the fire. The letter ends with a light reference to his despair with the work he is doing. The manuscript page (now in Texas) was enclosed; it was "full of flaws." No mention of *what* flaws. The *Autobiography* also speaks of despair and hard work, even of the frustration of collaborating with Whitehead, who is "hopeless" about answering correspondence. But nothing about the substance of the *Principia* per se.

I felt a little cheated by Russell. I would have liked to know how a man of such deep feelings could have plunged himself so totally into a search for the foundations of mathematics, how that search related to what else he did and thought and felt. He tells us how hard a time his grandmother gave him about the "uselessness of metaphysics." A young philosopher in a family of statesmen and politicians would have *had* to justify to himself the worth of what he was doing. How did he—or simply, did he? And did he think, for another example, that his theory of reference and meaning was alien to his reading of poetry at Lady Ottoline's? Must his "personal" reactions to philosophy be relegated to asides in *History of Philosophy?* The disjunction between "intellectual work" and "personal life" seemed strange in the *Autobiography.*

I think I know what produced it.

There is a way that things are different when one gets to the life of mind. You discover as an "intellectual" that you have walked on stage into a drama already well scripted by others, a drama that has been going on for centuries before you made your entry. Your own intentions and thoughts become linked to ideas, issues and institutions that have long had a reality of their own. Karl Popper calls this world where ideas and paradigms and truths live independently of their origins World Three, a world of "objective knowledge."

There is something objective and impersonal, telling of one's adventures in World Three. There is and there must be. Even generals telling about their campaigns are caught in it. They cannot dwell forever on the fears and foibles of their officers and men, or recall only the intrigues of the cabinet. There comes a point at which the principles of logistics and supply, of movement and firepower, must be center stage. Or perhaps better, it is like a chess master whose individuality is inseparable from the rules and stratagems of chess. The scientist or scholar in World Three is like the master playing chess. You cannot grasp his style, his daring, without knowing something about the game of chess itself. General Patton remains a caricature when appreciation of his devotion to the tactics of the cavalry is lacking. And so you must know something about the duchies of World Three, in which your scholar labors. Else you will not know what manner of man he really is.

In the next few chapters I must tell a good deal about the World Three in which I lived. Can one supply a road map so that the reader may know what tracks there were that might have been followed? Let me try, and for a start, let me say what I think about maps. That may help.

I suppose maps for journeys carry two kinds of information—at least, so it is with the maps or charts that mariners use. And the travels of scholars in World Three may be akin to the passages of mariners: There are no roads really. Ocean charts contain, first, information about the shape of bodies of water and the land masses that surround them. They also carry solid information about reliable ocean currents, about depths up to the limit of "off soundings," and about standard navigational signals. This is the steady, reliable fare to be found on any good ocean chart: the givens. If you need more of the same, there are backup almanacs crammed with daily, hour-by-hour positions of the useful heavenly bodies relative to where you are at what time. But charts also carry more ephemeral information, about likely weather and even about where other craft usually make their passages. Weather notation is found in "monthly charts" in the form of wind roses for hundred-mile squares, indicating averaged wind direction and force for the month in question. As for the passage "tracks" of other ships, the one for slow vessels heading for Scottish ports and Scandinavia from America passes just below Flemish Cap, at the south end of the Grand Banks. But that depends on whether the Belle Isle Straits are ice-choked or whether St. Lawrence traffic has been diverted because of ice danger. Ephemera on passage charts is dicey; land masses and ocean depths, the first kind of knowledge, is totally trustworthy.

Both kinds have counterparts in the maps we might make of the great spaces of World Three—call them topographic and atmospheric. The topographic is about the great and persistent issues into which knowledge has been carved up—the paradigms and classic conjectures. The atmospheric tells how winds may sometimes blow and ships voyage. Let me tell a little, by way of preparation for the following chapters, about the topography and the atmosphere of my part of World Three in those years after my return from the war.

Psychology at its academic beginning, in the German universities of the 1870s and 1880s, laid claim to a place at the table of scientists by dint of being able to study the senses and how they reacted to the world of physical energies, "stimuli." It proudly called itself psychophysics and laid bold claim to principles like Weber's Law. It was no mean claim: A just noticeable difference, the j.n.d. of any sensation —light, sound, touch, whatever—was a constant fraction of the intensity of the stimulus impinging. A light of ten units of energy would be seen as changed by the addition of one unit of energy or more; a light of one hundred units would require the addition of at least ten units to be seen as changed. Therefore:

$$\frac{\Delta I}{I} = K$$

It is a powerful idea, and within interesting limits it remains true, though it is expressed differently now. The effect of Weber's Law and of the decades of research in psychophysics that followed it was to tie psychology closely to the world of physical stimulation and sensation. But sensations are rather bare and ghostly things, however easily measured. Ordinary experience is an integral of "perceptions" —things and events that "mean" something. Perceptions were classically considered products of processes upstream from sensation that tied together sensations into objects and events. Indeed, the German psychophysicists had inherited British empiricism. Locke, Berkeley and Hume (though all three had other fish to fry as well) had deeded a sensationist tradition to philosophy before sensory thresholds were ever dreamed of as things to measure. The great tradition of Sensationism, that experience somehow copied the physical world, was as solid a bit of World Three topography as any land mass or ocean current on a mariner's chart.

It created an intractable dilemma. How does the world manage to appear as it does with its meanings, its events, its happenings— none of which are in sensation? Locke proclaimed that nothing is in the mind save what gets there through the senses. To which Leibnitz replied, "nothing but mind itself." What then organizes experience? What are the powers of mind that make things seem as they do? Locke dithered and proposed that there were two kinds of sensations: primary and secondary, the former directly reflecting the physical world, the latter being some sort of derivation of mind—like pleasure or pain. Higher upstream, the world is experienced as it is by dint of the cohering of sensations governed by the laws of association. Was that enough? Kant (in the spirit of Descartes before him) proposed a richer view of mind: It innately possessed concepts of space, time and causality as its powers and imposed these on the creation of experience. The great Helmholtz, struck by the dilemma of ordinary experience, gave mind the power of unconscious inference: Sensations were as indices from which mind drew conclusions about a world of objects and events. He hedged on how the mind knew to reach those particular conclusions.

The dilemma of ordinary experience was also a feature of World Three topography. For those raised in the Anglo-Saxon philosophical tradition, the canonical solution was the Empiricist credo: that the world appears as it does because our powers are principally associative and, in fact, experience memorializes the coherence of stimuli in the world of stimulation. What we know about the world we learn through experience, through the accretion of association. Experience is a reflection. The opposite of Empiricism was Nativism—as in Kant's doctrine of the innateness of space, time and causality. Nativism in the classic intellectual chart of Anglo-Saxon World Three was marked as a hazard to navigation, like the sands and onshore currents of Sable Island.

A third feature of the chart was Objectivism. It concerns the data of psychology, and was put on the map by Americans. Just as the data of physics were meter readings for all to behold and transcribe, so the data of psychology should be overt, public, nonsubjective. Even the high priests of sensationism were convinced that they should ban subjective and introspective data: It was *response* that should be measured and recorded, not the *experience* of sensing.

Finally, there was Physicalism, an offspring of Objectivism: Explanation in psychology was ultimately to be physical and biological. That, by the way, was why rats would do in settling disputes about the mind of man. The opposite was Mentalism, which asserts the causal efficacy of mind itself. On the Anglo-Saxon chart, it was marked by red "Beware"s.

The mainstream world of psychology that I entered as a student was dominated by sensationism, empiricism, objectivism and physicalism. But when I was an undergraduate, my heroes and mentors were almost to a man swimming against that mainstream. My heart was with them: Gestalt psychology, Sigmund Freud, the cultural anthropologists, even McDougall. The founding charter of Gestalt psychology was the irreducibility of ordinary experience to sensation. Freud stood for psychic reality as cause and never flinched in his insistence that reality as experienced was a selective construction in the service of the "economy of mind." The cultural anthropologists argued for the social origin of experience itself, that what we knew and experienced took its meaning from a world of culture, symbols and myth that had little to do with the world of physics and physical stimulation. This was all "minority" World Three. Part of me wanted to make the journey on this alternative chart of the minority. But another part did not want to sail in this world apart. Gestalt theory, Sigmund Freud and the cultural anthropologists, yes, but operating with the powerful instruments of World Three, sensationism, association, objectivism and physicalism. I was juggling two sets of maps at the start.

When I arrived at Harvard as a graduate student, I ran into the established charts of mainstream psychology. I did not know then that the intellectual tide was turning. I should have, for nearly every one of my fellow graduate students at Harvard was in opposition to it in one way or another.

The map changed in the next quarter century; none of us could anticipate how much. There was the unsettling effect of the war, of course. But that changed the weather marks rather than the topography. In the thirty-odd years since the war, the revolution has been so profound that today sensationism is rejected, nativism has become not only respectable but even in some fields dominant. Objectivism in its radical behaviorist form now seems quaint. Mentalism now takes the form of the argument that a program in a computer is not reducible to the computer's hardware. The heroes in psychology's World Three bear such names as Von Neumann, Simon, Chomsky, Piaget, Vygotsky. They rediscovered mind. Powers of mind now have pride of place over the sensations that they were alleged to organize. In place of mental association there are cognitions, control processes, rules, heuristics, grammars, strategies, hypotheses. The idea that a good theory of higher-level problem solving is impossible without an underlying theory of associative learning may not be dead entirely, but it is backwater rather than mainstream. Indeed, as Guy Groen put it in a recent thoughtful review:

> Direct experimental and theoretical investigations of thinking (e.g., Bruner, Goodnow, and Austin, 1956; Newell, Shaw, and Simon, 1958) seemed most successful when the research questions asked were about the strategies, hypotheses, and goals a subject used in performing a task, and the issue of how they were learned was left in abeyance. This implied that the best route to a satisfactory theory of complex human behavior might be through the analysis of performance rather than learning. Indeed, it might well be that learning in such a context was nothing more than a very complex form of problem solving!

What happened, of course, was that psychology's world was turned topsy-turvy not by psychology itself but by modern theories of computation, of linguistics, of anthropology, indeed, even of biology. It was this changing world that I try to describe in the chapters that follow. How little we understood the changes that were taking place around us! What one wrote during those decades was often far ahead of what one understood. It took time to catch up with the conclusions.

The five chapters that follow tell about particulars in various parts of World Three in those years. They tell about my gropings and those of my friends. The first deals with the freeing of perception from its roots in mindless sensationism. It is a curious story, much of it about flying on borrowed coattails, or perhaps about stray bullets shot in other battles.

The second deals with studying thought "directly," about a book that is said to have "sparked" the cognitive revolution.

The next chapter deals with how mind might begin, and it is really a continuation of the same story, this time in the crib and the nursery. My Oxford friend Alan Bullock says that the developmental story may be the most important drama of them all. But it is far from written.

This is followed by a chapter about language—how it is mastered and how it may become an instrument of thought. I was hesitant to write it and did so only because two close friends promised dire consequences if I didn't. In the end, I was glad I had, for even if I am still too close to it, it is very much at the center of my intellectual world.

Finally, there is a chapter about the practical consequences of all this—about "education." It is really about how one equips the powers of mind with suitable prosthetic devices so that they may reach such fullness as they can achieve.

The five chapters are not, strictly speaking, chronological, though they follow roughly the changing focus of my interest—save for the one on curriculum, which in any case is higgledy-piggledy in any chronological sense. One thing does not quite lead to another in World Three. Effects have a way of begetting causes, for in a research life one circles back on oneself and construes what one did in a new way—like the joke about a book by the physicist Pauli, whose first half could not be understood without understanding the conclusions that rested solidly on the argument of the second half. In any case, my five chapters (or their topics) unroll in some roughly chronological order.

I do not think psychology could have changed so drastically in so short a time without there having been concomitant weather changes in the real world as well as in World Three. For one, the world of mind and the world of power were drawing closer together. No sooner had I returned to Harvard, for example, than I received a telephone call from Henri Laugier, former chief of the Direction des Affaires Culturelles in Paris. In New York now, as Assistant Secretary-General of the United Nations, he was trying to push a resolution through the Economic and Social Council to establish U.N. Regional Research Centers, whose object would be to help in the development of underdeveloped areas, as they were then called. Would I gather together some colleagues and propose such a center in the behavioral sciences? Of course I would. Several of us ended up stalking the corridors of the U.N. in New York. The plan was defeated. Poor Laugier; even the French forsook him. But he was the voice of our times.

"Projects" were to be an intermittent diet for all of us. And of such variety! I found myself chairing a committee in the National Academy of Sciences studying stress in submariners, a run-up to the launching of atomic submarines that could operate for weeks without surfacing. So in the middle of winter in 1947, we were "hounding" shipping in the approaches to New York Harbor on the snorkel-equipped U.S.S. *Halfbeak*, the better to study the command and information problems of a boat in battle conditions. And information is what the problems are about. Develop a sufficiently complex technology and there is no alternative but to create cognitive principles in order to understand how people can manage it. A submarine is a microsociety. Each man must have a function and be seen by his mates to have a function. I must have learned more from the project than the navy did!

University research in the behavioral sciences, like all university research, was growing like mushrooms. The expansion released enormous energy; it also shaped its flow. Admiral Solberg, whom I had come to know during my submarine adventure, was the Chief of Naval Research. His panels (on one of which I served) lunched with him in the Admirals Mess at the Old Navy Building on Constitution Avenue. Owlishly serious about basic research and national security, he considered scientific knowledge to be a "stockpile." "We used up a good part of that stockpile in the last war and we need to refurbish it now." I thought the image utterly misbegotten. But it had a genuineness. Solberg, on the basis of that conviction, threw himself into the battle to create a National Science Foundation (though it trimmed his power considerably). Knowledge in a technological world was being seen as power—even "basic" knowledge.

I never doubted, nor do I now, that the ultimate aim of pursuing knowledge is its eventual use in *some* form. But there is a limit to how closely it can be "ticketed" to achieve particular useful objectives. Its most important use may be the cultivation of curiosity. When I was invited to give one of the addresses at the one hundredth anniversary of the Smithsonian Institution in Washington in the 1960s, I chose as my topic "The Perfectibility of Mind." But the conduct of inquiry, we all learned, is not just perfecting mind and cultivating curiosity. World Three was accommodating to the practicalities of a technological world. It seems plain to me now that the "cognitive revolution" that changed the map of World Three was a response to the technological demands of the Post-Industrial Revolution. You cannot properly conceive of managing a complex world of information without a workable concept of mind. And it is probably not an accident that at the very time the cognitive revolution was occurring, America's Gross National Product was for the first time coming to be made up of the earnings of industries involved in communications and in the high technology of control, computation and management.

The magic university word in those days was "interdisciplinary." Our Naval Research Panel reflected it. There were Margaret Mead, the political analyst Harold Lasswell, and a range of disciplinary worthies fiercely loyal to the principle of the mix. Border crossing was the heritage of the war years. Ironically, after the allure of interdisciplinism had begun to tarnish, the younger generation of civil servants who were by then running the new research agencies were still pushing it.

At Harvard, the interdisciplinary spirit expressed itself in a local revolution. In 1946 the old Department of Psychology split. One wing, the more sociotropic, joined sociology and social anthropology to found a new Department of Social Relations, an extraordinary collection: Talcott Parsons, Samuel Stouffer, Pitirim Sorokin, Gordon Allport, Henry Murray, Clyde Kluckhohn, with juniors just as lively. It became my new home. I embraced it. But I never could shed the "old Department" as a "reference group." I taught in both Departments, trying to use two sets of maps of World Three. Social Relations eventually became focused upon larger, macrosociological issues. Psychology, perhaps in reaction, narrowed its focus to the details of operant conditioning and psychophysics. The heart of psychology—the study of the powers of mind and their enablement—fell neglected between the two.

I went off to the Institute for Advanced Study in Princeton on a sabbatical in 1951–52. I brooded over the split. When I came back, I asked the dean whether I could have space to set up a "Cognition

Project." He agreed, and we opened shop at 9 Bow Street. It was there that I began work on the study of thinking and its development. Five years later, in late 1960, George Miller, who was also troubled by the hiatus in Harvard psychology, joined forces with me, and we founded the Center for Cognitive Studies. It was the new interdisciplinary way: Our comrades were not only psychologists but linguists, philosophers, mathematicians, anthropologists, and even a psychiatrist or two. We did not know it, but we were responding to some new marks on the map of World Three.

So nearly all of my "adult" intellectual life has been spent in the waters of the "behavioral sciences" or the newer "cognitive sciences." It becomes a way of life all right. When I arrived at Oxford in 1972 to find that many of the psychologists there had never met their colleagues in philosophy, linguistics, sociology, education or anthropology (and felt no deprivation for it), I found it parochial. Those who had ventured afield had gone toward biology, an old connection.

One last point about atmosphere. About a quarter of a century ago, I was plunged into the midst of an educational debate then raging. It was sparked by Sputnik. For a decade I was deep into it, sometimes after hours and on weekends, for a short period for eighty hours a week. I served on the education panel of the President's Science Advisory Committee in the Kennedy and Johnson years, went off to Africa to help formulate a policy of international educational aid, and as my interests moved toward development in the younger years, had a hand in the founding of Head Start. Indeed, even when I got to Britain I was made chairman of a commission to report on the nature and quality of the care of preschool children. I have never been a proper member of an education faculty or (save in an honorary capacity) a member of a professional society of educators, though I am a Founding Member of the National Academy of Education. I even took a year's leave from Harvard to build a curriculum, and spent a term of it teaching ten-year-olds part time in a Brookline school. I doubt I am a particularly odd duck in all this. All this has been part of the new atmosphere as well.

So let me turn now to the particulars. We can come back to the more personal themes later.

6

The Judas Eye

I did not need psychology to tempt me into thinking about perception. By whatever means it had happened, I became convinced well before I ever encountered that study that the world *looked* different depending upon how you *thought* about it. I never went so far as asking whether thought creates experience or experience creates thought, but had I been forced at age fifteen to choose between the two views, flatly one way or the other, I have no doubt I would have chosen the first. How things *seemed* struck me not as the starting point of the life of mind but as the finish line. In 1956, a quarter century after, struggling to write an introduction to *A Study of Thinking,* I must have been of the same conviction, else how could I have started that volume with an account of the difficulty in "recapturing preconceptual innocence."

I suppose philosophers (like schoolboys forced to it) would divide into those who would argue that mind is captive of the senses and those who would take the contrary line that the senses are servants of mind. Psychologists and physiologists are certainly no less immune to deep convictions on this score. It would be cheering to report that the latter, armed with their superior technology for studying such issues and for falsifying wrongmindedness, would have tipped the balance by now toward Locke or toward Leibnitz. But in fact, not much has changed on the abstract level where philosophical discourse lives. Indeed, nothing gets into the mind save what comes through the senses—save, of course, mind itself. All that was well established in those maps of World Three! What has changed, what has created a revolution in my times, is how we interpret such issues in the sciences, in the arts, in history, and even in philosophy. But let that wait for a moment.

The mystery of perception, at least for me, is not that our senses tell us so much about the world, but that they tell us so little. Yet what they tell us is, on the whole, what we need to know—thanks not to perception but to something else. Our genetic cleverness? How curiously clever our senses are with respect to the world we need to manage. To begin with, they are so riskily narrow-band. Much of the world goes too fast to be seen or apprehended, much goes too slowly; much is too big, too small or too high-pitched or too dim or bright or off color. Technology may devise ways of registering on what our naked senses cannot discern. But we know, somehow, that there is something different about "knowing" by instrument that there are molecules out there and "seeing" that the sky is blue. We use the first kind of knowledge to explain the second. The testimony of the senses seems less like the primary stuff of knowledge than like fodder for testing hypotheses that precede sense.

But that is only a part of the story, and it was not the main part as far I was concerned. It is not just that evolution has tuned our senses to the demands of our habitat. Nature, to boot, has given us so limited a span of attention that we can only sample lightly from the biased input that our senses permit us to apprehend. And "sample" is indeed the word for it. But it is not random, this sampling of the world by the eye and the ear and the skin senses and the rest. It is a filtering, a sorting out, and finally a construction, that world we perceive directly. The nature of the filter and of the construction processes that work with it—these constitute the *real* philosopher's stone. It does not turn base metal into gold, but turns physical "stimuli" into knowledge, a much more valuable transformation.

I suppose each generation of psychologists (and philosophers) lives in an intellectual climate dominated by a few roiling issues that create the *Zeitgeist.* In my time (and in spite of the well-formed maps of World Three to which I alluded earlier), no issue has gone through such a radical transformation as the significance of perception and the nature of the knowledge it yields. It has changed physics, the arts, the interpretation of scientific knowledge. The 1981 Nobel Prize in Medicine went to three men who had contributed deeply to our understanding of how the brain edits, sorts and reconstructs the news from the senses—indeed, even assigns the stories to be covered. In the half century before that, physics was dominated (it still is) by questions having to do with the manner in which the position, the bias and the instruments of the observer change the nature of what he can and does observe. What, in fact, do our observations tell us about the nature of the *world* and what about the nature of *mind?* And can the two be separated one from the other?

It is not surprising that the great end-of-century physicist Ernst Mach chose to call his major methodological work *The Analysis of Sensation,* this being the very same book that my psychology tutor, Donald Adams, once prescribed for me when my speculative fever ran too high. Mach argued, to oversimplify a little, that one could interpret experience either as external, an outer *world,* or, as an internal one, as *subjective.* Einstein's argument extrapolated Mach's in a more formal and a more empirically rich way: the world, externally considered, could never be autonomous from the framework of the beholder.

Nor was it physics alone. Manet, a contemporary of Mach's, caught the spirit in his Impressionist dictum: "Nature is only a hypothesis." And Freud was not far behind, likening human experience not so much to an illusion as to an arena in which the forces of reason and unreason strive against each other to shape "psychic reality."

That was the *Zeitgeist.* I may have had other, personal reasons for being gripped by these matters. One didn't need many of them.

In the late 1930s, a young psychologist with a strong theoretical bent could go one of two ways—either toward the study of perception or toward the analysis of learning. They were very different roads. The one had to do with what the world *looked* like; the other with what creatures *did* as a result of being exposed to the world. The first was mentalistic, phenomenological, essentially European. The second eschewed subjectivity, was dominated by behaviorism, and was quintessentially American in its objectivity. The closer the study of perception got to the study of the senses, the more acceptable it became to the behaviorist learning theorists. For then, after all, one could base the work on responses of discrimination: whether a given sensory stimulus produced the response "present" or "absent," "red" or "blue."

In the 1950s and into the 1960s, the battle of perception was joined. It started right after the war in a movement called the New Look. By the late 1960s it was mostly done. Perception—or "information processing"—had become mainline American psychology. The old objectivist "learning theory" was to be found only among zealous followers of B. F. Skinner. Social psychology, the study of personality, and even bread-and-potatoes industrial psychology took on a "subjective" cast—concerning themselves with how people *saw* the world and themselves rather than how they or their world *were,* according to some objective criterion. As changes go, even in so volatile an enterprise as psychology, the transformation was breathtakingly swift. Psychology came abreast of the times in which it lived.

I was so engrossed by and involved in the transformation that it is still difficult for me to disentangle my own biases from the events that were unfolding. And I am enough a child of the times to recognize that it is impossible, as Yeats says, to "tell the dancer from the dance." Several historians of that changing scene have even alleged that I had a major part in what happened, which should make me suspect as a commentator. But I am Tolstoyan rather than Carlylian in my historical biases. We were all caught up in history. And I can only tell the tale from the perspective from which I viewed it. It was often a beleaguered perspective.

In 1974, after the shouting was over, a young psychologist, Matthew Erdelyi, wrote a retrospective article entitled "A New Look at the New Look." His epigraph is from Kafka's *The Trial:* "The verdict is not suddenly arrived at, the proceedings only gradually merge into the verdict."

The proceedings, at least formally, started some quarter century ago with a series of publications (Bruner and Postman, 1947; McGinnies, 1949; Postman, Bruner, and McGinnies, 1948) which suggested that the perception of external stimuli is not free of the shackles of internal events: attitudes, values, expectancies, and psychodynamic defenses all impinge upon perception. This view became loosely known as the "New Look."

Things started "formally," in fact, with an austere, largely unread "methodological" paper by Leo Postman and myself in 1946. It bore the forbidding and (for the insider) presumptuous title "The reliability of constant errors in psychophysical measurement." However opaque the title may be to the uninitiated, to those who guarded the portal of "pure" psychology it was a bumptious historical challenge. The *coup de foudre* that was alleged to have caused the birth of scientific psychology (as I have already related) was generally taken to be the discovery, by Weber and by Fechner in the mid-nineteenth century, that the magnitude of an experienced sensation could be reliably pegged to the physical magnitude of the stimulus that produced it. The one rose, as it were, as a logarithmic function of the other. This is the cornerstone of psychophysics.

Constant errors, for the devout psychophysicist, are a nuisance. They are errors in judgments of size, brightness, loudness, whatever, that fail to conform to the logarithmic law, and that do so with such persistence and predictability as to be an embarrassment to anybody principally concerned with the "realism" of the senses. The second of a pair of identical weights you lift will almost always seem heavier, a "time error." There are space errors, order errors and other "illusions." You get rid of them if you have in mind to study "the senses." As we put it in our opening paragraph:

In Fechner's eyes, these variations were first and foremost *errors* by which he was "embarrassed" rather than phenomena of psychological interest. In his search for a mathematical law establishing the ultimate relations between the physical and the psychical, Fechner regarded these errors as impurities that had to be eliminated. For a long time psychophysicists followed Fechner's lead. Quantification of the constant errors was important only insofar as it provided assurance that their presence was "controlled" and therefore "eliminated." As Wundt [another of the founding fathers, who had turned coat] once put it picturesquely, "with the elimination of such psychologically conditioned errors, they eliminated psychology itself."

It was not a new point. But the times were changing, and so too the significance of "errors."

There was a reference in that early, forbidding paper to one by Bruner and Goodman, soon to appear. It bore the (for then) improbable title "Value and need as organizing factors in perception." It turned out to be the catalyst, the cloud seeder. It produced the New Look, and before that was done, it rained about a thousand articles and books.

It was psychophysics all right, but psychophysics in the marketplace rather than in the shielded laboratory where such matters were ordinarily conducted. Instead of having our "subjects" judge the magnitude of controlled, neutral "stimuli," we set them the task of estimating the sizes of coins, ordinary U.S. mintage right out of my pocket. And in place of "trained observers" as subjects, we used ten-year-old schoolchildren. Their job was to adjust a patch of light to match the size of a nickel, a dime, a quarter and a half-dollar. That was all. Half the kids were from schools in affluent parts of Boston; the others from the city's slums. My partner, Cecile Goodman, was a lively, clever and irreverent Radcliffe "girl" (as we used to say), who had taken on the topic as her senior honors thesis. I think she may have been my first "senior honors tutee"—which I have always considered the jewel of teaching tasks at Harvard.

The findings had an almost Dickensian quality. The more valuable the coin, the greater the overestimation of its size. And the poorer children overestimated more than the affluent ones. But there was something less Dickensian, more "insider," about the findings which made for some serious second thoughts about those constant errors. The most hallowed of those "errors" is the Law of Central Tendency. It describes a deep and conservative feature of human judgment. Given a *series* of magnitudes—size, brightness, whatever—human observers will tend to judge the greater ones in the series as smaller and the smaller ones as larger. In our judgments of magnitude, we err toward the middle: bigger than the middle is smaller, smaller is bigger. But not our children and their coins. The bigger coins, the quarter and half-dollar, were *over*estimated, the nickel *under*estimated. Was the value of the coins operating to turn the hallowed law of central tendency topsy-turvy? Can constant errors also *accentuate* value? We had put a cat among the psychophysicists' pigeons!

My friend Carvel Collins, the Faulkner scholar, was delighted. It was like the boy in *Intruder in the Dust* who feels a new half-dollar in his pocket to be the size of a cart wheel. And I suppose it was the literary immediacy of the findings that caused this little experiment to produce such a big splash in the press. It was all over the papers —at least the part about "rich" and "poor" kids.

It was a "cute" study, even a little unstable, for it is possible to overcome the effect by concentrating on size. But there was nothing casual about how it came into being. I had begun brooding about the problem as an undergraduate and I even have a "flashbulb" memory connected with it. It was a soft spring day in 1937. I had gone to a grove on the edge of the campus at Duke to read Kurt Koffka's remarkable and dogmatic *Principles of Gestalt Psychology,* just published. It opens with a discussion of the "behavioral" and the "geographic" world, the former a subjective transformation of the latter. It is illustrated by the tale of the traveler on the Lake of Constance who loses his way in a blizzard, lacking all landmarks, until he finally spies the lighted door of an inn. He knocks. The innkeeper asks what direction he has come from. The traveler points over his shoulder. The innkeeper replies, astonished, "You have just walked across the thin ice of the Lake of Constance." And the traveler falls dead of fright.

Koffka was a piece of a jigsaw puzzle that was forming in my head. Donald Adams and a crusty old naturalist, A. S. Pearse, from whom I was taking a course in animal behavior, had introduced me to a new conjecture. Might not survival of any species be as dependent on a way of experiencing the environment as upon a repertory of inherited specific reactions to that environment? It was an idea put forward by a German zoologist, von Uexküll, whose thesis was that each species had an *Umwelt*, a species-specific subjective world that selected and accentuated those aspects of the geographical world that were crucial for survival. It was an idea that Niko Tinbergen was later to develop, and many years after, he told me that he had read von Uexküll around that same time, and also with great excitement. In any case, the idea of a "behavioral" environment was very much on my mind those days.

Not all the reasons were intellectual either. That autumn I had become fast friends, indeed quite fallen in love, with a young woman. She had been an undergraduate on the West Coast, had dropped out, and was now at Duke to see whether she could "stomach school again." She was not succeeding very well. We were both reading Joyce's *Portrait of the Artist as a Young Man* when we met, which can make a heady bond. In the midst of that dreary North Carolina winter she got wind of a new *Hamlet* opening in Washington—John Gielgud as the Prince, Maurice Evans as Polonius, and I can't remember which of the Gish sisters as Ophelia. Please, please, could we go to Washington to see it? We went—at some peril, as it happened. The performance was pure miracle. It was the uncut version, with the full dumb show. After, we talked about those lines of Hamlet to Polonius:

Do you see yonder cloud that's almost in shape of a camel? . . .
Me thinks it is like a weasel. . . .

Those lines, she exulted, were Shakespeare's theory of drama. Drama? They were Shakespeare's theory of perception. All right then, if life imitates art, she said, then perception imitates drama. She left that spring. I missed her very much.

It is curious that the New Look should have started with a matter as abstract as the apparent sizes of things—even coins. Perhaps it was just as well; it is an easy metaphor, perhaps a universal one, else cave art and the depiction of saints in medieval painting would not have used its power. But I think it was not so much that as the atmosphere of Harvard psychology that predisposed me. And more particularly, Professor Boring. He was a man of ferociously strong convictions, as I have already related. The key task of psychology for him was the explication of sense—how the eye, the ear, the skin, even the gut, represented the world of impinging stimulation. He would argue, if pressed, that if it was not the key task, at least it was the *first* task. In some profound way, his presupposition about all the rest of psychology was rooted in the nineteenth century positivist idea that the world as we sense it reflects a state of nature in the external world. His historical scholarship, which was enormous in its scope and pervasive in its influence, for he had written the two primary source books that were in use in all the mainstream graduate departments in America, was sedulously premised on that idea. He was the spokesman of the founding fathers of academic psychology. And he was a compelling teacher—not so much in "pushing" his ideas but in seducing one into arguing from his set of presuppositions.

He took us seriously—his graduate students and the younger instructors in the department at Harvard. He was accessible for talk, and when the talk was done, you would often receive the very next day one of those long, single-spaced letters, restating his points and reflecting on yours. I think he thought of us as his young lions, and Hicksite Quaker that he was, he was genuinely "concerned" with our points of view. Out of sheer courtesy (laced by fear of being the fool), one knew his books down to the last argument before getting into talk with him. He did not suffer fools at all. And lazy scholarship angered him into gruff silence. He was one of the "older men" in my life for whom I felt genuine love. And a certain respectful fear.

I think it was him I was trying to convince that the structure of appearance was shaped from the inside out, and not just from the outside in, from "sense data" into experience. Boring's major theoretical book bore the characteristic title *The Attributes of Sensation*. It dealt with the manner in which the "founding content," the sensory stuff of experience, organized itself in terms of time, space, quality and clarity. Or, in his crabbed way of putting it, protensity, extensity, quality (as in different colors) and attensity. So sense-oriented was the account that he preferred to emphasize the *structural* properties of sense at the expense of the *functions* and *processes* that brought these into being. And so even the clarity of experience could be discussed as an attribute of sense, "attensity," rather than as a process of paying attention.

I was quite as ferocious as he about my convictions! I thought the notion of founding sensory stuff had the cart out ahead of the horse. The primary stuff of perception was the world of experienced objects, events, meanings. They gave experience its natural joints. Sensations and attributes and dimensions were abstractions from that world of ordinary experience. They were products of abstraction and not the founding stuff at all. And of course, that gang of Harvard graduate students with whom I had lived so closely before the war (under the benign and lively domination of Boring, whomever else's music we might be dancing to) were part of the same protest movement. We gave each other courage in standing up to Boring. "Standing up to Boring"—what an odd way to put it. For all the twenty-five years I knew him, I never saw him *act* the bully or the browbeater. Some people are just inherently formidable.

I think the "establishment line" about sensation against which the coin-size experiment needs to be seen is embodied in a celebrated series of studies that Smitty Stevens, Boring's gifted "favorite son," had published just before we had all broken up to go off to the war. It was a fitting gift to his spiritual father. The work ends with the claim that there were four "basic" attributes of tone—pitch, loudness, density and volume. It was not like Goethe's claim about "primary" colors, based on the quality or purity of the *experience* of spectral red, green, blue and yellow. It was argued, rather, from the outside in. There are only two physical properties of pure tones: the amplitude and the frequency of the simple sound wave that produces them. Pure tones may be rare; they are produced by a simple sinusoidal wave form. But they are, for all that, physically "deep" in significance. For it had been the genius of Fourier to show that any complex wave form, no matter how kinky its squiggle, could be shown to be a combination of a particular set of simple, sinusoidal waves.

Well, what of pitch, loudness, density and volume? Each could be shown to vary as a function of the combined amplitude *and* frequency of the simple sound wave. Now, sound waves get into the ear, as we all know, by shaking the eardrum, which shakes some bones, which then shake a window in a fluid-filled chamber, the cochlea. Inside the cochlea there is stretched out a curious neural carpet. It is narrow at one end and wide at the other. The carpet is composed of crosswise sensitive neural elements that fire off into the auditory nerve when moved more than a minimal distance. Again as everybody knows, there is a phenomenon called "resonance." A low-pitched tone resonates in big bottles, or on longer violin strings, or makes bigger panels shake. A high-pitched one does its resonating in small bottles, or on short strings and small panels. This is what makes Stevens's four attributes basic.

For pitch is "produced" by the *place* on the neural carpet that is the peak of resonance. (The neural carpet in the cochlea, of course, is called the basilar membrane.) High pitches peak toward the narrow end, low ones nearer the wide end of the basilar membrane. Moreover, if you change the amplitude of a constant frequency tone, you can demonstrate with a little physics that the peak of resonance will shift. Loudness? That can be reduced to the number of cross-threads in the neural carpet that are shaken into firing around the peaking point. And intuitively you can perceive that the ends of the carpet have fewer neighboring threads for shaking, so high-amplitude extreme pitches are not as loud as high-amplitude middle pitches. Density of a tone? You may well ask what that is and why, since it is "phenomenologically" nonobvious, it should be "basic." Well, it is produced by the *concentration* of elements around the peaking point on the basilar membrane that are shaken into firing. You can make a fairly good story about density changing with the interaction of the frequency and amplitude of sound waves. Never mind about volume—the scatter of elements in the entire carpet that get shaken up. A little dubious, but Stevens argued it as well as he could. There.

What made the four attributes of tone "basic" was that you could link the experienced sound directly to the physical properties of the stimulus acting on the structure of a sense organ way out at the periphery. It is about as raw a bit of implicit sense-data reasoning as one could encounter. It was brilliant. And it may be totally irrelevant with respect to how sounds are actually experienced.

But it was held up to us as the *right* way to go about the study of the senses. A student at Princeton had done a spoof on it, showing that with variations in amplitude and frequency of pure tones, he could get judgments of "orthosonority" from his subjects—given a little coaxing and training. I did not have to be convinced about the coaxing and wheedling needed in learning to make "judgments" of density and loudness. For I had been a subject (we all took turns for each other) in Smitty's experiment. And I had also served, at just about that time, as a subject in an experiment being conducted by the gifted Heinz Werner. He was working on "micro-melodies." He began by giving you "Yankee Doodle" in pure tones in the conventional scale. Then he would play it to you in a scale in which the ratios between tones were preserved but the whole scale was compressed into the range of one whole note. At first the compressed "Yankee Doodle" sounded like nothing but the repetition of one tedious tone. But wait a bit. What's that? And after a few sessions, "Yankee Doodle" was coming through bright and clear. Indeed, played immediately after, the "real" Yankee Doodle sounded gross! So what was pitch? Did it matter whether a given "pip" was in isolation or embedded in a melodic line? Did it matter that I had to know "Yankee Doodle" in advance for the compressed micro-melody to work its way into my experience as "Yankee Doodle"?

No surprise then that those first New Look studies were skirmishes in magnitude estimation. And of course, inevitably, some of the efforts to repeat them succeeded in replicating the results, others not. For much depended upon how salient *value* was in the setting of the experiment, how big an intervening space there was between where the coin was that had to be judged and where the comparison figure—a little memory gap increased the effect. And so did some fuzziness in the matching light circle.

Leo Postman (with whom I had joined forces) and I kept on attacking the bastions of psychophysics with other "demonstration experiments." We rediscovered what "primitive" painters had known for many centuries: Significant objects in a picture become accentuated in appearance—in size, color, saturation, clarity—however. We had made the point. Besides, the psychophysics of sensory attributes is much too winding a road into the study of perceptual filtering. After all, the method of comparison of sensory magnitudes, useful though it has been, was never designed for what we had in mind.

I say "we," for Leo Postman and I were inseparable in those years of the late 1940s and early 1950s. Though we were good friends, we differed in temperament and taste. We worked together for nearly a decade, and I cannot remember a single personal quarrel in all those hours of experimenting, working over data, writing, plotting next steps. Nor was there ever an issue about credit. No reason for it. The work rolled on so steadily and the papers emerged so regularly that Tweedledee and Tweedledum were undistinguishable from Tweedledum and Tweedledee. There was plenty of credit to go round. One of those indexes of citations that scientific bureaucrats like to compile reported us as more widely cited in the American psychological literature for a couple of years than Sigmund Freud himself. It was heady, even if not everybody was out to praise us.

I did not realize how different Leo and I were until he left Harvard for Berkeley in 1955. Or perhaps we both changed, like siblings "individualizing" after going their own ways. He was probably more conservative by temperament than I was from the start. Eventually his interests took him into detailed studies of rote memory, a field he pursued with zeal and style enough to win one of the profession's major prizes. But during those years of our collaboration, he was in search of a stance in psychology. His interests were broad, he was a "quick study," and he was astonishingly well informed about an astonishingly wide spectrum of issues.

Collaborations, even for short periods, are delicate arrangements. Work, and particularly "thinking" work, is probably collaborative in some deep sense even when done alone. You are involved, even when alone, in an implicit dialogue with *somebody* a good part of the time—however ghostly that somebody may be. A *real* collaborator can easily become an intruder upon that privacy. Sociologists are fond of such terms as "reference figures" to characterize "the other" in these implicit dialogues. "The other" may be a rather diffuse amalgam: "people who care about Mozart" or even "readers of *Partisan Review.*" They can also be quite specific. At the time of the New Look, the image of Boring often sat across the table from me, a voice of "official history." So did the shade of Gordon Allport. He was rather a voice of social significance who intoned (in my mind at least, if not in fact) uncomfortable questions about the bearing of what I was doing on the human condition. And there was Smitty Stevens, who stood for rigor and for Science with a very decided capital S. All of them, by the way, stood for clarity. But beyond all these household gods there was a "band" of more literary friends to whom I felt somehow accountable—less for clarity than for metaphor: Perry Miller, Morton White, Albert Guérard, Carvel Collins.

Leo and I shared "household gods": Boring, Allport and Stevens. That was enough. We rarely talked about literature or the arts or even "conceptions of man," though he was by no means uninformed on the last. And perhaps, in retrospect, our reticence was just as well.

For there was a difference between us, less noticeable then, but there. Beneath the skin, I was—what thin words!—an intellectual first and a scientist in support. I think the two were rather more separate in him. I used psychology to pursue matters that existed for me in their own right. Psychology was (and remains) only one way to use mind in behalf of these pursuits. We psychologists are different from but have no privileged place among our fellow supplicants— novelists, historians, linguists, poets, philosophers. Henry James understood the human condition differently from his brother William, but I have always believed that understanding either of them helped one understand the other. It is not a fashionable or even an intellectually compelling view in this age of complementarity and "disciplines," but I have always held it and cannot shed it.

Leo was principally a "scientist" in psychology; but he did not lack for cultural and moral concerns. He was not as impelled as I to make a "whole" of it all. Alfred Kroeber once told me that the difference between him and Clyde Kluckhohn was that Clyde wanted to weave everything he knew into one tapestry—anthropology, psychoanalysis, classics. He, Kroeber, was quite content to let them live on their own. He had practiced psychoanalysis in San Francisco right after the First World War, yet he was quite satisfied to espouse a nonpsychological, "superorganic" anthropology. I was more Kluckhohn to Postman's Kroeber. Postman had been an undergraduate with Gardner Murphy at City College in New York during its great flowering. Goronwy Rees, for many years the mainstay "R" of *Encounter,* asked me once how it was that City College, "of all places," could have produced such a profusion of intellectuals in so short a period. I muttered something about the Jewish intellectual tradition and the children of immigrants. But that scarcely scratches the surface. Gardner Murphy, in any case, was of that New York intellectual pressure cooker—Chautauqua rather than Jewish. He saw psychology as an instrument for liberating man to become a better member of a democratic society. Leo had been attracted to him, and then to Gordon Allport, who shared that liberal belief. Perhaps an alliance with me was a step on the way toward disengagement for him. I do not know. Whatever, I think our collaboration made him freer to do as he was inclined, without attachment to more overarching moral commitments.

We coincided at the right time. I may have pushed him toward radical stances he might otherwise not have taken. But I think they were stances that he wanted to explore anyway. He certainly helped me to be more detached about the way we went about stating and testing our hypotheses. We were a good pair.

Between us, finally, we broke out of our bind: the need to supplicate at the front door of psychophysics. We went next door. At least that is how our wandering began. Another of the "founding techniques" of psychology is to study what forever has been called *thresholds*. It originally referred to the threshold of consciousness, but out of deference to the objectivist charter that psychology had adopted, consciousness is usually deleted. Threshold is treated statistically now, rather than phenomenologically. How much does it take *on average* to see or to hear or to feel something—how much exposure time, how much brightness, how much of the "thing" itself? In its simplest form, the measurement of thresholds was and still remains the direct road to measuring the absolute sensitivity of the eye or ear and their systems of registration. How many quanta of energy of what wavelength does it take to see light of what color? I had served for Sunday morning hours on end as a subject in such "light" experiments for my friend George Wald when he was interested in the sensitivity of the human eye to ultraviolet light—a function I could serve uniquely, for I was not encumbered by a yellow-tinted natural lens in my eyes, both lenses having been removed when my sight was restored. I suppose the *idea* of thresholds must have been close to *my* threshold of consciousness.

It struck Leo and me that here would be the ideal way to study the *selectivity* of perception proper. We would not use light or sound in the raw, but present instead meaningful pictures or even printed words and see how long an exposure to them it would require for them to be seen. It was an old and honorable technique that had been used in dozens of experiments on "set" which, of course, had long since demonstrated that it takes less exposure to "see" something for which you are prepared. With the help of our distinguished colleague Edgerton at MIT, we designed a tachistoscope that could control exposure time and assure that the light would be constant in intensity for the whole exposure flash, something easily accomplished by the use of a preheated gas tube that explodes into full illumination in a fraction of a microsecond when electrically sparked. Such a minimal "rise time" for illumination when you are studying vision is trivial, for the thresholds we were studying were in the order of hundreds of milliseconds. Technically, we were under way.

I cannot for the life of me reconstruct how we decided to do the experiment that started the series of dozens of them we were to undertake over the next few years. It is as far from psychophysics as you can get! It was inspired by C. G. Jung, Freud's rebel disciple, and in particular by his famous study of word association. You could not have designed a better way for putting the unholy cat of personality among the pigeons of perception.

Jung had found that if patients were asked to give the first association that came to mind when presented with ordinary stimulus words, they tended to respond either abnormally quickly or abnormally slowly to words that represented trouble areas in their lives. He ingeniously proposed using the procedure for diagnosing the difficulties of his patients. The psychoanalytic common sense of the finding was that slow associative reactions were produced by repression, fast ones by a prepared "defensive" reaction. Given the way we were thinking, it was not much of a leap to translate all this into perceptual thresholds. Would words that aroused anxiety be more difficult to *see* as well. Why just association?

So we collected one hundred five-letter words, including some likely to disturb the anxieties of ordinary undergraduate subjects, to each of whom we read the words one at a time, with instructions (à la Jung) to respond with the first word that came to mind. They obliged, and we duly recorded not only what they said but how long it took them to give forth. We could then select for each subject which six stimulus words gave the slowest associative reactions, which six the fastest, and which six fell right in the middle of their range. A few weeks later, we had the subjects return and presented them "their" eighteen words one at a time in our new tachistoscope. How much exposure time was necessary to recognize them? Happily (but innocently), we encouraged them to guess even if they were not sure.

The findings startled us. Yes, the amount of time needed to *see* a word was most usually predicted by the amount of time it had taken the subject to free-associate to it. That would have been quite enough: an interesting finding. But for some subjects, words that had taken a long while to react to by association were seen with striking swiftness. And the reverse held as well: quick-to-associate words were sometimes seen only after preternaturally long exposure.

Fortunately, our innocence had served us well. Those guesses we had encouraged provided some crucial hints. Words, for example, that had yielded slow associations and took a long exposure to recognize produced curious guesses. CRIME, BITCH, ANGER and DREAM were reliably more likely to be seen only as garbled letters that made no "sense"—as if their sense were, so to speak, "senseless." In general, the trouble words in each subject's list were being either recognized very quickly or kept in that unprocessed state so long that their recognition was very delayed.

We blithely concluded that there might be two ways in which people went about perceiving things that might threaten them emotionally: "vigilantly" or "defensively." And so "perceptual defense" was launched. That was delayed recognition. Vigilance was the superfast recognition. Perceptual defense was to be a red rag of the next decade.

Small wonder. For how could people *know* that something was potentially threatening unless they could *see* it first? Was something passing through a Judas Eye, letting a perceiver decide whether to open the portal of perception to let it in? Or perhaps our subjects were only holding back in embarrassment. In the latter 1940s, ours seemed like an absurd claim. But having made the claim and produced the clamor, what could we do but go on? At least we could "clean up" the theory, for neither of us particularly wanted to sail in those waters under the banner of psychoanalysis.

So next time out we did something more "reasonable"—not about repression and defense, but about interests and values. If they were as psychologically obscure, at least they did not seem so mysterious. Gordon Allport had devised a remarkably sensitive test for the measurement of human values. It is a measure of something like personal commitment to six "key" values—religious, political, economic, aesthetic, social and theoretical. "Commitment" is a more comfortable idea, and the Allport-Vernon Study of Values test was both well known and well validated. We decided to use it as the backbone of our next experiment.

The experiment was akin in idea to the first one. We carefully chose six common words representing each of the key values, thirty-six stimulus words in all, and all equal in length, all about equally familiar. They were presented in the tachistoscope one at a time for recognition by subjects who had taken the Allport-Vernon test and whose "value profiles" were known. Would those strongly committed to a given value recognize words associated with it more quickly than words associated with values to which they were less committed?

Well, it took about 75 milliseconds of exposure to recognize a word representing one's strongest value commitment, about 100 milliseconds for one in the weakest, the rest falling in between. By any reckoning, 25 milliseconds of visual processing time is *not* to be ignored. It is the difference between running a mile in three minutes or four minutes. What was taking up the time? Or perhaps one should ask, What was saving time?

Fortunately, we had learned that it was revealing if subjects were encouraged to guess before they were dead sure. And again, there seemed to be some sort of "leak" going on through the Judas Eye! For, again, low-value words were producing "nonsense" guesses. But something else was happening. We were finding "semantic leakage" too. High-value words produced what we rather grandly called "covaluant" *prerecognition hypotheses*—for by now we had upgraded "guesses" to that name. EASTER would produce the guess SACRED for a religious subject. But low-value words seemed more often to be producing antonymous or "contravaluant" hypotheses: HELPFUL evoked SCORNFUL, BLESSED led to REVENGE. Statistically speaking, we could not dismiss the possibility that some "meaning" was getting through before the subject could "see" what was before him. We traveled far in that experiment, but the Judas Eye was still there in our conceptual baggage.

And it stayed there—in our studies and in others which were done elsewhere. One of the prettiest of those was by Dick Lazarus, now a distinguished student of personality at Berkeley, and then a young firebrand at Johns Hopkins. He found that if you sorted subjects independently into "intellectualizers" and "deniers" in the psychoanalytic sense, the former were more likely to recognize threatening stimuli quickly (vigilance), the latter to block them out (defense).

Karl Popper may not be completely right about science being an enterprise for *disproving* ideas, but he is not all wrong either. There are two ways of proceeding when an established theory encounters a conclusion or a concept that it finds awkward. The first is to show that the data supporting it are insufficient or just "wrong." If this fails, then the expedient thing to do is to show that the awkward conclusion can be explained in a less awkward or more comfortable way. Of course, you can ignore the whole thing. The supplicant with the uncomfortable finding has some obvious things he can do. He can go on amassing data to demonstrate that the conclusion is not wrong, is robust, etc. He can embody others' criticisms in the design of his next experiments to show that efforts to "explain it away" are vain. If he is *very* lucky, he can subsume the older conventional theory and his critics into a new theory he has devised—like Einstein subsuming Newton.

So what to do about the Judas Eye in perception? How well Whorf's hypothesis works in science! Words constrain and shape our view of reality in science far more than they do, I think, among American Indians. Science lives among paradigms. And the very word "perception" means immediate experience: what we sense here and now without thought or reflection, the difference between "blue sky," which is immediately apparent, and "molecules," which you have to think about in order to apprehend. Whatever runs counter to the lexical distinction between "perceiving" and "thinking about" will be suspect.

But it does not follow that, though perception has "immediacy" as experience, the *process* that brings it into being is also immediate. Even Helmholtz, discussing perception nearly a century before, knew that. What was perceived was for him a resultant of "unconscious inference," *unbewusster Schluss.*

The irony is that it was not until we were able to look at perception as a genre of "information processing" in the metaphor of a computer that we were able to see the *necessity* of its being the result of a prolonged process—for all its phenomenal immediacy. There is no formal reason to assume that "editorial way stations" in *any* information processing system do not abort inputs after they have used them. Inputs may be used and yet never get into the final display—consciousness. Even *semantic* inputs. But we shall come to that later. I give away the story here so that the reader may not be as blind as the characters in the tale I am about to recount.

The major attack on the Judas Eye, perceptual defense (and indeed the New Look), was to explain all of them away by accounting for things in a more comfortable and banal way. The weapon was the "frequency argument." The frequency argument in psychology is that what happened before is more likely to happen again, or will happen again more easily. It is the argument of the crease. Such arguments have been attractive to psychologists and to philosophers of mind since Aristotle—indeed, since the pre-Socratics. It is based on the doctrine of "habit," which is perhaps better called a doctrine than a fact, for it is so universally overextended. A habit, if that is what the specimen is before you, grows stronger or better or is more likely to be repeated the more often we behave habitually. It is a very poorly understood notion, and if it were the only doctrine governing human behavior, there would be no problem solving and no language. For both of those are principally organized by purpose-building your knowledge in the form of principles in order to deal with the task before you—in words or in concepts or in acts. And interestingly enough, the doctrine of habit was a monkey on the back of those who would have wished to understand either of those two enterprises.

Psychology, in its brief history, has gone out of its way to devise experiments demonstrating that mental phenomena follow the laws of habit—even problem solving and language, which have as their distinctive mark the production of novelty. It is an old struggle, this conflict between "reproductive" and "productive" interpretations of behavior. The allure of the former, the "habit interpretation," is that of course it predicts better, though it does so by singling out what is known to be habitual and leaving the rest for a later day.

Now it was the turn of the New Look to get the "habit interpretation." I think it was my colleague Dick Solomon who was first to the attack. He had a good point with which to start. Perhaps the "taboo" words in that first experiment—words like BITCH—were not what subjects would expect to find in a laboratory experiment. They would hold back responding out of embarrassment or even disbelief. The criticism might apply to that first experiment, but certainly not to the second and to others that had followed it. The house ensign of habit theory is *frequency:* The more often, the easier. The flag of frequency was soon set flying. And indeed, it *is* true within limits that when a person has no idea whatever what words are going to be presented to him in a tachistoscope, he will more easily recognize those words that occur more frequently in print. But you can demonstrate quite as readily that words in a particular *category* will be recognized more quickly than others if subjects are set for them, even when all the words presented are equal in frequency of appearance in text. Aside from which, our subjects in that second experiment had responded to words in their *own* highest value category:

A word quick and easy for one subject was slow and hard for another, given two different value profiles for them.

Well, then, the frequency argument argues, the reason for *that* is *idiosyncratic* frequency. A subject strong in religious interest sees *more* religious words. It is a very curious argument, the upshot of which leads one to the conclusion that the only thing that guides our perceptions is slavery to the probabilities of events we have encountered! How then do we search for particular events? How could perception be of any aid in finding novel objects and events for which we are searching? The model of man that emerges at the end of all that is *Homo historicus,* man as a creature entirely of history and habit.

There are two jokes about all this. The first is that the data upon which the frequency criticism was based turn out on second look to be peculiarly wrong, about which more in a moment. The second is that, a generation later, in the latter 1970s and early 1980s, there was to be a rash of experiment, inspired by two gifted Israeli émigrés in America who had earlier been at the Center for Cognitive Studies, Amos Tversky and Dan Kahneman, demonstrating how very little ordinary people heed solid statistical evidence from the past in making their judgments about the present. About frequency, it was shown in a study by Solomon and Howes that there was a high correlation between speed of recognition and the measured frequency of occurrence of words in English text. This "frequency criticism" was based upon word counts made during the Depression, using texts likely to be encountered by schoolchildren: the famous *Teacher's Word Book,* compiled by Thorndike and Lorge for the guidance of teachers of reading. The texts they had examined, of course, were children's books, widely circulating popular magazines and popular encyclopedias. You will not predict well from such counts what words university students know and are able to define. If university students *were* being guided only by the frequency of occurrence of words in printed text, those texts would certainly not be relevant. Indeed, if you try to predict what words university students can define on the basis of the frequency count they enjoy in the *Teacher's Word Book,* you will fail miserably. Words like FINANCE and SACRED, DOMINATE and COMPETE do not get a play in children's books but they are commonplace and well understood in university readings. What Solomon and Howes did when a word did not appear in the *Word Book* was to assign it to the rarest frequency: one in ten million. And when reexamined, their correlations between ease of recognizing a word and its frequency in English turn out to be almost entirely based on the peculiar inflation in rarity that they imposed. Never mind. If they had done their job properly, they probably *would* have found some correlation—at least for unprepared or naive subjects.*

I wish that Amos Tversky and Danny Kahneman had been around then! For it was to their topic that my interest began to turn. *My* interest, for by the time the frequency tempest in a teapot had spent itself, Leo Postman had gone off to Berkeley and his interests were moving elsewhere. I think he was fed up with controversy. I certainly was. Particularly with the mindlessness of the claim that perception was the slave of bygone probabilities. How, indeed, did we manage to contain within us some balance in our visual *search* of the environment, some balance between respecting real-world likelihoods and following our interests and values? Indeed, how did we manage the moment-to-moment changes required in pursuit of problem tasks? For in perception, we are obviously tuned to *both* the momentary likelihood of events *and* the dictates of the real world. There must be an enormous amount of moment-to-moment recomputing, enormous even for a nervous system as complex as ours.

I have to go back a bit to a little experiment that Leo and I did before he left for California, one that related to this set of conjectures. It took the philosopher of science Tom Kuhn (then a member of the Society of Fellows at Harvard) to appreciate its more general relevance, for he used it as a kind of metaphoric exemplar of his idea of paradigms in science in his *Structure of Scientific Revolution.* Leo and I thought of it as a step along the way to investigating the sensitivity of perception to contexts and rules. The little study that emerged provided us with more astonishment and amusement than any of the dozen or so others that we did together.

We hit on a wild idea. We would have a look at the way perceivers dealt with anomalies and incongruities encountered in the world— the "low frequency" world par excellence. We would do it all in a tachistoscope. There were lots of false starts working with recombined pictures that produced absurd images, but it was too complicated. Playing cards! What could be more strictly constructed, and what more readily violated! Reverse color and suit. We tried to get

*Much of the detail of this reconstruction is taken from Matthew Erdelyi's "A New Look at the New Look," cited earlier in this chapter.

a playing card company to print us such a set. They would not hear of it. We made our own.

There is something of Daumier about a six of clubs printed in red. Not quite obscene, but almost. We sat our subjects before the tachistoscope (incongruous cards and normal ones shown one at a time, each with increasing exposure until finally recognized) and asked them to tell us what they saw.

They behaved astonishingly. For one thing, and not surprisingly, they needed much more time to recognize a reversed playing card correctly—at first. Sensing a bit of red at fast exposure, they would try on subsequent ones to make a heart or a diamond of what they could see. They shed their "errors" with enormous reluctance. What tenacity, forcing the world to conform to their "reasonable" hypotheses. One subject, faced with a quick-flashed red six of clubs, persisted as exposure times lengthened well beyond what is ordinarily needed for spotting a regular playing card, insisted until next-to-last that it was "just" a six of clubs, but that there was now red light shining in the tachistoscope chamber. And then the breakthrough: hoots of laughter, "My God . . ." or soft curses at what idiots they were. *Next* time they would do better with trick cards. And by the end they *could* spot them just about as easily as the real ticket.

One finding we did not appreciate at the time, one that was to change the whole game later: Once you introduce a trick card into the game, recognition times for real cards also go up. For, as we were all to learn later from Shannon and Weaver and "communication theory," the time it takes to recognize something is not just a function of what that something *is*, but what alternative things it *might* be. Recognition time is also a function of the domain of possibilities you must search. But that gets us into the "birth" of the cognitive sciences, and we were nowhere near there yet.

As I look back on that period in the 1950s, it is plain that I was in search of "father figures." "Brother figures" too. I had, as one did during that period, generous research grants that even let me bring occasional visitors to Cambridge for the year, like George Klein, who (as we would say today) worked on the cognitive side of psychoanalysis; and David Krech, who, before his self-styled "evsky-otomy," was the very same I. Krechevsky whose work on hypotheses in rats had so engaged me as an undergraduate. And I was particularly delighted when Edward Tolman came to Cambridge from Berkeley in 1951, invited to take part in one of Talcott Parsons's "integrative seminars" dealing with the Theory of Action. Tolman's cognitive approach to learning theory particularly delighted me. Learning consisted for him of a change in one's *knowledge* of the environment represented in a stored "cognitive map," rather than in a change in habit strength produced by a summing up of past rewards. At the time of his visit, he was thinking about how stimuli encountered by a learner got represented in the learner's knowledge of the world.

I was a bit discouraged by all the "frequency" criticisms. What better than a couple of rat studies in the style of Tolman! They were about the "width" of cognitive maps—how many redundant cues besides the essential ones would a rat pick up in order to be guided to his goal? It depended, it turned out, on drive level. A very hungry rat threading his way through a maze to its goal box would take in very few, would form, so to speak, a "strip map." And if the situation changed, with his preferred cues left out, though other cues were still available, he would be lost. Moderately motivated rats took in more of the world.

Rat experiments were off the main line of my work. But this one was right on the track, rats or not: perceptual "uptake" under differ-ent conditions. But the experiments were also part of my stumbling around in search of "models" in both senses of the word: intellectual heroes and paradigm theories. Tolman, not only for his "cognitive" theory of learning but for his espousal of "means-end" readiness as the fundamental constituent of mind, was my hero.

Wolfgang Köhler was another. I visited in Swarthmore, the New World "home" of Gestalt psychology, presided over by the distin-guished and aristocratic Köhler and his assistant Hans Wallach. I had more in common with Solomon Asch, who, along with Krech and Crutchfield in Berkeley, had been moving social psychology toward a more phenomenological approach—toward concern with how peo-ple saw and interpreted the social world.

Köhler's single-mindedness expressed itself in the search for a neural "isomorph" to the figure-ground phenomenon in vision—the heart of the Gestalt metaphor. That is to say, if one found a phenomenologically "simple" *visual* form, then one should expect to find a counterpart neural process that corresponded to it, that was somehow *similar* to it topologically or even geometrically. Köhler was recording direct current in the brains of his subjects while they viewed sharp-contoured figures passing across the visual field. It was a gallant search for a geometric neural analogue of an experienced figure on a ground. Looked at historically, looking back to the early 1950s, it has an almost tragically quixotic quality. For it was not long after that Hubel and Wiesel were to find that the visual system of the brain operated as a coding system, particular receptors firing in response to visual slant, to edge, to contour, etc., the whole of it then getting put together at some upstream editorial center. The end-of-era feeling of that Swarthmore visit has been heightened for me in retrospect, for as I was setting down these impressions nearly thirty years later, Hubel and Wiesel were awarded the Nobel Prize for Medicine for this very work.

I also went off to see the legendary Adelbert Ames at Dartmouth. He had constructed a set of demonstrations, the "Ames Room" and several others, to show that the world of space that we perceive was built upon a set of "assumptions." His assumptions sounded like the prerecognition hypotheses with which Leo Postman and I had been struggling. I wrote him first, asking for reprints. His response was disconcerting:

> The reason we haven't published more is because we have empirically found that only through actually experiencing the demonstrations can people really get the significance of the phenomena (they can't get it from written descriptions). And if they don't get the significance of the phenomena ("in their guts" or "below the neck," as we say), our hypothesis concerning the origin and nature of sensation and perception doesn't make sense to them. . . . So of late our effort has been concentrated in interesting outstanding persons in the various disciplines in our stuff, and confirming the validity of our hypotheses through showing their general applicability. When you come up, you can see some material from persons in other disciplines. I apologize for this long letter, but some kind of explanation seemed necessary.

Never mind. Leo and I drove up to Hanover and were duly put through the demonstrations. They were ingenious all right. If you conceal cues about distance *and* about the real size of objects (providing only "retinal" or snapshot size as a cue), you do indeed force the visual system to make some weird decisions. Objects are always seen as having an intrinsic size and as being at a particular distance: the so-called size-distance invariance that even Sunday painters must master. If you cannot figure out that invariance for lack of cues, you impose your assumptions on what you do see in a most obdurate fashion.

I don't think either of us, Leo or I, was caught enough "in the gut" to satisfy Ames. I suggested that it would be interesting to study the "buildup" of his demonstration illusions by the use of tachistoscopic flashes. He did not think much of that. It was demonstration he was after, not experimental manipulation. And demonstration of a kind that, I think, speaks more to the artist's wonder than to the scientist's.

I recall my first meeting with Ernst Gombrich a few years later when he was at work on his masterful *Art and Illusion.* He wanted to talk about the perception of works of art, and we arranged to have lunch during a visit to his son, who was then a graduate student at Harvard. He told me that he was trying to understand how a painting could evoke the illusion of reality. "There must, beyond all the artifice of the painter, be something language-like about it, for the painting that succeeds in evoking the 'real' depends to an extraordinary degree upon conventions. The conventions of representing upon which the artist depends must somehow be the same as those the perceiver uses in seeing, don't you think?" Gombrich was fluent in his understanding of perception, fluent and open to wonder. We talked a good deal about Constable's painting of Wivenhoe Park, and Gombrich's capacity to conserve the artistry of that beautiful picture while analyzing both its tricks and its conventionalities was for me a miracle of living in two worlds at once. They were the two worlds whose simultaneous existence seemed to bedevil Adelbert Ames.

Save for a few brief encounters, I never saw Ames again—though Ernst Gombrich became a good friend over the years. I think my friendship with one made me understand the other better. A decade later, in 1960, a few years after my first wife and I had been divorced, I married Ames's niece and came to know the family in which he had been a legend. Two of his sisters were gifted painters—one a reluctant professional, the other an inspired amateur of extraordinary power. The first, Blanche, painted the famous collection of orchids that her botanist husband, Oakes Ames, was gathering from around the world for Harvard's collection, and her oils and watercolors are now esteemed in their own right. Jesse Ames's self-portrait is, I think, a work of self-analysis that rivals in depth some of the most discerning of John Singer Sargent's portraits. Adelbert, after finishing a law degree he never put to use, turned to painting. Very soon after (and with the aid of his sister Blanche), he veered off, turning instead to the exploration of a theory of color. And then to a theory of space and to the dilemma of how it might be that though the two eyes registered images of different sizes, they reconciled them by seeing one image of a particular size. (Indeed, he must have doubted this feat of nature, for at his Dartmouth Eye Institute it was customary to fit spectacles for those with different-sized images in their two eyes to correct the "fault.") He delved into the geometry of visual space and, finally, turned his uncertainties about the "appearance of reality" into a philosopher's stone that would explain how a world of meaningless "hieroglyphics" could be made into the appearance of sense. It was an "assumptive" world. Like Manet's "Nature is only a hypothesis" and Ernst Gombrich's conventions of representation!

But there was the zeal of an updated *philosophe* about Ames, for he felt that if his demonstrations were truly *felt*, they could liberate, in much the same way as those eighteenth century predecessors felt that the *Encyclopédie* could liberate from presupposition and ignorance.

In the end, he had little impact on psychology or philosophy, but he continues to fascinate artists. The Oxford philosopher A. J. Ayer, reviewing Gombrich's *Art and Illusion* in the *Times Literary Supplement*, draws a distinction between journeymen and pontiffs, praising Gombrich for making a place for the journeyman in art history. Ames's philosophy of perception, was, alas, for pontiffs only. Nelson Goodman, whose level gaze I have always admired, remarks in *The Structure of Appearance:*

> I look upon philosophy as having the function of clearing away perplexity and confusion on the most humble as on the most exalted levels of thought; and I hope the patient reader, much as he might like to take quick measure of the universe, may find that in philosophy as in science the microscopic method has its own fascination and rewards.

I suppose, as with one's family, one can never really set aside the influence of those with whom one struggled early. My search for a coherent view of the New Look was bound to work its way back to Professor Boring. Somehow, as I came on a new result or got a new idea about how perceptual filtering worked, I would have lunch with him or exchange letters about something of mine or his (though we were a hundred yards from each other). It was not at all asking "by your leave," rather a way of testing how cold the water might be, short of taking the full plunge. For here was a man who could be counted on to be intellectually severe and appreciative in one breath. In those years after the Harvard "fission" he was preoccupied with what he called "sociotropy" and "biotropy" in psychology.

I gave a colloquium in Memorial Hall to his "biotropes." It was on "social perception," and much too defensive, too insistent on the role of idiosyncratic personal determinants of perceiving. One of those famous single-spaced letters from Boring was in my box the next day:

> . . . A very much deeper thing . . . is the evidence of ambivalence in the relation of sociotropy and biotropy. You call this subject "social perception." That sounds like propaganda for something. Then you back down and say that it is perception, as indeed it is. Why all this talk about the matter then? The topic was "Some Social Determinants of Perception." If you did not appeal to the socio-biotropy dichotomy and just brought in a paper of discussion of certain social factors in perception, then this potential in-out-group aggression psychology would not get itself dynamized in the context at all. There were numerous little instances. You tended to make digs at what psychophysicists had thought about perception, or how they defined the stimulus, and it all seemed to me unsophisticated and unscholarly and biased, the way Harry Murray's aggressions about what he did not care to understand seemed. . . . You caught me in a week when I had just gone back to read Tolman and to try to understand him. So I kept putting your digs up against him and thinking that he had seen things as broadly as you could want, though you did not mention him. And I thought: Does Jerry really understand the history of these attitudinal problems in psychophysics and what, e.g., Kulpe did to the Wundtians in 1893 and all that, or is he just talking loosely as they must do in his in-group, increasing their own sense of solidarity by abusing the absent indefensible out-group? I know all about this group structure in systematic psychology. I was part of Titchener's in-group. I have seen how it worked both integratively and disruptively here in psychology at Harvard.

He then went on to a book that Hadley Cantril had just published in adulation of the Ames demonstration—the "Yellow Book," he called it, damning its "arrogance" for neglecting all that had gone before.

I was so cast down, I couldn't bring myself to write back for several days. Had I so badly overshot in my bid to get an equal hearing for personal and social factors in perception that I had deepened the gap between the sociotropes and biotropes? It was the very last thing I had wanted to do. I wrote and apologized for my edgy presentation. I did *not* want to forswear history. Cantril's book had appalled me as much as it had him. As far as I was concerned, I told him, my work was "as much a continuation of a century of work that had preceded it as, say, Brunswik's on the constancies." *I* knew perfectly well that *he* knew perfectly well that I knew the history he was citing: I had learned it from him in his famous history seminar, in which I had been one of *his* "in-group." But I also knew what he was trying to tell me.

The inevitable gracious letter after the storm arrived a week later.

Really I do not mean to ride a tired horse to death, but let me say one thing more about the nature of perception, because I reread a little Wundt last night getting ready for today's history lecture.

The opposition between *Vorstellung* (presentation—tabula rasa impressing—Locke, Hume) and *Wahrnehmung* (apprehending truth—objective reference—Leibnitz, Reid) has been going on all the time. The problem as Reid put it was: how do impressed sensations come to signify the external world, and he solved the mystery by saying that they do because God so wills it.

When Wundt came to create a scientific psychology, as he thought, in the 1850–60s, he saw—or thought he saw—that psychology transcended physiology because it dealt with perception. Hence his *Beitrage zur Theorie der Sinneswahrnehmung* [*Treatise on the Theory of Sense Perception*]. N.B. *Wahrnehmung*, not *Vorstellung*. You read that introduction as I did last night.

You get first: *"Alle Psychologie beginnt mit der Selbstbeobachtung."* If you translate *Selbstbeobachtung* as self-observation or introspection and think perhaps of Titchener (50 years later), you think that Wundt was missing the point of perception, dealing with it passively like Locke and Hume.

But you read on. *"Die Erscheinungen des Buwusstseins sind zusammgesetze Produktiv der unbewussten Seele."* ["The phenomenal appearance of things that characterizes conscious awareness is the combined product of processes in the unconscious mind."] What's that mean? It means that psychology considers in perception the way the products of the unconscious mind are put together in inner perception by unconscious inference to yield the phenomena of consciousness.

Do you wonder that I said to myself: "Ha! Wundt's saying that with Jerry Bruner in mind."

Boring (and Wundt!) were bound to prevail. But how were we to get at those "processes in the unconscious mind" that were producing the prodigies of experience? No question Boring was right about the "in-group." The New Lookers were certainly that, and in a way, that may have been the weakness of the movement. As a group—in correspondence and getting together a few times yearly at the usual professional meetings—we were much as Isaiah Berlin describes Oxford philosophy in his day: self-centered, increasingly convinced that no one outside our magic circle had much to teach us, "vain and foolish and, I have no doubt, irritating to others." And to that can be added his reflection: "But I suspect that those who have never been under the spell of this kind of illusion, even for a short while, have not known true intellectual happiness."

Unfortunately, perhaps, the New Look became the new way of looking at problems in social psychology and in the study of personality dynamics. I say unfortunately. *My* misfortune. The idea that action is better understood as an adaptation to what the actor is *experiencing* rather than as a "response" to "stimuli" in an external world fitted the spirit of the times. It was a long-delayed reaction against radical behaviorism. Herman Witkin conceived of personality differences as relating to differences in dependence upon inner and outer sources of stimulation. Some were even proposing that personality derived from cognitive style. I was delighted with these new developments. But what I felt was missing from the general progress was a comprehensive theory of perception per se, one comprehensive enough to deal with both figure/ground and ego defense!

I kept knocking at the door of the "classical" phenomena of perception with little experiments. There was one on "color assimilation" to show how the perceived identity of an object would change the film color it bore. There was another on classical "figure closure," showing that a crowded *13* would be seen as the letter *B* when in a letter series and as a *13* in the company of numbers. One on apparent movement (the movement we see when a point or line appears first at one position, then at another, with an appropriate interval between them) showed that apparent speed and even path of movement were in part determined by context and meaning.

That work was mostly producing lively examples for textbook writers to add to the tail end of chapters dealing with color assimilation or figural closure or apparent movement. Or perhaps providing training for Harvard graduate students—less the experiments than the chance they provided for reading the classical literature of perception with serious intent. Not one of my students ever went on to work on perception proper!

Ned Jones demonstrated in his honors thesis at Harvard that if two "balls" are made to cross over each other in apparent movement, they will be seen as *passing* each other if also seen as being thrown by baseball players, but as *caroming* off each other if seen as moving on the surface of a billiard table. While he was slaving away in the 1950s in the top of Emerson Hall with his cumbersome projectors and microswitches, an Austrian psychologist, Fritz Heider, steeped in the Continental phenomenological tradition and fresh on the American scene, was producing a film. It was also about movement —but with a difference. The featured players were a big square, a modest circle and a dauntless triangle, their world a blank screen save for a large boxlike outline with a doorlike opening in it. They moved about in a most "natural" way, and in a matter of seconds one irresistibly saw a full-blown scenario in which the plucky triangle is trying to rescue the pursued circle from the bullying square, using the house as a shelter against the square's assaults. I used to show that film to my undergraduate classes. Nobody ever reported *not* seeing *some* sort of drama being enacted.

How had *die unbewusste Seele* learned to "see" drama? Or baseball or billiards? Or were they built into the program for making those "unconscious inferences"—perception imitating drama, as my companion had insisted at that *Hamlet?* And how do we always— irresistibly, it seems—attribute dispositions and traits to others? And why, as Ned Jones was to demonstrate so brilliantly a quarter century later, do we tend to see the "reasons" behind the acts of others as reflecting their dispositions, while we see our own acts as dictated by circumstances?

Let me come back now to the Judas Eye and its conceptual miseries.

It helps to have a fresh metaphor with which to vault out of old trouble. The old one had got us into it. "Unconscious inference," *die unbewusste Seele,* was begging for it. McDougall's Cambridge hero, the British philosopher G. F. Stout, had fought a battle against something that bore the ancient label of "anoetic sentience." Its antique status came from Aristotle's argument that the "common sense" (in contrast to the special senses whose messages it collated) had to derive from soul or mind (*nous:* hence "noetic"), for it betrayed a working knowledge of the world rather than merely of sensation. And *nous* for Aristotle was active, was a program—what the Schoolmen later were to characterize as a *vis integretiva.* The gist of the argument was that you did not *see* things without *looking for* them, hear without listening, and so on.

Looking, listening, anticipating: all of these entailed the presence of a *hypothesis*. And what was that? Well, little more than the assertion that we were never indifferent, always tuned, ever readier for some events than for others. That was a first step: being tuned by a hypothesis. The second was input from the world, input that either *matched* a hypothesis in force or *mismatched*. If it were the former, the hypothesis would be *confirmed* and we would see. If the latter, then there would be correction: The operative hypotheses would change until a satisfactory "match" to input could be made. The world, in short, was providing not *sensation* but fodder for our hypotheses.

When I first tried out this "bizarre" three-step theory of perception at a gala symposium in Austin, Texas, in 1951 to inaugurate a new psychology building, I was reticent to the point of being apologetic. "The reader may object that our model of the information-confirmation cycle seems too saccadic, too jumpy, that perception seems to work more smoothly. . . . [But] there need be no phenomenal resemblance . . . between the feeling tone of a psychic process and the conceptual model used to predict or describe it." I brazened on to propose that hypotheses vary in their "strength." Being often confirmed in the past, having a monopoly over other hypotheses, and being supported by a network of supporting hypotheses—all these would make a hypothesis "stronger." The stronger a hypothesis, the less matching information was necessary to confirm it and the more mismatching information to disconfirm it. (Monopoly, of course, was put into the list to deal with highly "driven," fixated hypotheses of the kind that paranoids entertain.)

My New Look friends liked the paper—so did Edward Tolman and my other vigorous Berkeley ally, David Krech. It was not my style to turn its ideas into an explicit program of research. No matter. It turned into a subterranean one.

Robert Oppenheimer invited me to come to the Institute for Advanced Study for the year 1952–53. I "discovered" that physicists were just as concerned with my kinds of problems as psychologists! My new friends there, principally theoretical physicists like Bram Pais and Georg Placzek, liked to discuss perception and "observation." So did Robert Oppenheimer. They took it for granted that the "model" in your head determined the phenomena in nature you could know about. "Perception as you psychologists study it can't, after all, be different from observation in physics, can it?"

George Miller urged me to read the still new *Theory of Communication* by Claude Shannon and Warren Weaver. It is about the coding of events in the world and their informativeness—a physicist's topic. An event is informative in the degree that it permits one to decide among a set of alternative possibilities as to what it might have been. It is a deceptively simple and powerful idea.

The larger the number of alternative events possible, the more informative the particular event perceived will be. The value of a stimulus is what it *might* have been, rather than simply what it *is*. If a device must figure out which among a set of *possible* alternatives a given stimulus actually *is*, then its decision time would depend on the number of possible alternatives it has considered. A computer would go about its task in an economical way, as in Twenty Questions. It would divide the domain of possibilities in half each time, determine in which of the two halves the input event belonged, and eliminate the empty half. It is not clear how people would do the same task, for it is often unclear (even to them) how many possibilities they are entertaining and how they "partition" for search. That depends upon the representation of the world they carry in their heads. And how they derive sets of alternatives from it to face particular events.

Is this a psychological theory or a theory about the logic of choice?

When I came back to Cambridge from the Institute the following fall, George and I continued to teach our old standby "cognitive processes" course—"Psych 148." We were both full of "models-in-the-head" that people use for constructing and interpreting the world. He had a lovely metaphor: We had a model of the world that we spun just a little bit faster than the world went so that we could anticipate what was about to happen by changing to an appropriate hypothesis—and God save you if it was wrong; you then might miss the whole act.

What a job it has, that hypothesis generator! It has to search for what it *wants*, but at the same time keep track of what is going on in the world and what is going to happen first. Do only the first, and you have an illusioned monomaniac. Do the second, and the poor robot, governed only by the real-world likelihoods, will starve to death. You need both—some monomaniac to keep searching, some realist to keep track of where you are and what can be found there.

Without quite realizing it, we had freed ourselves from "sensations" and their overlaid "interpretive" perceptions. We were thinking instead in terms of coding systems, the flow of information through them, the heuristics, and the clever ways in which that information was combined and recombined in the service of coding. All of it was extraordinarily primitive. But the rudiments of a new approach to perception were there.

I think if there were a retrospective Nobel Prize in Psychology for the mid-1950s, George Miller would win it hands down—and on the basis of one article (though he had lots of other arrows in his quiver). It was a paper with the beguiling title "The Magic Number Seven $\pm$ 2." It is not even "about" perception but about immediate memory, so called. But it shed its light over the whole cognitive landscape. It is about the limitations on human information capacity. The "magic number" was the number of alternatives that a human being could keep in mind in immediate memory—7 ± 2. That, to use the jargon of those days, was the channel capacity of the human system. The existence of that limit forced two things upon us. The first was selectivity: Given this severe constraint on what you could process, to what would you direct your attention? The second was organization or "chunking": Given that you had only seven slots, you could fill them with gold or with dross. You could store and use a few values for falling bodies in different gravities, say, or you could store and use the comparable space, for the formula could handle any value possible:

$$S = \frac{gt^2}{2}$$

What Miller did quite incidentally in that paper was to reduce the old "frequency argument" to subordinate status. To appreciate this feat, you need to know about the founding hero of the frequency argument and what he set in motion. His name was Hermann Ebbinghaus and his accomplishments weighed heavily in the founding of "scientific" psychology in the last century. It was he who had devised pronounceable nonsense-syllable trigrams like DAX and PAF, which were as far from words as he could get them. He then committed lists of them to memory. As a young man he had gone to Paris, lived in a garret (or so Professor Boring's account would have it), and there drilled himself on his lists of nonsense syllables, so many per day, to ascertain how many he could remember and how many he would lose by the next day. From this work came his learning curves and, more important, his rates of forgetting reckoned in terms of how often he had drilled and how long ago. It was thoroughly associationist and Herbartian in spirit, and from it were generated such principles as: "Of two associations of equal age, the one more frequently practiced will be the stronger" or "Of two associations of equal strength, the older will be the stronger." Ebbinghaus started the systematic, quantitative study of memory. The frequency argument was its first product.

Using nonsense syllables was clever—and eventually self-defeating. All syllables are equally important or relevant. You do not have to consider the problems of selective memory or the organization of memory. You can't do anything with nonsense syllables except put them in a list or string them out like beads. By purifying the objects to be memorized, Ebbinghaus and his followers had ruled out the two key problems of memory—organization and selectivity. It was Miller's paper that made that fact crystal clear. George Miller turned that all upside down in that one brilliant paper. (Sir Frederic Bartlett had before, in 1932, but the conceptual apparatus he used was too soft to bring down the edifice of the nonsense syllable.)

George, Leo Postman and I did a study together combining some of these new ideas about informativeness and selectivity. It has now become the chestnut of introductory laboratory courses in psychology. Then, in the early 1950s, it was something quite new. We asked people to tell us what they could see when we flashed strings of letters of varying approximation to English on a screen—strings of different degrees of nonsense, though "nonsense" takes on a new meaning in this dispensation, for there is a huge difference between letter strings like YRULPSOC and RSEMPOIN and ones like APHYSTER, TERVALLE, MOSSIANT and VERNALIT, though they are all "nonsense." You can easily construct words that "imitate" the single-letter, digram, trigram, or n-letter frequencies of English (or French or German or whatever), without those words actually being "real." The more closely your nonsense strings approximate the higher-order multiletter structure of English words, the more rapidly they are recognized when you flash them in a tachistoscope. So far, simple enough—and not the least surprising commonsensically.

The very same Claude Shannon whose book I mentioned earlier had done a close estimate of the "redundancy" of English word structure. If Shannon's "informativeness" is akin to surprise, redundancy is its opposite. The only letter that can go into Q*OTATION is U. It has no informativeness, is completely redundant—if you know English. The redundancy of word structure is what letters you may expect to find and with what probability in sequences of letters composing words of language. We could easily determine the redundancy of the "nonsense" letter strings we had flashed at our subjects. In that tachistoscopic study, if you corrected the strings for their redundancy, you discovered that the time it took to recognize any letter string depended entirely on its redundancy. You don't need much more input to "see" what fills the space in MOSS*ANT than you do in MOTH*RHOOD, but you'll need plenty more to figure out Y*ULPSOC. It raises nice questions about *where* or *how* one is looking in the process of perceiving—inside or out, for example. Plainly, perception (or whatever it is) is tuned to expectable alternatives—but what are the expectabilities?

I think I am suspicious of "formal" models of human behavior—theories couched exclusively in mathematical terms or in abstract "flow diagrams." I have always been sympathetic to the metaphors of computation and information processing, but resistant to getting trapped in their necessary measurement constraints. Perhaps I feel that such systems of measurement trap you on their flypaper while you are still wanting to fly. Their precision exacts a very high price in the abandonment of imagination—eventually, no doubt, well worth paying. But not now!

I did not, in consequence, get deeply drawn into the Harvard-MIT "cognitive sciences" network—the remarkable group of people who were pursuing formal ideas about information processing and computing and decisionmaking. George Miller and Oliver Selfridge kept me abreast enough, I thought. I regret now not getting more involved earlier.

I turned to more concrete ways of formulating my ideas. There was the exploding field of neurophysiology. A new generation of investigators was discovering some of the ways in which the nervous system "filtered" input from the senses to accord with centrally induced states—and three of them were close friends, who were fairly bubbling with excitement: Karl Pribram, Walter Rosenblith and Bob Galambos. It was through one of them that I first heard of "gating." The Mexican physiologist Hernández-Péon and his colleagues had recorded electrical activity from the cochlear nucleus of a live cat's brain. The cochlear nucleus is the first junction point for the bundle from the auditory nerve after it leaves the cochlea and enters the brain. It is, in the words of Lord Adrian, the first editorial station on the way up.

When you sound a click, you can measure a burst of electrical activity from the cochlear nucleus. But now confront the cat with a mouse, securely inside a bell jar, and when you sound the standard click, there is no electrical discharge or a much reduced one. His attention is elsewhere engaged and some channel must have carried the message downstream to the cochlear nucleus to turn it off or dampen it. For the cat's auditory system the click was now "irrelevant." What a different nervous system from the one I had studied in my course in neuroanatomy. I rejoiced with my physiologist friends each time a tract was found that handled this "gating." One was even found that turned off the sensitivity to those clicks—a fiber bundle that carried messages downstream to the periphery.

I haunted the literature on brain mechanisms in perception, even wrote several long articles on the bearing of this work on the nature of perception to convince my colleagues we were approaching a new Jerusalem. That rich excursion eventually succeeded in turning my interest right back to where I had started from—but this time, better equipped with a new set of processes, new ideas, new procedures. The central issue that emerges from that rich work is "tuning," as I would prefer to call it. It comprises an array of processes far subtler than the physiologist can yet measure with even his finest electro-chemical recordings. They signal from upstream in the cerebral cortex to downstream in the sensory and motor systems to tune or prepare the organism for what it needs in the environment and what it will encounter there. It is a system of a complexity that can accommodate the need to give special place to surprises, to the probability structure of the world as represented in "models" that the brain stores, and to the requirements of acts-in-progress (as with Hernández-Péon's "tuned" cat).

To this rich picture was being added an element of "intention" —by the brilliant German biologist von Holst. The burden of von Holst's story was that before sending out motor impulses, the motor cortex was also transmitting "reafference copies" of its commands, f.y.i. invoices to prepare the neuromuscular system for acts that were about to occur, that were intended. My tennis partner and friend Richard Held, at MIT, even demonstrated that these reafferent impulses were needed for organisms to learn the environments in which they operated. His was the renowned study of kittens who could not learn to adjust to a visually distorted environment unless they could also *act* upon that environment. How one processed the visual environment depended on plans for acting upon it.

The frontier between psychology and neurophysiology was going through just as profound a revolution as that in the information sciences. The two of them were possibly converging.

I wrote my last "serious" papers on perception in the late 1950s. One was about its neural substrate and the other bore the telltale title "On Perceptual Readiness." It was about the "categorical" nature of perceiving. It was a theme that would occupy me for years after— more about inference and organizational strategies than about the appearance of the visual world. I had already shifted my allegiance to the study of thinking.

Just at that departure point, a new chapter in perception opened. I must say a few words about it. For I think, ironically enough, it was the chapter that resolved the dilemma of the Judas Eye. At the start, it was largely a British story, and its central figures were two close friends of mine, Richard Gregory and Donald Broadbent, both students of the Frederic Bartlett who had fought so valiantly to break through the mystique of Ebbinghaus and his nonsense syllables. They provided the needed demonstrations and then adapted the "computer model" to give new meaning to the concept of the filter in perception. Richard and Donald had been my closest companions during my year at Cambridge in 1956, and we had spent many hours together, talking about the sorts of issues that have filled these pages.

For practical reasons growing out of the work of British psychologists during the war (under the leadership of Bartlett), the British were considerably less interested in the philosophical problems of perception and more in their applications to "human performance" in practical tasks. They had had to figure out what to do when machines (like fighter aircraft) outsprinted human reaction times, or when displays (such as early radar) spewed out information faster or more monotonously than most human operators could take it in and digest it. They called what they did the study of *attention*—which disembarrassed them from the outset of some antique philosophical ghosts.

Besides which, British psychologists (more in awe of their philosophical colleagues than they should be) like to conceal their theoretical passions behind a practical cloak, and to this day Donald Broadbent (the doyen of British theorists) prefers to call himself an "applied psychologist." The British, too, have a pragmatic sense that alerts them to that most precious thing a good theory. If you do not have one, you do well to start from common sense. They did.

The crucial demonstration that reopened the debate on "how you know something when you don't really know it" was the cocktail party phenomenon, as it came to be known. They used dichotic listening as their instrument. It became an Oxbridge specialty. You simply fix headphones on your subject, lead a message to one ear and a different one to the other. If you put a different Parliamentary speech from Hansard's into each ear, the listener will flip back and forth between the ears and make some sort of amalgam of them. If the messages to the two ears are quite different, there is virtually no flipping. But then some curious things. If, when your listener is attending to one ear, you put a personal message or speak his name in the other, he immediately flips over. How did he know the message was there if he wasn't listening to it?

Could there be some sort of filter tuned to certain unheard features of input, programmed in such a way as to flip full on when the input displayed certain features? Well, what sorts of features? The cocktail party demonstration certainly suggested that the filter could be tuned to *semantic* features of input, like reference to oneself. Semantic features are categorical; they deal with *classes* of meaning. Might not there be comparable programming to deal with "values" or other classes of words—like those one might expect to find when perceptual defense or vigilance is operating?

The processing model that Broadbent and others proposed involved a stage of "buffer storage," where input could be literally held until necessary analyses could be done upon it in the light of the filtering program in force—done in any depth necessary. It was no longer bizarre, no longer a Judas Eye. For this is typically how a computing device goes about its business. If a lowly computer can do it, surely it can be done by a nervous system whose mantle alone contains 5×10^9 connections! We still don't know what kind of hardware in the nervous system brings off what the computer can do, but once you allow a system to have a buffer store that can be scanned before it lets its contents into "display" (let me call it "consciousness"), it does not take much imagination to figure out some possibilities. Indeed, years before multistep models of perceiving came on the scene, the ingenious Canadian neuropsychologist Donald Hebb had pointed out that the anatomy of the cortex suggested a profusion of short-loop circuits whose principal function might be to carry messages that reverberated as if in readiness to alter subsequent impulses that come into the system. Who knows? Perhaps those looping Lorente de No circuits, as they are called, will someday prove to be the home of that buffer store.

In fact, though my interests turned elsewhere, I never could quite leave the study of perception alone. I worked on eye movements with my old Cambridge friend and colleague Norman Mackworth, with my former student Molly Potter on the constructional processes whereby low-grade visual input is hammered into form by hypotheses (and often with disastrous results, as with aircraft pilots flying in foggy conditions), and on the development of various aspects of perception. But I never again thought of myself as anything more than, perhaps, an overqualified amateur of the subject, kept spottily informed by occasional reading and by the charged talk of old friends.

As I look back at those years of the New Look and after, it is hard not to be bemused by the accidents, the false starts, one's own pigheadedness, even the self-imposed blindness of in-groups. Our band of worthies, the "New Lookers," started out to liberate psychology from the domination of sense-data theory, the notion that meaning is an overlay on a sensory core. It was part, I have no doubt, of a broader and deeper cultural movement to change the image of man from a passive receiver and responder to an active selector and constructor of experience. No doubt, too, it "succeeded"—and the quotation marks are not there in false modesty. For in another sense it failed. New Look metaphor did not change theories of perception, however much it readied the ground for the change. The "cognitive revolution" changed them, and particularly the respected metaphor of information-processing automata—computers. Translating the Judas Eye into the language of buffer storage was as good as cleansing suspect money by deposit in an unmarked Swiss bank account.

Truth to tell, we probably need a New Look about once every other decade—the rekindling of concern for how, in detail, perception responds to needs, to wishes, to expectancies; how it plays its part in producing styles of mind and patterns of personality. It could be done better now—thanks, ironically, to the liberating effect of the computer on the psychologist's image of what is humanly possible. We might even learn one day how, if life imitates drama, perception does so as well.

7

The Turn to Mind

I had, I suppose, been studying perception as a kind of thinking
or problem solving. But how get more directly to it? Gifted writers,
such as Graham Wallas, had argued compellingly for the swift silence
of thought that emerged finally as illumination. And there was Freud
to warn us about accepting what most people said. The obvious way
to have started would have been, of course, to get people to think
aloud and then examine what they did on the basis of what they said.
"Thinking" was not a "mainstream" topic in psychology. Too mentalistic, too subjective, too shifty. A topic for foreigners, like the Würzburg School, philosophically committed to the idea that thought was
an act and to proving (against Locke) that it was imageless.

Köhler had got away with it by studying "problem solving" in
chimpanzees. When they found solutions to problems they had never
before encountered (and therefore without benefit of learning), he
called it "insight." And that had to be explained away in traditional
learning theory. But at least he could not be ignored. The others, the
philosophically motivated foreigners, *could* be ignored: exotic beyond the pale.

George Miller said, laughing, at lunch: "You're supposed to get at
the mind through the eye, ear, nose and throat if you're a real psychologist." And we recited together the stale joke about how psychology first lost its soul and then its mind.

I suppose it had. But the topic of thinking reeks with mind. To
study it and be taken seriously, you would have to camouflage it, like
Tolman's "Vicarious Trial and Error," smuggling the sheep of con-

sciousness into learning theory under behavioral wolf's clothing. It was 1952.

What most of the research on "thinking" was about was syllogisms —or problem solving in the manner of Köhler. You set tasks in syllogistic reasoning. "All men are mortal. Socrates is a man. . . ." Some interesting things had been found, like "atmosphere" effects: "all" in the major and the minor premises disposed people to accept "all" in the conclusion. Or people did better with concrete propositions than with the logician's "All x is y." The focus was upon the forms of human error: logical error, or was it linguistic? The problem-solving literature was somewhat richer but fuzzier. Its richness was due principally to Max Wertheimer, who had founded Gestalt psychology along with Köhler and was now an émigré teaching at the New School in New York. Typical problem: There is a tumor in the middle of the body that responds to X-rays of a magnitude that will burn the normal tissue around it. How do you get X-rays to the tumor without damage to other tissues? Wertheimer drove relentlessly at a central target that he could never quite hit: Problem solving and thinking required a "structuring" of the task at hand. The structure one found was "productive" in the sense that it permitted you to produce or generate a solution rather than reproduce one from memory. For all the fuzziness, there were also some rich findings—particularly about "fixation" in thinking. The contents of a bottle of ginger ale would not, for example, be used as readily to float a cork out of a narrow beaker as would water, the former being fixated in the problem solver's mind as something to drink rather than a medium for floating.

How little impact all this had on the mainstream of psychology! A little counting tells the story. Take the main texts, the advanced "high status" ones. When I was a graduate student, Woodworth's *Experimental Psychology* was *the* book. You virtually committed it to memory when you took the 1939 Harvard "prelims," the book having appeared the year before. It boasts 823 pages of text. By a generous count, the topic of thinking is treated in two brief chapters, one on "Problem Solving" (including animal studies), the other on "Thinking." All told, 77 pages. When the prestigious *Handbook of Experimental Psychology* appeared in 1951, under Smitty Stevens's editorship, it had 1,362 pages. This time, the topic was disposed of in a chapter called "Cognitive Processes": 27 pages. Add a few to that, for George Miller had a chapter on "Speech and Language," the last few pages of which were devoted to the relation of thought and language. The mind was not doing well in psychology. The eye, ear, nose and throat fared far better: nine chapters, about four hundred pages.

The early story of cognitive studies is full of clever ruses, procedural conventions for making mental processes look more "objective." The basic trick was to state your findings in centimeters, grams and seconds—c.g.s. Descartes had proclaimed that the hallmark of matter was extension, of mind, reflection. But the spirit of Descartes was not much about in 1952. Curiously, you could *ask* your subject to perform any mental operation you liked. So long as you expressed your results in "c.g.s." Perhaps the requirement made American cognitive psychologists cleverer than they might otherwise have been! "Whatever exists, exists in some quantity." It was Hume's voice, not Descartes's. Besides, a good measure provides a way of checking whether you are getting across to your subjects, and if you are, then the measure lets you study variations.

Take "mental chronometry" as a case in point. It is older than psychology. Its aim is to measure the time required by particular mental processes. It received its first backhand recognition in 1796 when the Greenwich astronomer Maskelyne dismissed his assistant Kinnebrook for observing star transits a second later than the master did. It turned out to be a matter of how one counted beats of a chronometer while watching a star crossing a wire in the telescope field—a classic of mental chronometry. The Dutch physiologist Donders published directly on the subject in 1868. Indeed, so impressed were Posner and Shulman more than a century later that they put Donders among the four "founding fathers" of cognitive science (the other three being Oswald Kulpe, Herbert Simon and myself, which makes it a rather long pregnancy!). "His basic idea was to assume that the time between stimulus and response could be divided into a series of stages, each of which added a component to the overall reaction time." Obtain a reaction time to the appearance of, say, a light. Now ask your subject to react only when a white light appears, but not a blue one. It takes longer. Donders subtracted the simple reaction time from the choice reaction time: the difference (he said) was the time required to make a choice between white and colored light. It is a very appealing idea—though one that has caused repeated grief and confusion in psychology. It assumes that component mental processes are successive or sequential (rather than running parallel). Most seriously, it fails to take context into account, and that may be the biggest part of the story of thinking. Some might say that Donders may be more of a Pied Piper than a founding father!

I confess I came within a hair of using "mental chronometry" to get at the processes of inference. Another classic detour lured me instead. It went by the name of "concept attainment." It is objectively impeccable. All that it requires of your subject is that he tell you whether a stimulus "belongs" in a particular class or doesn't. Class membership, of course, is a matter of rule, a rule that is in the mind of the beholder. The "category problem" has an ancient philosophical lineage, most of it forgotten or suppressed in the early research on "concept attainment." To me it seemed possible that the step from the particular to the general was the opening stage in the voyage beyond the information given.

Birthdays? My last year as a schoolboy was 1932. It was an altogether remarkable year. Just a half century ago. Take its novels. Aldous Huxley's *Brave New World*, James Farrell's *Young Lonigan*, Ernest Hemingway's *Death in the Afternoon*, William Faulkner's *Light in August*. Eventually I read them and they all gripped my imagination. And I should add John Dos Passos's *1919*, which I even got Kurt Lewin to read, the better to know what his adopted America was like. All appeared in 1932. I want to argue not dates, but *Zeitgeist*. After all, that was also the year in which E. D. Adrian shared a Nobel Prize in Medicine and opened a speculative inning on how it was that continuous events in the world registered their message on neurons that fired discontinuously all-or-none. It could not have been by chance entirely that 1932 was also the year when Werner Heisenberg won his Nobel Prize for Physics and made the subject of "uncertainty" grist for the mill of ordinary talk.

Two books published by psychologists that year were infused with that same 1932 *Zeitgeist*. Frederic Bartlett published *Remembering;* Edward Tolman, *Purposive Behavior in Animals and Men*. I did not read either of them until a few years later. They both (as do the novels) figure in this story.

For Bartlett, the problem of memory was the problem of organization, how lived experience is organized into a "schema" and how that schema represents the world in a manner to make memory recoverable and usable. Memory for Bartlett was not "laid down" once for all, but could be "turned around on" and reorganized at any time. Memory was inherently dynamic: it sharpened things for emphasis, assimilated the strange to the familiar, and conventionalized what was left in store. The memory schema for Bartlett was an updatable representation of the world, a real "model in the head."

For Bartlett, the engine that drove the mental enterprise (including memory) was "effort after meaning." It was constantly on the go —sorting, emphasizing, reconciling. It was about as far away as you could get from Ebbinghaus in his garret.

The clearest way to espouse purposive mentalism in an age of behaviorism was to conceal it in learning theory, the chosen instrument of antimentalistic psychology. That was what Edward Tolman did. He did it so well that he forced even that most redoubtable antimentalist, Clark Hull at Yale, into such Byzantine absurdities (like "pure stimulus acts" to stand for perception) that he finally came down of his own cumbersome weight. It was reminiscent of pre-Copernican astronomers adding epicycles to their orbits to account for fresh astronomical data. Edward Tolman called himself a "cognitive" learning theorist and he sheltered extraordinarily clever young rebels under his wing at Berkeley. Tolman was playfully freer of dogmatism than any influential psychologist of his generation. His style of debate was the stunning experiment that focused on the insufficiency of behaviorist explanation and gently added a new purposivism or some "mind-like" variable. Rereading that 1932 book, you easily forget that *Purposive Behavior in Animals and Men* is a half century old.

Take an example. Reward and punishment were supposed to work by "stamping in" or "stamping out" a particular response. This was the so-called Law of Effect. But, he argued, there must also be a Law of Emphasis: a principle for highlighting relevant cues. For what gets stamped in or out depends upon what cues an animal is attending to. It is not automatic. (That, by the way, was what had got Krechevsky started on his "hypothesis theory.")

Tolman had two powerful start-up ideas that fueled his intellectual travels. The first was "heuristic" purposivism: Treat behavior as if it were purposive—never mind about teleology. If you do your experiments well, it will not bite you. "Behavior reeks with purpose." For him, purposiveness implied that behavior is organized into means-end sequences and is "docile," or sensitive, to means-end relations in the world. We search means to achieve ends.

You do not go around "acquiring responses." You gather knowledge and then figure out how to use it to get to your goals. Learning is not modeled on a switchboard with incoming stimuli getting connected to outgoing responses. More like a maproom. Knowledge comes in; it then gets organized and plotted up. It is used to guide action toward goals. Knowledge is *based* on past experience; behavior is *based* on knowledge. Past experience does not affect action directly. It gets worked over. As one scandalized behaviorist critic put it at the time, "Professor Tolman leaves the animal wrapt in thought."

It was from Tolman that I adopted heuristic positivism—a modest "teleology" without tears and philosophical anguish. I had not liked McDougall's nineteenth century insistence that Purpose was somehow biologically as well as metaphysically real. It had only forced him to write a silly book in defense of animism. I wanted to look at "going beyond the information given" as functionally motivated activity, but I did not want to fight my way through a philosophical thicket. I suppose I am a typical "Anglo-Saxon" where speculative refinement is concerned: You do not have to get it all down *a priori* before you start.

The great Radcliffe-Brown, the British anthropologist, long ago proposed that "mother's brother" was a particularly crucial identity figure for "male ego" in primitive societies. What about foster mother's brother-in-law? Edward Tolman's gifted sister-in-law, Ruth, was the wife of Edward's physicist brother, Richard. We had worked together in Washington during the war. For the decade after, she was my confidante, friend, goad, confessor—indeed, my foster mother. Edward was the classic "mother's brother": supportive, admiring, full of great good humor. I suppose his "heuristic purposivism" was not only appealing to me intellectually but tinged with the hue of affectionate loyalty.

Be all that as it may, Tolman and Bartlett gave me the metaphors I needed for plunging into the study of how thinking takes you beyond the information given.

Let me come back to where I was, dangling on the edge of a new venture. That invitation to spend 1952–53 at the Institute for Advanced Study arrived in the midst of the dangling. I relished the freedom and also the chance to take up again with Robert Oppenheimer. We had maintained contact through our little "psychology committee" that met a few times a year at his office in Princeton to "keep him in the picture" about developments in psychology with the possibility that the Institute might make some appointments—visiting or permanent: Edward Tolman, Ruth Tolman, E. R. Hilgard, George Miller, E. G. Boring and me. Just to be sure, I took along a heavy load of unfinished work as a hedge against barrenness. A fortnight after I arrived there, I dreamed that Professor Einstein was implacably but gently pursuing me through the corridors of the Institute to ask me a question that I knew I could not answer. I worked so hard those first few weeks, I sprained my back over a manuscript in revision!

Eventually my unconscious settled down. No classes, no committees, not even the hourly tolling of the great clock atop Memorial Hall. What a sweetness to life! Niels Bohr, whose presence was always felt there physically or otherwise, forever made ambiguous the borderline between what physicists consider nature and what they consider mind. It made for a rich context of conversation for a psychologist. Bram Pais became my new friend. He would exclaim, "It is amazing that the human mind is able to grasp these complex and often wildly counter-intuitive things about nature—and yet there must be some crucial things that we cannot grasp because of the limitations of that mind."

The atmosphere was rich but uncluttered—and light. Eka Kantorowicz boasted that he had been a member of three master races—born a Jew, a Prussian, and now an American. Harold Cherniss had a vast card file on Aristotle in the center of his office and could pull out an apposite Aristotelian comment on any topic one could broach. Erwin Panofsky inspired me to read his rich study of Dürer's *Melancholia* and his little book on the Gothic cathedral. David Levy, that wise and humane child psychiatrist, who was visiting that same year, tracked back through his records in search of the origins of "the full maternal feeling" in women. Claire Zimmerman, my Harvard graduate student down for the year with me, was young, elegant, brilliant, enthusiastic. It was a happy year.

It was a turning point as well. It had been important getting away from Harvard (and my tachistoscope!), freed from that daily agenda into which one gets locked. Habits *do* develop a dynamism of their own. I wanted to stay clear of them, of the debates that lock you into the atmosphere where you are. I wanted to think about thought and get a little group that would join me in doing it.

So I wrote McGeorge Bundy, our Harvard dean, asking if I could have new quarters. For some arcane reason, I thought that change of place would work wonders. Bundy gave me 9 Bow Street, a little Victorian frame house across from the Harvard Yard, and there the Cognition Project was born in 1952. We started a regular Thursday seminar. Without ever quite deciding, we edged our way into the "category problem."

If you are going to study how people think, you can concentrate on how they become *illogical* or on how they become *logical*. Those syllogism studies I mentioned were about the former. If you take illogic as what needs explaining, then you are likely to believe (like Freud) that logic will out when the encumbrances to it are removed. He says in his *Future of an Illusion:*

> We may insist as much as we like that the human intellect is weak. . . . But nevertheless there is something peculiar about this weakness. The voice of the intellect is a soft one, but it does not rest until it has gained a hearing. Ultimately, after endlessly repeated rebuffs, it succeeds.

Thanks to Freud we do now understand more about how folly is generated than about how reason is. For me (and for many in my generation), ways of unreason were what one took for granted. But that left reason unexplained.

We could *evaluate* it by comparing the *results* of human intuitive reasoning with what one obtained by using formal logic or mathematics. But that did not explain *how* people came to their correct solutions, unless (like the nineteenth-century logician George Boole) you believed that the laws of logic *were* the laws of thought. That may be so in some sense, or become so when one learns how to *use* formal logic as a prosthetic device with which to check one's reasoning. But ordinarily, one uses various heuristic devices, or "tricks" as aids to reasoning—often very ingenious ones. How in fact do people go about it? What are the psychological processes involved? Oddly enough, there were very few studies on this topic—save, perhaps, by Piaget and Vygotsky working with children, work we shall encounter in the following chapter.

These were the considerations that shaped the approach I took to the study of thinking. In the past, for example, most research on thinking had given subjects to believe that the experiment they were in was about something else. I suspect that this practice grew out of the conviction that if they knew what the experiment was about it would be too easy. Incidental thinking was what they ended up studying. Why not tell them, instead of masking their task as a memory task or a discrimination task? It is a bit like William James's dictum: If you want to study religion, study the most religious men at their most religious moments. Why not something similar for studying thinking? Then look at their *performance* while thinking. Let it be generated by what they do when they are trying to think. What they do will be difficult enough to interpret, without having to worry about what they were making of a memory task or a discrimination task.

And if you want to study how people think, then give them a task that allows them to think! Let them know what is expected of them. Hide nothing. Tell them everything relevant to the task: what features or attributes are to be taken into account, what the rules of the game are to be. Their job is to *figure out* a solution. And bear in mind that "figuring out" is not a one-leap game: It takes time and protracted effort. So do not concentrate on one "response" at a time (even if you can measure it in milliseconds), but look at the sequence of steps through which they go. These may tell you about strategies rather than responses.

There is one discouraging problem that is created by doing what I proposed. How do you then analyze your subjects' attempts at problem solving? Do you not get into a thicket of impressionism and "qualitative" analysis—like Graham Wallas writing on "incubation" and "clarification" or Max Wertheimer on "good" and "bad" problem solving? Not that their pioneering work on "real" thinking (in contrast to incidental thinking) was not useful. Rather, it remained somehow inconclusive and imprecise.

Could one devise thinking tasks that were both challengingly complex and at the same time amenable to the sort of informational analysis that Shannon and Weaver had developed for dealing with information systems generally—of the kind discussed in the last chapter? Could we not control the amount of input of information we gave our subjects and then examine their uptake of it as revealed by their hypotheses or their subsequent acts? We might then know something more about such things as the natural order in which information can be most useful, how much redundancy is needed, what kinds of information are crucial at what points, and so on. We might, indeed, ask very qualitative questions in a quite quantifiable way. That, after all, is what a good research method should do for you.

So far as I know, there was only one other research group at work on a similar project in the mid-1950s—Carl Hovland's at Yale. We used to exchange visits. Herbert Simon was just beginning his work on the computer simulation of logic problem solving, and though we were in touch, we thought we were following what in those early days seemed to be quite different tasks.

Perhaps I can give a sense of the atmosphere in 1955 by a visit to a meeting that occurred in that year.

It was a Symposium on Cognition in Boulder, Colorado, organized by Howard Gruber at the University there. It was May. The variety of papers was rich. Charles Osgood presented one on attention, firmly based on contemporary learning theory. David Rapoport's was on thinking as an achievement of the conflict-free Ego, high Freud. Egon Brunswik continued his classical inquiry into the processes whereby mind samples the world to create representations of it.

Heider struck a new note. "Commonsense psychology is unashamedly and blatantly a cognitive psychology." It is what regulates the way in which people interact with each other, what they expect of each other. It contains such unignorable axioms as "What a person knows determines to a certain extent what he can do and what he cannot do." A psychology that ignores or dismisses what people believe about the "psychology" of others cannot be much of a psychology. That paper, it turned out, was to spark a generation of "attribution" theory: studies of what powers and traits people attributed to each other and under what conditions. But at a deeper level, it might have transformed social psychology into the study of how people *construct* a social world as they do—a world of stipulated realities.

Leon Festinger gave a talk about "dissonance theory." Forceful and concise, it too was an attempt to apply cognitive theory to everyday life. But in a different way from Heider's. The function of cognition was to bring beliefs into line with actions already taken: "The hypothesis states, essentially, that there exists a tendency to make consonant one's cognitions and one's behavior." We do it by exposing ourselves to information congruent with our line of action, or by distorting information that is *not*. Festinger was pledged to a new, simpler version of what Freud had sought: an account of how cognition leads us to unreason. Never mind that he wished not to take account of a great deal else that thought does—including making us "sicklied o'er." His object, I think, was to explain how thought brings us to terms with the decisions we are forced to make either by circumstance or by our own compulsions. It was a brilliant oversimplification. Thought was a set of procedures for reducing the dissonance between what we believed and what we did. "Dissonance reduction" would soon become all the rage in social psychology.

My paper was exceedingly abstract and detached, compared with Heider's and Festinger's. It bore the title "Going beyond the information given"—a good label for my preoccupation of those days. It was an attempt to characterize the basic cognitive processes that could account for the existence of intelligence. Intelligence (or cognition) was the act of leaping beyond perception in some principled way, "running beyond what is directly observed by the senses" (I quoted Frederic Bartlett's phrase). We fit events into categories as best we can and impute surplus properties to them by virtue of the category membership we assign them. Or we learn the probability or narrative texture of the environment so that, given one piece of it, we can figure out what goes with it. Then there are forms of "going beyond" that are based on being master of a grammar, a logic, some formal system that can be imposed on events. Our leap is then determined by the logic we apply. Each of these accomplishments of intelligence depends upon a coding system, a system that must be constructed either alone or, more often, with the aid of others. Mine was, I suppose, an early and rather half-baked version of the style of thinking of the "cognitive revolution."

That Colorado symposium was a laying out of landscape. Attribution theory, dissonance reduction, and the informational analysis of intelligent thought—those were its major topics. Festinger's account was an effort to lay out an old terrain in a new light—the perennial quest of psychology for the roots of unreason. Heider's was (or could have been, but really wasn't) the start of what later came to be cognitive anthropology: how the ordinary worlds of ordinary people come into being to create shared cultures. My presentation was a fumbling account of new theories of information processing. The three together provided the menu for the next decade of the psychology of thinking.

The research for *A Study of Thinking* was under way, in collaboration with two younger colleagues, Jacqueline Goodnow and George Austin. At the risk of boring the nontechnical reader, let me describe how we were proceeding. Start with that intelligent subject and tell him or her what you are up to. They have to figure out what things belong together in common classes and, if possible, to tell why they do. We begin by presenting them with a series of cards, one at a time or a whole boardful. The cards vary from one another in certain attributes, like the figures they bear, how many figures, what color, and what kind of surrounding border they have. A typical card might have two red squares with a single border around them, another one black circle with a single border. Each of the four attributes represented on each card—kinds of figures, number of figures, color of figures, and number of borders—is limited to three values. For instance, the colors were green, red, and black. It is a closed world of the eighty-one cards that you get by combining $3 \times 3 \times 3 \times 3$. Some of the cards "belong" together in a common class, others do not. The subject has the task of figuring out which do and which do not by picking them one at a time and being told each time whether what he has picked is "in" or "out"—a positive or negative instance, to use the jargon. The class may be all red cards, or all cards with red squares, or all black ones with a double border, etc., etc. There are dozens of ways in which the target category can be constructed. The experimenter knows what's what; the subject is to find out by choosing instances. That's all there is to it.

And indeed, you observe how the subject goes about choosing cards in order to find out that which will help him make up his mind about what defines the class. Regardless of what he tells you he is doing, you still have his string of choices, and they tell their own story. The subject can choose at random, of course, but in fact, he rarely does. Choice almost invariably reflects a notion about how to proceed, and notions are "governed" by rules. Rules generate a strategy: a way of sequencing your encounters with events that permits you to figure out what you need to know. Some strategies are quicker than others, some are riskier, some are more certain, some are less flexible.

There is something quite sterile about a "closed universe" of eighty-one cards—or for that matter, about any closed universe. We had ways of livening it a little, as I shall relate presently. But the gain you get from using a fixed universe is very great. For you can specify precisely the informativeness of any card chosen in terms of how many possible hypotheses about the category rule it eliminates. If, for example, a subject chooses one with two red circles and a single border and it turns out to be negative, then the correct category cannot be "red figures," "two circles," "red circles," etc., etc. And then you can see whether in fact the subject's subsequent choices reveal that he has assimilated all that information. It is a limited and powerful procedure and in 1955 it was brand-new. (I am told that a contemporary board game is based on our old experiment.)

Now, the strategies that people use in this task (as in others used to study "thinking") will depend upon the nature of the display, the amount or kind of information they already have at their disposal, the number of choices they have, the risks they can afford or are willing to take, the time they have available to them, and other matters that are, on the whole, commonsensical. We could change just such conditions as these and see how strategies change to meet them.

The strategies that came to light were interesting—surprisingly so. The "obvious" one, the super-rational one, is to list the criteria for grouping instances in a category and then tick off which of these are eliminated by any given choice of a card, and which remain. Any sensible computer program would do just that; it is a typical, brute algorithm. Our subjects did not have the benefit of paper and pencil, so very few people ever tried it: It so exceeds that magic number 7 $\pm$ 2 in its demand on memory as to be mnemonically impossible. The only subject who ever persisted at it was one of the leading physicists of my generation! A strategy must respect the limitations of its user. And human beings know some beautiful ways of respecting these limitations—though they often cannot tell you quite what they are doing. One of the neatest of them computationally is what we called "focusing." You pick a single *positive* card out of that dizzying array of eighty-one and use it as your home base, your *focus.* Then you make your choices so as to vary one feature of it at a time. You can't fail. If the new card is still positive, the varied feature could not be relevant. If it is negative, the feature is relevant. That is *conservative* focusing. If you are pressed for time or limited in the number of choices you can make, you convert to focus *gambling:* You vary from your focus by two or more attributes in your next choice. If the choice yields a positive instance, you get a huge informational yield. Imagine your positive focus card is two red circles with one border, and you now choose three black squares with one border and *it* is positive: You have it made. The rule for the category must be "all cards with a single border." But if the new card you choose turns out to be negative, you have learned nothing, for you cannot know what feature negated class membership.

Simpleminded though the experiments were—and I shall have more to say about that in a moment—we managed to gather quite a harvest of interesting findings. We managed to find out the procedures by which ordinary people go about being modestly rational. They did indeed tailor their search for information in ways that respected their limited attention and memory capacities. One example of that economical search was the "focusing" strategy already mentioned. Another was the nearly universal preference for positive knowledge: Positive instances of a concept were far more likely to be used than were negative instances, even when the latter were of equal informational value to the former. Our subjects, moreover, thirsted for redundant information to confirm their hypotheses, though logically they did not require the added information. But they also were masters of the art of tailoring their strategies to fit the limited opportunities for gaining new information—limited opportunities that we imposed on them in the experiments. They knew how to gamble on a few cues when it was necessary to do so. Some were leapers and some were plodders in their gathering of information, and they developed "rational" strategies that expressed their predilections. One interesting anomaly: most people, though quite systematic, were not very articulate in telling us how they proceeded. It was like not "knowing" the grammar of the language you speak.

Let me say a little about the tasks we used in this work and how peculiar they were, even if they did reveal a good deal about how our subjects were carrying on. The concepts we were asking our subjects to discover by letting them sample instances were utterly "non-natural." Philosophers like to distinguish natural-kind concepts (like "apples" or "trees" or "hammers") from ones that are non-natural. Obviously, we were aware of the difference and had discussed the difference early in the book—and opted for non-naturalness. Non-natural concepts are usually defined by a checklist of features—as with the concepts in our little tasks, which had "checklist" defining attributes like color, number, form and border. What kind of concept is "two red figures"? Why "two + red" rather than "three + black + single borders"? There is no natural kind of one or the other. Both are arbitrary, both peculiarly "senseless," though we can point them out or refer to them in a deck of experimental cards.

Now, *most* concepts that *most* people *mostly* deal with or search for in real life are not of this formal, checklist kind. To begin with, ordinary, natural-kind concepts have meaning and utility and connotation. They easily lend themselves, for example, to caricature and stereotype: the *ultimate* sports car, the *perfect* pear, the *typical* Latin lover. They fit into narratives like a hand in a glove. As the philosopher Frege has taught us, when you indicate a thing, the act by which you do so has both a *reference* and a *sense*. A referent is the extension of a concept to the world of instances; the sense of the concept is its relation to other things and other concepts.

Our concepts (like "two red figures") were all reference but no sense. Now, ordinarily, when we ask somebody whether something is or is not, say, a pear, the judgment that he makes is not based on "ticking off" its attributes against a list of the defining attributes of the concept "pears" and then making up his mind accordingly. Natural kinds incorporate their members more intimately, and even when we meet a peculiar instance, we can deal with it as, say, "a hairy pear."

In fact, the way our subjects went about solving our little nonnatural problems was in large part determined by the very nonnaturalness of the problems we had chosen to give them. We even discovered this ourselves, but because we had other fish to fry, made very little of it. For we happened to include a few tasks that involved concepts that were more in the spirit of "natural kinds." And we found (in retrospect?) some astonishing differences.

One natural-kind task consisted of instances that were variations on a human scene rather than being about figures and colors and numbers and borders. Each card contained an adult and a child. The adult (a male or a female) was dressed in day dress or nightwear; so too the child (who was either a boy or a girl). The adult, however dressed, was either handing the child a gift or simply standing upright. The child was either holding his hands up to receive something, or had hands at his or her sides. So the array consisted of a closed universe, but what a difference!

For now each instance "contained" not just checklist features but a little story. Take for example the "positive" card containing an "adult male in day dress giving a little girl in nightwear a gift, the little girl with hands at her sides." The subject says to himself, "Hah, a father giving his sulky, sleepy daughter a birthday present when she wakes in the morning. The concept must be about sulky children." So he then chooses for test all those instances where "parents" are giving "their children" gifts that the child is "not accepting"—

a reasonable "narrative" concept full of sense. But the sense soon overpowers the reference. Our subject hangs on to his little story. He encounters a negative instance involving an adult female and says, "Yes, I see, it is only when *fathers* are sulked at." The strategy is quite different. Now the "focus" is some reasonable, stereotyped scenario that fits a positive instance, and it is clung to so long as our subject can find any similarity in *theme* between that positive instance and any subsequent positive instance encountered. It is a very different story, a very different strategy.

Never mind, it was a useful beginning. Fifteen years later, two of our very brightest graduate students, each in a different way, pointed up the problem we had glossed over, and set it right—Elly Rosch and Jerry Anglin. We had made our point, and it had served its uses.

That was *A Study of Thinking.* Poor George Austin, whose health had always been precarious, had been in on the early planning of the work. To our horror, he was stricken with abdominal cancer and died in 1955, in his thirty-second year, before he really had a chance to see the shape the book had taken. We missed him. I have never had a collaborator to match Jackie Goodnow in intelligence, poise and good-humored open-mindedness.

The book came out in 1956—the year "cognitive sciences" were supposed to have been born. Historians of contemporary psychology cite it as one of the birth pangs. It obviously started something. Austere and full of mathematics (mostly expressed in ordinary English rather than in formulae), it sold like a hit novel. It is still not "remaindered." It made the study of thinking tough-minded. I quit the "category problem," and it was not until fifteen years later that my interest in it was rekindled, when Rosch and Anglin turned the problem on its head.

I was delighted when the book finally appeared. There was a long review of it by Robert Oppenheimer, the most thoughtful of the lot.

In the Spring of 1949, the Massachusetts Institute of Technology held a convocation devoted to the celebration of recent successes in the sciences and to reflections on their portent. Mr. Churchill, then Prime Minister of the United Kingdom, commented in the course of his address, "The Dean of the Humanities spoke with awe, 'of an approaching scientific ability to control men's thoughts with precision.' I shall be very content to be dead when that happens." This book which is before us need lend no haste to Churchill's thoughts of death, nor to those of many others who, without words or with words of less austere finality, share his anxieties.

Even the lay reader will recognize in this book some fresh and solid steps toward an understanding of characteristic traits of man's rational behavior. He will also see that the psychological sciences have a very long way indeed to go. For *A Study of Thinking* has in many ways the flavor of the opening of a new science. This is not because its authors so regard themselves. They are learned in the literature of their science; they make discriminating and frequent use of the findings of those who have worked in the study of perception, of concept formation, of linguistics and of learning. They are happy to recognize that the logical ideas to which they are led are as well explicated by Aristotle as ever since; it is clear that the models of von Neumann and the theory of games have contributed both to their explicit terminology, and to their ways of thinking and formulating problems.

But the book has a unity of view and a fervor of conviction which makes it point to the future. It raises more questions than it answers, the questions are new and newly sharp because there are some answers in the book. Although there is little in the findings here reported that shocks or transcends common sense, these findings are cast with the precision and objectivity which is indeed the mark of a science finding its bearings.

We are concerned throughout with the discovery and creation of order in man's cognitive life. We are dealing with a work which both studies a part of this great theme and, in itself, exemplifies it. The theme is vast. Man has a great capacity for discrimination. His potential sense of otherness is almost unlimited. Rational life begins with the selective practice of ignoring differences, failing in truth to perceive them; rational life begins with the failure to use discriminatory power in anything like its full potentiality. It lies in the selection, arrangement, and appropriate adequation to the objects of perception and thought, of limited traits, of a small residue of potential wealth.

He caught the theme that both Jackie Goodnow and I cared most about—that it will now be "natural for psychologists to turn their attention to man as a rational being, and not only to the problems of his appetites, his folly, and his will."

George Miller and I found ourselves running on converging tracks. His "birthday" for the cognitive sciences is September 11, 1956, the second day of the Second Symposium on Information Theory held at MIT. I was not there. The birthday started with Newell and Simon reporting progress on the "The Logic Theory Machine": a machine proof of Theorem 2.01 in the Whitehead-Russell *Principia*. It ended with Noam Chomsky giving an early version of the argument of *Syntactic Structures* (to which I will return in a later chapter). Miller writes: "I went away from the Symposium with a strong conviction, more intuitive than rational, that experimental psychology, theoretical linguistics, and the computer simulation of cognitive processes were all pieces from a larger whole, and that the future would see a progressive elaboration and coordination of their shared concerns."

The "larger whole" was not greatly fancied by all our colleagues. The Department of Psychology was locked in a standoff between Skinner's operant conditioning and Stevens's psychophysics. Two men less suited to conversation with each other would be hard to invent: each highly intelligent and articulate, and each with a tin ear for the other's message. That was George's department. My department, Social Relations, was moving further and further away from psychological concerns. My old teacher Gordon Allport found *A Study of Thinking* much too far from life, much too mathematical, and felt that I was taking leave of "real" psychological concerns. "The" review in *Contemporary Psychology* (it is the official journal of the American Psychological Association in which new books are reviewed) was principally negative and in general missed the point of what the book was about—interpreting its disinterest in the older psychological battles as "straddling the issues." George and I were both unhappy with the state of things at Harvard and in psychology generally.

I suppose everybody has a somewhat different notion of what the "center" of psychology is. We had our idea. We thought it was concern for the distinctively human forms of gaining, storing, transforming and using knowledge of all sorts—what makes humans human. Call them the cognitive processes. They were certainly being neglected—particularly at Harvard. Why not arrange to bring them together somehow? It was a vague idea. George had just been to the Center for Advanced Study at Palo Alto, and both of us had done turns at the Institute in Princeton, so though the idea was vague, it did not seem so strange to us. We sat long over dinner in 1960 with an excellent bottle of port to cheer us as we tried to hammer out the particulars.

Next day we wrote a two-page letter to John Gardner, then president of the Carnegie Corporation of New York, telling of our hopes to set up a center to which we could invite people occupied with the nature of knowing, whatever their discipline. Gardner came up for a visit shortly after. He liked the idea. I think he also had a hidden agenda: to foster new university ventures that would bring scholars out from behind the walls of their disciplines. In a matter of weeks we had our "Center for Cognitive Studies," as we had called it in the letter to Gardner. We were to be financed by a grant of a quarter-million dollars for a first five years of life—unrestricted money.

Armed with Gardner's promise of support, we went to McGeorge Bundy, the dean, to propose our idea for a center to be concerned with the nature of knowledge. He grinned: "And how does that differ from what Harvard University does?" Then he turned to his secret map to look for a home for us. Within the week we had a lovely wreck of a building up Kirkland Street, five minutes' walk from the Yard, President Eliot's old home, which had been converted into a state of improvised domesticity by several generations of temporarily located, married graduate students. An architect friend, Robert Woods Kennedy, combined Yankee thrift and French Modernist training to turn it into a very happy place to work—including an attic finished in the style of the stalls of the Académie Julien in Paris, where our graduate students could rub elbows and form their own little in-group.

George Miller and I were the managerial yin and yang of the Center for the next ten years. We were quite different people. He wrote in 1979:

I think Jerry and I made a good pair. I used to say that Jerry always used to plan for success and I always planned for failure, so, whatever happened, we were prepared. We shared a vision of cognitive psychology, but our intellectual playmates were very different. I gave him access to ideas growing out of communication theory, computation, and linguistics, whereas he gave me access to ideas from social psychology, developmental psychology, and anthropology. He broadened my view of cognition; I hope I helped to sharpen his.

As I look back, I am surprised that so heterogeneous a crowd of people could have collaborated so fruitfully at our busy little Center. We had a simple managerial principle that I will give you for what it is worth. Bruner expressed it best when he said that you have to trust the integrity of your own personality. The way this worked was that he and I got together at least once each year over a bottle of madeira (or was it a bottle of port?) and discussed people whose ideas we found exciting. Anyone whose ideas appealed to both of us was invited to join us for a year, and many accepted. By being totally selfish, we managed to invite some senior people we could work with. And then some bright post-docs followed the senior people and added enthusiasm to their wisdom. Our focus was on cognitive psychology, of course, but many of our strongest allies in reforming psychology were not themselves psychologists.

In 1960 we used "cognitive" in our name defiantly. Most respectable psychologists at the time still thought cognition was too mentalistic for objective scientists. But we nailed it to the door and defended it until eventually we carried the day. And now there are Cognitive Centers everywhere.

Swapping different perspectives on the same general topics can, in an unthreatening environment, be exhilarating. Visiting another institution for a year is a good tonic against one's own parochialism, and our visitors were no exception to the rule. Over those years, dozens of people came to the Center. Most seemed to be enlivened by the visit; some even claim to have been changed by it. A few went home and tried to set up something like it there. For us, it was a treat to have a Nelson Goodman, a Noam Chomsky, a Bärbel Inhelder, a Roman Jakobson right next door, at lunch, over coffee or a drink. A year is just about the right amount of time for a visit. You stay fresh, you can recover from initial bouts of misunderstanding, and you can store up some shared presuppositions for the future. You help the progress in curious ways—like regular lunches where people can take turns trying out ideas. Or weekly colloquia where visitors can show their stuff more formally. You don't have to plan to have people dine or drink together.

It took no great managerial genius to "run" the place—for it would not have got it either from George or from me. Over those years we had two administrators in a row, who kept the books effortlessly and dispensed grace. You need grace when, in a year, you are host to (a) a Soviet information theorist, (b) a Czech pediatric neurologist recently fled after the Soviet crackdown, (c) an Israeli who turns out a paper a week, and (d) a militant women's group of graduate students, visitors and secretaries. It worked. It worked for the two of us, very happily; and it mostly worked for our guests and collaborators.

But there was probably more to it than that. Something about *Zeitgeist*. We were lucky historically. Those were days of post-Sputnik academic expansion. To be independent of departmental support (as we were in the main, save where George's and my salaries were concerned) took considerable funding. It was available. We could not have brought off such a freewheeling exercise without "unrestricted" funds—money earmarked for nothing. That first Carnegie grant made the difference. (Five years later, we got another unrestricted quarter of a million from them.) Even *small* unrestricted grants help. When the Ford Foundation closed down its grant program in the behavioral sciences, it distributed funds in the form of small grants to some lucky investigators, including both George and me. We added our little packets to the Carnegie pot. Every cent of unticketed money is a fortune. Of course, we also applied for and got grants to do particular things—for which we were grateful—but they do not have the effect on the imagination of, say, five hundred dollars unrestricted. Do what you will with it but make it interesting. Will there ever be such luxury again?

We opened shop in 1960; George left for Rockefeller in 1968 and I for Oxford in 1972. There could never have been a more favorable time for the Center than its first five years. By the time of Vietnam and student unrest, the momentum had already been established and, in George Miller's embattled terminology, we had "carried" the day. But how do you describe what an institution *did* that made a difference, leaving aside the moot historical question whether it was successful or not? One way is to look at its spawn—institutions, people and ideas.

We were lucky picking people. It takes no luck to invite big reputations like Chomsky, Goodman, Jakobson, Inhelder. Or even to catch passing stars like Luria, Lacan, Piaget, I. A. Richards, for colloquia or "lunches." I mean the group "lower down," the Kahnemans and Tverskys and Bevers and McNeills and Todas and Trevarthens and Bowers and Levelts. I don't think George and I were psychic—though we *read*. We had talent scouts, our senior colleagues, to steer us to our reading. The rest was easy: a good lab to work in, and good talk. Then, of course, we had the advantage of the draw: Harvard and MIT graduate students.

There is an ironic twist. In those dozen years, anti-elitist times, the Center seems to have produced an elite, an establishment, an old boy/girl network. It reaches out over America, to Africa, Europe, Asia, even into socialist Eastern Europe!

About institutions. I think there are some that wouldn't be in existence but for *something* like the Harvard Center having provided an existence theorem. And a good many of them can trace direct descent: Chicago, the Max Planck Institute in Nijmegen, Edinburgh, La Jolla, McGill, etc.

About ideas, how can one tell? We certainly generated a point of view, even a fad or two.

How can one tell whether "cognitive sciences" will prosper? And what role the Center had? Michael Posner says, extravagantly: "If cognitive science should survive as a discipline, there is little doubt that around 2060 someone will be asked to review its history on the occasion of the centennial of its conception at the Center for Cognitive Studies at Harvard University."

George Miller, perhaps too ready for failure, takes a gloomier view:

I sometimes wonder, however, whether we really won the war. What seems to have happened is that many experimental psychologists who were studying human learning, perception, or thinking began to call themselves cognitive psychologists without changing in any obvious way what they had always been thinking and doing—as if they suddenly discovered they had been speaking cognitive psychology all their lives. So our victory may have been more modest than the written record would have led you to believe.

But even our limited victory was important, for it served to lift psychology's thirty-year ban on mentalistic terminology. A new generation of psychologists has now grown up without feeling naughty when they talk about mentalistic concepts like cognition, attention, imagery, memory, intuition, expectation, planning, intention, will, and so on, all of which had been banned by behaviorists as unscientific. In my opinion, however, the use of these mentalistic terms is still constrained by a positivistic philosophy of science, so that now we have in effect an oxymoron: non-mentalistic cognitive psychology.

In the end, we closed shop. The deans had never been very keen about a Center after McGeorge Bundy left. We were self-supporting, but a center such as ours is messy to a good administrator. It duplicates departments. Bundy, like John Gardner, our first Medici, had been out to reduce the power of departments. After we left, the Center ceased to exist. Nobody ever asked whether that was a good idea. It just happened. The dean said it should. Donald Broadbent, just returned to Oxford from a visit to America with a stopover at Harvard, asked me in 1979 whether I had any thoughts on what Harvard ought to do about a Center for Cognitive Studies, that it was under discussion. I *was* bemused!

Let me go back to the beginning: about how to study "mind and thought." There are three things that I wish I had known better when I started. One of them is about categories! The second has to do with reflection, or as we call it these days, metacognition. And the third is about whether one can study thinking by experiments, out of the context of its use.

A Study of Thinking was a "protest" book. We were trying to break out of the anti-intellectual corset by having recourse as much to rigorous logic as to psychology. Ours was in some ways more a logician's than a psychologist's approach. It was not that we did not know better. Jackie Goodnow and I both deeply admired Wittgenstein's *Philosophical Investigations* and knew its devastating critique of the idea of concepts as defined by common "features"—his famous discussion of concepts joined by family resemblance rather than by shared features. We were so keen to track our subjects doing their informational thing that we designed our experiments accordingly, with features in instances whose values could be easily computed. But as Roger Brown remarked some years after, the fixed array of "instances" we presented our subject already embodied "a certain model of the cognitive category." It was as I have already said, a lifeless and unrepresentative little world, lacking in "natural" joints. So hooked were we on our formal logic that we never fully appreciated what we actually found in that more lifelike microcosm of the adult and children. And so the strategies that we found were in the end appropriate only to the world in which we forced our subjects to operate.

Never mind that Jackie Goodnow and I "knew" about all these matters. Roger Brown, in a penetrating "after a quarter century" revisit to the old "category problem," said it in the right way. He distinguishes between our "text" and our "subtext" in *A Study of Thinking.* The text was the formal experiments and the rigorous idea of a concept set forth in the book. The subtext was our speculative introductory rumination on the category problem—the possible ways of looking at the issue. On that subtext he comments wryly: "It is like the music of Janáček, rich in thematic material which passes swiftly and is often undeveloped, but contains enough ideas to sustain a dozen operas." Why then did we choose so austere and far-from-life a text? I think the answer tells something about the price one pays for making any choices in science, even one as undeveloped as psychology.

I think we were willing to take whatever artificialization was necessary in order to show that the human processing of information was of the form of a strategy governed by a higher-order principle. It was our way of substituting something more directive and longer-term for the usual psychological idea of a "response" as the basic unit. Edward Tolman and John Von Neumann were very much in our minds, as was Egon Brunswik—men who wanted to highlight the sequential, strategic side of human performance.

And so we became so caught up in our austere text that we failed to see some intriguing things right under our noses, like the narrative concepts in those more natural experiments. But we were not prepared to pursue the more general point that a strategy would depend on the context of the task. A quarter century later, Nancy Cantor at Stanford was to find that hypotheses about human beings are fueled only by information that confirms them. The rest is ignored or passed over. We "construct" rather than test. It was there before our noses, but we were looking for something else.

Or take another matter: disjunctive concepts. A disjunctive concept is one that has no universal common property, in contrast to a conjunctive one, where all instances are required to have one or two or more common properties. In terms of the Bruner-Goodnow-Austin array, disjunctive category cards might be constructed by the rule that all cards, all containing three figures and/or red figures and/or squares, were "in." Each member has *something* in common with every other in the class, but not *everything*. Defined in terms of features, disjunctive categories seem like intellectual nightmares. Even our bright undergraduate subjects had a terrible time with them.

Yet in the junk world of real objects and natural categories, many of the simplest things of life belong unabashedly to disjunctive categories, like furniture, vegetables, dwellings and other homely classes held together by little other than partial overlap. They are dealt with, even by children, by tracking resemblances down a chain, not by incredibly difficult mental operations. The ultimate chagrin was when Richard Herrnstein and Peter de Villiers demonstrated that pigeons in a Skinner box easily master the rule of disjunctive categories if the categories are natural. They learn to pick out a body of water in color photographs taken at different angles from different heights in different light, etc. So do human beings.

What's "natural"?

Is it "natural" for people to have category problems thrown at them out of the context of ordinary life and told to "solve it now," alone and unassisted? I came on an entrancing article about how tailors in the Liberian bush solve problems. Entitled "What's Special About Experiments as Contexts for Thinking?" it makes clear beyond question that what goes on in a Liberian tailor shop is not what goes on in a laboratory—not even an improvised one in the African bush. Mundane problem solving in Liberia or La Jolla usually consists of converting problems into an old, familiar form. Your first assumption is that new things you meet are like the old you've already solved. Don't treat things as *new* problems unless you have to. Problem solving is for "kinky" cases that don't fit. Or for play where it becomes an end in itself. Most people are not little professors, not even the ones who design research on formal problem solving.

Finally, reflection—or "metacognition." There is a hum of work these days among psychologists, educators and cognitive scientists on what can be accomplished by people reflecting on their own thought. Plainly, we are able to monitor our own procedures for memorizing, for problem solving, even for creating works of art. If this were not the case, I suppose there would be little point in financing think tanks and universities—or even in setting aside time for reflecting.

As I reflect back on the "battle" to establish a cognitive emphasis in psychology, I am struck by an irony. The disciplined procedures for reflecting on one's own thoughts (including one's thoughts about cognition) are principally to be found outside psychology, principally in philosophy. My psychological "parents" at Harvard were all veterans of the battle to lead psychology out of the Philosophy Department there. I do not for a moment doubt that there are vast domains of knowledge that lie open to the *empirical* psychological investigations of psychologists, and I am sympathetic to the struggles of E. G. Boring to be free of the philosophy of mind or of Gordon Allport to study values free of philosophical ethics. Had I been with them then, I would doubtless have wanted to be free of philosophical epistemology.

But after all the struggles, I am finally convinced that a psychology of mind can never be free of a philosophy of mind. Wittgenstein, in one of his more posturing passages (*Investigations,* II, xiv), says of psychology:

The confusion and barrenness of psychology is not to be explained by calling it a "young science"; its state is not comparable with that of physics, for instance, in its beginnings. . . . For in psychology, there are experimental methods and *conceptual confusion.*

The existence of experimental methods makes us think we have the means of solving the problems which trouble us, though problems and methods pass one another by.

If philosophy is concerned with the problems of the alternative ways in which we can formulate our concepts and our language about the nature and uses of mind, we must obviously be in partnership with philosophy (however hidden we may wish to keep the partnership). The contradictions and the dilemmas that are the products of disciplined philosophical thought about mind cast their shadows over the psychologist as much as they do over the philosopher. It is not that a knowledge of the philosophy of mind will guide us to our data or the design of our experiments. Rather, I think, it will guard us against the triviality into which we are likely to stumble when we narrow our focus to do this study, that experiment, or offer this other theory.

Perhaps one of the biggest boons that has come from that much-heralded cognitive revolution is that the cognitive sciences can now count among their practitioners philosophers who still believe that, in the end, there can be no permanent division of labor in the study of mind.

8

How Mind Begins

My wonder about human development was a by-product of other concerns. I was driven to think about the initial "powers" or "functions" of mind and how we got from there to adulthood. It had little to do at the start with children or with improving education. I had always been intrigued by the enigmatic artistry, the humor and the play of children—but never professionally. I never "studied" my own children. My naive belief in the late 1950s, after completing the book on thinking (when, like others before me, I had concluded that thought was most often wordless, systematic and above all *swift*)—my naive belief was that by studying children one could find the slower, even the primitive forms from which the lightning of thought develops.

This, of course, is utter nonsense. I suppose it is the same genre of nonsense that sent the young Lévi-Strauss off to the Mato Grosso to find "the start" of culture. But this was 1956 and I was a grown man. I knew better, really, but deep down hoped for some miracles. Human beings, whatever their age, are completed forms of what they are, just as societies are completed forms of what *they* are. Growing is becoming different, not better or faster. You may become better or faster or more fluent at accomplishing certain external feats —like mastering mathematics or history—but the accomplishment is achieved by processes that are qualitatively different, not simply quantitatively improved. I know that is not the standard view and I shall come back to it later.

I think I know why the "idea of development" did not attract my interest sooner. But there is an irony about my late start, for in fact the first piece of research that I ever did was about a developmental question. I was a junior in college, taking one of those "reading and research" courses designed by some ingenious college dean to reduce the restlessness of hyperactive undergraduates. My teacher was a biologist whose passion was *Reptilia* and he happened at that time in his career to be interested in the reproductive cycle of his favorite species. When I came along, he was reading in the endocrinology of reproduction. He set me to examining the behavior of female rats during their estrus cycle. Perhaps he thought an aspiring young psychologist should learn about rats rather than reptiles—though he did let me come along hunting for giant snapper turtles. I took to it happily and in no time was assessing how the estrus cycle expressed itself in the vaginal smears and the behavior of my litter of Wistar Institute females.

Just about then, an endocrinologist, Rountree, had published the claim that the thymus gland, always large in preadolescent mammals, was responsible for inhibiting sexual maturity. My teacher pooh-poohed it. I thought it was interesting. Indeed, it was the first *theory* of development I had ever encountered. Besides, there is something attractive about proving an unlikely theory—more so usually than just disproving an accepted one. The notion that there is a built-in "buffer" system protecting against the attainment of sexual maturity until the organism is "ready" seemed interesting. It still does.

The upshot was that I should do an experiment to test Rountree's idea. The Biology Department would get me a weekly supply of frozen calf thymus from Armour's in Chicago, which I would reduce to "thymocrescin," as Rountree's substance was called, and we would see. I was on the edge of my first experiment—doing vaginal smears, working up a measure of sexual receptivity in my female rats, fumbling around with an aqueous extract of those precious calf glands in the big centrifuge.

The experiment came out—whether for the right or wrong reasons—as I had hoped, and I published my first paper jointly with my supervisor, Dr. Cunningham. I never did another experiment on development for twenty-one years. But I never thought of the work as related to "development."

The émigré psychologist William Stern arrived at Duke just about then as a refugee from Hamburg, and gave a seminar on development that I attended. I recall only one of his lectures. It was on "space and time as personal dimensions." He contrasted personal, phenomenological space and time with their abstract Newtonian counterparts, commenting on how the former developed a personalized idiosyncratic quality with growth. I was concurrently reading that fascinating book by the German biologist von Uexküll, about how each species organizes its perception of the world into a species-specific *Umwelt*. I found the general idea very appealing, very much in the spirit of Mach's *Analysis of Sensation,* which I had read shortly before.

The idea of an *Umwelt* stuck, but not as a particularly developmental idea. It came back to mind a decade later, when I read the classic Austrian study of unemployed workers in Marienthal by Paul Lazarsfeld and Maria Jahoda. That study revealed that children and their unemployed parents had suffered a constriction of their sense of future time—they planned less, thought in the shorter term, anticipated fewer landmark events. And then an anthropologist friend steered me to a new study by Meyer Fortes and his wife on the education of West African Talensee children. They argued a comparable point. The Tale people migrated with the changes of seasonal agriculture but had no fixed calendrical dates by which to mark the changes. Time was "functional." In consequence, crises about "time" and "dates" never occurred to them. Things were not "late" or "early." And their children were not expected to reach certain "stages" by certain ages. They did what they did when they did it. They were helped to a next level of accomplishment when they were ready, with neither fret nor fanfare. They too grew up without "time crises." That was more grist for the *Umwelt* view—with a developmental twist.

"Nobody" did developmental psychology at Harvard in those days before the war. And with the exception of Freud and Piaget, nobody had much of interest to say about the subject. Arnold Gesell at Yale was dismissed as merely in the business of gathering age norms, pretty prosaic work. The developmental question largely boiled down to when things got better or faster or stronger, or more controlled.

We all knew about Piaget. I cannot remember a time when I didn't! I had read him on language and thought, on moral judgment, on physical causality. I had found him fascinating, but not as a *theorist*. He was an astute observer of children and his observations were intriguing—particularly those about egocentrism. It never occurred to any of us graduate students at Harvard that he had any bearing on anything aside from the phenomena to which he addressed himself. The controversy surrounding his work was of that boring kind in which pedants complained about the small number of children he observed. That was "dust bowl empiricism." Piaget was simply a self-contained one-man show.

Freud was quite a different story. It was the anti-illusionist quality of his thought that was so attractive, as well as the "content." Hidden sexuality was still a "new," still an exciting idea. But beyond his insistence that our sexual and aggressive motives were hidden from us, were "unconscious" and masked by defenses, there was something else. It was the claim that each of us lived in a psychic reality that was discoverable by our struggle to deal with our plights. The metaphor of an "outer" reality that could never be directly known and an inner one that one "constructs" to represent it has always been a root one for me—the drama of Plato's prisoners in the cave.

Freud's substantive account of the details of human development, on the other hand, struck me as Gothic and unsubstantiated —more like the Book of Job than real. I read him as allegory. Development as a voyage through the erogenous zones, for example, seemed fixed and unreal. But even so, I liked his hypothesis that overindulgence or overdeprivation at any stage of development was likely to fixate you there.

My anthropologist roommate at Duke, Leonard Broom, laughingly told me that Freud's was a parochial, "culture-bound" view of the family—"fin de siècle." Gothic tales laid in Vienna! But again, it was not the idea of development that caught me, but the general theory. Freud as a way of thinking about the human condition.

When I first arrived at Harvard as a graduate student, and again after the war, there was a busy traffic in "culture-and-personality" theory. There were lively people involved. The torchbearer was Clyde Kluckhohn—a romantic, a restless believer in the power of culture to shape mind, but too subtle an intelligence to embrace any simple generalizations about how the two were related. In an unspecified way, culture shaped some sort of internal Freudian dynamic—not as in Vienna, but as it should operate for a Navaho or a Balinese. And the rest of the influence came through a "world view" contained in the language. Margaret Mead visited often, as dogmatic as she was clever, and always ready to attack an ordinary psychologist on grounds that he knew only Western culture. And Ruth Benedict would come: elegant, allusive, poetic. Both were allies of Kluckhohn's in what seemed as much an ideological as an anthropological quest.

There was no lack of empirical work. Johnny Whiting worked tirelessly and with a bouncy optimism on correlating culture traits with presumed "basic personality" characteristics—of which more in a moment—and tried to put the results in the churchgoing clothes of Yale learning theory laced with psychoanalysis. Alexander Leighton was also on the scene, though his principally descriptive work did not enter much into the theoretical discussions.

I think the marriage of psychoanalysis and cultural anthropology brought out the worst in both spouses. Psychoanalysis, designed for Freud's Vienna, did not improve by being exported to the exotic cultures of the world. Do "child-rearing practices," like weaning, toilet training, forms of disciplining the child, determine whether a culture "believes in" witchcraft or creates certain forms of economic exchange? Are traditional ghosts a displacement of anxieties created by early, severe weaning? Is culture just one big projection?

The particular craze for correlational studies linking child-rearing practices in preliterate societies with cultural traits coincides with the development of the famous Yale Cross Cultural Index. In it, the monographic literature of anthropology had been parceled into categories, each describing aspects of the social, religious or economic life of the preliterate peoples of the world. It was ideal for doing correlations between this trait and that. But the file created its own Humpty-Dumpty problem: How do you get it all back together again? The typical culture/personality study, for example, might first sort preliterate cultures into those in which weaning occurred earlier and those in which it occurred later than the median age of weaning for all recorded cultures. It might then sort the same cultures into those whose folk tales or beliefs contained devouring ghosts. The hidden assumption, of course, is that "age of weaning" has the same significance in all cultures, and so too "devouring ghosts." It works well on an IBM sorting machine, but does it do justice to the cultures whose traits one has yanked out of context?

That, of course, was the issue that brought the enterprise down. Structuralism was just waiting to be born. I recall two anthropologists warning me off. I had come to know Alfred Kroeber when he was visiting at Harvard in the early 1950s. He had to climb the stairs in

Emerson Hall very slowly because of a heart condition, and we first met as we chatted our way up the long stairways together. He admired Clyde Kluckhohn, but looked askance at his push to "unify everything"—culture, personality, child rearing. For Kroeber, culture was "superorganic," with laws and structures that were independent of the idiosyncratic sources of individual human behavior. He too had been fascinated by psychoanalysis, had undergone a training analysis with Brill and even practiced for two years in San Francisco. It only reinforced his sense of the discontinuity between individual plights and the structural nature of a culture. The other "viewer with alarm" was Claude Lévi-Strauss, whom I met in 1945 at a dinner party at the home of the French consul-general in New York—a man with the appropriate name of de Saussure, a nephew of the great structural linguist of the same name. How can you say systematically how culture affects a particular personality? You may specify how individuals enter into a system of exchanges. And when you have done that, perhaps there is nothing more that needs to be specified as far as the culture is concerned. The culture has its own inherent logic.

The development of personality was a topic that never caught my full intellectual interest. Not that I am less interested than the next man in what makes people tick. Given a choice of how to spend time reading, a novel appeals to me more than a treatise on personality. What puts me off "personality theory" is its decontextualized way of dealing with motives and dispositions. It lacks a sense of place and of setting. Stephen in *A Portrait of the Artist as a Young Man* was a creature of Dublin. Dublin exists in Stephen's devouring mind, and as he walks its streets he creates "epiphanies of the ordinary" out of what he finds there, the Dublin in his own mind that forms his reality.

In those twenty-one years between my first study of development and my next one, there was very little about mind in the study of development. Mostly it was about motives and their control. The mind came into the picture almost exclusively as a generator of fantasies and as a defender of tender turf—the brave ego doing its best between the forces of the superego and the id. The two men who made the *development* of "mind" interesting to me were Jean Piaget, the postwar Piaget, and Lev Semyonovich Vygotsky. The two of them, Piaget and Vygotsky, were alike enough in general program to be equally tempting as mentors. In the end, they were sufficiently different to be in a state of perpetual conflict with each other inside my head!

Piaget, personally and in terms of his *oeuvre,* was massive. The programmatic pace of his work moved like a glacier. He absorbed, he assimilated everything into the system of his thought. It has always been a connected system of thought, with a sufficient ambiguity to permit easy assimilation to the Genevan point of view. Its objective has been to characterize the underlying logic that gives coherence to knowledge, and to do it in such a formal, abstract way that the characterization reveals the deep kinship of all forms of thought—save, perhaps, the arts. He wrote an astonishing number of books, and each bore an astonishing resemblance of continuity to the one preceding it. He was Swiss, Protestant, logical, obsessed, driven into his eighties. His passions were epistemology and logic and how they grew by the actions of the growing child on the world. The nature of that world did not concern him much, only the selective operations on it. It provided a generalized nourishment for the processes of knowing.

Vygotsky published little, and virtually nothing that appeared in English before 1960; indeed, until the late 1950s, most of what he wrote in Russian was suppressed and had been banned after the 1936 purge. Sickly and brilliant, he died of tuberculosis in his thirties. His pace was swift and his intellectual style that of an intuitionist. He was a Russian and a Jew, deeply interested in the arts and in language. He was a friend of the film-maker Eisenstein and the literary linguist Bakhtin. His objective was to explore how human society provided instruments to empower the individual mind. He was a serious intellectual Marxist, when Marxism was a starchy and dogmatic subject. This was his undoing at the time of the Stalinist purges. One reads Vygotsky for clues, for intellectual adventure, for his extraordinary evocativeness. Though I knew Piaget and never met Vygotsky, I feel I know Vygotsky better as a person.

At heart, Piaget was an epistemologist, and a genetic epistemologist at that. He was convinced that by studying the growth of mind in the child one could retrace the evolution of the sciences. The psychological machinery in his system of thought is almost scandalously scanty. It is logical machinery in the main: ways of characterizing the logic implied by the child's way of attempting to solve a problem or of explaining why he has done something one way rather than another. The child moves up through stages of growth by dint

of some virtually unspecified process of "equilibrium" between assimilation and accommodation—the former a process of shaping experience to fit one's mental schemata, the latter changing one's
schemata to fit experience. You can look high and low in the dozens
of Piaget's books, but you will have great difficulty finding anything
more concrete than this description of these two central psychological processes.

Yet he made a tremendous contribution to our understanding of
the mind of the child and how it grows, and indeed to our understanding of mind in general. And I think he did it in much the same
way as Claude Lévi-Strauss has made his contribution to our understanding of human culture—by insisting on its structure and connect-
edness, its deep rules, its derivative structures. Piaget could be completely wrong in every detail, but he would still have to be reckoned
one of the great pioneers. This is not to say that he saw it all, for he
certainly did not.

The world is a quiet place for Piaget's growing child. He is virtually alone in it, a world of objects that he must array in space, time
and causal relationships. He begins his journey egocentrically and
must impose properties on the world that will eventually be shared
with others. But others give him little help. The social reciprocity of
infant and mother plays a very small role in Piaget's account of
development. And language gives neither hints nor even a means of
unraveling the puzzles of the world to which language applies. Piaget's child has one overwhelming problem: to bring the inner representations of mind into equilibrium with the structures of experience. Piaget's children are little intellectuals, detached from the
hurly-burly of the human condition.

I made a first visit to Geneva in 1956. Piaget arranged that the
two of us should have a "debate" at the Bern meetings of the Swiss
Psychological Society. We trundled off to the railway station to catch
the train—an hour in advance, as was his habit. The debate was to
be on our notions about perception. He proposed as its title
"L'homme calme et l'homme agité"! I talked about the selectivity
and the role of hypotheses, he about the difference between perception and intelligence. His perceiver was indeed calm—and collected
and self-sufficient. I teased him: "You know, having purposes does not
necessarily make a perceiver agitated."

But I think that a commitment to structuralism is in some deep
measure a commitment to a quietism that is always offputting to a

functionalist. The one studies how structural requirements determine the forms of action. The other, as in Claude Bernard's celebrated dictum, studies the manner in which function creates form. Nor is it that one is truer or righter than the other. They are two different ways of parsing nature. Yet there is something else about Piaget's view that goes beyond this point. In some quite stubborn way, he has always resisted the idea that there is a psychological reality to culture, that it exists in some "World Three," Popperian way such that it can be "internalized" or serve as a prosthesis for mind. For Piaget, knowledge is always an invention, and the forms of invention do not include taking over the stored representations of the culture and then achieving knowledge by reconstruing them. So the child who is father to the man in the Piagetian world is indeed a calm child and a lone one.

Vygotsky's world was an utterly different place, almost the world of a great Russian novel or play—Tolstoyan or Chekhovian. Growing up in it is full of achieving consciousness and voluntary control, of learning to speak and then finding out what it means, of clumsily taking over the forms and tools of the culture and then learning how to use them appropriately. I first encountered it in the late 1940s, reading a celebrated paper by him—one of the two then available in English—on thought as developing through the internalization of speech. Like all his writing, it is sketchy, evocative and brilliant, as if written in the heat of inspiration.

Then in 1961, after his official "rehabilitation" in Russia and a great deal of backing and filling diplomatically to obtain rights, his *Thought and Language* was translated into English by my colleague Eugenia Hanfmann. She asked me to write a preface. I read with new absorption, not simply because I had to write a preface, but because I became caught up in its complex dialectic. I was discovering a new Vygotsky.

What captivated me most was his approach to the role of context in mental growth. It was the avoided topic in Piaget. Vygotsky begins with a paradox: "Consciousness and control appear only at a late stage in the development of a function, after it has been used and practiced unconsciously and spontaneously. In order to subject a function to intellectual and volitional control, we must first possess it." What then *aids* the child to gain control?

Vygotsky's sketch of an answer was incorporated in an idea with the drab name "zone of proximal development." It consists in the child's capacity to use hints, to take advantage of others' helping him organize his thought processes until he can do so on his own. By using the help of others, he gains consciousness and perspective under his own control, reaches "higher ground." "The new higher concepts transform the meaning of the lower. The adolescent who has mastered algebraic concepts has gained a vantage point from which he sees arithmetic concepts in a broader perspective."

I returned to Harvard from my visit to Geneva in the midst of a cold and unhappy winter. It was late 1956 and *A Study of Thinking* had just appeared. I had no idea how it would be received and it never crossed my mind that we were all hovering on the brink of the "cognitive revolution" in psychology. My marriage was breaking up and my two children were very much on my mind. I cope with anxieties by throwing myself into work. Searching out what to do next, I decided to work on the development of thought, how strategies develop. It was a natural follow-up.

It was then that I thought I would find those primitive processes that were slowed-down versions of thinking in adults. I would concentrate on inference, on how children learn to go beyond the information given, particularly on the difference between slow "plodders" and swift "leapers." But I could not come up with a technique that pleased me. (In an odd irony, a quarter century later, while working on *this* chapter of *this* book, I was asked to referee a masterful review article in the *Psychological Bulletin* entitled "Hypothesis theory and the development of conceptual learning." It was all about what I might have done at that time and didn't do! It reviewed work of the period on the development of problem-solving strategies in children, on how hypotheses emerge, combine, how children are tested; how they use feedback in problem solving; etc. It was the developmental follow-up of the ideas and the methods that Jackie Goodnow and I had worked out twenty years before. I guess I must have had enough of it by then.)

My research students and I decided instead to study "learning blocks." Perhaps pathologies of development would tell us what we wanted to know. The Judge Baker Guidance Center had a large case-load of "underachieving children" and they were delighted to let us take on some of them for exploratory "tutoring," while they handled the "therapy." I have always been bemused by the distinction. In any event, we "tutored," they "therapized." In fact, we spent much time and effort trying to show the children how to deal with their anxieties and how to forestall their worst crashes. I think we helped them by letting them learn what kinds of learning situations set off their fears.

That project and the work it kicked up had the good effect of letting me gather my wits, particularly letting me look at children learning and solving problems in quite ordinary settings. I needed a respite from experimental work.

Soon enough I was back to it, trying to reconcile Piagetian structuralism and Vygotskyan functionalism. I realize now that I fell into an easy trap. I used the usual Genevan "conservation" tasks as my instruments for studying development. They consist, for those not acquainted with them, of an initial display of a quantity of some substance or liquid in a container—say a standard beaker half filled with water. This beaker is then emptied into a narrower one, in which the water level is higher. The child is then asked whether there is still the same amount of water as before, or whether there is more or less. It is a task beautifully designed to land you on the flypaper of Piagetian debate.

In the Piagetian "preoperational" stage (around five or six), the child is alleged not to grasp the reversible nature of quantity—that though it *looks* like more because it is higher, it is the same because it can be poured back to its original state. The child's conceptual grasp of reversibility, when achieved, is said to be general, to characterize all logical operations—give or take a little variability in the extent to which the general idea finds expression in different media or materials.

For Piaget, development is assured so long as the child has an adequate "aliment" of active experience with the world. You simply wait. The same order of developmental stages will unfold—possibly accelerated by richer experience—though Piaget dismissed this last point as *"la question américaine."* Could this be so? I had already seen the striking effects of too many curriculum projects to take this whole. How could one dismiss Vygotsky's "zone of proximal development" so cavalierly? Equip a child with the conceptual means of making a leap to higher ground, and he would often generalize and transfer his knowledge to new problems quite on his own. Were "stages" so monolithic after all? Did development move along with the slow and steady pace of a glacier pressed forward by a single source?

It seemed to me that there was a richer picture behind mental growth than this one. Human beings represent their knowledge of the world in three ways. One is through habit and action: knowing what to do. A second is through imagery: depiction of events and relations. Finally, we "know" things by representing them in a symbol system like language or mathematics. Making progress in the mastery of any domain most often involved using all three modes of representation—typically progressing from enactive, through iconic, to symbolic. Indeed, understanding could be deepened by using all three modes, even (and sometimes especially) when they were in conflict with each other. If some modes were easier for the child than others, then the way of helping him across the "zone of proximal development" was to start with it and then move on to others. Let him first master a problem by practical action, for example, and then move on to pictures and words. Or mask the child from cues that "fix" him in one mode, like the *height* of the water in that tall, thin glass, so that the evocative power of the act of pouring it back could enter his consciousness and reckoning.

I must confess to a complicated relation with Piaget, for it "explains" a next step in my own thinking. Particularly for younger men, he was an enormously attractive presence. There was a purity about him that was so genuine and singular in its expression that it was as if in his company one had shaken off ordinary trivia. He was almost totally devoted to the development of his ideas. To enter that world was a privilege. Besides, he was not in any sense an austere man. There was a quality of enjoyment in whatever he did—in his work, in the trencherman way he ate, in his way of joking about ideas, in his appreciation of charming women. But there was also a preemptive quality about his consciousness. To be with him was to be a part of it. It was difficult to define one's ideas without reference to his. He made many of the men around him feel like rebellious sons when their ideas diverged—rebellious, but not independent. It was not by any means that he was disrespectful of divergence. I never saw him dismissive toward an idea anybody proposed to him seriously in the spirit of exchange. He would consider that part of it that made some contact with his own mode of thought, give it a fair hearing, accept it or agree to disagree. Those parts that did not make contact, he could not hear—like the role of language in shaping thought.

I suppose it was too much of a father-son relation for me, one that generated too much ambivalence over autonomy and independence. Bärbel Inhelder, his principal assistant and one of the most perceptive women I have ever known, was the buffer between us, and it was with her that I would try to work out our differences.

I mention this because it relates to one of the turning points in the development of my own thinking in those days. Geneva psychology was founded on the idea of "stages" of development, each with its own underlying logic of operations. The part of me that was in league with Vygotsky rebelled at the "quietism" of stage theories, quietism in the sense that stages were simply something a child lived through until he had had enough *aliment* to progress to the next one.

My solution was to convert my ideas about modes of representation—enactive, iconic and symbolic—into stages of development. Enactive representation, in effect, is storing one's knowledge in the form of habits of acting (as in riding a bike); iconic is storage in images; symbolic, by means of a symbol system like language. Rather than concentrating on the manner in which hypotheses of each type were generated and tested at *any* age, I let my ideas fall into a chronological straitjacket: the enactive mode first, then the iconic, and finally the symbolic. The last was particularly important, for it provided the means whereby culture and cognitive growth made contact, the medium whereby the culture's tool kit could be made the child's own.

My graduate students and I plunged in. Working together with them on a research project is for me one of the joys of teaching. We had weekly seminars, at which ideas or findings were thrashed out. I went off to Africa with Patricia Greenfield to pretest procedures for comparing schooled and unschooled Wolof children. Lee Reich also studied Eskimos in Alaska. And hundreds of Cambridge children went through our procedures. The exchange with Geneva continued. Bärbel Inhelder and her assistant, Magali Bovet, came to Harvard for a year and several of us went over to Geneva occasionally for seminars. Communication did not necessarily draw us closer intellectually, but it did so personally. Given my interest in heuristics, in hypothesis formation, in the power of certain forms of experience to give a special lift to growth, it was bound to be that way. Such preoccupations do not fit well in a stage theory premised on the general nurturance of experience.

As I drew away from Geneva, I drew closer to Moscow. It was partly intellectual, partly personal. The personal part was Alexander Romanovich Luria, a Russian uncle in the grand manner. It was with him that I could talk and correspond about Vygotsky's ideas and my

variants of them. Luria had unflagging energy, intense loyalties, un-
quenchable enthusiasm. In the fifteen or so years that I knew him
well, I do not think that two months ever went by without a letter
from him, a new book or translation of his, a coffee-table volume of
Rublov's icons or the architecture of the cathedral at Rostov, whatever. He was the czar of Russian psychology, but a more benign czar
would be hard to imagine!

Luria visited the United States in 1960, staying with us in Cambridge for a week. He bubbled with enthusiasm for the beauties of
the Harvard Yard and took dozens of pictures of it. The "Second
Signal System" was very much on his mind and it only slowly dawned
on me how crucial this idea had been to him and to his friends—both
politically and intellectually—in turning Russian psychology around
to cognitive ideas. It had the sanctity of being formulated by Pavlov
himself. Pavlov, of course, had been the idol of the environmental
determinists after the Revolution, though he was no behaviorist. His
First Signal System comprises stimuli that register nature directly,
those to which animals become conditioned. The second system was
a transformation of the first. Through it, stimuli were converted into
language and made culturally relevant. Luria and his students were
hard at work on experiments demonstrating how language provided
children with the means for gaining power and self-control over the
worlds of external stimuli and internal impulses. Later, once language became more syntactically organized, they were enabled to
solve problems by converting them (or being helped to convert
them) into language, on which they could then operate. One study,
for example, involved the relationship between color and form. A
particular shape was a "positive" stimulus when it appeared against
one background color, but not when it appeared against another.
This kind of relationship is a very difficult task for young children to
master. If, however, the problem was presented in a form like "Air-
planes can fly on sunny days, but not on cloudy days," the children
would quickly recognize that an airplane silhouette was positive
against a yellow background, but negative when against a gray one.
It was a simple but powerful demonstration, a little replica of the
difference between the meaningful and meaningless cards in *A
Study of Thinking*.

It is difficult to appreciate how politically and ideologically important the Second Signal System was to my Russian friends. Marxist
dialectic requires that experience "reflect" physical reality. It also

requires that it do so in a fashion reflecting the history and culture of people. Pavlov's formulation of a Second System, the rather crude afterthought of an old man, provided the occasion for rehabilitating Vygotsky without rejecting Pavlov! For Vygotsky indeed saw language as the means by which mind mediated between culture and nature. Vygotsky's views were far more genuinely Marxist.

On a visit to the Soviet Union two years later, I learned that the proposal made by Luria to rehabilitate Vygotsky (with Leontiev and Smirnov) had meant the deposition of Ivanov-Smolensky as director of the Institute of Psychology in Moscow. He had been the strict ideological Pavlovian of the years since the purge of 1936. Ivanov's Pavlovian orthodoxy could now be applauded as admirable—and condemned as old hat.

Needless to say, Luria's news about Russian research on the role of language in early development was more than welcome to me. So were his other enthusiasms. One was about the importance of selective attention or the "orienting reflex." It was very closely linked to my earlier work on the New Look in perception. The other was about the selectivity of perception as revealed in eye movements. Luria had with him in Cambridge dozens of slides of Yarbus's work on eye movements. Yarbus had found that where the eye looked (as well as what the eye saw) was a function of what question the perceiver had been asked and was attempting to answer. The track of eye movements was like the path of a detective searching out clues related to a particular hypothesis.

Luria and I became fast friends almost immediately. We were compatible temperamentally and very much in agreement about psychological matters. His curiosity ran along much more psychological lines than did Piaget's and his interest in the cultural enablement of mind led him to be far more open to links between anthropology and psychology. Besides, he created none of those father-son problems that had dogged my relations with Piaget.

Studies in Cognitive Growth, my book on stages of representation, was published in 1966 and dedicated to Piaget. The last paragraph of the Preface says:

> Many points of disagreement are . . . minor by comparison with the points of fundamental agreement we share with Professor Jean Piaget. This volume would have been impossible without his monumental work. His genius has founded modern developmental psychology. It gives us all deep

pleasure to dedicate this book to him on his seventieth birthday and to present it to him on that occasion at the XVIIIth International Congress of Psychology in Moscow on August 9, 1966.

It was a rather stiffly formal luncheon party, the presentation. I had traveled to Moscow with Roman Jakobson, whose wit can always be counted on, and he and a dozen others joined us for toasts and birthday wishes in a small private dining room at the Ukrayina Hotel. It was plain that Piaget did not like the book much. Jakobson saved the day with witty anecdotes. The occasion had its ironic appropriateness. Dedicated to Piaget, presented in Moscow!

It is a curious book. It had a modest influence in psychology, though it was influential among educators. It got lukewarm reviews. By then, the Piaget wave had reached cresting level. The book was too close to Piagetian thought, yet too remote from central issues in his theory, to have much impact. The Vygotskyan side of it was mostly ignored, though that has changed recently. The use of cross-cultural evidence—comparisons of Western children with the Wolof of Senegal and Eskimos—gave heart to some who were more culturally oriented. And that too grew in time. Our book was really out of step with the drumbeat to which developmental psychology was then marching.

Perhaps the book was written at a bad time in my life. I was split in my interests. My work on education had become "renowned." I was being hailed as the "greatest force in education since John Dewey." There was even an article in *Harper's* magazine about me. I was on the Education Panel of the President's Science Advisory Committee and also at work putting together a new school curriculum in social studies. I should have been working more directly on the problem of how intellectual development and education could be linked.

It was 1966, ten years since *A Study of Thinking*. The new book had not got me back to the beginnings of mental life at all. This time I would do better. I would have a look at infancy, *early* infancy, and see what I could find there about how mind began. All I knew about the topic was what was to be found in the standard reference books, and there wasn't much there: mostly reflexes, autonomic functioning, sensory processes. Young infants cannot talk to you, cannot do much with their hands, cannot move about. They cry, feed, look, comfort themselves by sucking, fall asleep with prodigious speed. The best you can do is to hitch them up to rather sophisticated physiological apparatus that measures their heart rate or breathing or skin conductance and take what you find as an indicator of some internal state of mind.

That search for internal states through physiological measurement was a little like an electronic Olympics. One investigator in Holland, for example, regularly recorded fourteen simultaneous measures in his newborns. To make such measures, the infant must be put into a highly shielded environment, else the recordings will reflect a barrage of overactivation.

I am no physiologist and I am not particularly good at delicate instrumentation. But good fortune came my way. Drew Marshall arrived on the scene—a young man fresh back from Vietnam who had just barely managed to struggle his way through the requirements of school and college but who, in fact, was extraordinarily gifted in electronic gadgetry and was blessed with a very high intelligence indeed. Between us we managed to design and build the machinery we needed.

The last babies I had had any real contact with were my own two kids, and I had enjoyed, rather than studied, their infancy. I needed tuition. I "found" Berry Brazelton. I had known him before as a pediatrician and a tennis partner. He offered to give me a peripatetic "course" on what infants "were *really* like." Hard at work on his now famous Neonatal Assessment Test, he was longing for the company of somebody interested in just my kind of questions.

Saturdays we would go off to the Boston Lying-in Hospital on our own private rounds. After a while, the more venturesome young residents on the staff began tagging along. Brazelton is a clinical artist and a charismatic teacher. I paid my fees by asking him questions, "outrageous" questions he called them, that never would have occurred to a "doctor." He came to work the next year at the Center for Cognitive Studies. My luck was building.

A very clever and rather erratic young Scot had just arrived at Harvard, Tom Bower, with a fresh Ph.D. from Cornell. As an undergraduate at Edinburgh, he had been taught by David Hume. That in itself is not remarkable. I have had four Scottish doctoral students, all at Oxford, all loathing the place. Every one of them had been imprinted on Hume. Tom was not only interested in human infancy, but interested specifically in how mind begins. We talked a great deal and exchanged notes. I learned much from him. There are psychologists who doubt some of his research findings, since several have not been replicable. I think he may have been a little carried away in interpreting his findings. But as an intelligence he is wide-ranging, reflective, ingenious both in his questions and in devising means for answering them. He was a superb companion.

There are some odd things about babies. They are, for example, highly labile in their adjustment to the world immediately around them. So we designed an experimental room that was softer, simpler, less perceptually tempting than a world fit for older children. It was a cubicle draped in soft, cream-colored drapes. The baby was put in a comfortable, semi-upright chair in which he was held securely—what soon became known as the "Harvard chair." So soft was the visual environment that there was nowhere for the infant's eye to light! Within thirty seconds, he would be in tears. We shifted to a more burly, cluttered style. The infants were immediately more content. It was a little fable for our times, to which I shall return presently.

Infants do some things very well. One of them is to suck. They suck not only to feed, of course, but to comfort themselves—two quite different patterns. It occurred to us that perhaps we should use their sucking as a means of getting them to control the environment. It was not difficult to design apparatus that would allow us to measure an infant's sucking while he made use of it to control some feature of his environment. One of my graduate students had already discovered that infants regulated the duration of their sucking bursts according to the amount of milk delivered per suck. That was surely a way of controlling the environment. What about sucking to control aspects of the world not related to feeding or self-comforting?

My research assistant was a cheerful and bright Estonian refugee, in Cambridge with a postdoctoral biologist husband. She was doing a degree at Toronto. She was going to be at Harvard for another couple of years, so there was no rush. Ilze Kalnins was never in a hurry anyway. We could get on with the job as slowly as necessary. Working with young infants *is* slow work.

We hit on a bizarre idea. We had inadvertently noticed that when infants watch pictures, they turn away when they go out of focus. (What about that "booming buzzing confusion" of infancy?) Could we get an infant to clear up a blurred picture by sucking on a pacifier connected to the focusing mechanism? What would they do when their sucking created blur? We did the study—slowly. Infants *will* speed their sucking to clear up blur at six weeks. But they also combined their sucking with their looking in an ingenious way. While sucking to clear the blur from a picture, the infant keeps his gaze averted for a second or two, and then looks back to the cleared picture. When his sucking on the pacifier drives a clear picture into blur, he keeps looking until the last bearable moment, and *then* turns away. So not only could six-week-olds suck for "arbitrary ends," but they could combine sucking quite flexibly with another activity, looking.

To me, the infant's performance seemed like skilled activity. It had an organizing intent, an anticipated end state, flexible means to be deployed, and so forth. That is the stuff of all intelligent action—that and the capacity to combine these prerequisite routines into still more powerful skills. Even that seemed within the infant's reach, judging by his ability to combine sucking and looking to such good effect. I duly went off to a meeting in Minneapolis to report our findings. (A pleasant young woman came up after my paper and said, "That was nice. But what a pity you're leaving developmental psychology to do infant research.")

I think it was that study more than any others in the series undertaken over those years that set the course of my thinking. It seemed to me that the heart of the matter was the elaboration of intention-directed behavior. In early development, the child has a highly limited set of goals to which he directs his actions—establishing contact with others, grouping and taking possession of objects, exploring with hand and sense organs, feeding, comforting. More strikingly, he has a limited repertory of means of achieving intended objectives. But as Edward Tolman had put it forty years before, he has from the start a remarkably sensitive "means-ends readiness," a capacity to assemble means for achieving ends. He is active in doing so, a hypothesis generator from the start. It is this means-end readiness that gives a directedness to behavior, and when his behavior seems disordered or random, it comes from his inability to formulate a plan in which ends and means match. It is then that he suffers distress and frustration.

Part of the difficulty that the young child experiences is in controlling his level of arousal or activation. He is labile—becomes over-aroused, frustrated, or dormant with fatigue or boredom, to degrees that he cannot control. But when his knowledge of means and ends is sufficiently developed, it is striking in what degree he can mobilize and control his state. As with our creamy research cubicle, the world activates him or fails to. There are stimulating and supportive environments, and ones that put him to sleep or bore him beyond limits.

Two other related things those studies highlighted. One was the extent to which infants are canny in combining their own actions or their knowledge of the world to form either higher-order action routines or more generalized "cognitive maps" of their world. The other is the extent to which they play. It is as if the play—usually in the form of performing a wide range of acts on a single object or a single act on a wide range of objects—has the effect of sensitizing them to the combinability of the things of the world for goal-directed action.

And finally, people. The dependence of the species on a long immaturity makes it inevitable that we be sensitive from the start upon interaction with others. It is that sensitivity, as we shall see in the next chapter, that nurtures the acquisition of language.

The research gained momentum. There was a lively group of postdoctoral fellows at work with me. An irrepressible New Zealander, Colwyn Trevarthen, was at work on the fundamental distinction between "central" and "ambient" perception: focus on figural, central detail, and attention to surrounding context. He saw the two as reflecting the integration of the old optic tectum and the visual cortex proper. Perceptual development appeared to be dependent indeed on the integration of the two. Berry Brazelton was tracing the early development of mother-infant interaction, distinguishing it from the infant's reactions to inanimate objects. When Czechoslovakia was overrun, Hanus Papousek, who had directed the Mother-Infant Research Institute in Prague, joined us, working in learning and self-recognition. Alistair Mundy-Castle came from Ghana and began a series of studies on the child's capacity to figure out visual trajectories. It was a lively shop. With our own group at the Center, with Tom Bower's, with Jerry Kagan's, and with Roger Brown steadily at work on "a first language," Harvard had become, I suppose, the world center. If that was in doubt, then when MIT got added (for it too had its flowering of infancy research, led by Richard Held), Cambridge had certainly become it.

As far as the press was concerned, the thrust of this intense effort was that infants were far more competent, more active, more organized than had been thought before. Indeed, that was surely so. We had a visitor from India one day, a London-trained pediatrician. She asked to see one of our research procedures, and Ilze Kalnins demonstrated a six-week-old sucking a blurred picture into focus. The visitor watched for a while, then blurted out almost in indignation, "But babies of that age can't see!" We had accomplished *something*.

Given the political climate of the 1960s, the research was immediately and passionately taken up. Two social revolutions were in full swing; the infancy work armed both of them with compelling arguments. One was the black movement, the other women's liberation. The early "deficit" of disadvantaged children, principally black children, was already well publicized. Head Start was under way, about which I shall have more to say in the following chapter. The new research on infancy strongly suggested that those early years of "deficit" were the very ones in which children might be acquiring highly complex and presumably useful skills. The broader implications for early education were not missed either. Maya Pines did a major feature in *The New York Times Magazine*, replete with one of our children in color on its cover. John Davies did a comparable one shortly after in the London Sunday *Times*. And the "upmarket" press in Europe and America were soon editorializing on the importance of nurturing competence in early childhood not only as an aspect of preschool care but as an instrument of education generally. Daniel Patrick Moynihan had, a few years before, written a celebrated memorandum to the President on treating the failing black family with "benign neglect." In the new atmosphere, such a proposal would have been treated as genocide, which indeed it might be.

The women's movement was agitating for day care centers to support women who worked outside the home. The potential benefits of such day care was soon added to their brief. Our Center for Cognitive Studies had its own Women's Group—and a high-powered group they were. Several of the members helped establish the new University Daycare Center at Harvard. And they were very soon emulated by tens of thousands of women around the country.

To my surprise again, the practical impact of developmental research turned out to have more to do with politics than with scientific certainty. Policymakers are not that impressed by one's doubts. Under pressure, they can wait neither for the unseating of old paradigms nor for the establishment of new ones. When a small group of us had waited upon Sargent Shriver, director of the Office of Economic Opportunity in President Johnson's administration, with a plan for something like Head Start, he scoffed. "Washington in the baby business! That's all we need with our other troubles." We proposed a small pilot project, in acknowledgment of our ignorance about how to proceed with the idea. A few months later—principally following the urging of Lady Bird Johnson, so the story has it—when the idea came to be seen as a strong addition to the Great Society, the notion of a pilot project was rejected entirely. "If it's to be justified both as needed and as possible, you cannot play around with *pilot* projects," Shriver told me. Head Start was to be mounted in every state of the Union.

Where indeed were we, leaving aside all the politics of early childhood? How does one think of the beginning of mind? For one thing, the new spate of research had already made it clear that mind was not, so to speak, something from nothing. Simpleminded empiricism was surely dead. But if, in Leibnitz's terms, nothing is initially in the mind save mind itself, what were its powers? Certainly the intelligence-bearing constituents were there from the start: the component intention-driven skills and the appreciation of means-end relations. And certainly the capacity for the combining of actions was part of the initial equipment. A capacity for representing what one had encountered was surely in being from the start, as evidenced by a spate of studies on the child's sensitivity to deviations from the ordinary. The initial representational skills probably included a good deal of built-in appreciation of space, time and even causality—if not innate, then very easily primed by experience. The child's curiosity didn't even need to be stoked up, and all the evidence suggested that even the newborn's line of regard went to the informationally rich rather than the redundant features of his visual environment. What a five-year-old looked at was much what his mother was looking at, all else being equal. But of course, all else was *not* equal. Five-year-olds don't ask the same questions about the world that grownups do, and the eye, for all its swift skills, is no better than the questions put to it by the mind.

The question then is not where or when mind begins. Mind in some operative form is there from the start, wherever "there" may be. The question, rather, is about the conditions that produce human minds that are richer, stronger, more confident.

I remarked at the start that I had not "studied" my own children while they were growing up. Not that I didn't watch them with wonder. But I could never quite bring myself to formal study with note taking, recording or the rest.

I cannot claim any higher principle. Perhaps like Niels Bohr and his son, I was not able to know them both as parent and investigator. I felt "attachment" in a very direct and unencumbered way. When Jane and Whit were infants, I used particularly to take pleasure in giving them their baths; there was something marvelous about the abandon of their playfulness in a tub. I would somehow manage to be home if I could for that ritual. In general, I suppose, their fantasies, their constructed worlds, engaged me more than the orderly progress of their schooling or their mastery of this or that skill. Those were no problem. As it happens, they were both bright children—differently bright, and different in character. Whit was articulate and abstract, yet with a lively dramatic sense. A week before his sixth birthday I asked him what he would like to do on August 24. "Go to a foreign country." We drove from Vermont for a weekend in Canada. Jane "made" things, literally made them. When *she* was about six, we went off to shoot clay pigeons. A photographer friend was popping flashbulbs, Jane stuffing spent shotgun shells and flashbulbs into her pockets. When we got home she asked for a package of pipe cleaners. An hour later she had a small army of dolls: flashbulbs stuck into the tops of spent shotgun shells, faces painted on the flashbulbs, pipe cleaners sticking out for arms. Whit grew up to be an Arabist diplomat; Jane a painter-photographer.

I must have thought of myself as a provider of and accomplice in their possible worlds. I read to them a great deal, indeed made up not only stories but continuing sagas that ran for months at bedtime —about a talking crow and his adventures in Vermont; about his friends, including a heroic Robin Hood eagle who came to the rescue of the helpless and the harassed; about a series of indigenous or prehistoric heroes who introduced their inventions for the first time and prevailed though they were mocked ("What a silly thing to use that for, at the tip of a travois. A wheel is to spin when you pray, idiot"). As they grew older, the adventures grew more elaborate. My wife Kay was a willing and ingenious ally. We drove one summer to California via the trail of the Astorians, following the track of the historian Francis Parkman. We pitched tent each night near a site where the wagons had stopped and read aloud from the Parkman journals. In the early 1950s, the four of us went up into the Canadian Chibougamau Reserve over a one-hundred-mile corduroy road newly opened, rented a canoe from the Cree Indian agent, and explored "north of the trees."

I don't think my impulse was ever properly "pedagogical" either. I never felt strongly that the children ought to learn this subject or that. Perhaps it was because they were good students. I did want them to have a sense that they were in a larger world; we took them with us when we went to Europe to teach at the Salzburg seminar in 1952 or, even earlier, when we went off to explore Spain and France in our Jeep station wagon. Indeed, the idea of a "wide world" even inspired some Sunday afternoon pedagogical expeditions, I must confess. We would go off to the docks of Boston harbor and see the ships berthed there. I wanted them to know we lived in a great harbor—although the rotting wharves took some explaining to observant children.

I must report one unreserved pedagogical success, although I am not sure I had any educational objectives well in mind. It was a game, Gallery Whist, that I heard about from my friend and neighbor Robert Lee Wolff, one that, so far as I know, his mother had invented. It worked like a charm. I tried it first when we took the children along for visits to the Prado in Madrid in 1955. You set points for finding certain "unusual" things in the paintings of the museum. One morning it would be any painting of Veronica wiping the face of Christ with her veil—with double points when His face was also imaged on the surface of the veil. Another time it would be a painting of the Annunciation in which the Virgin plainly looked astonished to hear that she was to be Queen of Heaven. Dwarfs in any painting made easy points in Spain. Hard points were New World scenes in Spanish paintings of the sixteenth and seventeenth centuries. At the end of the day, points could be converted into local currency.

There were hazards to "the game." At the Prado Jane inadvertently stumbled on black Goyas. I saw this graceful eight-year-old running toward me full tilt down one of those long central corridors. "I found something really, really scary. Quick, come see." I felt a pang; not for long. Half an hour later I found the two of them glued to Hieronymus Bosch, so totally bewitched by the horrors he depicted that they could scarcely be dragged away.

It never occurred to me to believe in "stages" of development in the Piagetian sense. There was always *some* way in which *anything* could be made clear to them, given patience, willing dialogue, and the power of metaphor. They were bright and eager children, granted, but that surely was not the point. It was a question, rather, of finding a scenario into which they could enter. I recall once trying to demonstrate to Whit the experimental method, so called, by filling two milk bottles with colored water and capping them. Did water expand when it froze? It was winter, a bitter one; one went outside the back door, the other stayed inside. In the morning, the outside one was frozen, with cap thrust up in the air. Point made. Polite boredom. That weekend, we made one of our visits to the Peabody Museum of Anthropology. One of the cases had models of a tightly swaddled Plains Indian baby. I told Whit the prevailing theory about how that produced warlikeness among the Plains Indian braves, rather like a rage reaction against being restrained. On the way home after, he asked, "Why don't they swaddle half the babies and leave the others free, to see if that theory is true?" So the idea of "experiment" rooted in that eight-year-old head, but it took a livelier scenario than expanded frozen water to bring it out into spontaneous thought.

I suppose, as I shall relate in the following chapter, my interest in education was kindled by watching my children go through school. I'm sure that if I and my friends had pooled resources and set up a little kibbutz (as Elting Morison suggested once), we could have done far better at educating our kids than the schools did. My son even suggests, as a grown man, that I had a hidden theory of education from the start—something like "going beyond the information given." It never struck me as a theory but as a given! There were games, it's true, involving "guessing," like what could you tell about people, say, sitting in their cars observed on a ferry, or stopping by old cellar holes, in the woods in New Hampshire and Vermont, and making up stories about what it must have been like before the families had moved West.

Subjecting the children to experiment or assessing them according to norms would have created a distance between us that did not appeal to me. I can't do that and still have good conversation. I am not that detached. They have grown up quite interesting people. We still have good conversation. If I ever knew what their IQ was (and I don't recall that I ever did), I couldn't have cared less. Nor whether or when they could conserve quantity or comprehend sentences out of context. I knew that one of them had very low frustration tolerance, the other very high. I spent a great deal of time trying to arrange life so that they could live with what they had. I have no idea whether I succeeded—whatever that may mean.

Psychologists, on the same grounds that the cobbler's children shall go unshod, are supposed not to be good parents. That is surely tabloid nonsense. They are quite as variable and ordinary as the rest. Was I as a psychologist-parent any better able to "predict, control and explain" my children than other parents were? I wonder, for example, whether it was more obvious to me than it might have been to another parent that Jane would become a professional photographer and Whitley an Arabist-diplomat. There is too much fortuity that comes from the setting and the opportunities by which they were surrounded. Control? Both children went through blazing adolescent rebellions, in an individual way. I waited. I never felt I could make a dent.

I suppose, in a way, my own feelings toward them may have been guided by some sort of compensation for my own childhood. My father had (until his final illness) been away a great deal on business. We rarely did things together even when he was home. *I* did a great deal with *my* children. My mother, as I have related, avoided any show of affection and was not one for stories and fantasy. I suspect I was rather a demonstrative father, and I delighted in fantasy and tales shared with the children. But who knows really?

Still, if you are going to study how the mind begins, you would be well advised to have some children of your own. But that is surely no reason for having children! At that, they will be more likely to save you from your follies about how mind begins than to lead you to some evident truths.

9

The World and Words

That new wave of interest in "mind" in the early 1950s was, of course, the end effect of many stirrings. I sketched some of them in Chapter 7. One of them eventually developed a wave of its own. It was the study of language—language as an organ of mind and eventually language for its own sake.

At the start, language was not quite a self-contained topic for psychologists. It was viewed rather as an "influence" on thought and memory. In its own right, it was treated principally as a phenomenon to be demystified—"nothing but" the result of learning or association or imitation or all of them put together. It was just "verbal behavior," to be accounted for like any other behavior, only more so. B. F. Skinner was probably the last to go that route, in his *Verbal Behavior* published in 1957.

Certainly, my own interest in language started with concern for its impact on mind—again language as an *instrument* of mind.

It began, I think, with Sir Frederic Bartlett. His "schema" theory offered a view of memory as a process, an act of constructing or reconstructing the past in the form of a narrative or schematic framework that assimilated the idiosyncratic to the culturally ordinary. The past could even be changed by "turning around on a schema," an act of reflective reconstruction that transformed the past to new uses. It was never explicit *how* this was accomplished, but all the examples in his famous 1932 *Remembering* were linguistic, not in the linguist's sense but in the sense of a script being rewritten: sharpened, leveled, assimilated. Narrative rather than grammar was at center stage. Not that there were not memory images, but rather that they were reconstructed in language or some sort of symbol system.

Then there were Lev Vygotsky and Benjamin Lee Whorf. Theirs was the next step beyond the banality that language *influences* mind and thought. Theirs was the claim that language *must* influence, must even *shape* thought—language not just as narrative or label but as a system for cutting up the world into categories and relations by virtue of grammar and lexicon.

It was 1954. I asked Roger Brown to lecture in a course I taught on how language could affect social attitudes. His organizing theme was "Whorf's hypothesis" and, as usual, he was totally lucid even without benefit of a single line of notes. He gave Whorf two alternative readings. The strong version was that language was the mold into which thought was poured. The weak one was that language was a mantle thrown over our thoughts, their shapes showing through. The strong form asserted the necessity of linguistic coding as a feature of all mental operations. The weak form was a kind of "codability hypothesis": concepts and ideas that were most easily coded in a particular language were the ones that would be most easily remembered, used, absorbed into the culture.

I resisted the "strong" version. It seemed to deny the possibility of reviewing or correcting language by nonlinguistic means. There was no room for breaking the linguistic fetters that bound conventional thought. Codability, the weak form, yes; but the strong form seemed absurd. The Eskimo's six words for snow stood him in good stead; but the skier would invent six words as needed. Nonetheless, I had to grant that there were *some* concepts that could exist *only* by virtue of language and *they* would be instances of the strong form.

Vygotsky began, recall, with two independent "streams" of mental activity: a stream of thought and a stream of language. Thought early in life was in its own terms, whatever those might be. Language first became an instrument and then the medium of thought. It was the tool kit by which culture and history shaped and finally determined experience and thought.

Most of us in my generation had been raised on the philosophical mother's milk of two modes of logical thinking: the *analytic* and the *synthetic*. It was totally "obvious." Synthetic terms were *empirical* in the sense of being about the world and/or experience. Analytic terms were statements about the language itself and dealt with matters like synonymy, as in propositions such as "All men are mortal . . ."

I was quite willing to grant that when one embraced a system of logic with permissible terms and relations, then one was "stuck" with the results that the logical system could yield. The analytic was where the "strong form" of Whorf lived. Any system of logic, like any geometry, mortgaged one's freedom. But after all, it was experience of the world, not language, that gave shape to the synthetic. At best, it would be subject only to the weak form.

A flicker of uncertainty about all this came when I read Wittgenstein—not the *Tractatus* but the *Philosophical Investigations.* Is anybody properly trained for reading Wittgenstein? It was elusive, tantalizing and altogether provocative. One reads Wittgenstein rather as one reads poetry. It develops a "way of life" as you read it. Frank Kermode once characterized a "classic" as literature amenable to as many deep readings as necessary. I can even read the first few dozen sections of the *Investigations* as a theory of language acquisition!

The argument that caught me was a dark one. *Particular* domains of knowledge can be understood, but they cannot necessarily be *better* understood by subsuming them with others under more inclusive domains. There is a deep principle of "untranslatability" entailed. For any domain of discourse is a "language game" governed not so much by its own set of rules as by a "way of life." "Translatability" from one way of life to others remains indeterminate, even translation upward into higher-order abstractions. At best, concepts have family resemblances to each other.

Wittgenstein was to be brooded over, not adopted. For me, he was background not foreground. I had no idea he was having any effect—until later.

Then Noam Chomsky came on the scene in the late 1950s. I can recover three strong early impressions of him, two of them from reading, the other personal. His review of Skinner's *Verbal Behavior* was electric: Noam at his best, mercilessly out for the kill, daring, brilliant, on the side of the angels. The reductionism of learning-theory explanations of language was "exposed" as a kind of anti-intellectual sham, almost as a conspiracy to denigrate human rationality. The marshaling of linguistic evidence was devastatingly on target. I felt like cheering when I finished it. His little volume *Syntactic Structures* had much the same effect—particularly his demolition of what are called "finite state grammars." These are "associative" grammars based solely on the relations between immediately neigh-boring elements in a sentence, grammars that disregard the top-down structure of the sentence as a whole. His demonstration that associationist, learning theories of grammar *must* be wrong was tonic. His demolition of the old Augustinian associationist dogma (by invoking the recursiveness of embedded sentences which character-ize all natural languages) was in the same category as St. George slaying the dragon! So intrigued was I by the virtuosity of his proof that I wrote a letter that very evening to my painter friend Elizabeth Weems in Colorado, retelling it. She must have been surprised!

The more personal memory was of a colloquium Noam gave at the Center for Cognitive Studies. His strong case for the innateness of language was not new. The form of the argument was. It was based on the idea of an innate "hypothesis generator." Just as one cannot "perceive" the world, save as figures on grounds, so one could not experience language without imposing sentence structures on it, sentences with noun phrases, verb phrases and their natural joints. It is not past experience that leads one to do so, but the active nature of mind and brain. *That* made language interesting for me in its own right.

Language viewed that way had to be there in some form *from the start.* Something led us to *recognize* well-formed sentences or gener-ate them without tuition. It was an underlying "competence," a uniquely human grasp of a deep, universal grammar of which partic-ular languages were instances or surface realizations. The *perform-ance* of a speaker on any given occasion could not, then, constitute the data of the linguist. The data, rather, was what a speaker *could* do: his *generative* competence.

George Miller, lecturing to our joint course in the early 1960s, remarked that the number of word strings between three and fifty words in length whose grammaticality (or lack thereof) an adult could recognize was about equal to the number of photons in the solar system! If you had had to learn about their grammaticality one by one and if you could do so by a process of one-trial reinforcement learning, it would take the better part of one's life to scratch the surface, even if one encountered sentences at the rate of one thou-sand per second. Therefore, there *had* to be some sense in which we already *knew* the rules of language before we started. Nativism (the creed of my first teacher, William McDougall) was making its bid again.

Its initial appeal was in asserting the nonreducibility of complex mental processes—of which language was the supreme case. I welcomed Chomsky's formulation for another reason. Here was Vygotsky's "stream of language" developing from its own source.

Enter the Russians yet again. As everybody now knows, they were breaking away from *their* empiricist shackles at just this time—by invoking Pavlov's Second Signal System, through which the world of sense experience was transmuted into the categories and relations of language. Here was a stream of language that could fuse with the stream of thought. Given my belief in the role of categorizing in perception and thought, I quickly became a true believer. Chomsky whole was incorporated into *Studies in Cognitive Growth.* Learning to encode the world linguistically and then to operate on language rather than on the world—that was the ultimate stage of cognitive development.

It was all too easy to fall under the spell. There was the enthusiastic George Miller with his clever students, at work demonstrating the "psychological reality" of grammar. He was as ingenious at designing neat experiments for demonstrating the mental *operation* of grammatical rules as Noam was in marshaling linguistic instances to formulate them. The meeting place for experiments and theory at that time was the idea of "transformations," the means by which deep structure "kernel sentences" in the declarative form (K) "were converted into negatives (N), questions (Q), or passives (P)." For example:

The dog bit the man	(K)	(1)
The man was bitten by the dog	(P)	(2)
Did the dog bite the man?	(Q)	(3)
The dog did not bite the man	(N)	(4)

These transformations could then be combined; e.g.:

Did the dog not bite the man?	(QN)	(5)
The man was not bitten by the dog	(PN)	(6)
Was the man not bitten by the dog?	(PQN)	(7)

George had turned to "mental chronometry" to make his stand on the psychological reality of these transformations. Suppose a kernel sentence, K, required a certain amount of time to be comprehended. Each transformation would then require a constant increment of time beyond that to be understood. Presumably, one would "understand" by recapturing the kernel and then adding the transformation to it. Handling *two* transformations was equivalent to handling each of them separately, and should require the time needed for handling the kernel and each of the transformations. And give or take a little slippage, this is what appeared to be happening when subjects were given such sentences to comprehend. It was an exciting finding. Grammatical principles seemed to be operating not only in the grammarian's mind but also in the mind of the language user.

Unfortunately, the bubble of enthusiasm for this proof of the "psychological reality" of grammar soon burst. For one, Noam Chomsky wrote a new book, in which the notion of the *untransformed* "kernel sentence" was critically altered. There was no such thing; it was only an abstraction characterizing the deep structure of language. You could not "time" its comprehension by using a simple declarative and then adding "transformed" versions of it. You had to be close to the Harvard-MIT scene of those days to realize the devastation that this theory change produced among experimenting psycholinguists.

But a more severe blow was shortly to fall. The time required to understand a negative sentence, Peter Wason found, depended upon the *use* of the sentence. In a "context of plausible denial," for example, a negative would be understood more quickly than a simple declarative sentence: e.g., saying of one red circle among five blue ones, "that one is not blue," would be more quickly grasped than saying of one of the blue ones, "that one is blue." So now it seemed that context and speaker's intention needed to be taken into account, not only syntax and its transformations. The 1960s were drawing to a close.

I must go back for a moment to the gifted and aging Roman Jakobson and say a word about his place in the local linguistic ferment. He was at Harvard while all of this was in progress. A Russian émigré of enormous wit, learning and self-possession, he was one of the most knowledgeable and delightful companions in town. I never heard him utter a pedantic sentiment in the quarter century I knew him. He was the towering figure in linguistics of his generation: not only a great *formal* linguist in the sense of having unraveled the sound structure of language through his formulation of the concept of the phoneme, but also a literary linguist of world renown, a master of poetics. For Jakobson, grammar was not just a formal or logical *system*, but one that fulfilled different uses: It "marked" emphasis, it referred, it commanded, it could even be used to turn round on itself reflectively.

He often expressed admiration for Chomsky, but found his work abstract and narrowly conceived. In his amused and tolerant way, he contented himself with appreciative jokes about the limits of transformational grammars. For him, the most primitive and important distinction in language was between the unmarked and the marked: the function language served in distinguishing between what is ordinary and what is extraordinary, in the context of communicating— and the myriad ways one signaled the distinction. It was from that distinction, he argued, that many grammatical patterns grow, even such elementary ones as topic and comment, subject and predicate.

Jakobson's richness and intuition worked on me in somewhat the same way as Wittgenstein's dark insights did: not to be put to immediate use, but allowed to marinate everything else about language that one happened to be thinking about.

I do not know what finally drew me into the study of language per se. If language was *the* human means by which we finally represented and interpreted the world, then its acquisition must shed light not only on language but on thought. As I have already mentioned, I had become alienated from the Piagetian way of conceiving language as a by-product of general cognitive development. Wittgenstein and Whorf were working on me too: *Many* human realities (I was finally prepared to grant) could not exist *but* for language.

Some of the idiosyncratic reasons for my staying away from language also evaporated. The subject was in such good hands at Harvard with George Miller and Roger Brown hard at it. Moving to Oxford changed the scene. Not just moving *away*, but moving *to* an Oxford where, I shall recount in a moment, I found some resonance for my underground notions.

Besides, it was plain by then that the Chomskyan account of language acquisition had failed. Not that there may not be an innate Language Acquisition Device, the famous LAD, but rather that it must obviously be primed by some knowledge of the world and by some push to communicate. The reason that babies do not speak sooner, better, more appositely is not just that they lack the requisite "performance" capabilities with which to express their innate linguistic competence. Rather, it is that they do not yet know enough about the world, about other people, about themselves to appreciate how the rules of language are to be *used*. For LAD to work, it would need a LASS, a Language Acquisition Support System, which arranges encounters with the world and with language in a way to make it all recognizable to an infant LAD. You don't acquire language abstractly: You learn how to *use* it. You use it to communicate, to put order into events, to construct realities. As Erving Goffman once said to me, you acquire language as an adjunct to learning to be civilized.

What most struck me in Roger Brown's masterful book of 1973, *A First Language*, was the small number of "meanings" that early speech was *about*. It was about action and who did it to whom or what, about possession and a very few other "case relations," as grammarians call it. These were obviously the "real world" things about which the child already knew a good deal. Patricia Greenfield, my former student and good friend, was circulating the manuscript of a book just about that time, based principally on close observations of her son Matthew's acquisition of speech. In it she added a fillip to Roger's account—a pragmatic one. Her emphasis was upon the child's *intentions* in communicating, and upon the linguistic means by which he achieved them: means for evoking attention, declaring possession, directing action, singling out the informationally crucial aspect of a scene, and so on. Brown, to put it too simply, was all about what early speech was *about;* Greenfield was focusing upon what it was *for*. This was "pragmatics." Charles Fillmore, a gifted linguist at Berkeley, was beginning to write about how grammatical constructions served "to impose perspectives on scenes" through forefronting certain elements and backgrounding others. And there were other stirrings. A bright young psycholinguist at Chicago, Carol Fleisher Feldman, presented a paper at the Linguistic Circle there (how the unpublished literature circulated in the mid-1970s!) on "stance markers," whereby through grammatical construction speakers expressed their point of view toward topics embodied in their speech. Teachers talking to teachers used modal auxiliaries (like *might, could,* etc.) for marking their doubt; very few such could be found in their speech to pupils. And John Dore in New York was making something of the "orectic" in child speech: the feature of a locution designed to have an action effect on the listener.

Without quite knowing it, we were entering the "third" phase of studies on language acquisition. The first had been all about syntax and was principally Chomsky (or anti-Chomsky); the second had brought back semantics, and the importance of meaning in the child's grasp of early language (principally sparked by Roger Brown and Lois Bloom); the third was about pragmatics, about how language is used to "get things done" and to influence the acts, thoughts and beliefs of interlocutors.

I could not have chosen a better time to go to Oxford. Cambridge, Massachusetts, still marched to "syntax-semantics" music; Oxford was alive with the very pragmatic concerns that had been working away at my thoughts. It was the spiritual home of speech act theory.

Isaiah Berlin's tale of how it had got launched touches on some points I made earlier. A group of philosophers had met regularly in his rooms at New College in the fifties to present papers to each other. It was there that John Austin first presented the idea of the "performative" in language. He had begun by musing (as he did later in his William James Lectures at Harvard in 1962) that a good eighty percent of what people actually *said* to each other could be counted neither as analytic nor as synthetic propositions, but in no sense were they in the category of nonsense, as Vienna logical positivism would have had us believe. Those other utterances were the stuff of discourse: promises, evaluations, warnings, threats. Some of them, indeed, had no function save to perform some social act—as in the instance of "I christen this ship the S.S. *Queen Elizabeth*" or even "I'm with you; count on me."

What gave such utterances sense? The origin of any message was a speaker's intention in saying it: What was actually spoken had therefore to be interpreted not in terms of the timeless meanings of its grammar and lexicon, but in terms of the speaker's intent on the occasion of speaking. And so the famous "salt request." "Would you be so kind as to pass the salt?" is *not* a query about the limits of an interlocutor's compassion, but an "indirect" request for the salt—one that honors certain conventions or conditions on making a request of those not obligated to you. The message is a locution, but it has an illocutionary force, its intended meaning. That is made possible by virtue of conventions in the speech community. Intentions are what hearers dig out of utterances. Indeed, there was some nice question as to whether any save linguists, logicians, lawyers and pedants ever processed a locution for its "timeless meaning." Austin had set the Oxford tune.

The presence there of Peter Strawson, Rom Harré, John Searle (on a visit back from Berkeley), Jonathan Cohen, and many other nonphilosophers who had been touched by Austin (like Herbert Hart) made it a bracing place for what I was hankering to do. What that was had grown on me gradually. A few years before, I had read a beautifully argued paper by Joanna Ryan, a young English psychologist then at Cambridge and Herbert Hart's daughter. She had set out to apply Austin's insights to language acquisition. It was what first alerted me to what might be done.

Shortly after I got to England, Martin Richards and I started a regular once-a-term custom of bringing together my Oxford group and his from Cambridge for a day of chat. In time, we grew to include Nottingham (particularly John Shotter and David Wood), Sussex, and even St. Andrew's and Edinburgh. We tried out those Austinian ideas and, I think, were all rather surprised at what one could do with them. Those meetings shine in memory! Catherine Snow was visiting. Her work on mothers' talk ("motherese") had just begun. Here was something like LASS. With the help of a small group of research students, I was observing a half-dozen children at different points over their first two years. John Shotter was battling for a "common sense" psychology of development that gave pride of place to everyday concepts like intention, self, and so on. Joanna Ryan's disenchantment with academic life had already started, and she was spending more and more time involved with the women's movement in London, but she was there a few times, and I found her a delight to talk to—as I did her cleverest graduate student, Elena Lieven, half Russian, half Irish, and full of irreverence about traditional approaches to the study of language.

It was my first year at Oxford. I was bringing pairs of children and mothers into a "homelike" laboratory at South Parks Road—a huge and daunting zoology-psychology building—there to observe them feed, change, play with standard toys, "read" together, all on request. All this was duly videorecorded and audiotaped on beautiful equipment in an adjoining room, in the best laboratory fashion. I think I have a tendency, when I get into something new, to instrument to the eyeballs. Imagine dragging mothers and their year-olds (actually, the children were from six to eighteen months) into a great, dazzling white laboratory building (especially one grandly designed by Sir

Leslie Martin), leading them down corridors to a "natural" playroom entered through an outer room crowded with video screens—and then asking them to play with a set of standard toys, etc! Well, that was how we started.

The aim was to study the transition from prelinguistic to linguistic communication—or really, to have a look at it in order to figure out *how* to study it. But while communicative behavior—prelinguistic as well as linguistic—is very context sensitive and our Rube Goldberg laboratory setting doubtless produced a great deal of stilted talk and action, that first effort was not all in vain.

The gorgeous equipment (imported from my infant laboratory at Harvard) could be put to other uses. We went native. We took portable cameras to the children's homes and observed what they did when a psychologist was not imposing tasks on them. What was very soon plain was that mother and child were negotiating their respective intentions through communication: using whatever conventional means could be brought to bear and inventing conventions where none had yet been established. The *last* thing our children were doing, it seemed to me, was concentrating on literal utterances, extracting deep rules of universal grammar from them. And the last thing our mothers seemed concerned about was giving "grammar lessons." They were preoccupied with getting things done with words (or gestures or pushes or blandishments), as were their children. The situations in which they were operating, moreover, were loaded with familiarity. Communication was linked to those familiar routines, those familiar settings.

What had *this* to do with Chomsky's Language Acquisition Device? This was not a child without knowledge of the world, without a privileged relationship to the speaker of the language. He was not some sort of spectator at the feast of language, feeding on whatever came his way. Language was being mastered for the *uses* to which it could be put, not as an abstract system.

Just about that time, 1973, my neighbor and associate Niko Tinbergen received that greatest accolade his fellow countrymen could bestow: the Swammerdam Prize. The Dutch boast that its recipients are more distinguished than Nobel laureates. One of the prerogatives of the winner is to organize in Amsterdam a symposium on a topic of his choice with the cast of speakers he wants. Tinbergen and I had been talking about language, about human development, about the emergence of the human capacity for culture. Also about autism, a topic with which he was much concerned because it had touched his family. He was a lovely friend and near neighbor and I enjoyed our talks in Oxford as at Slakes, his place in the heights looking down on the Lake District. But I never felt we made much progress: I was suspicious of the reductionist language of ethology, he equally suspicious of psychological talk. Linguistic terminology he found particularly offputting. I recall a visit to Slakes. I was trying to develop a point about how our tendency to think in terms of topic and comment in thought becomes converted in language into the forms of predication. His gifted cellist daughter, Janet, was practicing a Bach sonata in a far room. I was not getting across at all. I think he was listening to Bach with more than half an ear by the time I was done!

So when he asked me if I would present a paper on the "beginnings" of language to "his" Swammerdam Symposium, I jumped at the opportunity. I would not have refused in any case, but here was my chance to tell him more connectedly what I was observing, reading about, thinking. I decided to have a first shot, to do something on "the ontogenesis of speech acts."

The Dutch do ritual occasions with style. The hall was packed. More to the point, it was well laced with family, with former students and colleagues, even a few of his former teachers, though by now Tinbergen had retired from his Oxford chair. It was 1974, the midst of an Arab oil embargo. Amsterdam had responded by declaring Sundays "motorless." The morale of the city was crackling with cheerfulness. A fit occasion for honoring a great man.

That address, "The Ontogenesis of Speech Acts," was the first in a decade-long series of papers and monographs that finally led to a book, *Child's Talk*. That first paper, once published, probably brought John Austin and the theory of speech acts closer to the center of effort in the study of language acquisition. But it was flawed in a way that testifies to the difficulties of shifting one's perspective.

I could not free myself from Chomsky's Language Acquisition Device. I felt compelled to enter the fray at the level of syntax. I *had* to make pragmatics and the issues of how language is *used* contribute to our understanding of why syntax is as it is. The *use* issue, how we master the *functions* of language, is just as important and still remains to be explained. We now know that just being *exposed* to a language is not enough for learning it. Something is needed to make language worth acquiring, whatever its syntax. I kept confounding the distinction, trying to show how the requirements of use had *created* syntax. That, of course, is an extension of Claude Bernard's great biological dictum "Function creates form," but it was misplaced.

Grammar is what it is, I argued, because it "emerges" from a prior appreciation of the structures or "arguments" of action: agent, action, object, instrument, location, etc. As one *acts*, one picks up "protolinguistic" knowledge about these arguments. In time, this knowledge is abstracted and converted into a "case grammar" that reflects the very same arguments. I even urged that the easy acquisition of Subject-Verb-Object order in sentences must be an outgrowth of the child's natural perception of the order of action in life. It is a very Piagetian approach, one that makes language an offshoot or a by-product of something else.

The truth of the matter is, of course, that grammars are extraordinarily arbitrary or "artificial." There is, as we know, a very limited set of them, considering how many are logically possible. Yet the limited number cannot come about by virtue of the "naturalness" with which they fit the world. Cause-and-effect may be a natural way of interpreting events in the world, but some languages will note this natural pattern "ergatively" by marking the subject of the sentence as a "causer," some will add something to the verb to indicate its "causativeness," some will mark the *effect* of the cause by making the object of the sentence accusative. They all distinguish causativeness from noncausativeness by grammatical means, but they all do it very differently. Grammar, in short, constitutes its own problem space. Knowing about causation in the real world gives no clue about how it is represented in the grammar of a particular language. Knowing about practical causation does, however, provide you with clues about what the language may be *about*, what it is referring to, how it is being used. That was the issue I should have been addressing and eventually did address.

We ended up, as I said, looking at children and their mothers not in the laboratory but at home, mostly at play. We then became participants in the play. How could it be otherwise? To do otherwise is to make the situations stilted, to distort what one wants to study. It is what typically happens when a social scientist becomes interested in how things happen in ordinary life. But do not take this to mean that "experimental settings" are useless! You may need a laboratory to give new wings to your curiosity.

Let me give an example of how this happened to us. One of my postdoctoral students, Michael Scaife, became intrigued with the roots of linguistic reference: how two or more people in communication manage to focus their attention on a common object or event by the use of some signaling device. It is about as ancient and central a question as exists in either linguistics or the philosophy of language. Scaife had just finished a D.Phil. under Tinbergen with a thesis on how the "eye spots" on butterfly wings inhibit the attack of predators like birds. The eye, simulated or real and for reasons that lie buried in evolutionary history, is a potent releasing or inhibiting stimulus among vertebrates. Man is no exception. Indeed, the first phase of mother-infant "bonding" seems massively abetted by such contact. Mothers frequently say that they feel their babies to be human when prolonged eye-to-eye contact first occurs.

Scaife had noticed in our "naturalistic" videotapes that once reaching begins, infants often follow an adult's gaze as if to find out what she might be looking at. Many parents say they "know" this. But alas, they also "know" a great many other things that are just old wives' tales. If young children did light on objects their parents attend by following their gaze, then the achievement of joint "linguistic" reference would be much easier—linking a sound or gesture to an object already jointly attended. But then, how comes a six-month-old to be following his mother's line of regard to find objects? According to the Piaget canon, they are not supposed to comprehend or otherwise take into account another's point of view. Here, indeed, was a fit topic for a laboratory study, one to substantiate an "existence theorem."

We did the study—or rather, Mike Scaife really did the study. This time parents were right. Children *do* follow an adult's line of regard, and by the time they are supposed to be at the fullness of their "egocentrism" (at one year) they do so easily and habitually. Then another study was reported by a gifted young Irish investigator, Maire Logan Ryan, which showed that one-year-olds were using a rising intonation in their mother's voice as a cue that she had shifted her attention (and gaze) to another object. When that telltale intonation occurred, the children would look back to their mother to find out where she was looking now.

Another postdoctoral fellow arrived at Oxford at just that moment. She got us started on a next venture that took us from the

Scaife laboratory study back into the setting of natural life. Anat Ninio was a young Israeli, a gifted poet who later received her country's top poetry award. "Let us now see how the labeling of these joint referents develops *in situ* in *one* single child over a whole year." We had the videotapes and got down to the hours-on-end task of analyzing them.

What we found was in some ways the acme of ordinariness. There was, in fact, a kind of "tutoring" taking place. The standard view, of course, is that language acquisition is "untaught." It is not an obvious kind of teaching either, but the kind of "scaffolding" that David Wood and I had found a few years before when he was with me at Harvard from the University of Nottingham as a NATO fellow. In that study, an adult tutors three- to five-year-old children in how to assemble a complex pyramid puzzle. Scaffolding consisted of an adult carrying out those parts of a task the child could not quite manage by himself, then giving control of them back to the child when he could manage. It is the natural stuff of apprenticeship. Something like that was happening when we observed how the child was learning to "name" things.

The linguistic version was a particularly interesting form of scaffolding. It depended on the establishment of *formats*. A format is a little microcosm, a task, in which mother and child share an intention to get something done with words. At the start, what the child cannot manage in the format, his mother does for him. Once he can, she requires him to do it thereafter. The format "stores" presuppositions that become shared by the two partners. It is *praxis* rather than *lexis*.

The format we studied was "book reading"—the mother pointing out and labeling familiar pictures in a book. It was a perfect stage on which to see the child's referential language unfold.

What a strikingly stable routine it was. Each step of the way, the mother incorporated whatever competencies the child had already developed—to be clued by pointing, to appreciate that sounds "stood for" things and events, etc. The mother remained the constant throughout. Thereby she was his scaffold—calling his attention, making a query, providing an answering label if he lacked one, and confirming his offer of one, whatever it might be. As he gained competence, she would raise her criterion. Almost any vocalization the child might offer at the start would be accepted. But each time the child came closer to the standard form, she would hold out for it. What was changing was, of course, what the mother *expected* in response—and that, of course, was "fine-tuned" by her "theory" of the child's capacities. When he switched from babbling to offering shorter vocalization as "labels" (still quite nonstandard), she would no longer accept babbles but would insist on the shorter "names." Then finally, sure that her son knew the standard label, she would shift to delivering her "What's that?" with a falling intonation on the second word and a special smile to distinguish a rhetorical from a nonrhetorical question. And so it went.

We became quite obsessed with formats. They seemed to serve, at one and the same time, as a way for the child to enter the culture and its language—an entry into *real* use. We began looking at the formatting of other utterance types—like requests. They brought one other matter into view. When mothers "taught" their children to request "properly," they were (as speech act theory puts it) teaching principally the *conditions* on requests, not its grammar: how one prepares the ground by making one's objective clear, how one fulfills sincerity conditions by indicating the genuineness of a request or fulfills "essential" ones by demonstrating that one could not do on one's own what one has asked another to do. The child's actual grammatical accomplishments (once they surfaced) were almost immediately put to use, adjuncts to making the substance of his request clear. My philosopher friend Rom Harré rejoiced: "Speech acts develop and then use grammar as their instrument."

Formats are little pieces of the culture—but crucial little pieces, for they are the first chunky bits of culture from which the child will generalize. Sufficiently circumscribed to permit an easy assessment of what one's partner is up to, they allow for correction of misinterpretation, and for negotiation of intention and meaning. They are indeed a means of entering the language and the culture simultaneously. They become increasingly dependent upon skill in language and, in time, can be *constituted* when needed by language, without the stage setting required earlier. One does not need the mother-created, scaffolding format of the early years. One *creates* them, imposes them by learning the linguistic conventions for doing so—converting by convention whatever situation one encounters into an occasion for indicating, requesting, warning, congratulating, whatever.

That was where that decade of work on language acquisition took me. It convinced me that you cannot properly study language acquisition as a *psychological* process simply by examining the *order* in which grammatical forms emerge. Not that the order of appearance is not astonishing in its own right: that in English, say, aspect markers appear before tense markers, or that gerunds appear in speech before the past tense. Such facts may have less to do with genetics, or with the derivational complexity of grammatical forms, than with the strategies that children *use* in attempting to accomplish things with language. Formatting, fine-tuned responsiveness, modes of embedding language in action and interaction—all these, I finally concluded, comprise the Language Acquisition Support System, the LASS that makes possible the operation of a Chomsky-like LAD.

How puzzling that there should be so *much* emphasis in the eighth decade of the twentieth century on the underlying *genetic* program that makes language acquisition possible and so *little* on the ways in which the culture, the parents and more "expert" speakers (including other, older children) help the genetic program to find expression in *actual language use.* The educational level of parents deeply affects how well, richly and abstractly their children will talk (and listen). It is not just the *grammar of sentences* that is at issue, but discourse, dialogue, the capacity to interpret spoken and written language.

In the end, I came to the conclusion that the need to use language fully as an instrument for participating in a complex culture (just as the infant uses it to enter the simple culture of his surround) is what provides the engine for language acquisition. The genetic "program" for language is only half the story. The support system is the other half. Or as Peter Medawar once put it about nature and nurture, each contributes one hundred percent of the variance!

So where did that leave me, given where I had started from—with an interest principally in how language served as an instrument of thought? I think the answer is "unresolved." I suspect that the "linguistic community" may not be that uniform, that "subcommunities" within it goad or tempt its members to use language for more than communicative ends. The "hidden curriculum" of some of these communities is to encourage the use of language to its fullest powers as a way of "arranging one's thoughts about things," in Dewey's celebrated phrase. That is what universities are for—far down the road. Long before that there are families, friendships, *Demon* crews, roommates, lovers, and all those rich relationships that make possible the exchange of thought and feeling. Eventually, the *ex*change becomes an *in*change, and we are individually the better for it.

I must end on a lighter note. There now exists a major center for psycholinguistic research at Nijmegen in the Netherlands. It is one of the Max Planck Institutes, financed and managed from Munich with German money and German administrative support, though it is in Holland, and is superbly directed by W. J. M. Levelt. I have always secretly feared that the Americanization of the social and human sciences might diminish the world's rich diversity. I accepted in the mid-1970s (with some trepidation) the chairmanship of the Scientific Advisory Committee of the Max Planck "Study Group" of Psycholinguistics (the parent Max-Planck Gesellschaft in Munich sets up its tryout institutes as "Study Groups" for five years before committing itself to their full status). I knew it would seem odd that an American (albeit an Oxford professor) should be promoting a countervailing European center for research.

Pim Levelt, in addition to his gifts as a psychologist and linguist, is a man of honesty and tact. I had known him and admired him first when he had been a fellow at our Harvard Center for Cognitive Studies in 1965–66. For all his gifts and his tact, he faced a most difficult diplomatic problem. Neither the linguists nor the psychologists of the German Federal Republic were overjoyed about the proposed establishment of such an institute outside Germany. Indeed, there was a good deal of opposition, for a Max Planck Institute is a rich research plum. It is the elite of the German academic world.

In the end, all went well and the Institute was duly created in Nijmegen, with full status and due pomp. The "management" in Munich could not have been more open-minded and more internationally spirited. Since such distinguished German intellectuals as Jurgen Habermas, Detlev Ploog, Dieter Wunderlich and others were on the board, it was a project difficult to refuse.

But it was a "sticky wicket," as cricketers say. Part of the virtue of Nijmegen and Holland was the willingness of the Dutch to make things easy—the university, the Dutch Science Research Council, the government. Part of it was Levelt himself: It would have been hard indeed to find anybody more qualified as a scientist, a leader and an internationalist in spirit. But some of the reasons for choosing Holland were delicate too: The international scholarly community could, many thought, be more easily lured to Holland either for permanent posts, for a year's leave, or even for a month's conference. I have no doubt that this will change, but in the 1970s, more than a quarter century after the war, it was still true. Holland was good neutral ground.

Besides, what could be a more international topic than the study of language and its psychology? And what could be a more international emblem for the Max-Planck Gesellschaft than to set up its new Institute outside Germany—only twenty miles from the frontier, but it is a *long* twenty miles. In the end, the internationalists prevailed —with due regard for a German quota for staff and student fellows. Insofar as there are "official" languages at such places, German is one of them. (But in fact, English is *the* language of most international scholarly enclaves, whether "official" or not, given the preponderance of it in the printed literature.) I think I may have helped in the proceedings by being the "disinterested" and internationalist American chairman of the *Fachbeirat.* I could put up the spirited claim for an international European gesture and speak disinterestedly for the "international community."

The Institute is flourishing; the German academic world has (as one usually does) accepted the inevitable.

Driving to Schipol airport after the final meeting in Nijmegen, at which a joint agreement was reached by our advisory board and a special committee appointed by Munich—being driven by a cheerful member of the administrative staff at Nijmegen who spoke only Dutch, which I do not speak—I spent most of the two hours en route brooding about the astonishing role of language in joining and dividing people. The "realities" we had discussed at that final meeting (even the *economic* ones) were realities created by language and its dependent symbol systems. What would happen to German graduate students who went to do their theses at Nijmegen? Would students be prepared to take the dreaded *Habitur* examination? And so it went.

My former Harvard colleague Jerry Kagan, reviewing research on infancy, wrote recently that by the end of the second year, symbolic functioning, self-awareness and concern with evaluative standards were already in place. They have a long spring to adulthood, plenty of opportunity to create a world where words make events, make standards and, to some still unknown degree, make the self through permitting us to differentiate ourselves from others in negotiation.

The French have a lovely proverb: "The fish will be the last to discover water." When the Institute at Nijmegen was "founded," I presented it with a gift of a seventeenth-century print, a map of the heavens, in the four corners of which are engravings of the observatories at Greenwich, Leiden, Copenhagen and Padua. It was to wish them good luck in mapping the world of language. That mapping task will be harder than mapping the heavens. The heavens stay put while you are looking at them. Language changes when you think about it. Certainly as you talk it. In the end, probably, full linguistic mapping will be impossible. For you cannot exhaust the subject by studying language "just" as a symbol system with its inherent structure—or "just" in any single way. Language is for using, and the uses of language are so varied, so rich, and each use so preemptive a way of life, that to study it is to study the world and, indeed, all possible worlds.

I think the best that we can do is get on with it, but with a Wittgensteinian skepticism. Learning about each use or facet of language—whether poetics or parsing—will itself be revealing. We will delude ourselves if we think it will come out singular and comprehensive. And we make the pursuit less revealing and doubtless less enjoyable if we insist that any one approach to language is the one to which all others should be reduced.

10

The New Curriculum

If you hold it to be the case, as I do, that the human species evolves by taking charge of its own evolution through the invention of technology for shaping its environment, then certain crucial things follow. One of them is that the passing on of acquired human characteristics that make technology possible becomes a matter of survival. You can suppose either that the passing on of this inheritance was accomplished by the transmission of culture or that, somehow, it came to be inscribed in the genes and passed on in the gene pool, as Lamarck and many European philosophers supposed. Perhaps I had had to think more about Lamarck and the "inheritance" of acquired characteristics earlier in my career than most psychologists—and probably more personally. William McDougall, the reader may recall, came to my rescue when I was suspended from college for refusing attendance at compulsory chapel and had me reinstated on grounds that I would help in his lab instead. He was conducting a Lamarckian experiment on the genetic inheritance of an acquired sensitivity to certain learning cues in rats. I was to be dogsbody and handyman for his two assistants.

The Lamarckian claim seemed to me at that time to be the defiance of a great man swimming against the mainstream. McDougall was in revolt against the three "givens" of scientific respectability: a Lamarckian against Darwin, a nativist against empiricism, a mentalist against materialism. I so admired the calm and courteous way in which he espoused his claims (I thought then it must have something to do with his being a Fellow of the Royal Society!) that I could not be dismissive of his Lamarckian stand. Nor could I accept it. I recall reading a poem by D. H. Lawrence lampooning evolution, the cart groaning and giving birth to the horse, and thought McDougall must feel that way. I thought him mistaken in looking to Lamarck (as he did) for explanations of human evolution. I thought the idea of culture much more to the point—uniquely human culture. It was 1935–36, and the idea of culture (as anthropologists then saw it) was a new and compelling idea to me. I was much too much in awe of the great man to discuss the matter with him.

The idea that man had the capacity to create an environment of his own was more than purely intellectual. It was almost a moral stance. The arts, science, politics, philosophy, technology—all of them were instruments for changing the world. I even entertained the view that passivity was probably original Original Sin!

But it never crossed my mind that "Education" in any formal sense was the chief or the most powerful means for passing on or recreating the culture. Schools, teachers, subjects, grades were routines rather than instruments. Not that I despised such matters: I had been a diligent if rebellious schoolboy. One of my more terrifying early nightmares was "pedagogic": I was the last survivor of a great catastrophe and had to pass on all that had been known before. In any case, I never in the undergraduate years sought out instruction in Education or in its history. It never occurred to me that I might one day need to know these things.

But for all my inattention to education, I suppose it was completely in the cards that I would get into it one day. Was it not inevitable that a man who had studied "cognition" with the biases I brought to that topic should, when the educational debates of 1960 arrived, be swept into them? Just as surely, I suppose, as a committed moral philosopher at Oxford in, say, 1640 would inevitably have been swept into debates on the Established Church and the Commonwealth!

But the inevitable manages always to wear a private face. It seems unique to those involved. Quirky particulars make up life. I was, for example, helping out some friends. They were trying to improve science education—physics education, to be precise. It was 1958. We were lunching together. Just two years before, Jerrold Zacharias and Francis Friedman, my luncheon companions, had started the Physical Sciences Study Committee—Zack and Franny, whom I had known before in the Society of Atomic Scientists, campaigning to cool the rapidly heating Cold War. Zack had started things with a letter to Jim Killian, the president of MIT, in which he proposed that:

> we make ninety films of twenty minutes duration complete with textbooks, problem books, question cards, and answer cards. Success or failure depends to a large extent on having the entire apparatus of the experiment really right. Like a high fidelity phonograph one must have besides the machine a good piece by a good composer played by an artist. The room must be good, not too noisy, and the people have to want to listen, but that all depends upon the piece.

They were, I think, running into their first troubles—discovering what a mouthful was the claim that wanting to listen "all depends upon the piece."

Our talk was about how kids learn. Zack always cultivated a facade of high self-assurance, by no means entirely feigned. He exaggerated it, I think, to test the mettle of anybody whose expert advice he was soliciting or being offered. He was a man shaped by success —one of the famous ZORC, the foursome who were so dominant in their influence on wartime science policy: Zacharias, Robert Oppenheimer, I. I. Rabi and Charley Lauritsen, as diverse a foursome as ever shared an acronymic noun! Together they had linked research at Los Alamos with engineering at Oak Ridge to produce the Bomb. Zack loved the "group think" of study groups, very much in fashion then. He dominated these by a delightful mix of forthrightness, self-assurance and a gift for maxims. Indeed, maxims. They had become very much part of the politics of science. Perhaps they have always lubricated the "interface" where ideas and politics meet each other. In our times they seem to have provided a workable coin for first exchanges among the military and scientific communities, each trying to understand the other's views—as in such extraordinary bits of imagery as the "stockpile of basic research" or the "missile gap" (which was, of course, quickly turned into a "knowledge gap"), and so on. I think, in fact, maxims have an important emblematic function, like the Union Jack: the Scotsman sees the Cross of St. Andrew, the Welshman St. David, and the Englishman St. George. Zack was at work creating maxims for educational reform.

Zack's current maxim was "Make physics teacher-proof." That was the objective of the ninety films, each featuring a "real" physicist. I think it was typical of the times. Zack along with other reformers was convinced that the trouble with schools was the shoddy stuff they taught. The cure was to narrow the gap between knowledge locked up in the university library or the scholar's mind and the fare being taught in schools. If, as in physics, an untrained teacher stood between the knowledge and the student, then bypass the teacher. Put physics on film instead. And that's what the Physical Sciences Study Committee was doing—that and organizing "summer institutes" to make teachers into better physicists.

Never mind the oversimplification. It was extraordinarily energizing, and its generous view of educational possibilities seemed "revolutionary" to all of us who were involved. It had enough appeal in those post-Sputnik days to convince the National Science Foundation to go into the curriculum business in its support. Indeed, I think it was Zack more than anybody else who converted Sputnik shock into the curriculum reform movement that it became rather than taking some other form. It is worth a moment's pause to get its spirit right.

The idea, of course, was classically "top down." Curriculum projects traditionally began by recruiting a star-studded advisory board and a staff of dedicated young idealists. By the early 1960s, "summer groups" sponsored by the projects were hard at work on mathematics, biology, chemistry, be it in Stanford, Boulder, St. Louis, Syracuse. Again, it was Zack who had set the pattern that tempted this profusion of university talent into summer curriculum-making. By the end of a decade, America had on hand the finest collection of science curricula ever devised. Then the national agenda changed, a new one created by the upheaval of the civil rights movement and Vietnam.

I must go back to Franny Friedman. He and Zack made an extraordinarily effective pair. They respected each other—enough so that they stood up to each other. Franny loved the play of ideas, whether among friends and colleagues or among kids in a tryout classroom. He was slow and deliberate of speech, with no embarrassment about his pauses for thinking. He disliked humbug, was withdrawn in the presence of maxims, and had a mind of great elegance. We became close friends and, since we lived close to each other in Cambridge, visited a good deal. While Zack, I think, found the vagaries of children's minds a necessary nuisance to be overcome in the interest of teaching physics, Fran was genuinely interested in and attracted by children's originality once they were caught up by a problem. From time to time I would pass on things for him to read, things I thought he might enjoy. His comments always surprised. I lent him a volume by Inhelder and Piaget on the growth of logical thinking from childhood to adolescence. It is a book principally about the emergence of so-called formal operations—thinking proposition-ally rather than concretely, in terms of ordered possibilities rather than known entities. "They've got noodles in their head about phys-ics and how you understand it," he exclaimed. "Grown-up adults don't understand the *idea* of reversibility any more than children do. How many adults understand what it means to unburn a match? They're just like kids with water jars, when you've poured from the wide beaker into the tall thin one. Everybody has trouble with the idea of conservation in some form. What's all this about before con-servation you had real trouble, and after it you don't anymore? That wasn't even true of Einstein!"

Curriculum reform for Franny and for me as well was about letting kids see through the flawed instances of nature to the pure, unflawed idea behind it: the deep structure. The strategy was to find means that would help the learner to get through the surface clutter to the simpler, more beautiful underlying forms. Issues of race and poverty in education had not come into our consciousness. At least not into mine.

What the inspired curriculum-maker (whatever his science) did was so refreshingly different from what we psychologists habitually did! We psychologists typically construct tasks or tests to separate the children who *can* from those who *cannot,* the former then being labeled "smarter" or "more mature." The ideal curriculum-maker—like Socrates instructing the slave in the *Meno*—arranges things in such a way that everybody will understand, all will be among the "cans" rather than the "cannots." It is Vygotsky writ large and ideal-ized, reaching an acme "under adult guidance or in collaboration with more capable peers." That divides the burden of learning be-tween the individual and his society.

During the late 1950s I dabbled around the edges of the new curriculum-making. Then in 1959 the National Academy of Sciences in Washington decided to have a closer look at what the ferment was all about. A "summer study group" to examine the new science curriculum was proposed and I was asked to head it. I think Fran Friedman was behind that. And many of the scientists involved felt they had outrun their resources. Perhaps psychology could be of help.

September on Cape Cod can be a glory of late summer: crisp, cool, brilliant. And 1959 was one such year. At Woods Hole we gathered at the old Whitney estate, the summer headquarters of the Academy, a big and rambling house that could take all thirty of us. And it was a curious thirty. There were the curriculum-makers— biologists, mathematicians, physicists—plus a sprinkling of psychologists and several professional educators. We had invited a couple of historians and a classicist, to leaven the mix. One of the historians was my son Whit's history master at Phillips Exeter, whose virtues he had praised above all others; the other, my friend John Blum, later of Yale and the Morgenthau volumes. They earned their keep, the two historians, by never letting pass unchallenged any scientist's intoxicated claim that the *summum bonum* of the mind was the pursuit of a higher scientific or mathematical truth.

The scientists were beset with little problems that their own particular curriculum projects had generated—material problems. They were devoted to those projects; men at the top of their professions giving of their time freely: biologists like Bentley Glass and Ralph Gerard, mathematicians like Carl Allendoerfer and Edward Begle, physicists like Zack and Franny. Most of them believed simply that a decent education should include decent science.

The professional educators had some gentle warnings to offer. John Fischer, dean of Teachers College, Columbia University, and Henry Chauncey, director of the Educational Testing Service, tried to outline the obstacles that lay beyond curricula—teachers, alienation, and so on. But most of us were convinced we were at the start of a new era in education.

The psychologists were curiously uneven. It is something about psychology and its stance toward the "real world." Psychologists, in the main, are embarrassed by education. They prefer to think of "learning theory" in the abstract—which has little to do directly with such concrete matters as the teaching of science. Most academic students of learning in 1960 embraced the belief that all learning was basically alike. It was plain to me that there was no ready-made psychology of learning to fit the needs of the occasion. But it was equally plain that "thinking psychologically" helped enormously— whether it was Lee Cronbach talking measurement and psychometrics, Kenneth Spence asking about rewards for performance, Bärbel Inhelder talking about the role of reversibility in arithmetic, or George Miller discussing the heuristics of intuition.

Historians of education now say that Woods Hole was "seminal," that it "revolutionized" education, etc. But education is an enterprise whose ways and whose knowledge base are still much too unorganized to revolutionize. Insofar as there was anything revolutionary, it grew out of the same "cognitive revolution" discussed in Chapter 7. There were three aspects of that upheaval that expressed themselves in our discussions.

The first, I think, was a point I trace to the philosopher Gilbert Ryle. It is a conception of mind. Mind, as he colorfully proclaims, is in the lorry driver's hands, in the moves on a chessboard, in the strategies on a football field; it is not just in your head. Mind is method applied to tasks. You don't think *about* physics, you think physics. Physics is not just a description of the world; it is the way you get to the description.

Piaget was the origin of the second emphasis. The vulgar way of presenting him in educational clothing is to make the argument (which he never did) that certain subjects can only be taught to children after they have reached a certain level of maturity. What Bärbel Inhelder emphasized was not that. Rather, it was that the child's understanding of any mathematical or scientific idea would be framed by the level of intellectual operations that he had achieved. There are ways of framing ideas that are appropriate to the level of development or abstraction that the child has reached. Lower levels of understanding are routes to higher-level ones. The lower level is not a degraded version of the higher. Each has a logic of its own. Each is to be respected.

The third emphasis was on the "generativeness" of knowledge. Knowledge is not a storehouse. You already "know" most of what you "learn" in science and mathematics. "Learning" is, most often, figuring out how to use what you already know in order to go beyond what you currently think. There are many ways of doing that. Some are more intuitive; others are formally derivational. But they all depend on knowing something "structural" about what you are contemplating—how it is put together. Knowing how something is put together is worth a thousand facts about it. It permits you to go beyond it.

Halfway through the conference, a young mathematician, David Page, rounded up a group of local schoolchildren to demonstrate his way of teaching mathematics. As far as he was concerned, no child could make an error in mathematics. Mathematical reasoning was simply too transparent. An "error" is made by somebody working on a problem other than the one that has been set. Page chose a lesson in algebra using his by now well-known "box notation." His class grew in intuitive confidence as we watched. Doubtless David Page was a genius at teaching, and a finely tuned mathematician besides. What was impressive, leaving that aside, was what the children were capable of doing under such instruction.

It had been an intense and interesting time. Atmospherics. Our little steering committee met the morning after the end. A "summary" report was out of the question. Would I try my hand at a "chairman's report," and set down *my* impressions at least?

It was autumn. I lived alone in a small flat in the heart of Cambridge. I loved working there. Everything was right to hand. And in a couple of months I had put together a first draft of a "one-man report." After circulating it for comment, I revised it and walked it over to the Harvard University Press. It appeared in 1960: *The Process of Education.*

The reaction took me completely by surprise. The ebullient Paul Goodman announced in the New York *Herald Tribune* that it was a "classic, comparable in its philosophical centrality and humane concreteness" to Dewey's essays on education. *Fortune* called it "a centerpiece in the debate on education in America." I was asked to give the keynote address to the annual mass meeting of the National Education Association in Madison Square Garden (my voice reverberating back to me in a boom that reminded me of the announcer in the Tunney-Dempsey fight years before). John Kennedy, running hard for President, telephoned to talk about ideas for legislation. I had helped him in his first campaign for Congress from our Eleventh District of Massachusetts. There I was, in the midst of the debate—flattered, skeptical about the immediate and "huge" (my publisher's word) success of the book.

My skepticism was not about the positions I had taken. It was about their easy acceptance. Rationalist, structuralist and intuitionist, I was quite off the main line of American education theory. The American educational tradition had always favored experience over reason, facts over structure, and thoroughness over intuition. I had set forth a strong argument favoring the idea of "models in the head" based on general understanding, from which hypotheses about the particulars could be generated and then tested against experience. The great disciplines like physics or mathematics, or history, or dramatic forms in literature, were, in this view, less repositories of knowledge than of methods for the use of mind. They provided the structure that gave meaning to the particulars. That, after all, was what culture was about. The object of education was to get as swiftly as possible to that structure—to penetrate a subject, not to cover it. You did this by "spiraling" into it: a first pass to get the intuitive sense of it, later passes over the same domain to go into it more deeply and more formally.

I suppose the most controversial statement in the book was that "any subject can be taught to anybody at any age in some form that is honest." It is easy to take literally, and I kept running into dubious schoolmasters who asked did I think six-year-olds could learn the calculus. My answer has always been that there are lots of intuitive notions in the calculus (or in *Hamlet* or the theory of evolution or whatever) whose early grasp would help the learning of the later, fully developed idea.

The Process of Education seemed to give heart to teachers and even (I was delighted to be told) lured some good people into teaching who might not have ventured there otherwise. And most of all, it seems to have served as a manifesto for those out to improve the intellectual quality of our schools.

The foreign editions (the book was translated into nineteen languages!) were particularly interesting, for their reception often revealed much about the countries of publication. The first translation was into Russian. It tripped off a debate on the dogmatism of Russian education, a displacement, I suspect, of more general dissatisfaction with dogmatism in the Party line. When I visited Luria in Moscow in 1962 ("You will live like a king on the royalties of your book," he told me), we did a "discussion program" together on national radio. "Do not pull any punches," he told me beforehand. "It will be good for us to hear."

In Italy, my irrepressible publisher, Armando Armando, used *Process* to attack the "decaying formalism" of the Right and the "utilitarian pragmatism" of the Communist Left. In Japan (where I became such a public figure that schoolteachers recognized me on the street!), the book caught a wave of reform and became an emblem against traditional learning by rote. And so it went, each country with its own troubles to cast on the screen of the book—Israel, Egypt, Greece, Turkey, wherever.

I think the book's "success" grew from a worldwide need to reassess the functions of education in the light of the knowledge explosion and the new, postindustrial technology. Its attention was on the knower and knowing. Its ideas sprang from epistemology and the sciences of knowing, rather than from ethics or from Freud, as in the round before. It reflected the intellectual ferment of its times, and if there were echoes of Chomsky and Lévi-Strauss as well as Piaget, that was no surprise. For all of us were, I think, responding to the same "epistemic" malaise, the doubts about the nature of knowing that had come first out of the revolution in physics and then been formalized and amplified by philosophy. Eventually it pervaded the "postindustrial" society. And so finally it came to education. I think that is why the book was such a "success" and why it hit a nerve wherever it was translated.

Late in 1961 I had a phone call from McGeorge Bundy at the White House. "Would you be at all tempted to come down and join the rough-and-tumble here?" I think I did better to stay in Cambridge. I'm better at thinking up new things than following old ones through to "implementation." But soon after, I was commuting weekly to Washington as a member of the Education Panel of the President's Science Advisory Committee. Jerry Wiesner, one of the wisest men I've ever known, was Kennedy's science adviser. Advisory committees are useful in a rather indirect way. They rarely create policy, but they can serve to shape "reality" for a policymaker by establishing an atmosphere of discussion. We discussed a great many of the educational issues that worked their way to Wiesner's desk. I think it may have helped some of the policy-oriented people on the panel, chosen for their strategic positions: the U.S. Commissioner of Education (first Frank Keppel and then Sterling McMurrin); Jim Allen, the Commissioner of Education of the State of New York (big state); the Superintendent of the Chicago schools (big city); the director of the National Science Foundation (big educational funding); the dean of Teachers College, Columbia University (establishment education). To which Wiesner had added spokesmen of various special constituencies, like the admirable Ted Hesburgh of Notre Dame and Sister Jacqueline Grennan of Webster Grove College, high-spirited, fearless, a devoted Vatican II partisan—both of them members of religious orders and both strikingly progressive politically.* And then finally the "intellectuals," like Franny Friedman, Lawrence Cremin and me.

*Sister Jacqueline, later Jacqueline Grennan Wechsler, was to become president of Hunter College in New York.

It is hard to say what such a panel accomplishes aside from keeping concrete issues from bogging down in their particulars and in bringing to attention interesting issues that do not have an emboldened constituency. It also can apply veto power.

My veto came toward the end of my tenure. A special-interest group proposed that we export American "educational technology" to developing countries to bring them into modern times: projectors, television systems, programmed instruction (there turned out to be virtually none of it prepared anyway) and kindred gadgets. By the accident of strong backing, it could not be turned down without a strong brief. So off I went for a three-week tour of third-world Africa (with Louis Cowan, a former president of CBS Television, a man of high intelligence and principle). I wrote the strong brief and proposed we provide aid only in response to locally formulated education plans and, whenever possible, only through international agencies like the OAS or the World Bank. So many of those developing countries would have been flattered by a sprinkling of slide projectors and teaching machines. More to the point, African postcolonial thinking too easily ran along the lines of aping the old masters: Oxbridge, *les grandes écoles,* Moscow University, teaching machines.

The Education Panel spanned the Kennedy and Johnson years. Lyndon Johnson was far more interested in public education than John Kennedy ever was. Choate, Harvard and the Hyannis family compound are not as likely to predispose one to being an "education President" as are small-town Texas and a schoolteacher mother. Johnson saw public schools as the "way up" in American life. He told me at a party he gave for our Education Panel at the new LBJ Library in Austin that the legislation he was privately proudest of in his whole career was a bill making low-cost loans available to college students.

Endicott House is an old estate in Dedham (Dedham is the town the Boston matron mentions when asked what route she drove to California). It is ten miles from Harvard Square and now belongs to MIT. Endless conferences and "study groups" have been held there and, so far as I know, still are. It is a charming if incongruous place. You may find yourself talking to an African intellectual about Nigerian education as you both stand in the "gun room" under the stuffed heads of African beasts shot by Mr. Endicott, who had manufactured shoes and modeled himself on his vigorous contemporary Theodore Roosevelt. Chief Shaloru was the African, a charming

Nigerian who directed the Oxford University Press in Lagos. He was telling Elting Morison and me about his schoolboy experience of first encountering the tale of Mungo Park's discovery of the Niger River in the pages of a Nelson history text. In his mind's eye, he said, he had put his grandfather along the shore, waving welcome to the intrepid Mungo. Morison, MIT's most distinguished historian, was there because we were discussing, among other things, the writing of history as an expression of national aspirations. In fact, it was a get-together to explore how we might be of some help to African educators planning future projects. It was 1961. "We" were Educational Services Incorporated, ESI, the nonprofit holding company that Zacharias had originally set up to handle the new Physical Sciences Study Committee. It had now become the vehicle for many other worthy and generous projects.

The meetings with our African colleagues were tumultuous and emotional—with all the emotions that are generated when anticolonialism and cryptocolonialism clash. Elting said, on the way back to Cambridge, "That will cure Zack and ESI of wanting to reform the social sciences—in Africa or anywhere else!"

He was wrong. Next summer we were back at Endicott House. Zack was determined. The agenda was the reform of the teaching of social studies in *our* schools. The participating cast was bound to produce a clash. Studying society has always produced two kinds of chemistry. One is humanistic, value-laden, narrative, concerned with the elucidation of the particular. It grows from an ancient tradition. Its prototype is History, a study that shares its muse, Clio, with Poetry. The other is called "social science," and it has no muse, but only totemic figures like the austere Auguste Comte or Max Weber or Émile Durkheim. Its spirit is positivistic, objective, value-free.

It took only a day for the clash to out. A sociologist, a very serious one named Bob Feldmesser, sparked it with a talk ticking off historians for having created the poor state of social studies in the schools of America. The "sacred cow of history must be slaughtered" and children introduced to the analytic methods of the social sciences. Get rid of history! I caught Elting Morison's pained eye across the room and thought of Henry Adams's "All the steam in the world could not, like the Virgin, build Chartres."

Elting was masterful in riposte—perhaps too masterful, in retrospect. "If you really did a careful historical study of the building of the battleship *Kentucky* in 1900," he began, "you would have to take

into account the social structure of the times, the psychological motives of the protagonists, the folk myths that animated the culture,
and the economics of the fast-growing nation." The day was "saved."
A "master plan" was devised to put the two visions into a single
frame.

Alas, there is a deep gap between the history-minded and the
social-science-minded. It takes more than master plans to bridge it.
Doubtless, there are many "uses of history." One of them is to form
the historical imagination, to give the past its form and its reality. In
that respect it gives pride of place to the historian. But the historical
imagination, I have always thought, is by no means a province of the
historian alone. The felicitous construction of the past gives to those
who construct it an extraordinary power over the minds of men.
Churchill's power, as Isaiah Berlin puts it, rested upon his evocation
of a British tradition and a British history that activated a nation that
might otherwise have despaired. Or, again, it was my African friend
whose pride in past put his grandfather on the banks of the Niger to
greet the English explorer. Or, as sensitively perceived by the essay-
ist Frances FitzGerald, looking back to her schoolgirl days: "Those
texts were the truth of things; they were American history. It was not
just that we read them before we understood that not everything
that is printed is the truth, or the whole truth. It was that they, much
more than other books, had the trappings of authority." The trappings of authority: heroes, villains, spunk, social reality, leaders,
legitimized in a landscape of the past. In English common law there
is a principle that legitimizes present practice by invoking that "the
mind of man runneth not to the contrary." There has never been a
historian worth his salt, I suspect, who was not awed by his respon-
sibilities as a putative (however unwilling) moralist.

The social scientist is a different animal. That "analytic framework" with which Bob Feldmesser was going to slay the sacred cow
of history is constructed of refutable hypotheses. And because a hypothesis is open to refutation by evidence, it is objective and ethically
neutral. It may, of course, turn out to be the case that *your* hypothesis
may be *my* undoing—whether it is true or not. Its very *existence*
troubles. Like entertaining the empirical hypothesis that the Pope is
fallible. But even granted that a hypothesis can defame in some
indirect way, the social scientist can still insist that his hypotheses are
in fact open to test, are framed so as to be open in that way. I have
never met a social scientist worth his salt who believed that a social

science generalization could lead men either to war or to build Chartres. Or should.

Conferences—from Versailles to the little gathering at Endicott House—generate a dynamism of their own. The compromise "plan" for a social science curriculum to run from kindergarten through high school (K to 12, the professionals call it) was its instrument. It boasted a starting six-year sequence on "The Human Past," not a chronology but a series of "postholes" dug deep into revealing eras in the past. The stones and bones of the Choukoutien caves were to be reconstructed in the light of the living ways of the Kalahari Bushmen, Jericho side by side with Hopi sites, Minoan Crete, Periclean Athens, the Renaissance and the Incas. It was a noble vision. It was to unite social studies and social science. Like the beautiful truths of physics, the beautiful materials of those epic eras would catch the imagination of students. That was to be the principle of the pedagogy.

There was one dissenting voice: the psychologist Richard Jones. He wanted to know about the emotional development of the children and how the proposed curriculum related to such matters. He was assured (by me, as I recall it) that these were problems that could be met in the process of building the courses!

In those heady days of 1962, anything seemed possible. Seminars were organized to "get the ideas right." An astonishingly gifted collection of people gave their time. The "stones and bones" were catered to by Robert Adams, the director of the Oriental Institute in Chicago; the living counterparts by the Harvard anthropologist Douglas Oliver. Sherwood Washburn came often enough from Berkeley to advise on fitting in primate evolution and recruited to our seminar table his former student Irven DeVore. We were blessed with gifted men and women of good will.

What happens so easily in planning groups is that they get taken over by the centrifugal forces they generate. Only a powerful central idea can prevent it from happening, and there was none. "Stones and bones" become "stones and bones" for their own sake, with mind for little else. The master plan of Endicott House became an exquisite collection of unconnected scholars' pieces: here a distinguished documentary on the emergence of maize culture in Mexico, there some stunning bits on scroll notation and dwelling patterns in Sumeria, later the beginnings of what was to be prize-winning film footage of baboon troops in the Amboseli Reserve in East Africa by Irven DeVore and of the Netsilik Eskimo in Pelly Bay by the Canadian

Film Board, guided by a perceptive anthropologist in our group, Asen Balikci. There were even plans for explicating Akkadian and Linear B; all gems-to-be. What it did not make was a curriculum. It was also costing a great deal of money.

I have no memory of how it happened, but there came a point at which the drift in this social studies project became sufficiently alarming so that a new "management" was recruited. Elting Morison was prevailed upon to be overall boss. There were to be three units: a high school year on the shaping of the modern mind; a "middle" one on the emergence of the New American at the time of the Revolution, "From Subject to Citizen"; and a "lower" course to replace the original one on the panorama of man's past, emphasizing human evolution. Elting recruited the philosopher Morton White for the modern mind, Franklin Patterson agreed to do the New American, and I was asked to take on the "early" curriculum. I agreed. I even had a germ of an idea of what I wanted to do. For I had been giving a General Education course at Harvard on "Conceptions of Man" in collaboration with George Miller. Part of it was about the emergence of human culture. It had filled my head with notions.

The notions were simple. Three questions could provide a structure: What is uniquely human about human beings? How did they get that way? How could they be made more so? I knew ESI already had material on the Eskimos, on primate evolution, on other things that could be used to explore my questions.

Pedagogy? I would get the most gifted, most experienced, most cultivated, most energetic school person I could lay my hands on and let him or her gather gifted teachers to shape and try out whatever we were producing. They would be partners of the scholars involved in the production. I had no question in my mind (nor do I now) that teaching is a form of dialogue, an extension of dialogue. Dialogue is organized around questions. And those we had.

I was invited to the Annual Meeting of Friends in Philadelphia, to talk about education. A young man came up afterward. He was the head of the history department at Germantown Friends School, "the Quaker Kremlin" he called it. He wanted to get into something more venturesome. I invited him to Cambridge to have a look at what we were doing. His name was Peter Dow. He was the answer to my prayers.

Soon we had that lively little group of teachers working with us. Our three questions kept us together; we virtually put them on a pennant and hung them out front! "What's human? How did we get that way? How to get more so?" You could ask anybody with a new idea how it fitted in, and in time people came to expect to be asked. In the end, we managed to avoid the instinct to go centrifugal. Peter, Annette Kaysen (my assistant) and I staffed our curriculum production shop with a Cambridge mix. We had a linguist-actor, an unorthodox designer, a miscellany of anthropologists fresh from the field— along with our schoolteachers, and scholars and editors, and a tiny staff to keep us in order. From outside, we must have seemed "raggle-taggle gypsies, O!" And I suspect Elting Morison thought we were just that. I think it worked. It never would have without the odd mix of magicians and menders.

What odd questions you encounter trying to produce "teaching materials" for schoolchildren (or for anybody else, for that matter). We had a treasury of film footage—the Zack heritage—and an obligation to use it, having shot it. It was beautiful footage besides, one important part of it done by the Canadian Film Board in the O'Flaherty tradition of deeply personal documentary. A Netsilik Eskimo family is followed through the four seasons of the year. What it depicts is humanly familiar though exotic in locale. Nonetheless, I was worried that film, no matter how "good," would sink children back into their seats and turn off their minds. How do you use film to get people to ask questions rather than to accept the surface of things? I asked my wise and worldly linguist friend, Roman Jakobson, how one should ask questions in film. He said, "Look at the conventions of film-making, the sequences that are taken for granted. Perhaps that is what you can *vary* to make the viewer come awake in the mind. Go again to see Robbe-Grillet's *Last Year at Marienbad.* It is full of questions."

You learn from particulars. It is not social science at all, not even anthropology in this case. You learn a genre or style—perhaps, to put it grandly, you learn the requirements of an art form. We kept the films silent. There was sound all right, but it was the wind or the cracking of the spring ice or the laughter and animated talk of an old Netsilik storyteller talking in Eskimo. But there was no commentator to take possession of your mind. And indeed there were sequences that violated expectancies about how the world goes, others that violated how film ordinarily goes. An Eskimo child builds a bird snare, catches a seagull in it, and stones it to death. It was not staged; that's what Netsilik boys do. Later, when Boston schoolchildren argued bitterly over whether little Zachary was a nasty brute, one of them said, "Listen, he's got to grow up to be a hunter." Or in the igloo, in dead of winter, with the social pressure of others heavy in the air, the adults make elaborate cat's cradles of soft string, some so skilled that they can move a stylized caribou right across from one hand to the other. A boy asked, stunned, "How'd they ever learn to do *that? We* can't."

There is no way to make film about "social science" or even about "anthropology" without its becoming banal. To "teach" anything real, film needs to do something other than declaring or proposing or displaying. For film to be challenging, it must not be "about." It *is,* in its own right. If it is not, it is nothing, or rather, it is "educational film." And that may be quite all right if it is dedicated to how you assemble the M1 rifle. But not if it is about life, with the aim of making you think.

My precautions against films as a "passive" medium spread to all the other things we were doing—posters, pamphlets, books, "field notes," class plans. Were they sleep-producing? We were all seized by the battle against passivity—from the cutting rooms through the design studio to the lesson planning for our tryout summer session. It became a pedagogical style rather than a theory.

The most moving teaching experience I have ever had was that summer session in 1965 at the Underwood School in Newton, Massachusetts, where we tried out what by now was called "Man: A Course of Study."

Peter Dow describes that summer this way:

The summer program, held at the Underwood . . . between 28 June and 30 July 1965 was unique even by ESI standards. For three classrooms totalling seventy-five students at the fourth-, fifth-, and sixth-grade levels we assembled a staff of seventeen teachers, twelve content scholars, seven research assistants, ten instructional researchers, four audio-visual specialists, and eleven administrators—sixty-one in all. Our objective was to get massive classroom exposure of the ideas and materials that had been generated by the working parties, and to record and evaluate these experiences in a way that would guide revision and future testing during the fall and winter. Bruner placed great emphasis on learning from children. Whatever the developers brought to the classroom must be rigorously evaluated by impartial observers.

Mornings were devoted to classroom instruction, afternoons to critiques of the morning's work, and evenings to writing and revising materials and lessons for the following day. Each classroom had a head teacher, several assistant teachers, curriculum writers, scholars, instructional researchers, and media specialists. Responsibility for the preparation of each lesson was shared within the working party, and each member felt a personal stake in its outcome. Seldom if ever had such an enormous concentration of talent been assembled to fashion a social studies curriculum for ten-year-olds. Years later many of the participants recalled this period as one of the most stimulating experiences of their academic lives. . . .

To those who know the subsequent high political drama of "Man: A Course of Study," all this must seem rather a digression. I think not. Briefly, after a year or two of very favorable notices (including international prizes for the film and even a special award to me from the American Educational Research Association) and widespread adoptions, the course came under attack from the extreme-right-wing John Birch Society in league with the newly emerging "creationists," opposed to the teaching of evolution. Between them they mounted the now familiar right-wing harassment of any school district proposing to use the course. In time they gained the backing of several "ultra" congressmen and senators. A press campaign followed which, in spite of stout defense from students, teachers, parents and principals involved with the course, led the Congress to cut off the funding of the National Science Foundation, which had originally financed the making of "Man: A Course of Study." The Foundation buckled under this congressional pressure, and agreed to submit all future curriculum proposals to a congressional committee in advance! Governor Reagan of California, whose state sheltered the core of the John Birch, came out squarely against the course—and did so again in a speech before the Conservative Assembly in the Southwest during his 1980 presidential campaign. And so symbolic had the course become for the extreme Right that they managed to pass on their "literature" about it to a right-wing group in Australia, then in opposition to the widespread adoption of the course there.

What stung the ultraconservatives, the "creationists" and the prudes, I think, was not just the *intellectual* depiction of man's humanity and its evolutionary origins, but the artistic power and integrity of that depiction. Anti-intellectualism is, I think, a response not to well-argued *reason* but to the narrative and metaphor that combine with reason to make an argument powerful. We had succeeded in creating material that was powerful enough to rouse bigots who might otherwise have slept through the padded patter of instructional words and instructional films. Charles Eames, the designer and film-maker, whose friendship I treasured, told me when I showed him what we were doing: "It is beautiful. You will be asked to tone it down. Don't. Far better to fail well than to succeed badly."

By the time many of these events had transpired, I had already moved to a professorship at the University of Oxford. And indeed, in the four years before I departed, in 1972, my Harvard duties had made my participation in the daily business of the course principally advisory. During that period, Peter Dow, Anita Mishler and several others took on the main burden in arranging for publication and distribution of the course and for inventing a highly original teacher-training arrangement through regional centers. It was Peter Dow, a far more experienced and a tougher man than the one who had come to us in 1965 from the "Quaker Kremlin," who bore the brunt of the attack by the ultraconservative textbook-watchers. Dow is soon to have a book published by the Harvard University Press, in which the grisly details of the battles, along with his wise perspective on them, are set forth.

One of the poignant moments of those times occurred in a "talk show" on the radio in Phoenix, Arizona, before whose school board Dow had appeared the preceding day to defend the course against its organized opposition, led by Phyllis Musselman and Anna Day, two veteran textbook-watchers. The host of the program was a local radio personality, Logan Stuart. Dow was to confront the two ladies. Their objections were principally about the course's depicting the dark side of Netsilik life, to which Dow answered that these were people who lived the harsh life imposed by an Arctic desert and who yet remained deeply human—though their values differed from our own in certain respects. Abandoning his role as host and moderator, Stuart asked Dow whether he was not worried lest exposure to other values might alter children's values. Dow replied that this was anything but obvious. Stuart blurted out, "What I am trying to extract from you is an admission that the most important thing to teach a child is faith!" To which Dow replied that in his view the purpose of schooling was also "to cultivate doubt, to raise questions, to help the child see the world from another point of view." That was how it ended, how it always ended.

As the educational storm was rising to the far right, I was living through the Vietnam malaise and the violent protests that it bred on the far left. I was the first master of Currier House at Harvard-Radcliffe. They were days of intense strain. America seemed to have plunged into an era of non-negotiable demands. I thought often in those days of Richard Hofstadter's book on anti-intellectualism in America, of the anti-constitutional fringe we have always bred in our unruly republic. There was little time or inclination to think about "Man: A Course of Study," about the curriculum reform movement, about what our well-meaning Cambridge group had done that was right and that was wrong in those ten years since Woods Hole. Besides, something else was entering the national consciousness, something that dramatically supplanted the dream of an intellectual New Jerusalem in our schools.

I published a little volume of essays just before departing for Oxford in 1972—*The Relevance of Education.* The volume, arranged roughly in chronological order, begins with an essay entitled "The Perfectibility of Intellect" (vintage 1965, presented at the Smithsonian Centenary in Washington and deeply infused with reform optimism) and ends with one entitled "Poverty and Childhood" (vintage 1970), strongly affected by Basil Bernstein and Ivan Illich and concerned with the risk that conventional education practice might perpetuate and institutionalize social and racial inequality). The last two articles I wrote before setting sail for England were one with Michael Cole, on cultural differences in cognition, and one with Urie Bronfenbrenner in the *New York Times,* entitled "The President and the Children," which attacked the cynical Nixon for his veto of the Child Development Act of 1971. The perfectibility of intellect, still an ideal worth cultivating, had come to seem self-indulgent.

Those five years—1965 to 1970—were years of desperate groping for anybody interested in education. It is never easy to think simultaneously about two such different educational ideals as the cultivation of excellence and the promoting of equal rights to opportunity. It is not that they contradict each other in any logical sense, but that each ideal taps such divergent human sympathies. And each makes claims on resources and budgets that collide. But the pull between the two ideals was not what swamped the curriculum reform movement. That pull is still to be resolved, and it will be one day. In some way, our life as a nation depends both on cultivating high intelligence to keep the complex social order running, and preventing the formation of a permanently alienated, undereducated, unemployable "under class."

What "killed" the curriculum movement is not easily analyzed.

But one of the big factors in its demise was the storm of anti-intellectualism, primitive patriotism, and "back-to-basics" that was kindled in those years of war, conflict and violence. "Man: A Course of Study" was right in its line of fire. The ferocity of the attack was classic overkill—partly produced by the screaming assault of the John Birchers and partly by the defensive posture it evoked in the Establishment. In the early 1970s, there were no fewer than three official committees investigating MACOS (as it had come to be acronymed by then): a House ad hoc committee appointed by Representative Olin Teague, an internal review committee at the National Science Foundation (our Government funding agency), and a special group in the General Accounting Office.

Teague's committee was charged with determining whether Government-sponsored curriculum projects were legitimate or whether they were a form of "mind control." "Man: A Course of Study" was the specific case. Gerard Piel, the public-spirited publisher of *Scientific American,* the man on Teague's ad hoc committee in the best position to assess the matter, said, in an address to the National Science Teachers Association in 1976 reflecting back on the matter:

The science curriculum reform movement was never a government enterprise. It was an enterprise of the voluntary initiative of university professors and school teachers. They initiated the ad hoc groups that set up the curriculum projects in each field. They had to seek the funding they needed from the National Science Foundation, but that agency had been created by Congress to support education as well as research in the sciences. At every stage in the development of each curriculum, the peer review procedures that have insulated the independence of scientists in our universities from the government granting agencies served to decouple the control of the content of the new courses from the authority of officials in the National Science Foundation.

When Piel, alone among committee members, wrote to schools using MACOS, he found an overwhelmingly positive response to it. But for all the favorable clearance, the course remained tainted as a "troublemaker," to be avoided if one was to avoid attacks by the extreme Right.

The General Accounting Office audit was after our finances. Had we let our publishing contract properly? Had we obtained advice from potential users before we started? In the end they found we had not been crooks. But they never found it necessary to note in their innocuous report how many distinguished and busy men and women had given their time and effort without recompense or profit of any sort. For not a penny of income from the sale of any materials of the course ever came to any of us involved. But that proved, I suppose, that we were socialists doing in the starving publishers who had to pay *their* scholars to get competing courses prepared. The GAO could not have saved us anyway.

The National Science Foundation decided to fund us no further, pending an examination of their general role in science education. That role has now been greatly reduced.

But curiously, though we bit the dust in a practical sense, the course of study we produced has had a powerful effect—in Britain and Australia, on the Continent in translation, as well as in America. Here in America it is in use principally in more independent-minded school districts as well as in many private schools. It seems to have the power of enlisting strong interest and support from teachers as well as students. And I think it succeeds in doing so as much by the honesty of the doubts and conjectures it projects as by any excellence it may possess as an inquiry into what makes human beings human. Yes, in that sense it is dangerous stuff. We failed well, in Charles Eames's sense. The paramount virtue of the course, as one teacher put it to me, was that it posed problems in such a way that teacher and student both knew that they were together at the frontier of their thinking, brooding about the nature of man. If I did not know at the start, I certainly know now that you cannot address that question in school without plunging into the central political issue of education.

In the end, I am back to where I started. If indeed it is the mark of our species that we create our own environments in very considerable measure, then surely education is one of the most crucial aspects of that creation. But I think the lesson of the curriculum reform movement is that you cannot accomplish the deeper ends of education by altering only the content and spirit of the courses you teach. Schools as now constituted are not so much the solution to the problem of education as they are part of the problem. If I had it all to do over again, and if I knew how, I would put my energies into reexamining how the schools express the agenda of the society and how that agenda is formulated and how translated by the schools. That, it seems to me, would be the properly subversive way to proceed.

IN THE END

11

Ornaments of Consciousness

I have wondered for a long time what design nature may have had in creating consciousness. What functions was it to serve? To what biological imperative did evolution respond in creating this extraordinary way of highlighting the immediate? For what niche in the world did it fit man?

I do not mean mind, but consciousness. Mind is a concept, an idea we construct in order to house the remarkable accomplishments that make it possible for human beings (and other creatures, who knows?) to go beyond the information given. I do not doubt that every human being has a somewhat different conception of what mind "is." Indeed, it took the refinement of radical behaviorism to insist that it was nothing at all! And every indigenous society (like every philosopher) has its own conception of mind which, no doubt, "fits" somehow its ideology about what men are worth and how they relate to other men and to their gods. I mean something much narrower by consciousness.

Consciousness is an instrument of mind, whatever you may take mind to be. It obviously is not all of mind, else it would not have been necessary for thinkers from Aristotle to Wundt and Freud to have proposed an *unconscious* mind, whether in the form of a high computer or in the style of a demonic Id. Consider consciousness to be, rather, a form of private, almost solipsistic display, the output of some sort of device for creating a "here and now" in an accentuated way. It is so difficult and shopworn a philosophical issue, what consciousness "is," that it is mostly avoided by levelheaded Anglo-Saxon philosophers, who win their laurels not so much for elucidating it as for telling us how to talk about it. There is not even a foolproof way to prove rigorously that anybody else but me is "conscious." Consciousness, I suppose, is the classic case of something, like the marriage of true minds, "whose height's unknown although its worth be taken."

Edward Chace Tolman dared to argue that consciousness was Vicarious Trial and Error, the covert form of what a rat does at a choice point in a maze when it looks back and forth between alternatives before choosing its next path. But psychologists, in the main, have avoided extended talk about what function consciousness might serve.

As I read and probed, I found two implicit theories of consciousness. One was a Trouble Theory, the other a Zest Theory. Tolman's was for dealing with troubles—for making hard choices. Huizinga's in *Homo Ludens* was the first about zest I encountered. Consciousness arose from playfulness and disengagement, "not to eat, not for love." But what function did *that* kind of consciousness serve? It was more like an ornament than like a tool. Could that be the cornerstone of civilization, as Huizinga argued?

We forget, I suppose, how puritanical the "scientific attitude" is —and particularly the facet of it that seeks to understand things by exploring their function. When Faraday showed Gladstone his electrical generator, the Prime Minister was reputed to have asked him what use it served. Faraday's famous answer was, "Of what use is a baby?" But even that was an appeal to long-range utility, and not to the value of ornaments and toys.

When I was fifteen, I "discovered" the French Impressionists. There was nothing profound about it: I just happened to "see" some pictures by Monet and Degas and Renoir when I went to the Metropolitan in New York. They seized me: I looked and looked. As I looked, I created those pictures, created them and a "real" world in which they existed. Forty years later, visiting in Paris, my wife and I went to see the great exhibition of French Impressionists at the Grand Palais. The queue was a half mile long. The Palais was packed. On the wall facing the entrance to the first gallery there hung the crowded Moulin Rouge painting of Renoir, surrounded by Parisians. It was as if the dancing crowd in the canvas overspilled into the room —not "as if": they *did*. I said to Blanche, "They've come out of the picture," and when I turned to her, she looked stunned. "Yes," she said, "they've danced right into the room." The picture had not only created a world of its own; in that charged situation, it had even captured the "real" world.

I do not mean to go on about Renoir, for there are painters whose company I prefer more, even among the Impressionists. But he figures in another episode. In the early 1960s, I had done a little experiment with two of my students, bringing pictures slowly into focus to ascertain how hypotheses fed on low-grade blur might affect the recognition of a picture. We used a curious contraption dubbed the Ambiguitor, which slowly moved a picture from total blur to full clarity. One of the "stimuli" (unbeknownst to me, for Gerry David-son and Phil Daniel had chosen them) was a well-known painting by Renoir of a mother and daughter seated in a box at the Opera. My starting hypothesis was "some sort of wheeled thing" (I mistook the curved and velveted leaning rail of the box for some sort of wheel, and I was in pursuit of vehicles), and that hypothesis was so compelling that even when the picture came into clear view, I was still hanging on to it. (I was not peculiar in this; others got equally stuck.) But then, when the next blurred picture appeared, I fell into a worse trap. This time I was convinced it was *another* Impressionist painting and "found" one. I performed just as badly and hung on to the end again. In fact, the "stimulus" this time was a snapshot of bicycles in the very rack outside Emerson Hall in the Harvard Yard where I parked my own bike every day. This time it was form and style, rather than content, that had taken me in. My performance on that second picture was like "computerized Mozart." I had created my own ersatz Impressionist painting out of the ragtag of that bike rack. In that fuzzy microcosm, Renoir had done the same thing to my field of view as he had done to that crowd of Parisians milling around his Moulin Rouge—inside the frame and out.

So perhaps a work of art creates its magic by providing a vehicle for transforming, transmuting, rearranging consciousness? And what kind of vehicle could that be? Or is it an ornament? What extraordinary power to wield in the service of nothing!

Is that sharp separation between tools and ornaments an especial figment of the Anglo-Saxon mind? As in the elaborate pretense by Gilbert Ryle (at least I think it was a pretense) at a dinner given by Stuart Hampshire in honor of Nelson Goodman, briefly visiting Oxford. W. H. Auden, who had been living in the Brew House at Christchurch, where he created a kind of luminous ordinariness, had died shortly before. Ryle was praising this quality, yet he needed to say as a preface, "Of course, I couldn't understand his poetry," as if admitting to being able to do so would have weakened his stance as an analytic philosopher. The trouble theory makes consciousness a tool; the zest theory, an ornament.

In the mid-1960s, I published a book of essays entitled *On Knowing: Essays for the Left Hand.* It was about acts of creating and their products—novels, poems, pictures, myths, pure mathematics. More generally, I suppose, it was about the production of surprise, about effective surprises at that, ones, yes, that served a "function" for the beholder, whatever function they may or may not have served for the creator. The essays did not set out to "explain" anything. Not even to demystify. The French critic René Girard comments in his remarkable book *Deceit, Desire, and the Novel:* "The eighteenth century demystified religion, the nineteenth century demystified history and philology, our era demystifies daily life." It was not that *On Knowing* was against demystification.

There are probably only two ways to demystification. One uses the apparatus of explanation, of cause-and-effect, of logical entailment, and in its most refined form, mathematics. It is at its base paradigmatic, formal, noiseless and Platonic. I have no trouble whatever understanding its function. It is the most powerful *practical* tool in man's possession. In effect, the first way converts what one knows into an abstract propositional form and then manipulates the propositions formally rather than pushing the "real" world around empirically to see how it works. It is Vygotsky's "scientific thinking," Piaget's "formal operations," James Mark Baldwin's "propositional mode."

Then there is the other mode. It tells a story; it is textual rather than logical. It does not deal in paradigms like perfectly round balls rolling down frictionless planes or the strict implication of the logician's "iff," his "if and only if." It is not that this mode does not have its rules, for the syntax of sentences, the constraints of dialogue and the grammar of stories are all demonstrable. (They can even be snatched into the formal mode by conversion into mathematical form, but at that point their kinship to narrative disappears.) Stories have a craft, even a pure form. What else but "pure form" could Yeats have meant when he wrote:

Players and painted stage took all my love
And not those things that they were emblems of.

Or the young Stephen in Joyce's *Portrait of the Artist,* struggling to
ready his speech on pure form in art for the College Debating Society. It is fashionable nowadays (and it was certainly one of the preoccupations of those "left-handed" essays of twenty years ago) to imagine that myth was the deep form of this mode. Its form of referring
is somehow to encompass not only its referent but the penumbra
around it. That, perhaps, is why its principal instrument is the metaphor.

There used to be a widespread belief that the formal mode dealt
with realities that are independent of the observer, that they capture
the *Ding an Sich.* The narrative mode of "making sense" dealt instead with the relation of the observer to what was being recounted;
it included a point of view, an evaluation, however implicit. But
modern physics would deny the independence of the known from
the knower, and critiques of modern social science likewise deny it.
Girard says of the demystifier of everyday life that he creates "the
greatest myth of all, that of his own detachment." Never mind. For
all that, the accomplishment of science and logic and mathematics
is a kind of power over nature that the narrative mode does not yield.
We can make television sets, recombine and splice genes, send men
to the moon. That is not the same as composing Beethoven's Opus
59 or writing *Paradise Lost.* What then could Henry Adams have
meant in his *Autobiography* by "All the steam in the world could not,
like the Virgin, build Chartres"?

I have a hunch that there is a process by which ornaments become tools. Perhaps I had just better say it first. Several times before,
I've commented on troubles, puzzles and problems—how we find a
puzzle form that "fits" a trouble and thereby converts it into a problem. The classic puzzle form, of course, is mathematics. It is so good
for converting troubles into manageable problems that we can justify
studying the puzzle forms of mathematics on their own. I have never
heard of a recommendation to an educational authority that mathematics be cut from the curriculum because most of it is, for any
practical purposes, useless. Nobody in his right mind has ever
damned Riemann or Lobochevsky for proposing geometries that did
not conform to everyday space. It is not a heresy, so to speak, to

propose a possible state of affairs in which the angles of a triangle failed to sum to one hundred and eighty degrees. It may be "useful" for elucidating something. But alas, there is a legion of troubles that do not yield to the crystalline structure of mathematical restatement.

They are principally human troubles, concerned almost exclusively with an elusive construct called "meaning." There are several useful "definitions" of *linguistic* meaning (perhaps nowhere better treated than in John Lyons's masterful two-volume work, *Semantics*), but a psychological definition of the term still eludes us. All we can say is that the meaning of anything inheres in its relations to other things—historical, causal, inclusive, scalar, spatial, affective, or whatever relation one can imagine. Even in linguistics, one is forced finally to admit that the meaning of any unit—be it morpheme, word, phrase or text—lies in its use. And even Wittgenstein had to conclude that the meaning of a word could not be detached from one's use of language as a whole or from the particular language "game" one might be playing.

T. S. Eliot's widow wrote an amusing letter to *The Times* (of London) when Lord Russell died. The great philosopher was to dine with the Eliots and, being a little late, jumped into a cab and told the driver his destination. At the first traffic light, the glass partition shot back, and the driver leaned over and said, "I know who you are. You're Bertrand Russell, the philosopher. I've always wanted to ask a philosopher something. . . ." The light turned green and they drove on further. Next red light, the partition slid back again and Russell asked, "Well, what's the question?" "Tell me; you're a philosopher. What's it all about?"

Human troubles do not yield easily to "Cannibals and Missionaries" treatment. But usually they cannot be put aside until they do, the way problems in science can be, in expectation that one day we will do better with them. They are usually on our backs: we can neither solve them nor will they go away. They are simply *predicaments*.

And here, I think, is where the power of narrative enters. Tales, myths, drama, the diverse forms of art provide the natural mode for depicting human predicaments—how they are managed and mismanaged, how laughed at or held at arm's length or succumbed to. Human culture (whatever else it is) is a stock of "forms" for giving structure and meaning to human predicaments. I think it was this "stock" function that led Joseph Campbell in his stunning book

The Hero with a Thousand Faces to urge so forcefully the importance of "the mythologically instructed community"—the power of the culture's stock to render meaningful *and* communal the predicaments of its adherents.

But obviously we don't go to the theater or take down a book of poems in the same spirit in which we go to a psychiatrist when a trouble proves unmanageable. Every art form has its proscenium arch, its way of encouraging a proper "distance" between the beholder's trouble and what is happening onstage. I think it is principally through conventions of style and artifice that distance is assured, and the country bumpkin who throws bottles at the villain is not stupid, but simply ignorant of those conventions.

It is not puzzling, then, that art so often moves toward "formalism"—to craft of actors and the painted stage, almost for its own sake. The formalisms are exercises in canonical form, of virtuosity in the tools of the craft. It is like the two real sisters in Sully's story. One says to the other, "Let's play Sisters." But the game is not about their life; it is a meticulous exercise in equal sharing of everything.

Over a period of a few years, I literally wore out a full recording of Bach's *Art of the Fugue.* I might as well confess that in the days of the Royal Canadian Air Force Exercises, I played a couple of records each morning to "pace" me, for which odd sacrilege I can only plead that I would never have got through the kicking and pushing and flexing without. However little physical fitness I may have retained, I can still claim that running in place provided me with a very specialized chance for thinking. Specialized because when you are doing RCAF "jogging" to the *Art of the Fugue,* you can think either about your jogging or about Bach: The rest of the world is simply trampled out—at least it was for me. What I concluded was simple, and probably simpleminded.

I decided that the exercises that constituted Bach's *Art of the Fugue* bore the same kind of relationship to his *B-Minor Mass* that, say, spherical geometry bore to Copernicus's theory of the movement of heavenly bodies, or that combinatorial mathematics bears to gene coding, and so on ad infinitum. He was solving the formal little puzzles of the fugue form, mastering what he would later use to such overwhelming effect in the Mass. Practice in form must in itself then have the same utility in the arts that "playing with mathematics" has for the sciences. And if for music, went my giddy thoughts, why not for the novel, for painting, for poetry, for any art form. The push to formalism in the arts is precisely the same impulse that leads one to enjoy mathematics for its own sake, or even to do Martin Gardner's mathematical puzzles or play chess. The aestheticism that some artists find barren and empty must be somewhat like the formalism that some physicists also find barren and empty.

I leaped at the chance for a psychoanalysis when it came my way in the early 1950s. Here, surely, would be the way to explore some of the perplexities of everyday life, to find clues in my own personal experience to the problems that concerned me professionally as a psychologist. The Commonwealth Fund had established fellowships for social scientists to have analyses and to attend the training seminars at their local psychoanalytic institutes, the object being to create a closer bond between clinical psychoanalysis and academic social sciences.

I think it may have been Talcott Parsons who conceived of the idea. He was the honeybee, searching out new flowers with which we in Social Relations could cross-pollinate. In any case, it was he who flatteringly approached me (and "other bright young men" in the Department) about it. So in the autumn of 1953 I started the long and curious process of "being in analysis."

My analyst was the gifted Edward Bibring: gentle, intelligent, deeply European and cultivated in the manner of those who had been educated in the ambience of the Austro-Hungarian world of Wittgenstein, Freud, the *Wienerkreis*, Kafka; the world that Carl Schorske describes so vividly in his *Fin-de-Siècle Vienna*. Bibring was ailing. But through the tremor and discoordination of Parkinson's disease, from which he was suffering, there radiated a kindly graciousness and human wisdom. We had everything going for us. We both knew and cherished common cultural heroes; we shared a shorthand of their ideas, their plots, their characters. We came, indeed, from the same "mythologically instructed community": skeptical, literary, detachedly Jewish, theoretical but not unworldly.

I do not think the analysis "took." It certainly did not produce any deep change in my orientation toward life, nor much of a clarification of who, what or how I was. I have wondered many times why it happened so. Why, at least, did not the experience of those hundreds of hours "on the couch" enrich my sense of myself, give me new ornaments of consciousness comparable to those I got reading, say, Joyce's *Portrait*, or Kafka's *Castle* and *Trial?* Or even from reading the "social realism" of Dos Passos's *U.S.A.* trilogy or of the wanderings of Farrell's Studs Lonigan. Why never the flashes of lightning as in reading Hesse's *Death and the Lover* at fifteen, Santayana's *The Last Puritan* at twenty, or Camus's *The Stranger* at thirty-five? Why could I not find "epiphanies of the ordinary" in what was uncovering itself on the couch?

Was it that psychoanalysis was not my form? That could not have been it entirely. For a few years later, when I was in naked need of help, soon after divorce when another relationship was breaking up with intolerable pain to my stiff-necked pride, I went through several months of "no-nonsense" analysis with somebody else (Bibring since having died of the complications of his illness), with enormous benefit in insight and relief. I think there was something deeper in that first failure.

In spite of the injunction to "speak unguardedly whatever came to mind," what in fact came to mind was already shaped to fit the canon of psychoanalysis and my analyst's expectations. But was it psychoanalysis itself that had this effect? There may have been something else, even more compelling. Bibring's illness risked too much becoming a recapitulation of my father's illness and his death. He was too close to my image of my own father—another gracious, intelligent, cultivated Central European who, once I knew him well enough to treasure as a "friend," would die and leave me dangling. I think that fear undermined the "transference" on which psychoanalysis is supposed to depend. Then again, I can imagine some wise psychoanalyst making the equally reasonable claim that, after all, just *that* might have strengthened the transference.

But for all that, I think there was another barrier, which inhered in psychoanalysis itself. I commented earlier that my "escape" from childhood was by embracing and in a way becoming the symbols, the events, the ideas, the happenings of my times. I had left available some important part of myself to be constituted by others, by happenings, by resonance. At times I was tormented by the instabilities that it produced in my life. At its worst and most self-alienating, it can become like Fitzgerald's *Gatsby* or those figures in fiction whom René Girard describes as slaves of "triangular desire"—Don Quixote mirroring the "perfect knight, the famous Amadis of Gaul." But things are rarely at their worst, and there are also many compensations. One learns to enjoy surprises.

In analysis, in *my* analysis, the search was for analogues of the past in the present. Those were the trophies of the hunt! I think I learned a great deal about my "defenses," how old ways of viewing the world imposed themselves on what I was experiencing now. But I also wanted an explication of the text as it was being played out in the present. Can you be at home with your insights about how the past is altering your perceptions of the present if the present is eluding you? The present becomes so full of mysteries that the past, already known in some workable measure, seems stale by comparison. At times, indeed, I had the feeling that I needed an anthropologist of the present to complement the psychoanalyst of the past. For the present in which I was then living was far from an open book! I wanted the text of the present and future; my analyst wanted the history of its narrator.

When I was midway through analysis, there came into being a "Top Secret" group charged with reexamining United States information policy in its most general sense—from the Voice of America to the mode of operation of the Foreign Service and even to our methods of intelligence gathering. It was code-named Project TROY, and two or three days a week I spent my time at a classified headquarters not far from Boston (dubbed "The Bunker") or in Washington. The exurban Boston site was, I suppose, in recognition of the high concentration of Harvard and MIT professors pressed into service. We were joined by others from outside, with us for a day, a week, a month, the whole tour. What a cast it was! And how little effect in the long run! There, entering the conference room, "on call" by our own Lutine bell in the doorway, to be rung by anybody or any subgroup with an idea it thought needed a plenary airing, were such as George Kennan, Clyde Kluckhohn, Elting Morison, J. T. Pierce, Edward Purcell, Robert Lee Wolff, Max Millikan, Donald Marquis. There was, as well, a salting of this assistant secretary of state or that, and we had a faithful attendant for a week in the person of that remarkable man James Webb, then Under Secretary of State to Dean Acheson. It was the Truman era. For all the gravity of the proceedings, Project TROY was the best club I have ever belonged to—so much so that a handful of its "old boys" set up a Supper Club that dined together at the St. Botolph's Club in Boston the first Friday evening of each month for the next fifteen years.

Never mind whether TROY succeeded or "failed." I have learned, not altogether gloomily either, that *all* great "one-shot" massive efforts to generate policy advice to an ongoing government "fail." Policy, I suppose, is such an intricate negotiatory process that the only way you produce quantum changes is through the ratcheting effect of specific legislation or decree. And the princes we were advising had neither legislation nor decrees in mind. We were advising Mr. Acheson, whose high ideals and agile lawyer's mind were very evident, and his Policy and Planning Staff at the State Department. The real object of such enterprises, I think, is "consciousness raising." In that, perhaps, TROY succeeded a little.

But that is not the present concern. I did learn some deep lessons about gearing foreign aid to the level of technological and social development of recipient nations, which more than a decade later helped me when I advised on policies for aiding educational development in the Third World. But in terms of the tale of psychoanalysis that prompted this diversion, something more personal needs telling.

I (in my mid-thirties) was learning to live in a new world—not just the heady "corridors of power," with Mr. Acheson returning from a briefing of the President to have cocktails with our group at his house in Georgetown. I recall his telling us how remarkably well Mr. Truman was able to wear his "three Presidential hats," as commander in chief, *chef d'état* and *chef de gouvernement,* or that "foreign policy was more a day-to-day response to telegrams from abroad than it was an explicit formulation covering a wider range." Or Mr. Webb objecting, at one particular presentation, that what had seemed to us a pressing problem for the future was too "iffy" a question to occupy the Policy and Planning Staff. I, for the second time, was discovering that the management of great enterprises was an extension of ordinariness. I had learned it the first time during the war, or at least "encountered" it and "played" at it rather mindlessly. The second time, I was perhaps old enough to be set to brooding about it.

What was this all about? Who were we, we "Trojans," and what was it we were trying to accomplish? What to make of George Kennan sketching fastidiously a history of Sinkiang province as an unstable buffer between Russia and China, or of the incomparably dry Lloyd Berkner concluding that technological progress was little more than "the scanning of small changes." During that year, I vacillated between a sense of exhilaration and a sense of incompetence in the face of serious issues.

A few of us used to spend time "after hours" in Elting Morison's study on Buckingham Street in Cambridge. Elting, a man with an exquisite sense of the mix of "high-mindedness and low cunning" that animates great enterprises, led what really should be called "group therapy" for men of ideas caught up in issues of power. His knowledge of history—but more to the point, his sense of the bearing of history on the conduct of human affairs—is a gift that he knows how to share. The internal strains within our group—Kluckhohn's deeply felt anthropological romanticism about the "integrity" of cultures clashing with Elting's own historical view that the essence of cultures was their dynamism, their lurches in conflict with their continuity, to take one example—were what came alive over those after-hours drinks at Buckingham Street. Or the pull between the agile legalism of Mr. Acheson's mind and his Christian high-mindedness, inherited from his bishop father.

For *textes* like these, the apparatus of the novelist, the historian, the dramatist, helped more than the retrospects of the psychoanalyst. It was not that extrapolating the family politics of my childhood was not interesting or important. I honestly believe, rather, that there is (at some times in one's life) a highly limited relationship between the politics of childhood and the conduct of a growing life. I think I know what that limited and archaic relationship is. But after it has been explored and its analogues explicated, a vast terrain of one's contemporary life remains unexplored and unexamined.

I think there must be something about stages. My friend Berry Brazelton has found that advice to parents about child rearing is most effective when it coincides with the point at which the child is just about to leap into the thicket of problems for which the advice is relevant. It may have been that I, like some of the parents Brazelton studied, was not at the right point in my life for psychoanalysis. Perhaps the midst of life was not the right "touch point" for exploring the origins of my own defenses against life. Or perhaps, who knows, perhaps undertaking a psychoanalysis for "intellectual curiosity" is not a good motive, or not a good enough one for an intellectualizer like me.

The seminars at the Boston Psychoanalytic Institute were mostly atrocious. They were divided into "theoretical" and "clinical." The latter, taught by a gifted and intuitive older woman analyst, were full of the problematic in life. Her comments and questions on the cases before us were wry but kindly appreciations of everyday drama. The theoretical seminars, on the other hand, could not have been more doctrinaire. They were in the charge of a gentle and intelligent younger analyst, who conducted them exigetically almost in the style of a pious and clever young priest. Freud's texts and their changes provided the writ. When one of our Class B foursome of social scientists (as the anthropologist, sociologist and two psychologists were classified, the second alphabetic position denoting that they were not to conduct training analyses)—when we would raise some such question as whether the Oedipus complex was not more *fin de siècle* Vienna than universal, our leader would agree that it was interesting, and that perhaps we could come back to it later. But we never did.

Nothing much grew in the theoretical seminars, and a few close friends that I made then among the aspiring analysts, with whom I have talked since, felt as I did that its main function was less speculation than indoctrination. A few years later, in 1955, when I was a Visiting Fellow at St. John's, Cambridge, I was asked to review the second volume of Ernest Jones's splendid biography of Freud for the Sunday *Times* of London. There were echoes of the seminar experience in what I wrote:

Jung's "defection," which Freud saw as a retreat on the issue of sexuality, hurt badly, and it was to be the last time that an heir was chosen. For the sensible Englishman, Ernest Jones, whose good judgment then was as apparent as it is in the pages of this well balanced book, proposed a *sub rosa* committee to guide the destinies of international psychoanalysis. Freud acceded with pleasure and relief and solemnized the occasion by a gift of antique Greek intaglios mounted in gold rings for the members of the secret council, writing in his illusionless way to Jones (who had had Charlemagne's paladins in mind in making the original suggestion) that he sensed a "boyish and perhaps romantic element . . . but perhaps it could be adapted to meet the necessities of reality." Freud to Jung in 1909: "Your surmise that after my departure my errors might be adored as holy relics amused me enormously. On the contrary, I think my followers will hasten to demolish as swiftly as possible everything that is not safe and sound in what I leave behind." Perhaps he underestimated the extent to which quasi-conspiratorial beginnings would breed a later tendency to orthodoxy among the in-group.

Jones dropped me a note to "thank you warmly for the care you devoted to reviewing Volume II," and I discovered upon my return to Cambridge and Boston later that winter that the older analysts thought I had made some worthwhile points. The senior analyst who had run the clinical seminar with such wry wisdom lamented that psychoanalysis was, alas, falling into the hands of doctors!

There was a shattering novel published in 1981, by the English poet D. M. Thomas, entitled *The White Hotel*. It is at the same time a deep appreciation of Freud and a harrowing evocation of the un-harnessed carnage of the Holocaust, through which one of Freud's "cases" subsequently lives out her life and death. It explores the unchartable landscape of a world that lies between inner, psychic reality and outer historical existence. It is, among other things, about man's liability to self-delusion—the theme that more than any other shaped Freud's skepticism. In the end, Anna's hysterical symptoms, so carefully unraveled by that great physician, foretell the unspeaka-ble butchery through which she dies. She has managed to master or at least to live with her internal world, only to be destroyed by an outer world which, almost to the very end, she has denied. Even the final roundup of the victims to be gunned down at Babi Yar, of which Anna is one, is transformed in their minds into another stage on the road to escape.

Like myths and allegories that use the instrument of horror for "teasing" consciousness, *The White Hotel* looks beneath the edges of the human capacity to tame evil by illusion and denial. But unlike Perseus, who slays Medusa by guiding his deadly spear by means of her reflection in his burnished shield and does not have to gaze directly upon her deadly evil, Anna falls victim. Perseus's shield was the gift of his mother. Anna's, ironically, was the gift of the illusionless Sigmund Freud: her cure. *The White Hotel*, as an image, is the symbol of the safe womb, we are told. Perseus's mother gave her son the gift of the gods, a shield that would reflect the world clearly enough so that he could combat the desperate, historical reality of Medusa.

I recall an episode from childhood. Into the quiet suburban world of Merrill Road there burst a sudden horror. Our neighbor, a quiet and unobtrusive man, hanged himself in his attic. There were police cars hurrying officiously into our quiet street, lights flashing. At breakfast I learned what had happened. "Why did he do that, why did he kill himself?" "We do not ask such questions; he must have been a very unhappy man, and that is enough," said my father. I am not altogether sure that I might not have responded that way if my six-year-old had asked me.

If there is any purpose to consciousness, beyond its being an instrument for the analysis of necessity and trouble, it must surely be to provide us with a vehicle for making present the absent, making visible the unseen, making possible the unimagined. We begin to understand how it does this in the derivational mode, how (guided by the procedures of reason) it can be led through the successive steps of entailment that permit us to "understand" much of the physical world around us. In its own right, it should quickly become "reinforcing" for its usefulness—though its self-rewarding quality needs more understanding. But the narrative mode, the one that gives access to human predicaments? It seems to be even more compelling, certainly more widespread. It is far easier to attract readers to *explications du texte* of the trial of Mrs. Harris than even to Carl Sagan's dramatized accounts of the regularities of the heavenly bodies.

The usual answer, of course, is that (first) we need explanation and that (second) we like those that fulfill our wishes and comfort us. The first probably reflects our use of language and the manner in which it operates "constitutively" (to use the jargon expression) to create a conscious reality of its own. Narrative explanation fills in the gaps and yields "meaning." As for the second part, the wish fulfillment, it too must be partly true. But if it were true, "if and only if it were true to the exclusion of all alternative truths," there would be no great art, no great drama, no interesting myth, no interesting religious mysteries—but only pabulum.

I want to make a wild guess, based on some ideas that have been surfacing in literary criticism for the last two generations. Literary criticism is not a bad place to look, after all, for to it falls the task of analyzing great texts, great works of art and appealing ones as well. I want to take the great Russian formalist Bakhtin as "the lesson." In Bakhtin's studies of Dickens, for example, he notes that whether you examine narrative or dialogue, you will find the presence of two or more voices—at very least, the character's own and the authorial one. In the convention of fable, for example, one voice sets the stage, speaking in the timeless perfective tense of "once upon a time," and the others speak in the midst of action. There is something inherently dialogic in the art embodied in language.

I have never doubted (as I remarked some chapters earlier) that thought, once one has joined the linguistic community, was in certain deep respects a continuation of dialogue. Or as Vygotsky, an admirer of Bakhtin's, put it, thought is the internalization of dialogue. (I have never been convinced that this is equally true or even true at all for the kind of thought that is "driven" by mathematics and logical derivation. I rather suspect that these forms were in fact developed to free thought from the specific context where it began and from the dialogue in which it may have started.) It is not surprising, then, that bumpkins throw bottles at the villain and flowers at the leading lady. They are *there*, like Mallory's Everest, those heroes and villains. Except, rather than being a five-mile-high rock challenging that dauntless Englishman to climb it, they are of our flesh! They are temptations which make us hope that human predicaments are not inevitable. If they achieve great art, those heroes and villains, they make us conscious that predicaments *are* there, but they provide a basis for wisdom about human communality.

So in the end I come to the conclusion that the "ornaments" of consciousness—Huizinga's products of zest rather than tools for repairing trouble—are also tools, but such extraordinary ones! For they, the works of art and the canonical cultural forms, are instruments for envisaging possibility communally. They are a means of continuing conversation by social means that can then be internalized in thought, in internal dialogue.

I have always used that most solitary of forms, the essay, to carry on where conversation left off. Dialogue with others, however confined it may be to one's writing table in the absence of others, permits an escape from one's own implicitness. But just as it saves one from oneself, it also provides a means of ignoring the constraints that others place upon you by their presence and their point of view. My good friend David Olson has assured me for years that the invention of written genres like the essay have almost as their primary function permitting one to go beyond the restricted range of spoken dialogue to a consideration of the text, its form and its "transcendent" truths. At the same time, by starting in dialogue, one is forced to take account of "the other," to unpack one's presuppositions in their behalf.

In another of his late poems, Yeats writes:

> Think where man's glory most begins and ends
> And say my glory was I had such friends.

I want in the next chapter to consider "friends." I put them in inverted commas, for some of them I never knew. They were "there," again like Mallory's Everest, though for internal talk rather than climbing. I call them "extravagant people." They were ones who had the extravagance to give themselves away, and I mean that in both senses. They were the ones who made good dialogue possible —sometimes, indeed, by making it so difficult that one had to turn inward on paper.

12

Extravagant People

The first extravagant man I ever met was named Frank Henning. He ran a dock and boat livery on a little tidal inlet in Lawrence, Long Island, that runs into the gut of tidal water separating the South Shore of Long Island from the string of sandy islands that enclose Great South Bay. His extravagance was profound: He held back nothing. In all material respects, however, he was penurious. Our little clique of "water rats" kept an old dory at his place, and later one of us, Lenny Jacobson, kept an outboard on a "runabout" there. Henning never failed to let us know what was on his mind—about us or anything else.

Henning had served in the Canadian "Princess Pats" in the First War, and on the basis of reflected glory, we all were sure that they were a "gallant regiment." For he had lost his left hand in combat and it was replaced by a hook-shaped prosthetic device that he wielded with zest and panache. The "Princess Pats" was, in our minds, a band of Frank Hennings. We water rats were about thirteen or fourteen. You never had a doubt where Frank stood on anything —who was a "crook," who was a "real fine gentleman," who an "idiot." On one occasion a local lad, a "spoiled rich boy" whom none of us much liked, ran his new Chris-Craft past the dock at full speed, creating a terrible banging and clattering among the docked skiffs that were rented out weekends to bottom fishermen from the City. Frank had a sash weight in his good hand, the kind he used for sinking the killy traps in which he stored live bait. Before the Chris-Craft had run the thirty yards needed to pass the dock on which he was standing, he had thrown the sash weight through the windscreen of the "fancy" runabout. You never had a moment's doubt where he stood on things. He was not "hot-tempered." His views were simply for expressing something to be made known then and there. That was his extravagance. It was simple but real, and there were no strings attached. We loved him.

Extravagance must be based on an unshakable belief in the limitlessness of creation—not on possessions, but the power to generate and to give away at will. Extravagance of this kind requires no "return on investment." It is limitless.

Extravagance, I suppose, is a state of mind. It could not be "real," for limitlessness in the human scope is an abstraction, not a reality. I have always counted myself lucky in the presence of extravagance, however it expressed itself. I have even come to believe that it is not so much a general trait of character—*real* extravagance, that is—as a way of reading local settings and reacting to them. Intimacy, for example, is one of the deep and beautiful forms of extravagance. It is the perfect setting for giving yourself away.

But some people can give themselves away even without such an assured and warm microcosm. They are there, giving gifts of self to others. Some can only make such gifts in the bosom of the family, in the common room of their college, among their close friends, in an accustomed club. Occasionally, extravagance occurs by dint of temperamental good luck and favoring circumstances. Occasionally, indeed, circumstances are such as to create a setting that turns a group of people extravagant with respect to each other. I belonged to a Friday Supper Club that was like that.

The Supper Club came into being in the mid-1950s, "founded" by that little group that had gathered after hours at Elting Morison's to talk over the day at Project TROY. We lasted for fifteen years out of pleasure in each other's company. It was not that we were "models" for each other at all. Nothing could have been further from our minds! What we talked about before, over and after dinner was almost without limit. Oddly enough, anything was admissible so long as it was not intimate! Our agenda was something else: to reconstrue what we already knew. You could take one of Wittgenstein's dark sayings as an implicit "motto" of the group: "The problems are solved, not by giving new information, but by arranging what we have always known." We never had "topics," never gave "talks," rarely had guests. We talked about what "we always had known," however novel its surface might appear.

The chemistry transcended the ingredients. We were serious. I refer to us all in the past tense, for what existed then was for those times and for that group then. There was Elting Morison, Yankee gentry, Theodore Roosevelt's biographer, historian of technological change—literate, skeptical, forgiving. A colleague once described him as MIT's "humanistic historical conscience," and not without good grounds. For it was Elting Morison who could always be counted upon to discuss the central, moral dilemma of MIT: the relation between power and knowledge, which in the context of that institution is no abstract debating issue. While the Supper Club never in any sense had a "leader" or even "officers," Elting was the spiritual "convenor" in the sense in which the English use that term.

We never had more than a baker's dozen of "members." Kingman Brewster, then at the Harvard Law School, livened those first Fridays of each month with a wit born, I think, of an appreciation of the absurd and of the transitoriness of all human arrangements. He had "form" and a "tribal sense," as one of the group put it, a combination that rallied Yale when he was its President in troubled times. Max Millikan directed the Center for International Studies at MIT. He was learned, and had in addition an insider's knowledge of contemporary politics and economics that was rather "CIA." But for all his engagement in the contemporary scene, he had the detached and calm curiosity of his father, "the Millikan physicist." George Homans, Harvard historian-sociologist, was an Adams: no mistaking his Adams chin. Nor his iconoclastic resistance to what he referred to as "guff." He was a scholar by temperament, but like many anglophiles he had a deep distrust of high flights of the conceptual imagination. I have never known a more consistently good-humored man. Myron Gilmore, historian of the Renaissance, was later to be first director of Villa I Tatti, the Berenson palazzo in Fiesole, converted to a Harvard center. He had an almost feminine sympathy and intuition for the play of historical personalities, a feel for the airs and graces, as well as for the substance of Renaissance thinking. His scholarship had an enormous charm. Robert Lee Wolff gave us yet another historian. He, more than either Homans or Gilmore (and certainly more than Morison), saw history as a negotiation and collaboration among powerful figures. He took, perhaps, a more judgmental view of the unfolding of Western history—and of events on the contemporary scene as well. He saw virtue and evil struggling beneath the surface of events.

I must put McGeorge Bundy in a category of his own. At the start, he was the Dean of Arts and Sciences at Harvard, a brilliant political scientist, a sharply focused analytic mind. Indeed, he might well have become a mathematician but for the bizarre chance that, as an undergraduate at Yale, he had encountered his classmate Andrew Gleason (who later became perhaps the leading topologist of his generation). Gleason's brilliance so discouraged Bundy (he took it to be "typical") that he went instead into political science. I have never known a man with a greater gift for concision than Bundy or one with a more developed ability for formulating precisely the current state of play. It was not that he lacked a sensitivity for the fuzzy edges of human affairs. Rather, he was eager to find a conclusion on the basis of what could be known—however *pro tem.* His enormous self-confidence made it easy for him to be a good listener and an extraordinarily "quick study." Some of his contemporaries, I know, found him arrogant. Perhaps it was, as Kurt Vonnegut once said, that those who come to their ignorance slowly and tediously hate those who get to theirs quickly.

The scientists in the Supper Club were all from the "hard" side. Victor Weisskopf and Edward Purcell were physicists, deeply involved in their work, Weisskopf as a theorist, Purcell as an experimentalist. Both loved dilemma. Like most great physicists I have known, they were both forever bemused by how the disorderly processes of human thought could ever have discovered the exquisite orderliness of nature. Both were men of strong moral convictions that had been intensified by their closeness to the politics of the Bomb. Weisskopf was Austrian by origin, a gifted pianist, and of an Old World charm. His "meta"-physical interests were shaped by a fascinating mix of classical philosophical reading and immersion in the deep issues that physicists like Einstein, Bohr and Heisenberg had raised. Purcell was American Midwest, boyish in looks and enthusiasm, and in an almost puckish way unpredictable as to where his unbound curiosity would take him—whether to the statistical unaccountability of batting slumps, to Wally Gilbert's work on DNA, back into some new mystery in his beloved electromagnetism. For all that, there was a quality of deep seriousness about him. The two of them brought to the conversation at the Supper Club the dilemmas of quantum mechanics, of a Nature that might in the end be asymmetrical, and of Bohr's complementarity.

Edwin Land (of Polaroid fame) was the only "nonacademic" among us. Din Land had a mix of elusiveness and directness, of concrete common sense and abstractness, of ambition and genuine modesty, that made him difficult to penetrate. He was the classic autodidact who had defined his own curriculum. He was forever musing. For several years he was at the beginnings of what was to be his now celebrated theory of color mixture. He saw it in the grand sweep of inquiry that had started with Newton's resolution of white light into its spectral components. And at the same time he could throw himself into the battle of introducing polarizing films into both headlights and windshields in a way that would eliminate glare. Or notice that the elevator operator at the Polaroid offices could be brought closer into the spirit of the place if he was also given the task of sorting and handing out the mail. Or provide the funds necessary for the starting of Freshman Seminars at Harvard, on the grounds that learning to ask questions should be a staple diet of the curriculum from the start. He had the quality of a twentieth century Ben Franklin, or of an Erasmus Darwin—scientific innovator and practical man of deeds. For all that, there was also a strain of the romantic in Land—in his admiration of genius, in his crusading beliefs about the manner in which industrial organization could bring out the best in men, and in his extraordinarily generous support of the academy.

We had two engineers as well. Will Hawthorne was a Cambridge professor and eventually master of Churchill College there. He had a permanent visiting arrangement with MIT and was, indeed, our only "visiting member." He brought us wry tales of the difficulties in bringing technology to bear on Britain's defense and industrial policies—as in his witty accounts of the plastic "sausages" he had designed for carrying crude oil to be towed by British ocean tugs from the Middle East. The other engineer was Julius Stratton.

Julius Stratton, like McGeorge Bundy, needs a separate word. He was, in a sense, McGeorge's opposite number at MIT—second in command under Killian. Though his background was in chemical engineering, he had earned his reputation as a university administrator and policymaker. If Bundy's forte was a brilliance in formulating issues and then proposing daring solutions to them, Jay Stratton's was prudence. I think he saw himself as a balancing force that helped hold MIT together. Elting Morison used to chide him occasionally by referring to him as "Julius the Just." While McGeorge Bundy saw his role, I think, as shaking Harvard into some needed consciousness and daring, Jay Stratton saw his as a judicial one. Perhaps each of those institutions needed the man it had got.

That made twelve, a good company for dining, at the St. Botolph Club in Boston the first Friday of each month. (We had a few years at the Club of Odd Volumes as well.) We dined well and drank well. Bobby Wolff saw to our wines with a fine eye for a good claret. We were in one respect like the Junta in Max Beerbohm's *Zuleika Dobson*, which met regularly to consider new members, only to blackball any that were proposed. After a year or two, we had become so accustomed to each other that we shilly-shallied each time it was proposed that we needed a biologist or an artist or a judge. The sole exception, the only new member ever elected, was the economist Wassily Leontief, and he contributed such fresh air and spunk to the proceedings that we felt it would not be worth the risk of trying another.

So we had our baker's dozen. Over those fifteen years of dining together, we had an occasional guest—never more than one at a time: Robert Oppenheimer (when he was giving the William James Lectures at Harvard), the art historian Ernst Gombrich, the aging Walter Lippmann, the critic Alfred Kazin, the architect Serge Chermayeff, the economist Carl Kaysen, a few others. They livened the company, obviously. But for all their liveliness, the group went its own way. Lippmann inclined us somewhat toward politics and Gombrich toward the arts, but it was not as if they were there to give set pieces for a set discussion. For the allure of the group was the absence of any agenda whatsoever. We were our own agenda. We talked extravagantly about what was on our mind. If it was worth thinking about, it was worth talking about. Or to paraphrase Wittgenstein again: Good conversation battles through language against the bewitchment of our intelligence.

We took in each other's business—intellectual, professional, academic, political, but as I have said, not personal. Some of us rarely saw each other between dinners; some were close personal friends. Those who believe that you come to "know" people only by a mutual baring of souls must surely be wrong. Nor were we in any sense a "mafia" which decided matters of great local moment and then pushed them through our various "connections."

The "issues" that surfaced in conversation over the years were, I think, less important than the underlying attitudes they evoked.

The effects of those conversations were more stylistic than substantive. I doubt whether any of us "learned" very much. The underlying premise was that there is no topic so specialized, so arcane, or so rooted in prior knowledge as to be beyond intelligent comprehension and discussion. This made the group an incomparable sounding board: whether it was Jay Stratton trying out an idea for appointing distinguished foreign humanists as visiting members of MIT—"You mean like Old Masters to be hung in the corridors," somebody said —or the question of selling the Boston site of the American Academy and moving "to the country."

There *were* worldly themes, which were replayed quite regularly. "The MIT question" was one. The more general question of which it was an aspect was: How do you impart knowledge to human beings in a way that assures that they both *understand* it and can *use* it to some practical end. That great institution (Elting Morison used to refer to MIT as "the great beating heart of America") had a generation before decided that engineers should first be taught physics and then its application. The complaint was that now graduates became tolerable little physicists, but incompetent engineers. I had always felt that our group was being implicitly autobiographical on the subject. The relation between "knowing" and "doing" was a most personal issue in that company. So each time any of us went forth to do "good works"—whether Weisskopf to Geneva to direct CERN for a few years, Brewster to preside over Yale, Millikan to reorganize the CIA, Bundy to become Kennedy's Security Adviser, whatever—we would return with new versions of the old dilemma.

But the most profound dilemma, which, paradoxically, held the group together intellectually, was never mentioned explicitly in our decade and a half of talk. Lionel Trilling is one of the few people I have ever heard talk about it openly. The deep and powerful ideas of science are not understood, cannot be fully understood by men not educated in those sciences, no matter what else they may be educated in. Trilling describes this as a "wound," an impotence that is felt deeply by the nonscientific intellectual. And I have no doubt he is right.

Science was often discussed, never in a pedagogic or didactic spirit. I think Weisskopf and Purcell particularly welcomed the chance to put their dilemmas and quandaries in the form of comprehensible metaphors—serious metaphors that could become generative. I recall discussions of the red-yellow-white shift in the heating of metals and the story it told of altered atomic patterns, of the puzzles of quantum mechanics and its noncontingent transitions, of the limits of complementarity, all treated not so much to "demystify" as to distill the philosophical or "programmatic" dilemma from the hardware of physics.

I think I shared with the other nonscientists among us a sense of philosophical relief. If I could not understand the formal apparatus of physics, at least I could be helped to appreciate its implications for the use of mind. It created an unspoken solidarity in that group that was quite extraordinary. Curiously, it was never as compelling an experience to hear Wassily Leontief comment on his input-output theory or George Homans on English villages of the thirteenth century. Not that these were not interesting subjects, interestingly treated. It was only that they required a form of thinking that we all did as naturally as breathing.

But I must not give the impression of great earnestness in those dinners. We were never in violation of easy conviviality. In fact, we also drank a good deal. And that must surely have helped.

Alas, history overcame us. The moral indignation of the Vietnam War, the tensions of the student protests, and our own political commitments finally divided the group. The last meeting, as I recall, was the only one that ever had a special agenda, and it was called by McGeorge Bundy, who by then had become President of the Ford Foundation. It was in 1970. We met in New York, the only meeting that ever took place outside Boston. Harvard was in the midst of the ROTC issue and other troubles that I shall want to tell about in the next chapter. Our little group included leading members of Harvard's liberal and conservative caucuses. Wassily Leontief and I were in the former; Bobby Wolff in the latter. McGeorge was eager to minimize the Harvard conflict. The Supper Club came together for the last time to discuss whether there might be some way out of it. It was an honest meeting, but it was no longer a meeting of friends.

I admired Bundy's spunk in bringing us together that way. I doubt it helped move events toward a resolution at Harvard. It was certainly not a happy way for the Supper Club to end.

Nearly ten years later I was at a dinner party in London, at the home of the then economics editor of *The Times,* Hugh Stephenson, a summer neighbor of mine in Ireland. The guest of honor was Paul Foot, a radical Marxist and the leader of a far-left faction, a delightful and amusing man. Foot was full of that day's hearing before a High

Court judge on the issue of whether he was guilty of libel for having written that a prominent trades union leader had negotiated cheap holidays for his members in Spain just when Franco was threatening to guillotine Spanish union activists. Stephenson and Foot had been together at New College, Oxford, and were old friends. They held wildly different views about how Britain and the world should be run. That did not keep them from enjoying dining with each other occasionally. Perhaps the British know something about the relation between knowing and doing that we don't.

Never mind. The Supper Club created an extravagant environment for exchange. It was one of the things in the world I would have been poorer without.

Extravagance in the sense I've used it is a "gift of self." It is the ultimate extravagance—unless one is convinced that it is endlessly generated within one, that there will "always be more where it came from."

"Self" is not, oddly enough, a self-evident idea. Earnest efforts to define it, to date its beginnings in an infant's life (a favorite sport of psychoanalysts), or to set its limits—all these usually end either in muddle or in philosophical priggishness. Indeed, even the vintage of "self" words in our language—self-respect, self-aggrandizement, self-centered—is surprisingly late, mostly after the sixteenth century. "Self-consciousness," for example, is dated by the OED as of 1697. The birth of words may not mean much, but it does suggest at least that before their arrival, the ideas to which they refer were probably not in wide or explicit circulation. The only point I would want to make about the concept of Self is that it should not be taken for granted with respect to either its nature or its origins.

There must, I think, be some tuned element in the evolved brain of higher apes and hominids that starts the Self growing. There was an imaginative little experiment a decade or two ago in which the chimpanzee and the Old World monkey were compared reacting to a reflection of themselves. Before they were placed before a mirror, their foreheads were stained with a bright patch of color that had no odor or distinctive touch quality. The stain was put on when the animals were under anaesthesia, so they would have no memory of it. After her initial fright, the chimpanzee looked at her image with care. Then her hand moved tentatively to her forehead to "explore" the colored patch. There then ensued a long, fascinated inspection of her mouth as she opened and closed it, of her eyes, etc. The "tuned element" in her chimpanzee brain was translating an *external* image into an image of "Self." Not so the Old World monkey. The typical macaque response was to fly at the "animal" in the mirror, to make threat gestures at it—to treat it not as Self but as "Other."

What makes the Self grow beyond that primitive level, we do not understand very well. Most would agree that it has something crucially to do with others. The gifted French writer Vercors wrote in the 1960s a novel in which a young woman, raised by foxes, recognizes her humanity only when her captor and would-be lover exposes her to a mirror. It is then that she begins to feel inside her the sense of another's caring. It was not a very good novel, but it made an interesting point about Others being required for the realization of Self.

The usual psychoanalytic "story" about the growth of Self is plotted, of course, around the infant's first achievement of independence from mother. Then, late in the first year, the child shows his first fear of strangers. This is taken to mean that the mother and other familiar figures are now part of the child's "extended Self," whereas strangers are not. The child enters a period in which those very things most likely to produce laughter when done by a parent will produce tears when done by a stranger.

How much speculation there has been about that extended Self! That genius William James devotes the better part of his chapter on "The Self" in the *Principles* to it. And Sigmund Freud enriches that story immensely by adding to it the idea of "identification," the incorporation of the Others into the Self to the point where, indeed, one can almost characterize a human being as a cast of characters (as Freud does in his vivid essay "The Poet and the Daydream").

It was not an altogether new idea. At the turn of our century, a "school" of social philosophers and psychologists argued that self, however it may originate, must be shaped by the reaction of others to our presentation of ourselves. Charles Sanders Peirce, John Dewey and George Herbert Mead elaborated on the idea one right after the other. A tedious sociologist of the day, Charles Cooley, even coined a dim-witted label for the idea: the "looking glass Self." It survived nonetheless, and today the idea has received renewed attention from such gifted writers as Erving Goffman and Rom Harré, exponents of what has come to be called "symbolic interactionism." I was given the rare chance in 1981 of naming the new University Professorship to which I was to be appointed at the Graduate Faculty of the New School in New York. I proposed it be named for George Herbert Mead—in many ways the "founder" of the transactional idea of self. His posthumous book, *Mind, Self, and Society,* helped start it all.

Yet there is something telltale about the heat that this idea generates. One of my teachers, Gordon Allport, in spite of a grudging admiration, could not discuss it without disparaging its invitation to think of personality as only the "subjective side of culture." He was champion of the "autonomous ego." My good friend David Riesman's *The Lonely Crowd* is really an essay on Mead's proposal that we find the meaning of self in the reactions of others to us. The moral indignation of Riesman's splendid book was aimed not at the *idea* of the transactional self but at the American sickness that ensues when nothing else is left. To both Gordon Allport and David Riesman (each a moralist of autonomy), "others" are like certain poisons: stimulating in small doses, deadly in large. For them, as in the lines at the end of Sartre's *Huis Clos: "L'enfer, ce sont les Autres."*

Who can deny the "American sickness"? During the period of student unrest in the late sixties, I encountered it in its inverse form —in the ideal of the "autonomous self." It was in the turbulent year when I served as master of Currier House at Harvard-Radcliffe. There was a refrain I kept running into even among the most articulately radical students—about "getting away from everything" for a year in order to "find out who I am." That was one side of it: the autonomy side. But then, a year after the "bust," when the police were called in by President Pusey to drive occupying students out of University Hall, there was a counterrefrain. The protests, I was told by some of the former activists, had really been an "ego trip." It had not expressed deep social or political commitments. But, I asked, were you not also committing yourselves by taking action in behalf of things outside yourself, expressing conviction by acting jointly with others? I wondered afterward why they wanted to define themselves only in terms of what was irreducibly private. Why did they have to factor out what was public, have to call it alien and an "ego trip"?

Everybody, I suppose, has *his* kind of person, his partner in dialogue who in the end becomes a member of his cast of characters. Some people in the world are uncanny in their gift of entering others. They give not only their ideas but their secrets: they unmask

themselves, or go maskless. They seem never to hedge, as if they would be the richer for giving. Sometimes this gift is of the innocent —as with Billy Budd, "top-foremastman of *The Rights of Man* of Philadelphia," or my boyhood's Frank Henning. When this human extravagance is combined with great talent, it becomes a form of community renewal—if the time and climate are right. The extravagant great create self in others in a manner that, finally, makes others more easily able to share self. It is not that the world becomes like them. Rather, they create a medium of exchange.

Universities turn into drab places without extravagant people. They operate efficiently enough without them, but joylessly—and rather silently. It cannot be an accident that in virtually all folk societies, the word for "chief" is the word for "talker." Universities, of course, have more chiefs than tribesmen. They are talkative places when they go well. Silence is a dangerous symptom.

One of the sources of silence (and a formidable barrier to wide-ranging extravagance) is built into modern scholarship. It is specialization. Some institutions in the society—like the Navy or the Foreign Service—are so sensitive to the dangers of specialization that they go to elaborate lengths to counteract it by regularly rotating their officers from one kind of job to another. Indeed, the Navy, when an officer becomes irreversibly specialized, marks him EDO, Engineering Duty Only. The unmarked case is the generalist. An officer is to command, not to specialize.

Universities proclaim in their charters (and in their initial morpheme) that they aim to be repositories of the general culture. Alas, their systems of promotion, of reward, of instruction, even of administration, are based on specialization. Generalism is not a career. If one ever has the good fortune to be appointed a "university professor" (without attachment to department or discipline), it is an event that comes late in life in reward for having worked one's way through a distinguished career as a specialist of some kind. The appointment is an occasion for champagne and a party. You begin as an instructor in mathematics or an assistant professor of psychology, and your promotion depends upon how well you do within your specialty. Those brave universities that create positions for lecturers in general education, or its equivalent, all learn the same lesson: They have willy-nilly created a category of second-class citizenship whose principal role is to teach undergraduates some "general cultural" course that is regarded at best as a lamentable necessity (like English compo-

sition), at worst as a silly or "soft" option (like the local drama critic giving one on "The Idea of the Theater").

I think that the preceding chapters must have made it plain to the reader that I (like most university professors) have spent a very large part of my life brooding about and researching very specialized matters—perception, learning, thought, language, and so on. I have the usual boxful of prizes and honorary degrees to assure me of my specialized accomplishments. Indeed, I was "given tenure" at Harvard (an expression that makes many cringe) when I was in my early thirties, not because I was thought to be an educated man but because I had done a lot of psychology. (The year following, I experienced the worst depression I have ever suffered in my life, caught between feeling trapped and feeling a fraud; it is not uncommon.)

But I have always thought of myself as an "intellectual" first, and then a psychologist. An intellectual is somebody who follows his ideas where they may lead without regard to disciplinary boundaries and who, having done so, accepts the consequences of his conclusions in how he thinks, feels and acts personally. It is an impossibly romantic idea, rather like the scholar Gypsy or the French Encyclopedists. How could a scholar Gypsy have had an expensive laboratory, foundation grants, research assistants, superb graduate students?

But fortunately, even the most specialized universities have their ways of keeping alive the dreams of scholar Gypsies. They provide their scattering of extravagant people who make life possible for them.

Take I. A. Richards as a type case: poet, critic, cranky proponent of Basic English, mountaineer. I first encountered him when I was a graduate student at Harvard. He was offering a graduate course with the beguilingly unrestricted title "Interpretation." I had read two of his books before: *Practical Criticism* and (with C. K. Ogden) the famous *The Meaning of Meaning*. The metaphor of his very first lecture was Goethe's line "Gray is all theory; green grows the golden tree of life." He drew from his enormous knowledge of poetry and prose classics, exploring the distinction of the literal and the figurative, and as I walked out of Sever Hall into the Harvard Yard, the bells of Appleton Chapel pealing as they do between classes, I knew that what I had heard was a scholar and a man. It was not just his learning or the slightly donnish way he had of enriching what he said with playful asides. He was, I thought, giving himself away—in both senses of the expression.

A few lectures later, I timidly asked him some questions after class. His answers were so full of care and so lacking in any sort of defensiveness that one had the sense of being in the presence of an "artist of mind." I never saw him again until after the war. All I remember of our first postwar meeting is that he was writing something that he proposed to call "How to Read a Page." It was a reply to a potboiler entitled *How to Read a Book,* an early example of the banal "frequency argument" applied to children's reading. Richards ended up by writing a lovely piece on what should have been a commonplace: that there are lots of ways to read, some very slow, some like lightning.

A few years later, I told him that I had just given the members of my freshman seminar six books to "read" for their first week's assignment so that they might find the topics they might want later to pursue. They had moaned in despair, "But you can't read *six* books in *one* week with all the other things you have to do." I suggested that they just try. Of course, it worked a little miracle. "You couldn't have done them a better favor," Richards said.

In the 1960s, when he was working with Christine Gibson on the "stick figure" scenarios to help children learn to read for overall sense, he needed some help to check out the progress of the work abroad. I introduced him to two aspiring young psycholinguists, Dan Slobin and Eric Lenneberg, whom he dispatched to Israel and Brazil respectively—helping to launch two of the ablest younger scholars of their generation. But Richards was unhappy with the state of linguistics and, I think, with cognitive studies too. He feared the former was becoming too formalistic to deal with the poetic power of language. When I showed him a manuscript version of *Studies in Cognitive Growth,* on which I was at work, he said, "You make symbolic representation in the child ever so formal and mathematical. How shall you deal with the forms of symbolic magic?"

He was at dinner one evening at our house in Cambridge. We had not known it was his seventieth birthday. The English philosopher Freddy Ayer and his wife, Dee, had said they would love to see him again. He was bubbling. That morning at seven, his phone had rung. Who would call at that hour? It was Grenville Clark, curmudgeon lawyer and retired member of the Harvard Corporation, calling from New Hampshire. "Ivor, I know you've just turned seventy and I thought you ought to start with a word from an old hand of seventy-nine. This has been the best decade of my life. Happy birthday."

From seventy on, Richards turned back to poetry, whence he had started. His first volume was of love poems!

His love of poetry was remarkably informed with a sense of its structure. I recall the almost passionate care with which he read Gerard Manley Hopkins aloud at a seminar in 1975 at my college in Oxford, where he and Roman Jakobson shared the topic of the language of poetry. He wanted to vivify the power of sprung rhymes, where elements of thought and elements of sound stress coincide. His joint pursuit of the music and the thought of Hopkins's poems was exquisite—and emblematic of the man.

I have published only one poem in my whole life. It was about the artistry of sailing and sailing vessels, a birthday poem to my yawl *Wester Till* . . . about "turning mindlessness to geometric ends . . ." I enclosed the poem in a letter to Richards. His reply was on hand-painted Chinese stationery, a treasure from his early Peking days. "It is a voyage in itself," he said. "What I especially like is, of course, the exactness of every phrase."

Roman Jakobson was another. I met him for the first time in an oral examination. The thesis being examined was a rather dull one. But Roman Jakobson could make a table of random numbers interesting. He even managed to make the examination interesting. The candidate jumped his final hurdle on Jakobson's coattails.

Jakobson had been the towering figure of linguistics in his generation. His extravagant genius has influenced far more than linguistics proper. He had always regarded himself as the inheritor of the tradition of Charles Sanders Peirce, a tradition that sees the structure of the linguistic system as a reflection of the functions to which language is put. He has done some of the most fundamental work of the century on poetics, on the contrastive sound system of the language, on the phonemic constituents of meaning, on metaphor and metonym and their role in language development and aphasia. For him, the deep function of language was to mark or to leave unmarked, and this it did by a myriad of devices to give nuance to awareness. His essay on Blake begins with an analysis of the sound structure of

> My mother groaned, my father wept.
> Into the dangerous world I leapt,
> Helpless, naked, piping loud:
> Like a fiend hid in a cloud

and ends with the implied assertion that there must exist not only a language of poetry but a poetry of language itself.

In the latter 1960s, we were together at dinner. "May I try out an idea after dinner?" he asked. Standing before the fireplace, he talked explicitly on "the language of poetry and the poetry of language." It was about the structural integrity of language and the requirement that integrity imposes on poetry. He was giving us his most cherished thoughts—giving them away as he was constructing them. He believed deeply that language was the instrument of humanity, and he acted accordingly. He touched more minds in his lifetime than most mortals ever do—anthropologists, literary critics, neurologists, psychologists, linguists.

Jakobson's style was like Rostropovich playing Bach on the cello. (Richards's was that of an exquisitely played English flute.) The drama of Jakobson was that one felt in the next months some great connection would be found. Yet he had great lightness of heart. On his seventieth birthday, a great gang of us descended upon a Chinese restaurant in Medford—Peking on Mystic, it was called—and had a magnificent meal together, the earthenware teapots (at his suggestion) being filled with vodka rather than with green tea. It was very funny, which is all I can remember about it!

Claude Lévi-Strauss in the Preface to *Sound and Meaning* comments on the vividness, brilliance, discernment of Jakobson's style as a lecturer and, indeed, as a writer. He could never forsake the poetic function. One had the feeling in his company of one's consciousness being off the "automatic/hold" position and on "disautomatic/scan." Even in his most technical papers, there is this sense of forefronting, marking, drama. There was never a danger of dryness. He could be exhausting, yes, gloriously so. He was, truly, a poet linguist, a linguist poet.

Roman once said of a mutual friend that he organized his life into journeys, each kept separate in his mind, each self-contained, each computable. He, Roman, he said, had no such episodes. As with his historical mentor, Charles Sanders Peirce, it was all the same journey, whether the object was lyric, hortatory or epic poetry of the first, second or third person, or distinctive features of phonemes. His greatness as a companion was not just his loyalty and kindness, but also his readiness to welcome you into that world whose unity he was seeking to unmask by exercising his consciousness and by goading yours. We flew together on a long flight from Boston to Moscow in

1966—over the ocean, over the Alps, over wherever, for hours. We talked about language, about human development, about thought and consciousness—gossiping, discussing, joking, trying out hunches. It was much too short. I shall never forget his generous capacity to share his conjectures, his tentative as well as his settled conclusions, his shrewd reminiscences about this Czech futurist poet or that departed linguist. Kindness, connection, consciousness—and in such concentration! Such a man!

Remember Wittgenstein's "Philosophy is a battle by means of language against the bewitchment of our intelligence"? I think both Roman Jakobson and Ivor Richards were quite as much interested in how language could also bewitch our intelligence. They were more extravagant than Wittgenstein.

A good friend of mine, Karen Peterson, an undergraduate at Currier House when I was Master there in 1970–71, was given a College grant at her graduation to make a trip around the United States. The only stipulation was that she visit women who had been active as alumnae of Radcliffe. I asked her later what she had learned. She said: "A very few people make a very great difference. Without them, the towns and cities where they live would be much, much drearier places."

The greatly admired sociologist Robert Merton once did a study of a community (in New Jersey, if my memory serves). I recall his telling a group of us, at a seminar we had arranged on one of his frequent visits to Cambridge, about the "locals" and the "cosmopolitans," the two types of leaders in the town.

The "locals," I think, is what Lionel Trilling had in mind in making the distinction between authenticity and sincerity. Authenticity inheres in having place and function and history, like characters in a Jane Austen novel or in Mrs. Gaskell's villages. Sincerity, by contrast, is what one must create as an impression when one's place, function and history are not shared with those around one or, in an uprooted world, are simply not established or even capable of being established. The nineteenth century novels—of Jane Austen, of Thomas Hardy, of Trollope, of Chekhov, of Flaubert—are woven on the shuttles of authenticity. Writers of our century, I suppose, are principally preoccupied with sincerity and "the presentation of face" —perhaps one should say "the politics of face." I recall a review by Lionel Trilling (more than a decade before he gave his Charles Eliot

Norton Lectures at Harvard on authenticity and sincerity) of David Riesman's *The Lonely Crowd*. He made one very arresting comment: It was precisely the demise of the "novel of manners" that had brought into being the kind of fine-grained sociology that Riesman's book represented. And, we would add today, that is represented as well by the penetrating essays of an Erving Goffman.

The "great" and universal university communities where I have lived my life needed their authentic locals, their creators of community, just as desperately as the towns that Karen Peterson visited on her Radcliffe travel grant or as Bob Merton's New Jersey town needed its locals. Often, the locals have had no "official" function, no famous professorships, or if they did, it was a function quite beyond what they were officially "known" for.

When I was at the University of Cambridge, in 1955, there were members of my college, St. John's, who, by the very style of their *memory*, were locals. One of them, a classicist and bachelor, a man of steady good humor, saw to it in a dozen little ways that I should feel part of that "combination room," as common rooms are called in Cambridge. He was a prototype local. "Bruner," he said, for the mode of address at John's was by surname, "you had better start practicing reeling off the College prayer *very* fast, for you may end up one day soon as the youngest Fellow at table and it would not do to keep the meal waiting by slow delivery." I dined at John's one evening twenty-five years later—I was there to "viva" John McShane's excellent Ph.D. dissertation—and found the very same John Crook sitting at the very same corner place at table in hall where I had remembered him sitting before. And making conversation possible—as before. Crook may or may not be a great classicist. I simply do not know. It would not matter. I remember another such at King's, where I dined occasionally with Oliver Zangwill and Meyer Fortes. His name was Dr. Saltmarsh. He was a Dean of the College and an expert in English local history. King's, even more than John's, was a college of vivid personalities and distinguished scholarship. None exceeded Dr. Saltmarsh in guarding the loom on which that college wove its daily life. He was a local presence. I felt a genuine sadness when, only a few years ago, I saw his obituary in *The Times* —one that sang praise for his role as *genius loci*.

It has made me think of the forms of extravagance. Certainly one can discern the extravagance of genius—the Jakobsons and the I. A. Richardses of the world, who not only see connections where none were seen before but find ways of infusing their friends with new insights about those connections. But John Crook and Dr. Saltmarsh were not that kind of genius. Their trade was in the familiar, helping others find fresh consciousness in what they already knew. It requires being an exemplification of what it can mean to live locally—whether in the combination room at St. John's or on that inlet by the salt marshes on the South Shore of Long Island where Frank Henning presided.

Ruth Tolman is a name not known to many. For a decade after the war, she played an incomparable role in holding together her friends—psychologists, psychoanalysts and physicists from all over the world. She did so whether at her home in Pasadena, or whether visiting in Berkeley, in Cambridge, in Princeton at the Oppenheimers', wherever.

Ruth Tolman was a clinical psychologist—a diagnostician, therapist, invisible organizer. Her husband, Richard, was a New Englander, "of the yeomanry not the gentry" as he would say, of Quaker extraction. He was ordinarily professor of physics at Cal Tech, a distinguished student of statistical and quantum mechanics, and second in command during the war of the Manhattan Project, under J. B. Conant. He was a man of wry humor and enormous generosity, an appreciator of the odd forms the human spirit takes. His role in the making of the Bomb could not have been without anguished concern. Ruth and Richard Tolman seemed totally suited to each other.

Ruth worked with me in Washington during the war, doing opinion surveys on civilian reactions to war programs. We remained fast friends for all the years afterward, until her death in 1957. She was the perfect confidante, a wise woman.

It is difficult for me to separate what is personal from what is "professional" or intellectual about Ruth. And that, of course, was part of her genius. We corresponded in fits and starts, sometimes twice a week, sometimes with a month or so between, and I suppose the classic psychoanalytic interpretation (which I will only confirm if I deny it) was fairly obvious. We joked about it occasionally. I may have needed a mother, and she a son (she was childless). But I think we wore it lightly enough. The desolate grief I felt at her death verified how much she had meant to me personally. Her genius in any relationship was just that she could give a sense of personalness to anything she touched.

Perhaps I can give some sense of it by an excerpt from a letter. When psychology at Harvard was splitting up, in 1953, she wrote:

I was tremendously interested in your story of the beginning rift in the Department there. I suppose it is not right to say "beginning rift," but the beginning of its explicit and aggressive phase. Having seen Gordon [Allport] in the Emergency Committee [of the APA], I can recognize his tense, tight-lipped, withdrawn reaction to opposition and hostility. He gets hurt and indignant and loses his sense of humor completely, thus destroying in himself the techniques that could be effective in such a situation.

But Jerry, it all distresses me, somewhat in the same way that our curious conflicts used to distress me in Program Surveys. I feel that as specialists in the knowledge of interpersonal relations we fail all the time to manage them well. I do not really see why there should not be biotropes and sociotropes, each of them keen about the new things in the findings of the other. I cannot see any more reason why some psychologists should not be eye-ear-nose-and-throat psychologists (if they get fun out of it) and others social psychologists, than why some physicists should not work on nuclear physics and others on thermodynamics or statistical mechanics. Hells bells, it's all good clean fun if you like it, isn't it, and the struggle for power that builds up around the issues seems to me a definite source of weakness in the field. This was one of the points that Vannevar Bush made for not including the social sciences in his endless frontier—that they were never able to agree among themselves and were always at swords points. Oh dear, oh dear, and it really is that way. The same day your letter came I had an interesting note from Boring—interesting in the light of what you had written. . . . He says this: "I guess biotropic psychology must be stronger than sociotropic psychology. The biotropes seem less frustrated, less aggressive, less ego-involved. Now you see why I should like to talk to you about this, since you are a sociotrope. (Do you know these words? The heliotrope turns toward the sun. It sees the sun though it is not of it.)" Interesting don't you think? I wrote him in reply much of what I have just said to you—that I didn't for the life of me see why there couldn't be all kinds [of psychology] very profitably for everybody.

There has been a lot written in the last few years about how women more than men value relationships as much as achievement. Ruth viewed the world of scholarship in much that way. Intellectual connections were real for her as relationships between their exponents. She would bring her psychoanalyst friends to dinner parties with those of us working on the New Look, promoting their enjoyment in each other as well as in each other's ideas.

Ruth and Robert Oppenheimer were close friends, friends from the days before the war when he was commuting between Berkeley and Pasadena. They trusted each other's taste. It was Ruth who originally proposed to Oppenheimer that the Institute at Princeton should consider psychology under its roof. It was at her instigation that he organized that first meeting to advise him on "deep questions" in psychology—a meeting in 1951 of George Miller, Paul Meehl, Ernest Hilgard, Edward Tolman, me, and several others. Over the ensuing years a trickle of psychologists visited for a year at a time, including George Miller, James and Eleanor Gibson, Jean Piaget, Wolfgang Köhler, David Levy and me. Ruth wrote me after the meeting: "Robert wonders (a) if the psychologists really have some feeling of urgency about problems which could be worked on helpfully and appropriately at the Institute, and (b) how the people to work on it could be found. . . . He is genuinely puzzled."

We even had an "advisory committee" in the 1950s of Ruth, George Miller, Edward Tolman, Garry Boring, to meet with Oppenheimer once a year to keep him abreast of the field. Eventually, twenty years later, and after Oppenheimer's death, Carl Kaysen appointed George Miller a Fellow. But that did not last.

But while Ruth's enterprises of creating intellectual connections by cultivating relationships may not have changed the face of psychology, they surely changed the lives of people whom she touched. For her extravagance was in grace. She had the gift of making us feel that what one was thinking about, working on, experimenting with, was part of how one was living as a human being. It was so lifelike a gift that it never seemed special in any way at all—as if it were Ruth herself that was the gift. How curious that we never fully appreciate that there are some people who make us more civilized with each other.

Elting Morison was another who had a gift for creating community—and such an extraordinarily mixed one at that. It was he who really started that Supper Club. He taught Humanities at MIT. By trade a historian, he wrote exceptionally fine biographies of Henry Stimson and of his former father-in-law, Admiral Sims, and edited the definitive edition of Theodore Roosevelt's works. But his scholarly relevance to MIT was his specialty of technological history—or more precisely, the impact of technology on society. He is one of those people who think conversationally. He also listens!

We met first in the late 1940s; I cannot remember how it came about. We became close friends through Project TROY. I would often stop by for a ritual martini as I bicycled home. His study at that hour was rather an open house, his wife, Ann, joining the conversation, and likely as not one of his three children, all of them quite as conversational as their parents from a tender age. He was six or seven years my senior. He managed, somehow, to be extraordinarily gregarious and at the same time to remain a very private person. I think it is as New England as broiled scrod.

Elting was from top to toe what my good friend Sheila Grant-Duff calls the "high-minded elite." His high-mindedness, however, was laced with a lively, somewhat bemused sense of the ordinariness out of which events of great moment are forged—which, I believe, is what made him such a splendid biographer. His curiosity about people, however, was rather specialized. He was interested in their "psyches" (to use his phrase), but principally as it led them to make decisions—*what* they decided about and *how* they went about making up their mind. Indeed, this furnished the "drama" of his own historical scholarship—how the Navy finally overcame its resistance to the flexible gun platform and chose it over the traditional fixed firing station, how Henry Stimson and the Joint Chiefs made the decision to drop the Bomb, and so on. By the same token, he was fascinated by MIT, "the great beating heart of America," and how it went about making up *its* mind on the crucial issues facing it. His sympathies, his high-mindedness and his sheer astuteness about human affairs made him the ideal friend-adviser if, indeed, you were involved in making a decision of some kind. In consequence, he was consulted often not only by friends and extended family but by the mighty at MIT. Doubtless, he would have denied exercising great power at that institution (and later at Yale), but in fact he *was* powerful. No matter that it was the power of style, for Morison was never a man of causes. The style was that of a man of vision, yet pragmatic. He surely must have been one of the most knowledgeable men concerning MIT and its predicaments in his generation there, and it was not surprising that Jim Killian and Jay Stratton usually tried out important decisions on him before launching them on the institution.

Elting too was an extraordinary confidant—and I am using the adjective to indicate not only the superlativeness but the unusualness of his gift. For when you "sat down" with Elting—and I have discussed with him everything from how to cope with the reactions of my son and his fellow editors of *The Exonian* when they were fired off the paper by the Headmaster for putting out an issue on some of

Phillips Exeter's less savory investments, to matters as distressing as my own divorce—when you talked out such matters, he was both sympathetically astute and also a repository of knowledge about how comparable matters were handled in our own community. He managed to do the latter without a trace of the gossip's spirit; he was interested in how things worked and in how to make them work.

If that were all, he would have been an absolutely essential figure in Cambridge. But there was one other trait he had—again, a superb one for a historian: a gift for reflecting on events, exploring the different senses in which they could be explicated. He invited me occasionally to the seminars he would hold for MIT students in his study. They almost always revolved around a particular book: a play, a novel, an essay (Mill's "On Liberty" was one of his favorites, particularly when he took to giving seminars for the "Advanced Management" program that brought successful young business executives to MIT for the year). *Hamlet* was another of his favorites, and he asked me to come and say a few words about Ernest Jones's famous psychoanalytic essay on the play. There was a quiet, rather sullen student there. He listened attentively and with what seemed to me increasing dissatisfaction to the rather highbrowed proceedings. Finally he blurted out, "I don't see why you need all these complicated explanations. Hamlet had been off in a German university where they dueled all the time. He just came home sword-happy." Then another one volunteered that if he was, he wasn't very efficient at it, "given the amount of blood he spilled to get the job done." Morison was dancing with intellectual delight. He loved the confrontation of alternatives—whether in history, in literary talk, in the business of MIT, or in the lives of his friends.

He claimed he was a ritualist, a conservative ritualist. It is intriguing what masks people choose to put on when they think of themselves. In fact, he was a conservative in the classic sense of admiring and defending what was great and fine. But his excitement came from observation of and participation in change. He rarely had a position to push, as I have already said, but he loved presiding over situations where change was inevitable.

When we worked together on social studies curricula for the schools, on "Man: A Course of Study," among other things, we were "quadrumvirs": Elting, Morton White (the philosopher of history), Franklin Patterson (later the first President of Hampshire College) and I. Elting turned the project into what must surely have been the best intellectual club going. We had each other and we brought in the liveliest minds we could, from Cambridge or elsewhere. Again, Elting did not "stand" for anything. He believed so deeply in exploring points of view that he preferred nurturing the debate to pushing views. "Discussion without attachment to results" was one of his favorite phrases.

His extravagance took the form of fair-mindedness. You will never get a hearing better than the one he offered. I rather suspect that in the end, institutions would mire down without extravagant people. The calculus of institutional life becomes predictable enough to become boring. Well-orderedness easily reaches an excess that converts its virtues into a vice. Universities (or perhaps any institutions) cannot get their yeast from strife alone; a little goes a long way. So all that remains to provide the antidote to ordinariness is extravagance of spirit: the spendthrifts, the outpourers, the ones who give themselves with abandon. They may no longer be the raison d'être of the university, but woe betide the one that squashes them.

13

Living in Universities

I have spent a half century in universities, wars and brief transitions intervening. They have been my "hometowns," and like hometowns they must surely have helped form my identity.

Well-established universities are hotbeds of contrast. The mean and the generous, the outward-looking and the parochial, the yearning and the self-satisfied haunt their halls. Having been a member of two particularly well-established ones, Harvard and Oxford, I suppose I have seen the contrasts most nakedly. For when universities become "famous" foundations, they seem to increase in their power to produce both envy and large-mindedness. The ever-present danger for any mortal scholar living in a great university is that he should define himself and his worth by his association with it. It is what produces the "Harvard disease" and the "Oxford disease," the conviction that to be elsewhere is to be nowhere—and nobody. The conviction also produces bores.

When I first encountered "the university" in my late adolescence, I was turned by the experience into an intellectual romantic. By the end of my second year as an undergraduate at Duke, I was convinced that the noblest profession was the use of mind to gain and increase knowledge for its own sake. My early rebellions were not rebellions against the *university,* but against those who (in my romantic view) were betraying its free spirit—by requiring students to attend chapel or establishing a system for students to inform secretly on examination cheats. Both of those affairs would have been better handled by quiet intervention and repair. But to a nineteen-year-old they were irresistible evils that demanded a public cry of indignation. But then, it was a cry of the powerless, and I was comforted by a belief in evil powers against whom one could do public battle. Romanticism leaves very little in the middle: Paragons and villains take up all the space.

It does not require much "reality" to reinforce a romantic image once created. "The university" in those impressionable first years was as much historical and stylistic as institutional in its embodiment. It was the *way* one discussed matters with oneself and with others, and that included both the seriousness and the wit. The historical aspect was not just the library (though the idea of the library as a "lens" focusing all recorded knowledge in one particular place did carry me away when I first thought of it), but that the learned man carried his historical antecedents in his head. My image battened on astonishingly selective fare. For Duke in the 1930s was no Athenian Academy!

The habit of "illusion-feeding" locked me into romanticism. I could be confirmed in my faith by talking with my mathematician roommate, Lee Arnold, about the possibility that the foundations of geometry were given in the character of mind rather than in the nature of the experienced world, or with my anthropologist friend, Leonard Broom, about how culture achieved autonomy from individual minds. Universities were places where people came together (like the prisoners in Plato's cave) to figure out ways of turning away from the wall toward the sun, to figure out how to find the reality behind appearance. There didn't have to be a multitude engaged in the enterprise to make it real. Just a happy few. *We* happy few. I was a little snob. But a *pure* one.

I think I would have withered in the heat had I gone to Harvard as an undergraduate. It was daunting enough and structured enough in its expectations to frighten me as a graduate student arriving there in this new Athens. I was saved, I think, by the illusional habits I had acquired at Duke—and by the snobbery, a snobbery that Harvard easily (and, I was going to say, cheerfully) continued to sponsor. I think (in retrospect) that the snobbery had other roots than just intellectual romanticism.

Universities in the late nineteenth century began providing for clever young people of humble background a quick passage into gentility. They were particularly useful for Jews. For there is an inherent conflict in the Jew of the Diaspora between a long-estab-lished spiritual, intellectual tradition and the materialism and shrewd practicality that grew from the circumstance of living in a restrictive, often hostile world. I sensed these two sides of my father, loved the first and hated the second. The young and idealistic Jew feels the spur of shame more than he feels guilt. He is ashamed not of being a Jew, though, but of being a Jew of the second kind— huckster rather than spirit. An intellectual career—better yet, one legitimized by membership in a great university: what better solution? Respected from within and yet a passport to the wider world. My mother used to say to me, "Your father would have been so proud of you." And I would wince a little.

So to the idealistic young Jew who "makes it" at Harvard, another symptom may be added to the Harvard disease. If he does not have a good immune system, he turns into a simulated Wasp: Wasp wife, Wasp tastes, even Wasp sports. And probably he will land on a couch talking with a psychoanalyst afflicted with the very same problems! I think that was what Alfred Kazin must have had in mind when he exclaimed to me, "Oh, you Harvard Jews."

My attachment to Harvard was total and I could scarcely wait to return there after the war. My intellectual romanticism had gone through a sea change, for I'd spent the better part of 1945 in the Paris of *Il faut s'engager,* dominated by Sartre and *Les Chemins de la Liberté,* by Camus, by *Les Temps Modernes* and by intense discussion of spiritual renewal. Back in Cambridge, I flung myself into my research and teaching like a deprived maniac. Back to that eighty-hour week. Back to my friends; to the old Department; to Winthrop House; to the literary circle around Perry Miller and Matty, the ever slightly downcast F. O. Matthiessen; and to a university atmosphere that (more than I could know at the time) was shaped by its president and his fighting cock of a provost.

A university, like any other complex institution, takes its cues not so much from ordinances and catalogues as from the people it converts into negotiable myths. The President and the Provost were grist for the myth-making mill. As a president of Harvard for the immediate postwar years, James Bryant Conant was the perfect tonic. He started with one enormous thing in his favor: He had *been* President before the war, he "knew" Harvard and was seen as an insider rather than a newcomer. He had, moreover, been a major figure in developing the Bomb, and while there was already considerable anxiety about the horrors that its existence portended, Conant was seen as on the side of those most keen to control it. His reputation as an engaged scientist and statesman was beyond the reach of even the most subtly malicious—principally the more traditional literature professors, who found him unsympathetic and "impatient with the humanities," as one of them put it.

Indeed, he *was* impatient. Perhaps he was hankering after a wider world for his talents (which he found later, first as our Ambassador to Germany and then in an attempt to reform American secondary schools). But it did not show. He launched *General Education in a Free Society,* the report that founded "Gen Ed" at Harvard, and then forced the faculty to face anew the question of how much education should be "concentration" and how much "distribution" (to use the old prewar language). The report had come out strongly for a conception of general education as not a smattering of "distributed courses" but a focus on the core of the Western tradition: its science, its arts, its literature, its history, taught where possible through case histories in greatness by scholars of renown. It did not come to pass quite that way, of course, but the consciousness evoked by debate on the report was far more important than any curriculum change it might have wrought. It gave Harvard an educational focus that it easily loses in pursuit of other ends.

And it was Conant as well—supported by a handful of scientists who had been at Oak Ridge, Los Alamos and the other places where the action had been—who brought Harvard into the era of Big Science without, at the same time, turning the "other side of Kirkland Street" into a no-go area of national defense fortresses. I recall the day in March 1949 when Conant announced that Harvard would accept no contracts for any research that required a security clearance for either its conduct or its publication. It was a singularly unemotional debate, there in that elegant Faculty Room in University Hall where Miss Johnson served tea for those who arrived a few minutes before the appointed four o'clock. It was Conant's cool head —and George Kistiakowsky's, Bright Wilson's and Percy Bridgman's —that prevailed.

Paul Herman Buck was Conant's Provost. There is a portrait of him hanging just by the main door of the Faculty Room, brilliantly executed by Gardner Cox. It catches Buck at his most bantam cock. He was a historian, and a very good one. Like so many good historians I have known, he had the spirit and the skill of a Restoration gossip. Conant was chilly, publicly remote, lofty in argument—not an accessible figure. Buck was personal, literally rather gossipy, warm, good-humored in a way that even infected his peeves. To Conant's New England Yankeedom, Buck brought the Ohio of *My Sister Eileen*. No question he was a man of principle; but no question either that he was a fixer, and a good one. "I have a date to see Paul" was the first step to getting things done in the real world of Harvard. It was Paul Buck who saw to the arrangings of the new Department of Social Relations, who kept the Committee on General Education within bounds, who "managed." Indeed, it was Buck who assured me, when I came to him with my first tenure offer from another university, that I really ought not to be thinking about leaving. He knew that I knew he was in no official position to say such a thing. And I knew that he knew that I would take it as a weather forecast. As it turned out, of course, I became a tenured professor a few years later. But that is not the point. It was Paul Buck who gave Harvard the personalness of a parish in those days. Without it, it would have been a much drearier place.

Harvard in those years—in the decade after 1945—was presided over by men who had become established before the war. I always felt very "junior" with them, though some became good friends, like Howard Mumford Jones, Kenneth Murdock, C. J. Friedrich, Harry Murray, or the senior Arthur Schlesinger. For me, they were on the roster of what the British call "the great and the good." And had it been England, they, like my later friends Alan Bullock, John Maud and Asa Briggs, would have landed up in the House of Lords. Just as well not. For there they were daily at the Faculty Club on Quincy Street, ready to talk—the hallmark of those times and that place. The Harvard Faculty Club had a "long table" in the style of the Athenaeum in London. Sit there and you might find talk with Bright Wilson about science policy, with Howard Jones about the roots of self-mockery in American humor, whatever. Today, I am told, it is where university administrators sit.

You did an enormous amount of dining out as well as lunching together at the Faculty Club in the Harvard of those postwar years. It gave a cohesion to Cambridge that was extraordinary for a period of such rapid growth, when new people and new enterprises might have overloaded the system and triggered withdrawal among the old-timers. That older generation took seriously (and gaily) its hostly duties: the Perry Millers, the Howard Joneses, the Harlow Shapleys, the John Coolidges, the George Walds—as they would have been known in those sexist days. There was also much departmental dining. I do not recall that the talk was "brilliant" or even particularly substantive in any scholarly sense. But it was lively, gossipy, "characterological" in a slightly malicious yet forgiving way, and rooted in the Harvard scene.

I recall George Kennan complaining during his visit to Oxford in the 1970s that he found the conversation at High Table at Merton rather trivial. Shortly after, I was at a dinner at Isaiah and Aline Berlin's elegant Headington House. It was in honor of Jacques Monod, who had just given a Herbert Spencer Lecture, and the company included such celebrated figures as John and Mary Warnock, Herbert and Jennifer Hart, Christopher Strachey, and the Hampshires. I cannot for the life of me recall one "serious" topic. The confrontation of Alan Bullock and Lord David Cecil, John Sparrow's dim view of his coming retirement from All Souls, the new French technique of controlling universities by dividing them and putting new ones out in the suburbs, the isolation of Dirac and Gödel, the fate of Oxford Girls' High School (of which Mary Warnock had been headmistress)—it was the clever ordinariness of dinner table talk that gave it its power to connect the Oxford community. Cleverness helps the ordinariness travel beyond the table, particularly wicked cleverness by admired outsiders. It was very much that way in the postwar years of Harvard. As when a distinguished English visitor to Cambridge said of President Pusey that he reminded him of the back of a spoon, or when C. P. Snow (while in town giving his "Two Cultures" lectures) said at a party in his honor at the Conants' that America was the most ideological country he knew, so much so that it had forever to hide behind a shield of pragmatism.

My academic youth ended with the retirement of Conant and Buck in 1953. It was "our" turn now.

I had found two kinds of "Fellows" in my college at the English Cambridge in 1955. There were the unworldly "locals," deeply and often fiercely involved in college affairs (often holding some office) and in "teaching" (by which word tutoring was intended). The others lived in a wider world—Britain or even beyond, though they too were scrupulous both to participate and to appear to participate in college business. Harvard, alas, has no place for locals. It is, as the ghastly aphorism has it, "up or out." It is astonishing that the policy did not breed more ill will than it did among the younger faculty, who were, so to speak, living on the block. Quite to the contrary, the younger faculty took a philosophical view of the matter—somewhat as in Russian roulette, "one in six." I think it may too have been a lucky by-product of the recruitment of the Harvard young: They were led to believe that they were appointed to their (in those days competitively paid) assistant professorships because they were the lords of creation. Some were. A good many others did not take much convincing. Besides, an early spell at Harvard was pretty good assurance that you would end up at Berkeley or Chapel Hill or Madison or Chicago—if not at Harvard.

I was past all that now. A new team was in office: Nathan Marsh Pusey and McGeorge Bundy in place of Conant and Buck. Pusey, I am sure, found me irksome—particularly after that Battle of the Chapel, which he lost and about which, over the years, he never uttered a single word to me, though we occasionally sat next to each other at official dinners. He was not an easy man to reach. I had known McGeorge for several years, first as our Head Tutor at Winthrop House, and later as a fellow member of the Friday evening Supper Club. As Dean of the Faculty of Arts and Sciences, he presided over the Committee on Educational Policy, the tiny and potentially very powerful body that does the faculty's planning and executing. McGeorge Bundy is not a man merely to decorate an office with his presence. He may have made some great mistakes (whether at Harvard, in Washington or at the Ford Foundation), but they were not for lack of doing what he thought was needed. Bundy was out to refresh the Harvard scene—particularly to cut down the exclusive jurisdictional power of the traditional departments over fields of scholarship. Harvard, he felt, was not growing enough interstices.

He put together a fresh Committee on Educational Policy, and asked me whether I would serve on it. (He described me once as an "amiable pirate" and maybe that was what got me signed on!) We succeeded and we failed—succeeded in setting up a rash of new interdisciplinary centers that subsequently brought great renown to the university, failed in being able to get faculty posts shifted from departments to centers, thereby condemning the latter to live ever after on "soft money." But that, again, is not what mattered. As with the earlier days, it was the lively spirit the committee engendered that made the difference. It was the early 1960s, the greatest period in educational expansion in our history, and the time was indeed ripe for reexamining how to institutionalize new domains of scholarship: "regional" studies like the Russian Research Center, which could bring to a single table the politics, economics, culture and literature of a nation state; the Center for Cognitive Studies, a new pattern of collaboration that was to spread to a dozen or so other universities for the study of knowledge-acquiring and knowledge-using processes; a center for the study of urban affairs and the life of great cities; and so on.

University departments in the classical mold are, I suppose, a necessary evil. I remember the passionate Pitirim Sorokin, upon failing to get some proposal through a department meeting in Social Relations in the mid-fifties, complaining in his rich Russian accent, "Correspondingly, if this were a music department, we would vote against appointing Wolfgang Amadeus Mozart as a member." It was William James who remarked in his *Principles* that habits develop a dynamism of their own. A department, after a few decades of operation, becomes a collection of dynamic habits. It is inconceivable that there not now be a course in Reaction Time with somebody to teach it if there has always been a course in Reaction Time with somebody to teach it. And conversely, if there has never been one on Culture and Mind, you would have to fight against raised eyebrows to get it listed and considerably more fiercely to get an appointment of somebody to teach it. That is why issues like the teaching of General Education and the establishment of "centers" are such valuable prods to consciousness.

I asked McGeorge Bundy many years later whether our "revisionist" Committee on Educational Policy might have followed a different course. Its major fault, he said, was that it hadn't gone far enough when the opportunity was ripe. I'm inclined to agree with him.

Harvard under Nathan Marsh Pusey was bound to get into trouble in the years of discord that attended the civil rights movement and the protests over the Vietnam War. He had started so well, armed with a reputation of having stood up to McCarthy at Appleton College in Wisconsin. But he lacked the qualities of a happy warrior. He did not make friends in the Faculty of Arts and Sciences, and responded by withdrawing. He never knew the art of first trying out his ideas informally and playfully, and then touching base with those who might be affected. Stubborn, isolated, and I think lacking in a vision of what Harvard might be in the new era of protest and redefinition, he drew around him not men of vision but his deans and administrators, many of whom, though able men and women, were, in their administrative roles, the President's men.

When 1968 and the disruptions arrived, the university under

Pusey was not in a strong position to cope with the shocks that were in store. The scenario was the familiar one. Sit-ins against the Dow Chemical recruiters, or against deans or committees that had disciplined the sitters-in, marches through the Yard, mill-ins in University Hall. It was a dreary procession of events, and the university soon became divided into "caucuses," the liberal and the conservative. Predictably, University Hall was duly occupied, on April 9, 1969, by students led by activists of the SDS, of whom Seymour Martin Lipset has written so well, the gifted young of middle-class professional families with liberal leanings.

Pusey, isolated from his faculty and from the counsels of moderation that he would surely have received from the leaders of either caucus, consulted his deans and then overreacted. He called in the police—the Cambridge and Boston police and the police of the ring of towns around Cambridge, who have traditionally been hostile to what they have always seen as the overprivileged, indulged students of Harvard. At five in the morning on April 10, the police entered University Hall. "They came in swinging," one of my students told me. At the University Health Service, the Cambridge city hospital and Mount Auburn, forty-eight people were treated for injuries after the Bust, five of them policemen. A strike was inevitable, and it came.

The manifest issue that had rallied students to occupy University Hall was the presence of ROTC at Harvard. It was an issue that also divided the faculty. Its settlement was, in fact, not difficult to bring about, and Paul Doty representing the conservative caucus and I the liberal managed by April 17 to put together a resolution that was acceptable to the faculty by a vote of 328 to 25 and that we knew in advance would be acceptable to the Harvard Corporation, the university's trustees. For when Doty and I had finally agreed upon a compromise draft that placed ROTC in the status of an ordinary extracurricular activity with no special privileges, we were able to get an unofficial agreement from Hugh Calkins and Keith Kane, the two corporation members who were standing by during the troubles. That was not particularly remarkable. What was remarkable, rather, was that it had not happened before, that the ROTC issue had been allowed to drag on and to fester.

Doubtless, had there been no ROTC issue, the determined leaders of the uprising would have found another. But that was surely not the point either. What had happened was that Harvard through its

leadership had behaved so woodenly and insensitively that one crisis
had been allowed to turn into another, bigger crisis and that into yet
a bigger one. From demonstration to little occupation, from little
occupation to big occupation, from big occupation to bust, from bust
to strike. It was not that we were the first to have traveled down that
road; there were the lessons of Columbia and of Berkeley, and Ar-
chibald Cox, the gifted lawyer, had been given the job of keeping a
brief on the options. I do not know whether Pusey consulted him
before calling in the police. The "official" account that appeared in
the special issue of *Harvard Today,* dated May 1, 1969, says only:

> After being ejected, the deans had regrouped at President Pusey's house
> at 17 Quincy Street. Under a long-standing contingency plan, Mr. Pusey had
> convened a meeting of the Executive Council, an advisory body that in-
> cluded the President of Radcliffe and the deans of the ten faculties of the
> University. At the same time, Deans Epps and Glimp were summoning the
> sixteen-man Administrative Board, consisting of deans and senior tutors, for
> a 1:30 meeting. The Nine House Masters were to meet at 3:00.
>
> During these consultations, Mr. Pusey was in telephone contact with
> members of the Corporation, and Dean Ford was drafting a statement to be
> delivered to the demonstrators. The intention was to give the demonstrators
> an ultimatum to leave the building by 4:30, after which the police would be
> called.

How had we slipped into the language of "regrouping" and "ulti-
matum"?

Perhaps the scenario was inevitable. I doubt it. For me, one of the
lessons was leadership. Pusey's was insensitive and impersonal, but
perhaps some of the blame rests with a faculty that could let him
become isolated, as an Israeli visitor put it to me, "on the basis of a
difference in style." "Style of leadership" is an evanescent thing. It
is a reciprocal affair. Nobody would doubt Pusey's uprightness and
fundamental decency. We used jokingly at the Project TROY sessions
at Elting Morison's to compare Yale's tribalism with Harvard's insti-
tutionalism. Yale was fortunate during its time of trouble to have a
"tribal" leader in Kingman Brewster. They even called him "The
King." It is not that the policies that were pursued at Harvard in the
late 1960s were "wrong" or that it is clear what the "right" policies
might have been. The Israeli (he was very shrewd) was probably at
the heart of the matter in singling out style. Was it Pusey's style or
the changing style of Harvard? Harvard, like the great state universities that Clark Kerr was writing about, was moving toward the "mul-

tiversity." It had lost its power to create mythic "university men" who could act as cicatrices to hold the institution together and take the issues in hand. Or perhaps it was not so much Harvard as the academic world—or just the unity of "culture." In any event, those were harsh and discouraging years in Cambridge.

I had spent nineteen years there as a member of the faculty. The divisiveness that followed the bust was dreary. We had become "politicized" by the student uprising. Not that there were not distinguished scholars in abundance. But somehow they had become privatized. The era of Great Men, of the exemplary figures, was over.

Psychology at Harvard, like psychology across the land, had fallen into a set of specialties, and Harvard had its share of brilliant practitioners of most of them. But again, the forces at work were mostly centrifugal. The unifying idea of "social relations" or of "cognitive studies" had not succeeded. Pusey, I think, had never had much stomach for the behavioral sciences; he found us quarrelsome and demanding and, I suspect, rather distasteful in style of work. Bok, who succeeded Pusey, though much more appreciative of both substance and style (he had done excellent work in labor negotiation and appreciated the dark sources of both human folly and wisdom), was devoted to noninterference as a policy. We psychologists (and our near neighbors) were endlessly involved in figuring out how to carve up and resplice our discipline. I was asked, in effect, to disband the Center for Cognitive Studies—by the Dean—so that we might have a more orderly, departmental structure. The times were not inspiring.

Late one afternoon in the winter of 1970, I received a transatlantic telephone call from Larry Weisskrantz at Oxford, asking whether I would be interested in the new Watts Professorship of Psychology that had been established there. Would I come over for a visit to discuss it? It was quite out of the blue. I phoned I. A. Richards, not only because he was a trusted friend and a wise man, but because I thought he would have a particularly sensitive feel for the Anglo-American "connection." With not a flicker of doubt, he urged me to have a look: "You must go." So off I went.

Oxford was an attractive alternative. It would have taken more than my seven years there to understand what makes it run as well as it does, and, I think, much more Englishness than I would ever want to achieve. Its charm and its courtesies are irresistible. There is a recent volume of pieces edited by Jan Morris, *The Oxford Book*

of Oxford, a charming hodgepodge of ambivalences. It is a particularly unsettling place for Americans in residence, Oxford. Within a
decade of each other, Ralph Waldo Emerson could write of it that it
was "rare, precarious, eccentric, and darkling," and his fellow New
Englander Nathaniel Hawthorne, "The world, surely, has not another place like Oxford: it is a despair ever to see such a place and
then to leave it." Gibbon, Southey and Alphonse Daudet hated it.
Max Beerbohm said, "I was a modest, good-humoured boy. It is
Oxford that has made me insufferable." And it would indeed have to
have been Henry James who called it "the finest place in England."
I have never met anybody who studied there or taught there who
was able indifferently to take it in his stride. It is preoccupying,
inspiring, hatefully parochial, delightful, welcoming and monumen-
tally snobbish.

The fact is, one realizes after a few years, there is no Oxford, only
Oxfords. Its complexities and privacies are so entrenched that established members of the place may each live in a world that overlaps
only slightly with the Oxford of somebody a hundred yards away. It
is not only Christ Church and, say, Nuffield. C. S. Lewis wrote of his
Oxford, where he long resided: "It brings home to one how little I
know of Oxford."

But if ever there was a *university,* with the singularity that the
word implies, Oxford is surely it. Even if it is made up of many
Oxfords. What was it like being a professor there? It bears no single
answer. What turf are you on? There are many, each with a wall. You
are mistaken if you think Oxford is quaint. You miss the point if you
let your eye run that course. For its dons (and for most of its undergraduates as well) it is tautly serious, its episodic gaiety notwithstand-
ing. It is judgmental, hierarchical and unforgiving. By comparison,
Harvard is uncorseted.

It marks you. Once you are on the scene, you understand why
Gilbert Ryle, in *Concept of Mind,* is so preoccupied with the category error. Oxford is the boot camp and the advanced training center
in that form of linguistic snare. This one is a "high flier," that one a
member of the Hebdomadal Council, the other "stroppy." But the
labels are, as linguists say, context sensitive. College was one context,
my Department another, and the idealized Oxford that emerges in
summaries still another.

Oxford idealized is indeed, as John Locke is alleged to have said,
an idea in the mind of God. It exists just as surely as the Harvard of

idealized figures existed in the late 1930s, but with a different source of legitimization. Style and accomplishment are what marked the Walter Cannons and Ralph Barton Perrys of my early Harvard days. But while style is of the essence in the Oxford scene, accomplishment is rather more mystical. It has to do with individuality (even eccentricity) that is at once personal and communal. Take the memory of Maurice Bowra as a case in point. He was remembered as the Master of Wadham, as a conversationalist and controversialist who excited undergraduate imaginations by his attentions, his waspish wit and his bravura homosexuality. Of the Establishment, he was nonetheless famous for flouting it. His accomplishment was not negligible as a scholar—he was a competent enough classicist all right—but it was as a human being who explored to the limits, yet with decorum, the possibilities of being his own eccentric self that he excelled. The books in his honor—one of which, a collection by those who touched him, was published during my stay in Oxford—these books were offerings to his unique personalness. So were the stories, like that of his reaction upon hearing that a certain male philosopher and female novelist were having an affair: "Very good. They will suit each other. I've slept with both of them."

There were "greats" in the Oxford at which I arrived—some living and some, like Bowra, of recent memory. Philosophers particularly have a strong grip on the Oxford imagination. I do not think it is their cleverness that accounts for the thralldom they create. More likely it is the upper-class bias against specialization. The gentleman is not a specialist but clever, clever enough indeed to keep the specialist in his place. I think this may also be partly at the bottom of the antimetaphysical, even antispeculative character of British philosophy. It must be sensible, not carried too far aloft. Critical cleverness is the hallmark. Empiricism, sense data theory and, latterly, "ordinary language" philosophy and "how to get things done with words." The philosophers of my generation at Oxford included among them such masterful practitioners of these arts as Freddy Ayer, Stuart Hampshire, Gilbert Ryle and, above all, John Austin. (I do not include Isaiah Berlin in this dispensation; he is a special figure, whose influence was no less enthralling, but different.)

The clever Oxford undergraduate (as any clever Oxford undergraduate will tell you) can muster something "interesting" to say on virtually any subject. The acme of this aspiration is the Oxford philosopher, who, by his general and critical sense of the nature of things, can make any specialist quake, scientist or otherwise. What other university in the world joins by hyphenation so many disciplines of learning with philosophy as fit subjects to be "read" by undergraduates? Indeed, there were even two routes by which one could read psychology: through PPP (Philosophy, Psychology and Physiology) or simply through EP (Experimental Psychology). I sensed our PPP papers were cleverer (though not better) than those written by the EP candidates. In any case, there is no college in Oxford that, to the best of my knowledge, does without a philosopher on its tutorial staff. And it is hard to imagine any nation in the world that could mount a chat program like Brian McGhee's on the BBC, the host spending the better part of an hour in prime time just talking with the likes of Ayer, Hampshire, Berlin, Michael Dummett, Charles Taylor—and even three Americans, John Searle (who inherited his mantle from John Austin), "Van" Quine (who is revered there, as elsewhere, as the best logician in the business) and Noam Chomsky. Philosophy at Oxford consists in being boldly clever without being tediously detailed. And of course, it steers clear of either speculative flight or tendentiousness. Not a French "deconstructionist" or a German phenomenologist in that BBC parade! Their cool spokesmen on the British scene were Taylor (a Canadian) and the puckish Tony Quinton, a man of enormous wit and charm who can make Habermas and the Frankfurt school witty and clear for the British ear and who, besides, is a first-class philosopher off his own bat.

So the brilliant crew of Oxford philosophers dominates the Oxford intellectual scene in a way that their equally gifted Harvard opposite numbers have not done since the days of Royce, James and Santayana. Many will claim (in and out of Oxford) that the team fielded in Cambridge, Massachusetts, could run circles around their colleagues in Merton Street: Rawls, Putnam, Quine, Nozick, Cavell would under other circumstances be most suitable for the Queen's Birthday Honours List!

Purity and intellectual impeccability, those are the ideals—no matter what eccentricities may embellish or, indeed, obscure them. Gilbert Ryle was a case in point, a man of penetrating analytic skill, astonishingly and outspokenly lacking in knowledge of or any evident sensitivity for the arts. He was celebrated for having answered all correspondence about articles submitted to the journal *Mind*, which he edited, on the backs of the letters submitting them. The confusions created, particularly after his death in 1976, were a source of much amused delight. Charity toward the great was one of the gentler sides of Oxford—and a part of the mythopoeia that burnishes Oxford greatness to its mirrorlike brilliance.

It was my good fortune to be at Wolfson College while it was presided over by Isaiah Berlin. There is surely no man of his generation who so combined human kindness with sharpness of wit. He must have been blessed by a magic childhood, for his old friends from St. Paul's and from Oxford undergraduate days testify that he has always combined the two graces. I recall my first College Meeting: a rainy day, a stuffy room, the fellows in a rather graceless "picky" mood. The topics were appalling. One of them had to do with duvets versus blankets in the new halls of residence under construction. Our President could not have been more gracious, more fair-minded in hearing all sides of every issue. We walked out together afterward and I murmured something about the meeting having been a bit surprising in its detail. "The first rule is that no subject is too small to be on the agenda. All else follows."

Isaiah Berlin epitomizes contemporary Oxford in some extraordinary way. His kindness, one might say, is legendary. But that is not right, for it is in fact, as I have reason to know, both real and prodigious. His judgment of character and events is profound and impartial, yet he is a man of passionate opinions and values. For all the penetrating quality of his judgment of people, he remains perpetually an appreciator. His book of "portraits" of his friends (*Personal Impressions*), as one reviewer put it, combines a reasoned hero worship with a perceptiveness for human foibles that forever challenges the beholder's imagination.

By any system of accounting, Berlin should be an "outsider" on the Oxford scene: a Jew, a Zionist, singularly un-English in appearance. He is nonetheless an insider's insider—formerly head of a house, fellow of All Souls, president of the British Academy, revered for his wisdom and trustworthiness as a counselor. His philosophy, moreover, never ran the risk of what Iris Murdoch once called, in a celebrated essay, "the dangers of dryness." He writes on the philosophy of history, on Vico and Machiavelli and Herder, and does so with a gusto for moral substance and historical relevance. It is not about logic, not about language. Another anomaly: Morally engaged though he patently is and has always been, he talks with an amused detachment and even gossipiness about the very matters that one knows him to care about deeply. His gossip—it is always parentheti-

cal to the topic at hand—is vivid and totally without malice: illumina-
tions. He told me once that he abhors silence as nature abhors a
vacuum. His concision is such as to make his ordinary comments
seems like *mots*. Of a visiting American colleague after a lecture on
the subject of psychology: "Clever, clever. Nothing has happened in
the last three hundred years." Or of the fractured Russian of the
Eugen Onegin being sung by an English opera company: "Speechless."

How can one know how a culture reads its texts and negotiates
its heroes, especially a culture so complex and veined as Oxford is?
Had I to choose a single figure who somehow contains Oxford's
ideals, its contradictions, and above all its wishes for redemption, it
would be Isaiah Berlin. When I accepted the Watts Professorship, I
received a four-word cablegram: HOORAY HOORAY HOORAY, ISAIAH.

Yet, along with the familism and focus of the place, Oxford can
produce the most appalling myopias. A distinguished professor of
literature, encountered at tea one day, had never until that moment
heard of Professor Tinbergen, though they had inhabited the place
jointly for fifteen years. She was pleased to learn that he had just won
a Nobel Prize. The Regius Professor of History proposed Mr. Bhutto,
the Prime Minister of Pakistan, for an honorary degree while Bhutto
was still under suspicion of having murdered opposition leaders in a
recent coup. In one of those rare instances where Congregation
acted on a political matter, the proposal, already endorsed by the
Hebdomadal Council, was rejected. Bhutto had been at Christ
Church as an undergraduate, as had the Regius Professor. The
proposers were indignant!

Yet when students (led by an International Marxist Maoist faction
in support of a student union of the fun-and-games variety, of all
things) occupied the Indian Institute, where some university offices
were then situated, the potentially nasty situation was brought to a
close when, after a few days of it, the ladies and slightly aging gentle-
men whose offices were occupied marched in and drove them out
armed with nothing more than furled umbrellas—accompanied un-
glamorously by their chief administrative officer, the Registrar. It
should not be thought, however, that this "bust" was unplanned. It
was a far cry from the Harvard one!

I was not a part of Old Oxford. Wolfson was a most definitely new
(though greatly admired) college for graduate students. I lunched
one day in London in 1975 with McGeorge Bundy and Lord Zucker-

man, on the occasion of a CIBA Foundation anniversary celebration at which I was to receive their annual Gold Medal for Research. My companions at the table were symbolic: one of them, Bundy, as President of the Ford Foundation, had given a founding grant to Wolfson College; the other had advised Sir Isaac Wolfson against doing the same. Fortunately, Sir Isaac had ignored Zuckerman's advice and given both his name and a small fortune to the college. It was said at the time that Zuckerman had never forgiven Oxford for not appointing him to a chair in zoology, but I doubt it. In any case, Bundy and Zuckerman had a history of being on opposite sides of issues. When Bundy was President Kennedy's National Security Advisor, they had clashed over the issue of whether Britain should develop a medium-range missile, and the gossip of those days was that it had been a bitter confrontation. But that day in London, they seemed to be on the best "Solly and Mac" terms. They were both full of curiosity about Wolfson and were pumping me about the college.

I was delighted to tell them how well the place worked. For the first time, research (graduate) students had a foundation of their own. Up to that time, research students had been relegated to a kind of second-class status in Oxford colleges, as members of the "middle common room." Hugh Lloyd-Jones, the Regius Professor of Greek, had said to me shortly after I arrived in Oxford that to understand the traditional spirit of the place you should know the equations: "college, undergraduate, tutorial, don: good; university, department, research student, professor: bad." The founding of Wolfson (and of Linacre College) in the 1960s had marked a turning of the tide.

Isaiah Berlin (and a small band of co-conspirators) had planned a great leap forward into the twentieth century. The college was to be formed not in the old monastic tradition (fellows of colleges had been required to be bachelors until late in the nineteenth century), but would have quadrangles for married students and dons and their families. (The children of the college, once it came to be real, were extraordinarily well-mannered, even at Saturday lunches, when they were admitted in the company of parents to hall.) There was some sort of unofficial "two-thirds" rule. We were two-thirds men, one-third women; two-thirds scientists, one-third others; two-thirds United Kingdom, one-third overseas. There was one common room: no junior, middle or senior ones. There was no high table. Save for feast nights, service was cafeteria. The table was excellent and the assistant chef rowed (most expertly) in the college eight. I lunched in college nearly daily, and with great pleasure, for I became fast friends not only with a number of dons there, but with a fair number of our research students—an art historian, some biologists, several of our young psychologists, a classicist or two. I do not recall in those years ever lunching or dining in college without finding some pleasure in the experience. The table was lively, the "side" minimal, and backbiting almost totally absent.

I have no doubt whatever that this happy weather was enormously abetted by the wit and sympathy of Isaiah Berlin and the dedicated little band of college officers he brought along with him. Isaiah was not often in college, for he had many other duties. But it was the rare day when one did not see the Vice-President, the Domestic Bursar, the Senior Tutor and the other officers of the college at lunch. It was at lunch or in the relaxed atmosphere of the common room over coffee that much of the college's business got transacted —or, more accurately, done lightly, so that it rarely had to become heavy business for the Governing Body.

The student members of the college knew they were part of something special in Oxford. They were responsive to it. Ruth Padel, a delightful and spirited poet-classicist, daughter of a London psychoanalyst, writing a thesis on "the wound" in classic antiquity. Or Henry Hardy, would-be publisher and editor of Isaiah Berlin's papers, son of a West Country doctor, whom one might have expected to have written with a quill pen and who yet wrote a delightful and perceptive piece in the *Times Literary Supplement* on the joys of the word processor for the literary man. One sensed they took Wolfson quite as seriously as did our most senior officers.

However powerful an institution may be, even one designed to transform old environments like Oxford's cannot, in a deep sense, resist the internal logic of the place. Hugh Lloyd-Jones was not making idle chatter. The "old" colleges make their tutorial appointments, create their fellows to look after the teaching needs of their students. That means, of course, the *traditional* teaching needs— philosophy, languages and literature, classics, mathematics, politics and economics (the last two elements of the renowned PPE of "Philosophy, Politics and Economics," introduced by G. D. H. Cole after the First World War to train a new generation of prime ministers and cabinet members as varied as Harold Wilson, Edward Heath and Tony Crosland, whose grandfathers almost certainly, had they been at Oxford, which they most surely had not, would have read "Greats" in the original Greek and Latin). At Oxford (as at Harvard), the sciences do not "teach" much. In place of tutorials, they have "labs." Colleges do not need many science tutors. Nor, in the main, do they want to commit either support or funds to what are seen as new, "upstart" fields like psychology, sociology, geography or even anthropology, which do not have large enrollments. Besides, and for reasons that reflect the English passion for imposing hierarchies, the behavioral sciences are seen as "soft options" trading in barbarous neologisms.

Given that set of biasing constraints, it was inevitable that many scientists and many of the practioners of the "soft options" would not find places in Oxford colleges. At Cambridge University, where the sciences had grown earlier and faster, this had been taken for granted and "compensated" by the creation of a University Common Room, where, if fellowship was not assured, at least one could take lunch. At Oxford, there is a principle of "entitlement"—each and every member of the university is entitled to a place in a college. With the steady growth of the sciences and the newer social studies, it was inevitable that there would be no places for them in the colleges. And so, in recent times, new colleges were founded to accommodate them—St. Anthony's for regional and more specialized policy studies, Nuffield for the new extensions of politics and economics, and (finally) Linacre and Wolfson.

So our fellows were, so to speak, structurally determined. We were two-thirds scientists and, predictably, we were a numerous body—some sixty fellows, which is double the number of a well-off older college, such as Brasenose or Oriel. And many of the fellows, besides, had been "passed over" and had not been college fellows before. We, again predictably, had a generous share of senior psychologists—my own professorial Fellowship, as well as ones held by Donald Broadbent (for those years, the only psychologist Fellow of the Royal Society) and Michael Argyle, one of Britain's best-known social psychologists. I should make it clear that a fellowship in Wolfson carries dining privileges and other graceful perquisites, but no stipend—in contrast to a tutorial fellowship in a wealthy traditional college, which may carry, in effect, a higher stipend than one's university lectureship.

There are, I suppose, two ways of responding when, at last, you become a fellow of a new college after years of having been passed over. You may now become like all the others, and perhaps even more so. Or you may seize the opportunity of the newness of your college to explore the limits of the changes you might ring.

Academic institutions are, for all the security of tenure with which they endow their members, curiously conservative places when it comes to formal decisions about how they should be governed. Our college meetings were generally humdrum and gray. For all the liveliness of Wolfson's informal life, the venturesomeness of the fellows, assembled in meeting, was in very short supply. In the main, being of Oxford, we behaved Oxford. Exploration of new fields of endeavor? I suppose it was typical that when Roy Harris, the newly appointed Professor of General Linguistics and a fellow of Worcester, and I proposed setting up a fellowship in Communication Studies (for which we offered to raise the money), we were not so much turned down as instructed that the field was too vague, too broad, too likely to be trendy, and that it would be more to the liking of the Committee on Academic Affairs if the appointment specified either the philosophy of language or some aspect of linguistics related to a particular language stock. Both those fields of study, ironically, were overrepresented in the Oxford of the 1970s, where at least eight in ten college tutors in philosophy would have ticked the philosophy of language as one of their specialties.

Wolfson's moment of tension came in 1975, when Isaiah Berlin was to retire from the presidency. Who would replace his magic touch? I suspect Isaiah had taken the presidency partly out of a sense of duty to help build a more fruitful Oxford and partly because he believed there was some deeper intellectual honesty to be found among scientists, which he as a humanist could help insinuate into the collegiate life of Oxford. That is not a trivial problem, even in the Oxford of today. For it was no happenstance that a distinguished professor of literature, on that occasion at Dick Ellman's house, had never heard of Niko Tinbergen, though he had just won a Nobel Prize. Indeed, I was elected a member of the Ashmolean Club shortly after my arrival in Oxford, to discover that it had been founded in the last quarter of the nineteenth century, following the famous Huxley-Wilberforce debate, to prevent a recurrence of any further bitterness between scientists and the rest of the university. We were about a dozen scientists and an equal number of college heads, and we dined together once a term, rotating colleges. They were most affable and excellent dinners—good company, good talk, and that sumptuous style of eating and drinking reserved for college feasts which so enrages zealots of the far Left. In honor of its origins, I offer a most amusing dinner conversation with Isaiah Berlin, Harry Fisher and William Hayter, in which we all agreed that the Devil was by all odds the most interesting figure in either the New or the Old Testament—certainly the liveliest mind to be encountered in the Bible (as Milton would have agreed, I think, having reread Book IV of his *Paradise Lost* to check). In any case, if the Ashmolean Club had a function, however muted, then the next president of Wolfson, as head of a houseful of scientists, certainly had one.

It was a bit like *The Masters,* C. P. Snow's novel of the changing of the guard at a Cambridge college, and there were moments during our proceedings when I had not a doubt about Oscar Wilde's dictum about life imitating art. There was the classic "insider-outsider" split; our vice-president, Michael Brock (later to be the master of Nuffield College), was the insider. I found myself in a "caucus" trying to find other suitable candidates to put into the running. It was astonishing to me how many distinguished scientists, scholars and men of affairs would jump at the opportunity to become the head of an Oxford college! And equally astonishing how passionate the opposition could be. Our caucus had dined a distinguished scientist at another university, a very attractive candidate, it had seemed to me. Within two days (how the "feeler" dinner had become known so quickly seemed astonishing), I received a phone call from a law don at the college where our putative candidate had once, years before, served as a fellow. "You are making a dreadful mistake, I can assure you, Jerry." His objections were based on the man's reputation in college twenty years before.

The "outside" candidate, as it turned out, was Sir Henry Fisher, a former judge of the High Court who had resigned from the bench when he found that it was not intellectually challenging enough to one who had not as much judicial temperament as he had originally supposed he had. His resignation had caused eyebrows to be raised among some jurists, who felt it had denigrated the bench. But Harry Fisher had always been of independent mind and one to cause an eyebrow or two to be raised. Son of Sir Geoffrey Fisher, Archbishop of Canterbury, he had fallen in love with and then married a Roman Catholic. A restless spirit with a lively curiosity, he had made enemies, it seemed, during his later years at Oxford, when he had served as Estates Bursar of All Souls, the fellow in charge of college finances. I was dispatched to find out what *that* was all about, and I consulted my friends who had been about during that period.

There had been a lively debate at All Souls over a proposal to create a half-dozen or more science fellowships in the college. All Souls is a uniquely English phenomenon: a collection of distinguished scholars leavened by young Prize Fellows, who gain their term membership by one of the fiercest competitive examinations set anywhere in the Western world. To this mix is added the most esteemed of the "great and the good," plus a sprinkling of such figures as, say, the editor of *The Times,* along with other powerful mandarins of the establishment. On the face of it, it would have seemed the most natural thing in the world to add a sprinkling of science fellows. John Sparrow, the altogether unique and curmudgeonly warden, was opposed. He pleaded a shortage of financial resources. Harry Fisher, in his capacity as estates bursar, is alleged to have taken the floor and urged that the college (which, of course, is enormously wealthy) would do well to sell some of its silver rather than let the proposed fellowships go by the board. Sparrow had regarded this as a disgraceful and light-minded suggestion and had not forgiven Fisher.

The more I heard, the better I liked Fisher. But the college was divided, for Michael Brock was a deserving candidate, with many friends. What was so typical, I discovered later, was the shape of the suspicion toward such an "outsider" as Fisher. Would he be enough of a "college man"? Would he be drawn off into affairs of state, into quasi-judicial assignments? English academic debate is much more abrasive than its American counterpart. I remember Eka Kantorowicz, the distinguished historian at the Institute for Advanced Study, saying to me that manners in America had known no equal since the Versailles Court of *Le Roi Soleil.* I recalled that remark during the debate leading to an electoral vote in college. Fisher was elected.

He was an excellent president: well informed, patient enough, intelligent. I had asked Isaiah Berlin jokingly before the election what sort of man should succeed him. "He should be tall, blond and a bird-watcher." None of those, Harry Fisher was still sufficiently different to survive comparisons with his predecessor. Yet how curious is the college parochialism of Oxford! Whereas Isaiah Berlin was, as I have already mentioned, deeply engrossed in university and national affairs and often absent from college, I never once heard a breath of criticism for it. Harry Fisher, though more often in evidence, was often criticized for "being away," though his absences were by no means outside the range of the public interest—ironing out the issue of false arrest and maltreatment, undoing the tangles of EEC regulations when they conflicted with national statutes, and the like. There is a chemistry of local loyalty in Oxford colleges that I have never understood—no more in my own college than in Worcester, where I witnessed the same suspicion and even resentment of my friend Asa Briggs when he became provost there after retiring as Vice-Chancellor of Sussex University. The balance of parish and nation (so precious in Oxbridge colleges) turns out in practice to be a very delicate one indeed—easily distorted by envy, by traces of stale electoral debates in college, and by a bloody-mindedness that an English friend of mine characterized as the yang to the yin of English fair-mindedness.

I can only describe my department at Oxford as institutionally appalling! I have rarely seen an unhappier one. Its unhappiness was, I think, brewed from several bitter roots. For one, psychology is not much appreciated or admired in Britain, and certainly not much in Oxford. Up to my departure, only three British psychologists had ever been elected to the Royal Society, and none has ever been elected to the British Academy. There is, in consequence, more than a little self-hatred among British psychologists, and it is usually displaced into dismissiveness toward specialties down-market in rigor from one's own. Some British psychologists, indeed, are never so flattered as when taken for a physiologist or pharmacologist or geneticist. This curious turn of mind reflects, I think, the "soft option" verdict of many other scientists in the university. It may, historically, be an echo of the hopeless struggle of psychology to fight free of philosophy, to achieve a unique "methodology" untainted by philosophical presuppositions.

As a result, Oxford psychology of the 1970s was sadly compartmentalized, the emblem of that compartmentalization being the seating "plan" at eleven o'clock coffee each day. Here the "information processors," there the "brain and behavior" group, in that other corner the social psychologists, in between the developmentalists. It can readily be said of Oxford that it is greater than the sum of its colleges. Of the Department of Experimental Psychology (about which the adjective speaks volumes), it could be said in those days that the whole was less than the sum of its parts. The individuals were often stars—like Jeffrey Gray, Donald Broadbent, Ann Triesman and Peter Bryant. Its members were fiercely hard-working, both as teachers and as researchers, but one had the strong impression that the atmosphere of criticism kept them prudently turned in on their own specialties.

Ironically, the one open season, when the task of psychology as a whole was discussed departmentally, was in 1976, and it was occasioned by my delivering a Herbert Spencer Lecture to the university. Its theme had grown out of my sense of the conflict between psychology and those of its neighboring disciplines that also purported to deal with the nature of man and of human action—the sciences of culture, like anthropology and linguistics, jurisprudence, etc. All those disciplines were premised in one way or another upon the social reality of human intentions and on human accountability as embodied in the reasons people give for their actions. Yet psychology, at least in its more positivist, "causal" garb, denies or ignores the role of intention in human action and treats reasons as symptomatic afterthoughts rather than, in any sense, as contributory. Still, the reasons people produce may make the difference between going to the gallows or going free.

The term following, a weekly departmental seminar was organized; my friends referred to it merrily as the "Bruner-bashing seminar." It was in the high English academic abrasive tradition. I never was much good at it. But at least the issues were aired.

My lecture duly appeared in the *TLS* and, if nothing else, it brought to the surface a good many of the tensions that had bedeviled the British psychological scene. My former student Ned Jones, by then a professor at Princeton, wrote to say he had enjoyed it but wasn't it, after all, slightly old hat! Well, in America and in France and Germany it was. But the idea of a "constituted reality" formed by the social negotiation of the meaning of action—that idea was either pure anathema to British psychological colleagues or it was their cup of pure nectar. Converting psychology into a cultural science was too much for the hard-nosed. A cause was a cause, as determined by the canons of science. Never mind the manner in which commonsense interpretations of behavior actually affected human action. *That* was not psychology.

Oxford can be a demanding place. Through four of my years there I had a steady and heavy spare-time occupation in addition to all else. I had been asked by the Social Science Research Council to lead a study commission examining the state of preschool education and care in Britain. So, in effect, I had my teaching, my research on the acquisition of speech acts in children, and the work on preschool care to look after. My chair, the Watts Professorship, was supposed to be a "nonadministering" professorship, in the sense of not having duties as head of a department. But that does not mean one stands back from involvement. Besides, I like the sense of having some hand in shaping events around me. I think that being in a foreign country strengthened that feeling. One feels less "foreign," being involved. I found college duties, on the whole, rewarding and (in some odd way) even instructive. I put in for the Domestic and Premises Committee at Wolfson! I am appallingly bad at keeping my *personal* domestic accounts and shamefully have left the job to others; but I thought that here would be a committee that would instruct me in the mysteries of how an Oxford college *really* runs. And so it did! Astonishingly well, economically, kindly. But departmental committees were, in the main, ritualistic and boring. They brought out the bureaucratic and the hostile in my colleagues to an astonishing degree. It is very difficult to paper over that much division. The bureaucratic side was a maze of departmental regulations and statutes that I found difficult to penetrate. I did not have enough of a firsthand sense of our undergraduate system to judge most of the changes that were proposed from time to time. That was, I suppose, inevitable. As for other matters, they too conformed to Isaiah Berlin's dictum of nothing being too small to discuss.

As a professor, I could (and did) lecture, but I did not "teach" in the Oxford sense. Professors do not tutor; to do so is to take bread from the mouths of babes. Tutoring is the prerogative of more junior members in their role as fellows of college or, on a piecework basis, filling in when a college had no psychologist fellow—which was the case for most colleges. The examinations—the "Prelims" at the end of first year or "Schools" at the end of the three-year course—are based on a syllabus and readings that are "covered" by tutorials. The lectures were, so to speak, an adjunct: once a week for the eight galloping weeks of an Oxford term, of which there are three, Michaelmas, Hilary and Trinity, dividing the academic year into thirds, with a few weeks off in between, save for the summer recess, "the long vac." It was a treat to lecture with no concern about examining students on the contents. The Oxford undergraduates I came to know were, on the whole, better prepared for university work than their American counterparts at Harvard. British secondary schools are far more demanding and hold their university-bound students to a standard demanded by the O-Levels and A-Levels—those bogeyman examinations around which the lives of middle-class families with teenagers revolve. English students, besides, have many more opportunities to write, and concision is demanded of them rather than expressiveness.

Oxford, like England, sorts into "classes." College tutors treat "Firsts" in much the same spirit as they might greet the news of a tidy little deed of gift left by a former scholar. You are "made" by a degree with First Class Honors. Within the last five years, I have dined out with friends in London who told me in advance of his arrival that one of my fellow guests had got a "First" at Oxford. I was expecting somebody considerably younger than the affable fifty-year-old to whom I was introduced. But while a "First" may give you an enormous running start and lift-off as a "high flier," failing to get one will certainly not break you. Margaret Thatcher, Harold Wilson, Edward Heath, Shirley Williams—all were solid "Seconds." You would probably do better in the Civil Service with a "First," but it would make one's common sense suspect in British politics. It has always astonished me how the English know about each other and in what standard terms—like their "degree." You might know of a Frenchman that he had been to one of the *Grandes Écoles* or of an American that he was a Harvard man or she a Bryn Mawr girl. But their degree? Was it the long struggle of the British middle class to find a substitute for the "breeding" of the gentry that led to its preoccupation with "cleverness" and/or qualifications? I remember my Nigerian friend Tom Lambo, while still a professor at the medical school at Lagos, lamenting the Anglicization of nursing qualifications: "I sometimes think they'd sooner see a patient die than have him looked after by somebody without qualifications."

On balance, looking back, I am glad to have spent that much of my life in universities. They enabled me to do the work I wanted to do and gave me a chance to teach—undergraduates and graduate students alike. By the ordinary standards, I have been a "successful" teacher: My classes have always been well attended and my former graduate students hold chairs at such suitable and far-flung places as St. Andrew's, Sydney, UCLA and Princeton. One young man, a charming political science graduate student, once took a Harvard "reading" course with me to "find out what psychology was all about." He ended up in the United States Congress, where, as Senator Proxmire, he has been a thorn in the side of the behavioral sciences ever since! But I find a certain wry pleasure in the absurdity of his attacking some of the projects dearest to the hearts of others who have studied with me. It speaks well for the open quality of our system.

The young Henry Adams, writing home from London, where he was serving as secretary to the Ambassador, his uncle, commented on the superiority of British life in cultivating individuality, even eccentricity. This applies as well today, and its universities are no exception. They are certainly more in the style of pressure cookers than ours are. Oxford is the prototype. The abiding peril of Oxford is that, as a system, it risks sacrificing the man to the boy. I have met too many full-grown men and women who have clung too long to the rancors, the conceits and the "cleverness" cultivated during their Oxford years. But at its best, Oxford can also kindle altruism, honest independence and a love of excellence that is enviable. Its principal vehicle is its fetish of individuality—the extraordinary man (or, now, woman). It conjures with its Freddy Ayers, Maurice Bowras, Hugh Trevor-Ropers, Alan Bullocks, John Sparrows, Isaiah Berlins.

Harvard rarely leaves so deep or so enduring a stamp on its students. When it achieves the intensity of a pressure cooker, it is through more "institutional" means, created more by peers than preceptors. Peter Jay, a former British ambassador in Washington, told me once of the impact of John Austin, the philosopher, as a tutor —his clarity, his pure intellectuality. Another commented on the pleasure and terror of reading his weekly essay to Lord David Cecil. At Harvard, it is far more likely to be the experience of being on the editorial board of the *Crimson*—and the abiding heroes there are *former* editors, like Franklin Delano Roosevelt and Robert Benchley. (The exception at Harvard is the man-of-letters-to-be; it was as likely that for a "History and Lit" student, F. O. Matthiessen or Perry Miller or Jack Bate or Harry Levin might have had a more "Oxford-like" influence on their tutees.)

Withal, there is a "corporate" rather than a familial or "clan" quality to Harvard. It stresses its instrumental role in the climb to success in a way Oxford does not. "Returning" to Harvard later as a nonacademic can be done, really, by only one route: to stand for election to the Board of Overseers. But, again, that is an elective office and one's success depends upon the favor of one's peers, not one's professors. It is a corporate role that one fulfills as an Overseer, however good a "club" the Board may also be. At Oxford, unusual meritoriousness (in virtually any walk of life) is rewarded by being elected (by one's former teachers) as a Supernumerary Fellow of one's old college or, if one is a perduring high flier, by being elected to All Souls. Even American "old boys" are not forgotten—as when John Brademas, formerly a U.S. Congressman and now President of New York University, was elected a Fellow of Brasenose, where he had been a Rhodes scholar years before. Harvard, for all its corporateness, has never enjoyed an assured place in the political sun comparable to Oxford's—speaking now of students, not faculty. Every Prime Minister of Britain since the war, save two, has been an Oxford graduate. Only one President since the war has been a Harvard man.

Yet the hermetic "verticality" of the British system is as likely to be its undoing as it is its source of excellence. Harvard's faculty, whose distinction easily outshines Oxford's, has a closer connection with the conduct of the state. The Kennedy Center, I suspect, is a far more effective channel into the political life of America than are the occasional dinners at All Souls or the columns of *The Observer* and the *Sunday Times* where the clever ones air their views. But at that, I am not sure. Oxford's power in the public as in the private domain is through its style. Harvard's is through generating new and powerful (and doubtless, sometimes wrong) ideas. Harvard, in consequence, cannot abide the local, the interestingly eccentric. It is "up or out." Oxford *still* cannot quite abide the world-famous "professor" unless he can be given a local identity and a local function.

It is characteristic of learning a second language that you begin by continuing to think and speak to yourself in the first, and then translate into the second. After a while, you can think and speak in the second, though it is easy to switch back and forth and to "check by translation." Finally, you think and speak in one *or* the other, and translating becomes difficult and, for some, even painful. Going from Harvard to Oxford was much that way. I have, for better or for worse, become bilingual. It is, as the linguist de Saussure urged, structural, not comparative. You cannot translate "term for term." You could no more translate Oxford "proctor" westward than you could translate Harvard "dean of students" eastward. The two ways of life, like Wittgenstein's language games, generate their own ways of talking and, in the end, their ways of thinking.

I had originally gone to Oxford, attracted to a new start in a new setting, wearied of the familiar outlines of Harvard's political squabbles and of the back-and-forth of the behavioral sciences there. Oxford in some ways was bound to be a pig in a poke: I did not know it well and, in some respects, found its preciousness more than a little offputting. As it turned out, the gamble worked well, personally and in terms of getting on with my work. I was spared some of the bureaucracy by dint of having come there on the understanding that my chair was a "nonadministrative" one. And I very soon found colleagues with whom I shared my interests—inside my department, but more often outside. The only person there whom I had known well before I came was Donald Broadbent, a friend from days in Cambridge.

But it did not take long, and I soon found that I shared many matters in common with the philosophers in Merton Street, notably Rom Harré, Charles Taylor, Tony Kenny and Jonathan Cohen. I regularly attended the meetings of the Oxford Philosophical Society (of which I became a member) and watched with fascination the exquisite counterpoint of Oxford philosophical debate. It makes an interesting evening of talk, having Ayer, Dummett, Strawson, Hampshire, Hare and such younger lions as Gareth Evans mix it up over issues in the philosophy of language—the Oxford preoccupation. It was grist for my mill, for my own research on language acquisition.

I had a superb group of research students. What I cherished most about them as a group was the happy (and workable) blend of philosophical and psychological interests that shaped our debates, our "in-jokes" and their research. I think I can give some of the flavor with a few thumbnail sketches. John Churcher was very much out of an Oxford undergraduate mold: passionate in the abstract distinctions he thought obligatory, intolerant of intellectual compromise, immensely self-critical. Churcher eventually abandoned altogether the idea of working for a higher degree, on grounds that it would be too compromising to the natural growth of his own ideas, which centered principally on the nature of concepts of space and direction. Fortunately, he can continue with his teaching and research in Britain without a D.Phil., and has done so. Alan Leslie, a young Scot, was preoccupied (as so many young Scottish intellectuals are) with the intellectual inheritance of David Hume and, as it turned out, he did his thesis in refutation of Hume's proposal that causality was a category that grew out of experience. Indeed, he found that infants of a few months of age seem to respond to displays of "apparent causality" in much the same way as adults. Roy Pea, an American Rhodes scholar, had come equipped with an astonishing background in philosophy and linguistics. His style was elegant but rather American in its vigorous systematicness. He ended up writing a handsome thesis on the course of development of negation in infant speech, from practical opposition to the proper abstract negation of propositional content. He too managed to extract from a technical philosophical problem a quite testable empirical hypothesis. Alison Gopnik had come to the group from McGill, her letters of recommendation urging us to take her in the department at Oxford on grounds that she had taken everything available at McGill in linguistics, philosophy and psychology. She arrived an unreconstructed Chomskian, departed a disciple of Vygotsky, but with a thesis demonstrating that some of the infant's initial relational language was developed not for communication (as Vygotsky says) but as an aid for sorting out his thought processes. They were typical of the more abstract wing of our "LAG"—the Language Acquisition Group, as our group referred to themselves and to the unofficial seminars we held each Friday lunchtime. But there was an equally interesting countervailing empiricist wing, also varied in origin.

Michael Scaife was a good case in point. He had come to me as a postdoctoral fellow from Tinbergen, with a thesis on response to eyespots on moths and butterflies. He soon became interested in the capacity of infants to use the gaze direction of another to guide their own direction of attention, and he was not one to let the more dashingly abstract in the group get away with attempts merely to deduce the evidence. He stood for evidence, however good the theory and its deductions might be.

Andy Meltzoff had come with me from the States, where he had been a Harvard undergraduate. His piper was Piaget; he was out to explore the literal implications of what Piaget claimed and what Tom Bower claimed. He found his thing all right—by demonstrating striking instances of imitation of facial gestures in the opening months of life, when, in fact, the child could not possibly be equipped with the conceptual apparatus required by Piaget (or by Bower, for that matter) for such imitation to occur.

José Linaza was in Oxford on a Spanish fellowship, his concern being to reexamine the growth of play in children, play as a system of rules. I doubt he ever dreamed at the start that he would be reading Herbert Hart on jurisprudence or critics of ethical theory. In the end, he showed the manner in which, in fact, the child's growing grasp of *futbol* amounted to a successive transformation of organizing rules from the simple "make a goal" to the later complexities of offside stipulations. Though he ended doing much of the actual research with little Madrileños, he was a marvelous sight on an English playing field. For part of his elegant approach to his topic was to organize games with children as the players, he acting as coach/referee/fomenter of violations.

It was a lovely decade, made so in large measure by such students. At times there were too many of them to cope with, for there were not that many people in Britain to whom they could go. They got better and better, and jobs became fewer and fewer. One year, indeed, there were none advertised at all. Many of them did not like the department, found it cold and unwelcoming, and would have left but for LAG. Fortunately, there was a quite steady stream of visitors who helped keep the atmosphere lively and, price beyond pearls in any university, a secretary, my secretary, Megan Kenyon, who managed to make everything seem easy and cheerful, and when necessary shared in the recognition of the absurdities of everyday life in a cold climate.

It was around 1977 that I made a first decision to leave Oxford—to leave "eventually." I had felt more than a little isolated on the occasion of the "Bruner-bashing seminar" and I did not relish battling over the old terrain of mentalism. I found myself bored by what struck me as the "official" attitude of "being scientific," which meant being biologically reductionist or reductionist in a computational metaphor. A little later, the Sloan Foundation asked me whether I would be interested in writing an "intellectual autobiography," offering to pay my salary for a year or two while I did it. I thought that perhaps I might detach myself from the department, find some other way of being a professor in Oxford. It did not work out.

So back to America (with a year at the Netherlands Institute for Advanced Study as a sabbatical en route). I would work on the book, using my papers, which were on file in the Harvard College Library, with a visiting appointment in my old department. But it was not an easy return. One cannot play *da capo* in the music of one's own life. You cannot go back. We lived an hour out of Boston on a family summer estate that had been in my wife's family for six generations. We became increasingly estranged. I was delighted when, in 1981, the New School for Social Research invited me to take up a university professorship. Being separated from a university left me with a sense of nonbelonging that depressed me. I had never thought of myself as needing an institutional scaffold. Why should I? I had always had one. But there was something more to it than that.

The New School appealed to me in some new way. I had always been a creature of establishment institutions—Princeton, Harvard, Institute for Advanced Study, Oxford. It was not so much their "elitism" that troubled me, for I am dedicated to the idea of cultivating an intellectual and moral elite. Rather, there was something about the "gentry" ideal they embodied. One part of me has always felt like an outsider amid all the grandness, the great history, the local iconography. The New School had opened its doors to the refugees of Hitler's persecution. New York, where I had grown up, beckoned in some arcane fashion, as if calling me to come home. I had the image of the New School becoming again, after its lean years, a pivot for a new and burgeoning New York. I think that in some deep way, perhaps a romantic way, I wanted to recapture the immigrant roots that had become gentrified and tamed in the formal rounds of establishment. I accepted the offer. In the end I have come back to the beginning, richer for the passage.

14

Da Capo

"*Da capo*" tells the musical performer to go back (after some variations) and play the major theme once more. *Da capo* then.

I had, at the start, a conviction that one could study mind by examining how it expressed itself in achieving, storing and transforming knowledge of the world. That theme (with variations) has dominated my working life. And even when I was "unconscious" of it, as frequently was the case at the start of a new enterprise, it was not long in making itself known again.

It was not just *my* theme. This same "epistemic concern" has marked my generation of psychologists, philosophers, anthropologists, even physicists. I fell victim, I suppose, to the *Zeitgeist*. But I was surely a willing, an eager victim! My "generation" created and nurtured the Cognitive Revolution—a revolution whose limits we still cannot fathom, for it lies at the center of a postindustrial society that is still in roaring growth. The central premise of this emerging society is that it is the generation and management of knowledge, rather than the mere brute conversion of power and material into goods for distribution, which is the key to the industrial and social process. The new capital is know-how, forecast, intelligence. As the revolution progresses, it is evident that "wisdom" gets added to its list of assets as well—harder to define, harder to achieve. In any case, the epistemic sciences and their metaphors have replaced the engineering of power and materials as the pragmatic base of the management of human affairs. The result has been not simply a renewal of interest in how "mind" works, but rather a new search for mind and for how mindfulness is cultivated.

What an odd route each participant in such a revolution travels! I had got caught up in it in my graduate student days when I (and my fellow students) rebelled against theories of perception that linked the orderliness of experience too directly to the presumed orderliness of the "external" physical world. There had to be, we argued, some principles of selectivity and organization that gave the perceptual system an opportunity to work from top down, from inside out.

Then the war came and (it seemed) we left such abstract issues behind. I, for one, worked on public opinion at home and then on psychological warfare and political intelligence abroad in France. But those war-driven enterprises only served to prick at my old interests. It was not very long after I reached Washington in 1941 that I began to suspect that opinions about the war, about our allies, about our hopes for the future, were formed not so much by weighing all the evidence before deciding, but rather by deciding first (however tentatively) and then sampling the world selectively for confirmation. It was the rare bird—usually a scholar of some kind, without commitment to a particular line of action—who could afford the specialized uncommitment of high doubt.

When I returned in 1945, to continue my academic career at Harvard, my first urge was to revisit my wartime conjectures in the quiet setting of a peacetime university. Others had similar agendas, I discovered. So a group of us at Harvard (and a varied group they were) began a "deep" study of ten men, to find out how they "really" formed their opinions—and we chose to examine their attitudes toward Russia and communism, for like so much of life, the topic was a mix of the fancied and the real. What we found reflected, I suppose, the interests of the clinical and social psychologists, the anthropologists, and even the budding cognitive psychologist in our group. Opinions served three inextricable functions. They provided hypotheses for filtering and organizing news and knowledge. But they were also a projection screen for inner fears and needs. And finally, they provided a means of aligning oneself with those whose views and values one wished to share. The findings were compelling, and if not startling, at least they struck a blow for functionalism and took a mighty step toward recapturing the study of opinion from the journalistic triviality into which the popular pollsters had plunged it.

I suppose, in effect, we were denying the usefulness of sharp boundaries between psychology, sociology and anthropology. It was not coincidental that the era of the study was the same one in which the new Department of Social Relations at Harvard was coming into being, participants in the first making up the younger generation of the second.

Temperament and tradition matter mightily in the paths one takes as a scholar. Temperamentally, I am uncomfortable with shot-gun approaches like our study of opinions and personality. I prefer pinpointing a particular finding and then arguing its more general implications to the hilt. It is a dashing conception, the *a fortiori* claim, but when it works out there are few things more satisfying.

So while still in the midst of the work on opinion formation, I launched into the study of perception—the study, indeed, of the sources of *selectivity* in perception. If you could show that percep-tion was biased toward confirming hypotheses in force, then *a forti-ori*, how much more so must preexisting hypotheses guide the shap-ing of opinions by selecting only confirming input. My partner, Leo Postman, and I used even to refer to that early work as "social per-ception," so close was its link to social psychology in those days. I think we helped drive out (or at least drive to the wall) behaviorist, "learning theory" accounts of social behavior, replacing them with epistemological ones. It would never again be easy to do a social psychological study without explaining why you had ignored how the world *seemed* to those engaged in the action.

All of which was, of course, very gratifying. But by then the logic of my own work had led me into a new set of problems. It is one thing to consider selective perception as an instrument in the formation of social reality and social values, and quite a different one to try to understand what makes perception selective or by what rules this selectivity is governed. How, for example, do our hypotheses stay so well tuned *both* to the structure of events in the real world and to our biases?

What about those "models in the head"—each mind's representa-tion of the world? Could they do both forms of service? George Miller's "Magic Number 7 $\pm$ 2" provided the clue. You may have an accurate enough representation of your world, but given the severe limits on your capacity for dealing with information, you still had to scan that world through a peephole. You could learn how to use your peephole better, but to do so you would need to know what to sample first and what to make of it. This is *strategy*, and coping with the world plainly required that you have one. A strategy of *perceiving?* Surely that must be what we mean by thinking.

New metaphors were coming into being in those mid-1950s, and one of the most compelling was that of computing. Computing took as one of its premises that the flow of information through any system involved continual decisions about what should enter and how it should be used by the system. No computing system of any power could operate without a great deal of such specification. Many of the forms of filtering required by a selective system could now be reformulated as ordinary operations of ordinary computers—and man surely was one of the most high-powered versions of a computer, whatever else he might also be. The old objections against filtering in perception as implying a Judas Eye that first had to have "a tiny look" before deciding what to exclude were at last being undermined.

A second metaphor grew out of the "theory of information" that Shannon and Weaver had proposed. It was, in a way, less metaphor and more cold turkey. The informational value of any input to a system had to be computed in terms of what the system was ready to entertain by way of a set of alternative inputs. So perceptual *readiness* was as crucial a feature of the act of perception as the nature of any input to the system. That, then, was what gave psychological reality to such notions as "strategy" in cognition. It was not just computer jargon or Cromwellian metaphor.

And so came into being *A Study of Thinking*—by now a very long remove from where I had started right after the war on the nature of opinions, though only a decade had gone by. I know it must have seemed to some of my friends (and critics) that I was "jumping fields," although I must confess that it never occurred to me that I was doing anything except following my nose where it led me. I have never had any profound emotional commitment to any of the traditional (or even nontraditional) "fields" of psychology—like "sensation and perception," "learning and memory," "higher mental processes," "child psychology," "social psychology," "abnormal," "intelligence testing," etc. Insofar as they generate their own little kingdoms, each with its own set of bottled theories, they impede the progress of psychology by creating ad hoc realities designed to deal with local technical difficulties. Look, for example, at the absurdity of a theory of intelligence testing separated from theories of learning or of thinking. Or an abnormal psychology that does not take into account the lessons that social psychology can offer on the subject of multiple social identities and the conflicts they engender.

Why not simply study what you want to find out, letting it take you where it may? More in retrospect than by previsioned grand design, I chose to study the sources of and the obstacles to human rationality by whatever means I could. "Fields" of psychology are important, for they deal with special contexts, make particularly revealing comparisons and sometimes even formulate powerful mechanisms. They were never intended to cast psychology as a whole into the posture of blind men trying to figure out the elephant! With luck, besides, those special fields provide some powerful tool kits for those who want to borrow them.

In any case, *A Study of Thinking,* which was an exercise in trying to understand how man managed to be rational, appeared in 1956. It and several concurrent developments are now alleged to have triggered the "cognitive revolution" in psychology. What Peirce, James and Dewey had earlier argued on speculative grounds—that meaning depended not on anything intrinsic in the world but upon the uses to which knowledge was put—now became not just a matter of speculation but also a matter of fact, if only a tiny one.

And so to the next obvious question: How did it all *get* that way? I became a "developmental psychologist." And I spent the better part of the 1960s and early 1970s trying to unravel how the primitive operations of the baby's "mind" got converted to the subtle arts and sciences and intuitions of an adult. In the end I concluded that man could not have made that voyage without the aid of the ready-made tools of a culture and its language, that mental growth comes as much from the outside in as from the inside out.

Once you nourish such a suspicion, things change for you. For one, you are forced to look outside the human skin for the sources of human competence—to the culturally provided prosthetic devices that make it possible for the human mind to vault beyond itself. My interests in the nature of art and science, and the "disciplines of knowledge" as ways of knowing and experiencing, became much livelier. I began to see the study of human development as not only part of the natural science of maturation and learning, but also one of the sciences of the artificial. We were, after all, a species that created itself by the constitutive power of our symbol-making, our institution-creating, our very culture-creating. Whatever you might say about the growth of mind, you could never say it without specifying the devices and tools that made it possible.

And so I was led by the nose again—this time to study those "outside in" devices. "Education" was one candidate. Another was language. But I never really "chose" to study either of them with anything this explicit in mind. They were temptations that happened to come along and that fit the state of my curiosity. Just as I was brooding on these more general matters, for example, the nation was being forced to reconsider the quality of public education—the famous post-Sputnik reassessment. For another, our conception of human language was being revolutionized not only by the penetrating insights of linguists like Chomsky but by philosophers like John Austin. Chomsky's account gave promise of reorganizing our views about mind itself, its natural categories and transformative powers. Austin's presented a view of language as an instrument for using culture and convention—the performative function of language.

So I "became" an educational theorist who thumped the tub for an understanding of knowledge as a prosthetic device: that the structure of knowledge (rather than its content) was what permitted us to grasp and retain and transform the world in a generative way not tied to the learning of details—at any age for any subject in some form that was honest.

And I "became" a developmental linguist in the pragmatic tradition, inquiring how young children learn to acquire the social and intellectual *uses* of the language whose grammatical structure they acquire so easily and, doubtless, therefore with some biological assist.

Both those "excursions"—into education and into language acquisition—took me that much closer to where I had wanted to travel. But not in a straight line.

For it is a winding road that one inevitably follows, even though it seems obvious and straight ahead at the outset. Not only that, but you get caught in controversies that are wildly irrelevant to what you thought you were doing—like becoming the target of the ultra-right in America for espousing a curriculum that included a beautifully crafted account of human evolution. The hounds of creationism were set baying! You could spend forever defending yourself. Much better to get on with it. I suppose that if one were giving advice to the new starter, it would be to have faith in where your nose leads you and don't expect to be forever traveling down arrow-straight highways. And above all, race your own race.

I had hoped that psychology would grow in unity, that it would lead the way toward a fresh and full assessment of man and of his perfectibility. I even expressed those hopes in a speech I gave at the centennial celebration of the Smithsonian Institution in 1962, knowing that the President of the United States would be in attendance; I entitled it "The Perfectibility of Intellect." But psychology is more splintered, less unified, more beset by contradictions than it was when I started. Even the Cognitive Revolution risks being trivialized by the narrowness with which psychology defines its specialized research problems. Much of it stems from our wish to have a distinctive identity as psychologists, to be free of our parent, philosophy. It sometimes has the unfortunate and inadvertent consequence of creating a kind of anti-intellectualism by denying the worth of those other disciplines that concern themselves with the nature of man.

I had hoped that psychology would (in the manner of those Harvard days in the 1950s) fuse with anthropology and sociology and such more humane fields as linguistics. I think it may yet do so, but fusions are not fashionable in these thin days. But a psychology that is negligent or inattentive to the other social sciences and to philosophy will inevitably be bland, particular and even trivial. Psychology is almost always the richer for being combined in new amalgams of learning: It needs rich context. We too often resist incorporation on grounds that it will reduce our "rigor." We act like poachers turned gamekeepers!

I had also hoped that psychology would find enough self-confidence to address itself calmly to issues of human values, and perhaps there is reason to be a little pleased in this respect. It had seemed to me that Gordon Allport was mining a rich vein in his *Study of Values* —providing a kind of natural morphology of the domains in which everyday human values cohered: political, economic, social, religious, aesthetic and theoretical. At least he had provided (following the German phenomenologist Spranger) a computable way of sorting out human valuations which went a good step beyond William James's tough-minded and tender-minded. And his "value scale" had a robustness to it that could not be matched by the more finical phenomenologists who, like Max Scheler, had done a microanatomy of the forms of human sympathy. Allport's test, it has turned out over the years, really correlates with the things that matter in ordinary existence: the jobs you choose, the way you spend your free time, the friends you make, the stuff you read. But there has not been much follow-up. The philosopher Charles Morris wrote a stunning little book (he used to say I was the only one who ever praised it) on "varieties of human value," based on a factor analysis of world religions and religious ideologies. It was methodologically weird (though no more so than the factoring of human intelligence into primary mental abilities), but it was substantively a beginning. Values did pop out of his number cruncher: like "reduce outside distraction and find the inner reality" or "cultivate effort of will in pursuit of one's own goals" or "live in harmony with one's fellows." Whatever its virtues (there were surely some admirable ones) or vices (it had its share), it was a less muddled book than Morris's *Signs, Language, and Behavior* (a timid "behaviorizing" of C. S. Peirce), which sold like hotcakes for a decade. *Varieties of Human Value* was a candidate for remaindering from the day it was born!

I suppose my hopes for a clarification (or even a taxonomy) of the nature of human values grew from a conviction that psychology could not live healthily in isolation from the normative or policy disciplines—jurisprudence, literary criticism, legal and moral philosophy, political science. Like many anthropologists and like "conceptual pragmatists" generally, I believe that we constitute and negotiate our own social reality and that meaning is finally "settled" by these constitutive and negotiatory processes. Just as in my early work on "New Look" perception, I still believe that the worlds of meaning we construct (and then institutionalize) are at bottom evaluative— what contemporary logician-linguists call "deontic." Neutral, "factual" meanings—the "epistemic" domain in contrast to the deontic —are forever caught or contextualized in these value systems. The effort of both philosophers and practical men to translate grand concepts like "justice," "equity," even "altruism" and "health," into workaday meanings depends upon understanding how human values operate and change in real life.

In English common law, there is that plea holding that "the mind of man runneth not the contrary." It is, in effect, an appeal to a durable social reality as a source of legitimacy. Psychology will come of age when it learns to explore and explain how such "durable social realities" come into being, how they work and how they are transmitted from generation to generation. The deeper issues beyond the nature of the act of valuing itself—whether one value is better or richer or fairer than another—will never come within the province of any science.

I must speak more personally, finally, about the voyage beyond adolescent innocence—what happened to that eighteen-year-old intellectual idealist/snob/rebel who left Duke for the Athens of Harvard in 1938. He certainly became less starry-eyed, much less of a snob, and in some ways more of a rebel.

The first thing I would have to say is that I very soon became a "professional." That is what American graduate education accomplishes. If you go through it seriously, you become at *least* that. You learn your "field," you get good at your trade. You "give papers" at this "meeting" or that colloquium, write them up crisply, answer your critics, know the "literature," apply the appropriate statistical tests, review important books for first-line journals, develop good academic manners. You go to department and to faculty meetings and ask reasonable questions or propose sensible answers. There could be no island tribe in the Pacific or hill folk in New Guinea with a more prescribed set of rituals and beliefs than those of the academic community.

Indeed, I did it all so well that it was early a foregone conclusion that I was very "good" at it, and I was duly given preferment—tenure, grants, attention in the "literature." It is the apparatus of the successful academic.

Mastery of it has real consequences. Within limits, it permits you to "get on" with your work: Research grants mean equipment for doing your thing, assistants to track down the details, and the opportunity to think programmatically in a practical way. A major university appointment with tenure carries the gift of time perspective. And Cambridge, Massachusetts, placed one in a network so rich in connections that there was virtually nothing out of reach in the realm of known scholarship or of apposite criticism.

It is all very domesticating. The tautness of its net is, I am sure, one of the major creators of Kuhnian paradigms. There are canonical views to live by if you are to be part of the net; and one does not dump them carelessly. There was "Harvard psychology" and "Yale psychology" and, indeed, "East Coast psychology" (of which Berkeley was a part!) in contrast to "dust bowl empiricism." The same for literary criticism and history.

If you are in a field like physics—and all the sciences are a lot or a little like it in the sense of depending upon discussion with those at the growing edge—then the proximity of intellectual peers is of enormous moment. It assures your being at the front end of the procession of knowledge. But if you are a novelist or a poet—and most fields are also a lot or a little like novel-writing or poetry—then the domestication will extract a high intellectual price. For an academic community is too ordered, too conservative in procedure to sustain you. I always had the feeling that my several "creative writer" friends who were also critics—Albert Guérard, John Hawkes, Ted Spencer, Ivor Richards, Richard Eberhart—were pushed by circumstances toward criticism and away from creating. I recall a visit in Oxford from Stephen Spender in the late 1970s during a tryout year of his teaching at University College, London. He complained (in a most generous way) of the "orderliness" of the existence and of the demandingness of that order. It was the same evening that he told me he had not been bored since the days when he first came up to Oxford as an undergraduate. I wondered at the time whether the mood might not have surfaced in the circumstances of his new life.

And so inevitably it was with me. I enjoyed Harvard and its domestication, the busy life of teaching, doing research, writing, occasional administrative choring. But it also made me restless, a little bored, unrequited in the left hand. I do not like routine and its cycles, yet they were also a comfort to somebody who is given, as I used strongly to be, to swings in mood from discouraged restlessness to highly focused engagement. My domestic life was also highly ordered, as were the lives of most of my friends. And in a setting like Harvard's, one gradually becomes gentrified, almost self-gentrified. For during the period of which I speak—the decades after the war —we lived among and shared schools and parties and pleasures with Brattle Street and Coolidge Hill, Cambridge and Boston "society." Children went to Shady Hill or Buckingham or Brown and Nichols, and then not to "St. Grottlesex" but to Exeter and Andover. Some protested and started their children in the public schools of Cambridge or moved to suburbs to fare better educationally. For many Harvard families (mine included) the social mobility was inexorably "upward," and there was no resisting it.

I enjoyed it—much of the time. At times the life made me feel an outsider, an impostor, a "simulated Wasp," an Uncle Tom. Had I known what it was all about, I might have managed it better, but by 1956, right after the completion of two demanding books, and after a great deal of tension in my marriage, I went through the ordeal of a divorce, my son having already gone off to school at Exeter and my daughter (just ten) remaining at home with her mother. It was a tense and a difficult period. I took up with some wonderfully free spirits in Boulder, Colorado, and I spent the next summers in bohemian freedom there, in Aspen, in Europe, on the Vineyard, visiting, reading, living among musicians, writers, painters. My companion, Elizabeth Weems—she was the presiding spirit in that Boulder group —was a gifted painter and a rebel, a refugee from Texas wealth and a temperamentally disposed doubter of social conventions. I could not have found a happier and more congenial antidote to my malaise. Our friends, I think, thought we had too much influence on each other. In the three years we were together, there was scarcely a topic I can think of that went unexplored—intellectual, moral, personal.

Elizabeth Weems helped me to make friends with my left hand. I painted; wrote poetry; read fiction, mythology and drama, as if starved for it; listened to music with a new ear. Ours was not a relationship that would have survived domestication. We remain fast friends.

I had a student in those years—he had been my undergraduate tutee while editor of the *Crimson* and he shared my bemused doubts about psychology's neglect of the left hand. Mickey Maccoby decided to do a Ph.D. with me, and for several years we had that rich experience of a close friendship across generations. Between him, Elizabeth Weems and a circle of old friends, life came back together into a new pattern. I suppose the most direct expression of that time and those circumstances is my little book *On Knowing: Essays for the Left Hand.*

It's curious about transitions. How productive that period was— the years 1956 to 1960: articles, reviews, books galore (including *A Study of Thinking* and *The Process of Education*). Release from gentrified domestication?

I was remarried—to Blanche Marshall McLane—in 1960, and we lived happily in the center of Cambridge until the end of the decade. I think I was able to cope with my earlier domestic restlessness by throwing myself into the round of work, excitement and crises that marked that decade. My duties in Washington and in Africa, the excitement of putting together "Man: A Course of Study," the troubled times, were all shields against entrapment in the gentrified domesticity of Cambridge. And summers were for sailing, which we did much of, cruising as far east as New Brunswick and Nova Scotia and south to Bermuda. We had no children of our own, and her children and mine made a lively extended family.

The grimmest note of that period was my son Whitley's service in the Vietnam War. He was disenchanted with it, like others in his generation, but went anyway: "Why should somebody else get drafted in my place?" Dreams about one's only son being "lost" in some distant place where he had no business being—they had about them the feeling of helpless terror. He came back safely, after serving principally in POW interrogation, but the mismanagement and the ineptness of the war convinced him that without expert knowledge of the world, America would get into one after another politically disastrous episode. So after a brief stint in graduate school at Harvard, he departed for foreign service with the government, in which he has remained ever since.

Spending 1970–71 as Master of Currier House, the first "coed" house at Harvard, was lively. I had hoped to make the house into something like an intellectual community, rather like an Oxbridge college, and in many ways, the group of tutors and associates there managed to do so to an astonishing degree. It was satisfying and time-consuming, and our life was back and forth between delights and alarums: mini-occupations, the pleasure of the company of the visiting Diana and Lionel Trilling, coping with the segregation communally self-imposed on itself by the Black group but resented by many of the individual Black students, dealing with the wooden conventionalism of minor deans.

An outsider came to stay in one of the entries, a "friend" of one of the residents. He was a thorough nuisance, and long overstayed his welcome. They would not throw him out: that would not be "friendly." That was an issue worth the conversation. Or the issue of the Currier House Day Nursery—the long ideological hassle over whether, after all, we would be instilling "middle-class values" in the children. As it happened, students and staff made it a delight, not only volunteering their help, but even taking their instruments along to play in a corner for those kids who wanted to listen. Good Mozart on a flute in the corner of an ordinarily noisy nursery classroom does indeed soothe the savage breast.

When in 1972 I was lured to Oxford, my wife and I sailed across the Atlantic in our sailboat, *Wester Till* with some friends as crew. It was a great adventure, birds with us virtually all the way—the good luck of a June passage by the northern route, replete with icebergs.

The Vice-Chancellor assured me on my arrival in Oxford that no other professor in the history of the university had ever thus sailed to his chair, though a professor of surgery in the nineteenth century, a Scot, had driven a wagon from John o' Groat's in the far north of Scotland to Merton, where he parked it outside, only to find it had been stolen when he returned to drive it to the stable. The customs officer at Lymington, where we landed, asked almost as an after-thought whether I had any drugs on board. I said yes, I had half a dozen vials of morphine in my medical kit to treat shock. "You're going to a professorship at Oxford, I understand. You do know some medical professors there. Would you be so kind as to give the mor-phine to one of them, else we shall be three hours filling out the required forms, I'm sure." I had met the British class system!

I have already said enough about life in Oxford in the preceding chapter. I do want to add one thing. There is an atmosphere of generalism about conversation in that place that is celebrated and real. If you ask a geologist, say, what he does, he will tell you that, say, he studies sliding plates under the ocean that shove continents apart or draw them closer, and he will tell you about it, most usually, with charm, directness and simplicity—and no condescension. Ask an ancient historian, a philosopher of language, a student of the foundations of mathematics, a reader in the conflict of laws, and you are likely to get a similarly open response. I have often wondered why this is, and an answer occurred to me one Sunday afternoon in our village in Ireland, amidst our English friends there. For one thing, the English do not segregate their company by age as much as we do, nor do they run as much in occupational packs. It is taken as a mark of respect that when somebody who is *not* in your business or *not* in your age range asks you something about what you "do," the answer should be not only comprehensible, but part of the gen-eral conversation. All this is the case if the members of the conversa-tion are of the same social class or if one of them is seen as a foreigner by the other.

This works very much for the foreigner who comes to live and work in Britain. I found the atmosphere hospitable and easy to move about in. I am not particularly an anglophile, though I am fond of Britain and the British people, despite their bloody-mindedness, which can be as exasperating after a while to a foreigner as it is to those native to the island. I had gone there, I suppose, for what my friend John Gardner calls "self-renewal," and I most certainly found it. It was not only the climate of thought in philosophy, which buoyed me up and gave such good support to the work on language discussed in an earlier chapter, but also the quality of the life there. Odd things: Sunday rambles into the countryside along the charming River Windrush, where the Mitford sisters had spent their unruly childhoods; or sailing the waters of the British Isles and entering the company of a convivial group of eccentrics called The Royal Cruising Club; or spending summers and some Christmases as well in that village in Ireland: Glandore in county Cork. There was an enormous refreshment too in the astonishing hospitality of the British, in spite of their absurd claim to being a basically inhospitable people. Oxford itself can be overwhelmingly social, and one needs to be careful lest one indeed become overwhelmed by it. I have never spent a more "social" eight years as in that city—to which add the attractions of London, Cambridge, Edinburgh and Bristol, where I had many old friends. Indeed, the English "stay" was not that all discontinuous socially with life as I had known it before, given those friends.

Perhaps I am a natural wanderer, although the record may conceal it, for in my academic career I served twenty-seven years at Harvard and eight at Oxford, which, I realize, is not a flighty career. But for all that, I have an attachment to friends in distant corners of the world that I have kept alive not only by correspondence but by visits. There was, for example, Henri Tajfel, whom I knew first when he was a young don at Durham in the northeast of England. He came to visit me to talk shop at Cambridge, England, in the mid-1950s and, if I remember rightly, a year never passed after that in which we did not visit. In some ways, we were brothers. He was one of the people in the world with whom sharing was essential. As was Alexander Romanovich Luria in Moscow, of whom I have already spoken. Bärbel Inhelder was another, a born sharer who could always manage to make Geneva completely hospitable, even when my differences with Le Patron were at their stiffest. And Oliver Zangwill in Cambridge, Donald Broadbent in Oxford, Peter Wason in London, Margaret Donaldson in Edinburgh, Niels and Annelise Christensen in Denmark. These were the people with whom I could share both my personal life and that World Three of which I spoke in an earlier chapter. Their books, their talk, their concerns, their records, even their children, were all part of it. It is not just an abstract cliché that the scholarly world knows no geographical limits. They were the world in which I wandered and, wandering, could still be at home.

One should end an autobiography, I suppose, by trying to sketch what one means by "oneself." In fact, it is a hopeless venture. For the moment one takes thought on the matter, it is clear that (as I should have known from William James) the boundaries of self are like morning mist. Speaking as an "intellectual autobiographer," I find "myself" not just inside but outside as well. It is not just in ventures —in books, in institutions, in issues, and in the currents of World Three where one has navigated—but in people. In the distant friends among whom I wandered and among the friends nearer by with whom I worked out ideas and projects. Like Yeats, I can say:

"My glory was I had such friends."

Or take one's students. I have had many of them: graduate students, undergraduate tutees, occasional ones I've befriended in classes or by good chance. Some have been spectacularly successful and they populate chairs on three continents, have won coveted prizes and have even made some fundamental contributions to knowledge. I have always felt a certain reserve with them all. It is not just that the relation is so asymmetrical, for in fact you have inordinate power over them. But rather, it is so fragile. I inadvertently made a woman graduate student burst into tears by tearing too avidly into a shoddy bit of writing she brought me, and my shame lasted for months. She eventually dedicated a book to me, which, finally, served as absolution!

I am under no illusions about the naturalness of the teaching relationship. Given its institutional setting, it is quite unnatural, quite difficult to treat as if it were just a matter of being friends. One of my former students, Howard Gardner, once commented (ten years after he'd earned his degree) that from his side of the divide, he could have had no idea what the demands on my life were when he was a student. We have become good friends since. And I could mention others among them to whom the same story is applicable: Kenneth Kaye, Patricia Greenfield, Eric Wanner, Susan Carey-Block, Edward Jones—to limit it to the last decade or two.

I mention it here because of a special "self-making" quality of former-students-turned-friends. They give continuity to one's life, much as there is continuity in old friendships where, though you have been separated for five years, you can take up immediately where you left off. They do it in a fashion comparable to the way your children, your nephews and nieces, your childhood friends, do it for you. I think in the end it has something to do with an old Piagetian motif: the pleasure inherent in maintaining invariance across transformations. They are still there, *malgré tout*. And so are *you*.

But that does not get us very far ahead with self! Perhaps one can define it by accomplishments, given the sense that it is not easily confinable inside the heart (or the breast, or wherever). But when I think of the accomplishments that feel most personal and "self-like," they are not very conventional, nor even very meaningful to anybody else. They are rather autarkic, in the main, and fit a childhood fantasy of self-sufficiency quite typical of a lonely child. Not very surprising that I became a blue-water sailor! When, having sailed the North Atlantic, we were approaching our intended harbor in The Solent, I ordered the boat polished up and all hands into their dressiest sea clothes. I wanted it to seem that it was nothing more than crossing from the Isle of Wight. But, that time at the Sorbonne when I was being given an honorary degree, all I could think of when the Orator was citing my virtues was that it was exactly in the style of an obituary. So I doubt we find our selfhood in accomplishment. Or perhaps some do.

I remember with what delight I read Bertrand Russell's *Unpopular Essays*. They were (or at least so it seemed to me) about issues where he had held his ground, about matters of conviction in style or substance. I think that gets a little closer. But if you define yourself oppositionally, you end up with a self-image of a battler, a street fighter, a stiff-neck. And that is surely not me. In the main, I have always preferred to commit Type I errors, the kind in which you say "yes" in doubt rather than "no." But perhaps *that*, then, should help me define the properties of being that I would want to call "myself." With students, for example, I have (in spite of that one humiliating incident) always assumed that beneath any muddle a good idea might be lurking, and that if I tried hard enough in conversation I could find it. Sometimes I have—and sometimes, I think, the poor student has adopted my interpretation in self-defense.

No, I think withal that what has been closest to self is a set of underlying convictions about man's capacity to think, to get himself out of muddles, to share ideas with others. But I also think that he could never succeed in doing so but for two other circumstances, the two of them inextricably linked. The first is a social world that he can understand and that, if he does not understand it, he can alter or reconsider. This is a matter of trust. Without trust, there is thought, to be sure, but in the end it destroys the world that supports the human condition. The second is a measure of compassion—not saint-like, but enough for there to be an appreciation of other minds, other motives, other possible worlds. I think that this must be the minimal inner inventory that led me to search for things in the world that would correspond to my small list. What defined self for me was finding enough of them to be able to walk about the world without feeling a stranger.

And after all, then, how did it seem, spending a lifetime as a psychologist?

There are those famous final paragraphs in Wittgenstein's *Tractatus*:

> We feel that even if all possible scientific questions be answered, the problems of life have still not been touched at all. Of course there is then no question left, and just this is the answer. . . .
>
> The solution of the problem of life is seen in the vanishing of this problem. (Is it not the reason why men to whom after long doubting the sense of life became clear, could not say wherein this sense consisted?)
>
> There is indeed the inexpressible. . . .
>
> Whereof one cannot speak, thereof one must be silent.

I, like the "long doubter," cannot speak about the sense of life—or more to the point, I cannot speak of it in a fashion that is a continuation of how I speak as a scientist about the mind and its movements. Freud once said (was it half in jest?) that one decides small matters by reason, great ones by instinct. Instinct may be as speechless as Wittgenstein would have us believe, but it is not voice-less. It is only that its voice does not translate, does not lend itself to the extraction of propositions.

In life—whether "personally" or as a psychologist—a part of me simply goes from one thing to another. I followed my nose: my instinct, my intuition, or whatever one calls it. It has not always led me to where I wanted to be nor even to where I thought I would get to. Any articulate man can make up stories to make such paths seem reasonable or even foreordained. Indeed, that is what the genre of autobiography is principally about. But when one reflects, my nose has been no worse a guide than my reason. In both cases, chance overran what I had prepared.

Take the very decision to become a psychologist. I cannot remember ever making it—which is not to say that I stumbled into it. Yes, I suppose it was natural. But once I became one, my plans and projects certainly were not "derived" from some master plan, not even in the way that tactics are said to be derived from a master strategy. You are drawn to this, repelled by that. Not that I lacked a map. Maps would generate themselves as needed, as if there were a kindly cartographer in my head. You could even invent a plausible past for what you did or believed—as Roman Jakobson used to reinvent "original discoveries" in the writings of the nineteenth century Polish-Russian linguist Baudouin de Courtenay. In fact, those retrospective maps (we all use them) are extrapolations from one's hopes about what will be true in the future back to what might have been true in the past. There is nothing so likely to persuade you of a pragmatic theory of meaning as a life of thought!

I have never been interested in constructing a "grand" or overarching system of thought (as I mentioned in an earlier chapter). It might interfere with instinct or intuition and in any case would surely attenuate the likelihood of surprise. I think that this may be the "reason" why I have felt the need to keep my left hand as fit as my right. And so I must confess that there has never been a major turning point in my life at which I could truly say that I knew exactly why I was doing what I was about to do. I am sure that I share that dilemma with the human race. I believe that "character" consists of going down one road, having decided that is the one to travel, and doing so without excessive fear and trembling.

Even when I was young and unformed, my convictions seemed to me out of the reach of conventional proof. I suppose that might have been a poor way of being equipped for becoming a man of action—but I wonder. I don't recall ever having been criticized for being irresolute. Absentminded, abstracted, a little *au delà de la bataille*—yes. But not lacking either in convictions or in a readiness to act. No, I did not become a man of action. It never occurred to me to go into business, though that was the familial and "obvious" thing to have done. And later, when there were opportunities to become a political figure or even a university president, I was not tempted. I think I was more interested in constructing possible worlds than in trying to prove that one was spot-on right. How to say it? I think hypotheses are infinitely more interesting than the facts that are used either to bring them down or shore them up. Temperamentally, I suppose, I was bound to become a constructivist, bound to conclude eventually that man created a reality in some measure for his own use, and by use alone could judge its worth—whether painter, physicist or man in the street.

Following a maxim such as that in one's ordinary life is sure to make one subject to illusions—Type I illusions, where you are prepared to believe, even in doubt. Sometimes they undo you, principally when you cannot negotiate your illusions into the realistic status they deserve among others. My heroes and villains, my alarums and dreads, have not always appeared so to all my fellow men.

I think optimists and alarmists are flesh and blood with each other. One believes in "best scenarios," and the other in worst. Timon of Athens went from one to the other: Shakespeare did indeed know a thing or two. I tend toward best scenarios, though, like Timon, I swing to the other extreme at times. It is astonishing, I suppose, that optimists remain so in spite of their exposure to such disasters. I have always envied steady people who counsel that things are not as bad as they seem or as good as you hoped. Envied them but rarely befriended them. At least science and logic have technologies of disproof that temper the two extremes. Not poetry:

> The dog starved at his master's gate
> Spells the downfall of the State.

Another reason for Plato wanting to keep artists out of the Republic.

Ventures of high optimism have had an enormous role in fueling my life. College, once I sensed what it might be, released boundless energy in me. Then the idea of the life of mind—the chance not only to think, but to think about thinking and to talk about thinking about thinking. The idea that you could penetrate the program of mind, of thought, created an even steadier energy. In some curious way, these primitive convictions have been linked with similarly optimistic beliefs in the mutability of human affairs: that taking action might have an effect. In consequence, I have been party to projects ranging from the intellectually quixotic (like a United Nations plan to create great social laboratories in the various regions of the developing world) to equally long gambles that paid off because their day had come (like setting up the Center for Cognitive Studies at Harvard).

I must have seemed at times the very soul of Dr. Pangloss—save for one trait that, perhaps, is more characteristic of survivors than of optimists. By general testimony, I am said to be very stubborn and persistent. I do indeed work very hard for my hypotheses, one minute judicially, the next like a bare-knuckled street fighter. In consequence, I suppose, I have seemed like somebody who had to be taken seriously, or at least humored. I am not a particularly good team man, but people seem to prefer having me on their team rather than on the other side. But that could not be quite true, for I mostly wear my convictions on my sleeve—again like an optimist.

All this dodges the initial question: whether being a psychologist gives one any special hold on Wittgenstein's "sense of life." Well, no. Perhaps you know the menu better, but that is not what makes a fine palate. At that, I rather suspect that living in universities may not provide the best vantage point for sampling the whole menu. You do far better cultivating your friends and their predicaments. I am lucky in making friends easily, although I do not know why that is so. Certainly not by virtue of being a psychologist. More likely a gene kink! Or perhaps my curiosity makes me an uncommonly good listener.

I suppose my life has been a good one—as seen from a commanding rock by some mythologically instructed member of my reference tribe who is watching the parade. Most of the time it has felt that way to me too: full of movement, of direction, of surprise, of affection and loyalty. Psychology has certainly helped it to be so, psychology as a way of inquiry rather than as a basis of wisdom.

In the end, I think I know what I would want to do if I had it to do over again. I would do much the same, knowing full well that another turn round the track would produce just as many uncertainties as the first trip round. Except I might be better equipped. Or, perhaps, "whereof one cannot speak, thereof must one be silent."

Index

Acheson, Dean, 210–212
Adams, Donald Keith, 24–25, 30, 67, 71
Adams, Henry, 188, 205, 268
Adams, Robert, 190
Adrian, Lord Edgar Douglas, 100, 108
Agricultural Economics Bureau, 42
Allen, Jim, 186
Allendoerfer, Carl, 182
Allport, Gordon, 30, 33–38, 63, 76, 77, 80, 122, 129, 228, 237, 280
Allport-Vernon Study of Values test, 80
Almond, Gabriel, 30
American Educational Research Association, 194
American Psychological Association, 32, 122
Ames, Adelbert, 88–91
Ames family, 89
Analysis of Sensation, The (Mach), 67, 133
Anglin, Jerry, 120
"anoetic sentience," 94
anthropology:
    developmental psychology vs., 133, 134–136, 138, 146
    psychology vs., 29, 59, 115
Argyle, Michael, 260
Aristotle, 83, 94, 111, 121, 201
Armando, Armando, 185
Arnold, Lee, 26, 243
Art and Illusion (Gombrich), 89, 90
Art of the Fugue (Bach), 207
Asch, Solomon, 87
Atlantic Monthly, 38
Attributes of Sensation (Boring), 72–73

"attribution" theory, 114
Auden, W. H., 3, 204
Austen, Jane, 234
Austin, George, 60, 115, 120, 128
Austin, John, 165–166, 168, 254, 255, 268, 279
Australia, aboriginal puberty rituals in, 5
autobiography, approaches to, 6, 55–56, 288
Autobiography (Adams), 205
Autobiography (Russell), 55–56
"autonomous ego," 228
Ayer, Sir Alfred Jules "Freddy," 90, 231, 254, 255, 270
Ayer, Dee, 231

Bach, Johann Sebastian, 207
Bakhtin, M., 137, 215–216
Baldwin, Al, 37
Baldwin, James Mark, 204
Balikci, Asen, 191
Barker, Roger, 23
Bartlett, Sir Frederic, 5, 98, 101, 108–109, 110, 157
Bechterev, Vladimir, 32
Beebe-Center, Jack, 33
Beerbohm, Max, 223, 253
Begle, Edward, 182
behaviorism, 27, 28, 60, 62, 67, 109, 110, 157, 276
Benchley, Robert, 268
Benedict, Ruth, 135
"benign neglect," 151
Bennett, Arnold, 19
Berenson, Bernard, 26

Berkeley, George, 38, 58
Berkner, Lloyd, 211
Berlin, Aline, 247
Berlin, Isaiah, 92–93, 165, 189, 247,
    254, 255, 256–259, 261, 262, 263,
    266
Bernard, Claude, 139, 169
Bernstein, Basil, 196
Bessie, Simon Michael, 47
Bhutto, Zulfiqar Ali, 257
Bibring, Edward, 208–209
Billy Budd (Melville), 229
blacks:
    in Head Start program, 151
    prejudice against, 17
Blake, William, 232
Bloom, Lois, 165
Blum, John, 45, 182
Blum, Léon, 30
Bohr, Niels, 44, 111
Boole, George, 112
Boring, Edwin Garrigues, 33–34, 37–38,
    72–73, 76, 97, 111, 129, 238
    on New Look, 90–92, 237
Boston Psychoanalytic Institute,
    212–213
Bovet, Magali, 143
Bower, Tom, 125, 147–148, 150, 271
Bowra, Maurice, 254
Brademas, John, 269
Brave New World (Huxley), 108
Brazelton, Berry, 147, 150, 212
Brewster, Kingman, 220, 224, 251
Briggs, Asa, 246, 264
Brill, Abraham, 136
Broadbent, Donald, 101–102, 126, 260,
    264, 270, 287
Brock, Michael, 262, 263
Bronfenbrenner, Urie, 196
Broom, Leonard, 29, 134, 243
Brown, John, 47, 48
Brown, Roger, 127, 150, 158, 163, 164,
    165
Brownian movement, 15
Bruner, Adolf (brother), 10, 11, 14, 21
Bruner, Alice (sister), 7, 10, 11
Bruner, Blanche Marshall McLane
    (second wife), 202–203, 284, 285
Bruner, Herman (father), 5, 8, 10–17,
    20, 24, 156, 209, 214, 244
Bruner, Jane (daughter), 51, 153–156,
    284
Bruner, Jerome:
    absentmindedness of, 7, 291
    areas of study of, 8–9, 24–25, 28–29,
        36, 61, 62–64, 178, 230, 274,
        277–279

Bruner, Jerome *(cont'd)*
    childhood of, 4–7, 9–21, 108, 178,
        202, 214, 218–219
    childhood friends of, 17, 19, 218–219
    classmates of, 22–23, 26, 29–30, 37
    as collaborator, 9, 19, 76
    on communism, 29–30, 38, 137,
        144–145
    curiosity of, 9, 15
    dreams of, 16, 24, 111
    at Duke, 19, 21, 22–31, 70–71,
        132–133, 243
    early blindness of, 4, 7, 9, 11
    early education of, 7, 13, 15, 17, 18,
        21
    in Europe, 38–41, 45–51, 138, 154,
        165–172, 202–204, 225–226, 235,
        286–287
    family of, 5, 10–17, 20
    as father, 140, 152–156
    at Harvard, as faculty member, 63,
        243–254, 275
    at Harvard, as student, 32–38, 59–60,
        72–73, 134, 230, 275
    honors awarded to, 51, 194, 230,
        258
    intellectual preferences of, 8–9, 18,
        25, 77, 276
    as Jew, 5, 7, 13, 18, 20, 23, 39, 208,
        244
    jobs of, 25–26, 39, 41–51, 64, 246,
        252, 273
    literary interests of, 5–6, 13, 18, 25,
        32, 48, 71, 108, 136, 208–209
    marriages of, 40, 89, 140, 209, 283,
        284
    mathematics enjoyed by, 18, 25, 26
    mentors of, 86–92, 136–139, 230–234
    New Look theory of, 67–72, 75,
        79–86, 90–95, 103, 145, 237
    at New School, 273
    at Oxford, 247, 252–272
    on poetry, 18, 26
    at Princeton, 43–44, 63, 110–111
    psychoanalysis of, 6, 208–210, 212
    published works of, 28, 45, 47, 65,
        68–69, 101, 115, 132, 145–146, 168,
        184, 196, 204
    rebelliousness of, 27, 242, 248, 275,
        282
    as researcher, 9, 19, 28–30, 130
    romantic relationships of, 18–19, 71,
        209
    sailing enjoyed by, 17, 19, 21,
        218–219, 285–286, 289
    speeches made by, 20, 63, 115, 168,
        184, 280

Bruner, Jerome *(cont'd)*
  as teacher, 26, 64, 96, 140, 143, 191, 288
  thesis of, 38–40
  vision of, 9, 10, 14, 45
  as writer, 9, 14, 216, 272
Bruner, Katherine Frost (first wife), 40, 43, 50, 89, 153
Bruner, Min (sister), 10, 11, 16, 18
Bruner, Rose (Glücksmann) (mother), 5, 10–17, 18, 21, 24, 156, 244
Bruner, Sarah (aunt), 10
Bruner, Simon (uncle), 10, 11–12, 16
Bruner, Whitley (son), 21, 43, 51, 153–156, 182, 283, 285
Brunswik, Egon, 114, 128
Bryant, Peter, 264
Buck, Paul Herman, 245–246, 247
"buffer storage," 102–103
Bullock, Alan, 61, 246, 247
Bundy, McGeorge, 111–112, 123, 126, 186, 221, 222–223, 224, 225, 248–249, 257–258
Bush, Vannevar, 237

Calkins, Hugh, 250
Cambronne II, 46
Campbell, Joseph, 206–207
Camus, Albert, 209, 244
Canfield, Cass, 47, 50
Cannon, Walter, 31
Cantor, Nancy, 128
Cantril, Hadley, 38, 43, 44, 91
Carey-Block, Susan, 288
Carroll, Madeleine, 49
Cartwright, Dorwin, 37
"category problems," 108, 112, 126, 127
  disjunctive, 128
Cecil, Lord David, 247, 268
Center for Cognitive Studies, 63–64, 84, 112, 122–126, 147, 150, 151, 160, 249, 252, 292
"c.g.s." (centimeters, grams and seconds), 107
Chauncey, Henry, 182
Chermayeff, Serge, 223
Cherniss, Harold, 111
Chicago Tribune, 42
childhood, views of, 4, 6, 19–20, 212, 227
children:
  development of, *see* developmental psychology
  early infancy of, 146–151, 166–167, 175, 270–271
  egocentrism of, 134, 138, 170

children *(cont'd)*
  mother's communication with, 166, 170–172
  play of, 20, 150, 169
Child's Talk (Bruner), 168
Chomsky, Noam, 25, 60, 121, 124, 125, 159–165, 168, 186, 255, 279
Christensen, Niels and Annelise, 287
Churcher, John, 270
Churchill, Sir Winston, 4, 120, 189
City College of New York, intellectual elite at, 77
Clark, Grenville, 231
Coblentz, Gaston, 50
cognition, cognitive development, 114–126
  defined, 115
  experiments with, 116–120
  meta-, 127, 129
  study of, 8–9, 28–29, 60, 61, 63–64, 87, 97, 107, 150
"cognitive revolution," 115, 130, 140, 183, 274, 280
Cohen, Jonathan, 166, 270
Cole, Michael, 196
Collins, Carvel, 70, 76
"common sense," 94
Comte, Auguste, 188
Conant, James Bryant, 38, 43, 244–246, 247
"concept attainment," 108
Concept of Mind (Ryle), 253
conditioned reflexes, 144
Conrad, Joseph, 6
consciousness, 201–217
  definitions of, 201–202
  mind vs., 201
  purpose of, 215
  theories of, 202–204
"conservation" tasks, 141
Constable, John, 89
Contemporary Psychology, 122
Cooley, Charles, 227
Coolidge, Calvin, 13
Cox, Gardner, 245
Cox, Oscar, 43
"creationists," 194
Cremin, Lawrence, 186
Cronbach, Lee, 182
Crook, John, 235–236
Cszenstokowa, Poland, 10
cultural anthropology, *see* anthropology
Cunningham, Bert, 132
curriculum reform movement, 179–198

Daniel, Phil, 203
Darwin, Charles, 177

Daudet, Alphonse, 253
Davidson, Gerry, 203
Davies, John, 151
Davis, Elmer, 50
Day, Anna, 195
Death and the Lover (Hesse), 6, 209
Death in the Afternoon (Hemingway),
     108
Deceit, Desire, and the Novel (Girard),
     204
De Gaulle, Charles, 42, 46
Demon, 19, 173
Descartes, René, 7, 58, 107
developmental psychology, 61, 131–152
     anthropology vs., 133, 134–136, 138,
          146
     Piaget on, 133–134, 141, 163, 169,
          170, 181, 183
DeVore, Irven, 190
Dewey, John, 146, 173, 184, 227, 278
Dickey, John, 43
Dilthey, Wilhelm, 35
disjunctive categories, 128
"displacement," 6
"dissonance theory," 114–115
Donaldson, Margaret, 287
Donders, Frans Cornelis, 107–108
Don Quixote (Cervantes), 209
Dore, John, 164
Dos Passos, John, 108, 209
Doty, Paul, 250
Dow, Peter, 191–195
Duke, James Buchanan, 25, 26
Duke University, 243
     Psychology Department at, 24–25, 26
     student life at, 22–30
Dummett, Michael, 255, 270
Duncan, Raymond, 39
Dunston, Irv, 29
Dürer, Albrecht, 12–13, 111
Durkheim, Émile, 188

Eames, Charles, 195, 198
Ebbinghaus, Hermann, 97–98, 101, 109
Eberhart, Richard, 283
Edgerton, Harold, 78
education, 178–198
     curriculum reform movement in,
          179–198
     defined, 178
     object of, 185
     theories about, 25, 61, 146
Educational Services Incorporated
     (ESI), 188
egocentrism, 134, 138, 170
"ego trip," 228
Einstein, Albert, 67, 82, 111, 181

Eliot, T. S., 49, 206
Ellman, Dick, 261
Elting, I., 240–241
Eluard, Paul, 48
Emerson, Ralph Waldo, 253
empiricism, empirical psychology,
     58–59, 134, 135, 158, 161
Encounter, 77
Encyclopaedia Britannica, 9, 15, 16
Endicott House conference, 187–188
Erdelyi, Matthew, 68, 85n
Evans, Gareth, 270
Evans, Maurice, 71
evolution:
     "creationist" attack on, 194
     Darwinian vs. Lamarckian, 27,
          177–178
     study of, 3
Exonian, 239–240
Experimental Psychology (Woodworth),
     106
experiments, 112, 116–120, 127, 145,
     155, 169
     with animals, 24–25, 28–29, 59, 87,
          99–100, 101, 128, 132
     with cognition, 116–120
     with infants, 148–149, 166–167
     with perception, 69–70, 75, 85–86,
          87, 93, 99–100, 101, 145, 148–149,
          203
Expulsion from the Garden, The
     (Dürer), 13
extravagance, as personality trait, 219,
     226
eye-to-eye contact, 170

Faraday, Michael, 202
Farrell, James, 108, 209
Faulkner, William, 70, 108
Fechner, Gustav Theodor, 68–69
Feldman, Carol Fleisher, 164
Feldmesser, Bob, 188, 189
Festinger, Leon, 114–115
Fillmore, Charles, 164
First Language, A (Brown), 164
Fischer, John, 182
Fisher, Sir Henry, 263–264
FitzGerald, Frances, 189
Fitzgerald, F. Scott, 209
Flanner, Janet, 50
"focusing," 117
Foot, Paul, 225–226
Ford, Henry, 39
Foreign Broadcast Monitoring Service,
     39, 41
formats of communication, 171–173
Fortes, Meyer, 133, 235

Fortune, 184
Fourier, Jean, 73
Franco, Francisco, 226
Frege, Gottlob, 119
"frequency argument," 82–87, 97–98
Freud, Sigmund, 7, 8, 26, 35, 59, 67, 79, 105, 114, 201, 213–214, 227, 290
  on child development, 133–134
  on logic, 112
Friedman, Francis, 178, 180–182, 186
Friedrich, C. J., 246
Future of an Illusion, The (Freud), 112

Galambos, Bob, 99
Galantière, Lewis, 47, 50
Galli-Curci, Amelita, 12
Gallie, Bryce, 46
Garbo, Greta, 23
Gardner, Howard, 288
Gardner, John, 122–123, 126, 286
Gardner, Martin, 208
"gating," 99–100
Geisteswissenschaft, 35, 36
General Education in a Free Society (Conant), 245
Gerard, Ralph, 182
Gesell, Arnold, 133
Gestalt psychology, 24, 30, 59, 70–71, 87, 106
Gibson, Christine, 231
Gibson, James and Eleanor, 238
Gide, André, 6
Gielgud, John, 71
Gilmore, Myron, 220
Girard, René, 204–205, 209
Gladstone, William Ewart, 202
Glass, Bentley, 182
Gleason, Andrew, 221
Goethe, Johann Wolfgang von, 8, 73, 230
Goffman, Erving, 164, 227, 235
Goldstein, Kurt, 33
Gombrich, Ernst, 89–90, 223
Goodman, Cecile, 69–70
Goodman, Nelson, 90, 124, 125, 203
Goodman, Paul, 184
Goodnow, Jacqueline, 60, 115, 120, 121, 127, 128, 140
Gopnik, Alison, 271
Grant-Duff, Sheila, 239
Gray, Jeffrey, 264
Great Gatsby, The (Fitzgerald), 5, 209
Greenfield, Patricia, 143, 164, 288
Gregory, Richard, 101
Groen, Guy, 60
Gruber, Howard, 114

Guérard, Albert, 5–6, 46, 48, 76, 283
Guillaume, Paul, 49

Habermas, Jurgen, 174, 255
habit, theories about, 83
Haire, Mason, 37
Halliburton, Richard, 18
Hamlet (Shakespeare), 71, 94, 240
Hampshire, Stuart, 203, 247, 254, 255, 270
Handbook of Experimental Psychology (Stevens), 106–107
Handel, George Frederick, 23
Hanfmann, Eugenia, 139
Harding, Warren G., 13
Hardy, Henry, 259
Hardy, Thomas, 6, 234
Harper's, 146
Harré, Rom, 166, 172, 227, 270
Harris, Roy, 261
Hart, Herbert, 166, 247, 271
Hart, Jennifer, 247
"Harvard chair," 148
Harvard Educational Review, 47
Harvard Today, 251
Harvard University, 243–254
  General Education at, 245
  Oxford vs., 255, 268–270
  Philosophy Department at, 129
  protests at, 228, 249–251
  Psychology Department at, 33–38, 63, 72–73, 237
  student life at, 32–38, 72–73, 106
Hawkes, John, 283
Hawthorne, Nathaniel, 253
Hawthorne, Will, 222
Hayter, William, 262
Head Start, 151, 152
Hearst, William Randolph, 12
Heath, Edward, 259, 267
Hebb, Donald, 103
Heider, Fritz, 94, 114–115
Heisenberg, Werner, 108
Held, Richard, 100–101, 150
Helmholtz, Hermann von, 38, 58, 82
Hemingway, Ernest, 108
Henning, Frank, 218–219, 229, 236
Herald Tribune, 184
Hernández-Péon, R., 99–100
Hero with a Thousand Faces, The (Campbell), 207
Herrnstein, Richard, 128
Hershey, Lewis Blaine, 42–43
Hesburgh, Ted, 186
Hesse, Herman, 6, 18, 209
heuristic purposivism, 109–110
Hilgard, Ernest R., 111, 238

History of Philosophy (Russell), 56
Hitler, Adolf, 6, 19, 23, 27, 38, 40
Hofstadter, Richard, 196
Homans, George, 220, 225
Homo Ludens (Huizinga), 202
Hopkins, Gerard Manley, 232
Houdini, Harry, 12
Hovland, Carl, 114
Howard, Cecil, 46
Hubel, David, 88
Huis Clos (Sartre), 228
Huizinga, Johan, 202, 216
Hull, Clark, 32, 109
Hume, David, 38, 58, 92, 107, 147, 270
Hurvich, Leo, 39
Huxley, Aldous, 26, 48, 108
Hylan, John, 12
hypotheses, formulation of, 95–96, 128,
    140, 149, 160

Icarus myth, 35
"identification," 20, 227
Ile de Bréhat, liberation of, 46
Illich, Ivan, 196
immaturity, functions of, 19
industrial psychology, 68
Inhelder, Bärbel, 124, 125, 142–143,
    181, 182, 183, 287
Institute for Advanced Study, 95,
    110–111
International Congress of Psychology,
    20
Intruder in the Dust (Faulkner), 70
Ivanov-Smolensky, Anatoliy, 145

Jacobson, Lenny, 17, 218
Jahoda, Maria, 133
Jakobson, Roman, 124, 125, 146,
    162–163, 192, 232–234, 291
James, Henry, 31, 35, 77, 253
James, William, 31, 77, 113, 227, 249,
    278, 280, 288
James, William, Lectures, 33, 165, 223
James-Lange theory, 14
Janáček, Leoš, 127
Jay, Peter, 268
Jews, Judaism:
    identity of, 7, 10, 20, 111
    intellectual tradition of, 77
    in Poland, 10, 11
    prejudice against, 23
    Reform vs. Orthodox, 13
    skepticism of, 7
    at universities, 243–244
John Birch Society, 194, 197
Johnson, Lady Bird, 152
Johnson, Lyndon Baines, 187

Jones, Ernest, 213, 240
Jones, Howard Mumford, 246
Jones, Ned, 93–94, 265, 288
Jones, Richard, 190
Joyce, James, 71, 205, 208
Judas Eye, 79–86, 94, 101, 103, 277
Judge Baker Guidance Center, 140
Jung, Carl, 6, 35, 79, 213

Kafka, Franz, 68, 208
Kagan, Jerry, 150, 175
Kahneman, Dan, 84–85, 125
Kalnins, Ilze, 148, 151
Kane, Keith, 250
Kant, Immanuel, 58–59
Kantorowicz, Eka, 111, 263
Kaye, Kenneth, 288
Kaysen, Annette, 192
Kaysen, Carl, 223, 238
Kazin, Alfred, 223, 244
Kennan, George, 210, 211, 247
Kennedy, John F., 184, 186, 187, 224,
    258
Kennedy, Robert Woods, 123
Kenny, Tony, 270
Kenyon, Megan, 272
Keppel, Frank, 186
Kermode, Frank, 159
"kernel sentences," 161–162
Kerr, Clark, 251
Kilcupp, Cory, 32
Killian, Jim, 179, 222, 239
Klein, George, 86
Kluckhohn, Clyde, 63, 77, 134–136,
    210, 212
Koffka, Kurt, 30, 70–71
Köhler, Wolfgang, 33, 44, 87, 105–106,
    238
Krech, David (I. Krechevsky), 27, 86,
    87, 95, 109
Kroeber, Alfred, 77, 135–136
Kuhn, Tom, 85
Kulpe, Oswald, 91, 107

Lamarck, Jean, 27, 177–178
Lambert, Gerard, 43
Lambo, Tom, 267
Land, Edwin, 222
language:
    acquisition of, 150, 164–174
    "performative" in, 165
    "pragmatics" of, 164–165, 168
    role of, 175–176
    study of, 8–9, 25, 61, 144–145,
        157–174, 206
    transformational approach to,
        161–162

Language Acquisition Device (LAD),
  Language Acquisition Support
  System (LASS), 25, 163–164, 168,
  173
Lashley, Karl S., 31, 33
Lasswell, Harold, 63
Last Puritan, The (Santayana), 31, 209
Last Year at Marienbad (film), 192
Laugier, Henri, 51, 61–62
Lauritsen, Charley, 179
Law of Central Tendency, 70
Law of Effect, 109
Law of Emphasis, 109
Lawrence, D. H., 178
Lazarsfeld, Paul, 133
Lazarus, Dick, 81
learning:
  defined, 183
  theories of, 27, 36, 60, 67–68, 87, 98,
    105, 109–110, 159, 182, 276
  see also education
"learning blocks," 140
Leibnitz, Gottfried Wilhelm, 58, 92,
  152
Leighton, Alexander, 135
Lenneberg, Eric, 231
Leontief, Wassily, 223, 225
Leslie, Alan, 270–271
Levelt, W. J. M., 125, 174
Leviathan, 12
Lévi-Strauss, Claude, 131, 136, 138,
  186, 233
Levy, David, 111, 238
Lewin, Kurt, 24, 33, 108
Lewis, C. S., 253
Lewis, Sinclair, 18
Lieven, Elena, 166
Light in August (Faulkner), 108
"light-years," 15
Likert, Rensis, 41–43
Linaza, José, 271–272
Lindbergh, Charles, 5
line of regard, 170
Lippmann, Walter, 223
Lipset, Seymour Martin, 250
literature:
  of 1932, *Zeitgeist* in, 108
  views on, 5–6, 13, 35, 48, 136, 159,
    204–205, 215, 232–235, 292
Lloyd-Jones, Hugh, 258
Lobachevsky, Nikolai, 26, 205
Locke, John, 38, 58, 92, 105, 253
logic:
  analytic vs. synthetic, 158–159
  Freud on, 112
"Logic Theory Machine, The" (Newell
  and Simon), 121

London Times, 151, 206, 213
Lonely Crowd, The (Riesman), 228, 235
Look, 49–50
"looking glass Self," 227
Lorente de No circuits, 103
Loti, Pierre, 25
Luria, Alexander Romanovich, 125,
  143–145, 185, 287
Lyons, John, 206

Maccoby, Mickey, 284
McCormick, Robert Rutherford, 42
McCulloch, Tom, 28
McDougall, William, 8, 24, 27, 31, 59,
  94, 160, 177–178
McGhee, Brian, 255
Mach, Ernst, 67, 133
Mackworth, Norman, 103
McMurrin, Sterling, 186
McShane, John, 235
"Magic Number Seven ± 2, The"
  (Miller), 97, 276
Malinowski, Bronislaw, 26
Mallory, George Leigh, 7, 216
Malraux, André, 48
"Man: A Course of Study," 192–197,
  240, 284
Mandate from the People (Bruner), 45
Manet, Édouard, 67, 90
Marquis, Donald, 210
Marshall, Drew, 147
Martin, Leslie, 166–167
Marx, Karl, 3
Marxism, 29–30, 38, 137, 144–145
Maskelyne, Nevil, 107
Masters, The (Snow), 262
Matthiessen, F. O., 244, 268
Maud, John, 246
Max Planck "Study Group" of
  Psycholinguistics, 174–176
Mead, George Herbert, 227–228
Mead, Margaret, 26, 63, 134–135
Meaning of Meaning, The (Richards),
  230
Medawar, Peter, 173
media:
  on infancy research, 150–151
  in 1920s, 12, 13
  wartime, 42, 49–50
Meehl, Paul, 238
Melancholia (Dürer), 111
Meltzoff, Andy, 271
Melville, Herman, 35
memory, study of, 97, 108–109
Meno (Plato), 181
"mental chronometry," 107
mentalism, 59–60, 67, 109, 126, 177

Merton, Robert, 234, 235
Merton, Thomas, 4
Messiah (Handel), 23–24
metacognition, 127, 129
Michaelis, Max, 45
Mill, John Stuart, 240
Millay, Edna St. Vincent, 18, 26
Miller, George, 64, 96, 97–99, 105,
    106–107, 111, 160–161, 163, 182,
    191, 238, 276
  at Center for Cognitive Studies,
    121–126
Miller, Perry, 46, 76, 244, 246, 268
Millikan, Max, 210, 220, 224
Milton, John, 25, 262
mind:
  concept of, 183
  consciousness vs., 201
  see also cognition, cognitive
    development; thinking
Mind, 255
"Mind, Mechanism, and Behavior"
    (Hull), 32
Mind, Self, and Society (G. H. Mead),
    228
Mishler, Anita, 195
Moby Dick (Melville), 35
molecules, motion of, 15
Monod, Jacques, 247
Morison, Ann, 239
Morison, Elting, 155, 188–189, 191,
    192, 210, 211–212, 219, 220, 222,
    224, 238–241, 251
Morrell, Lady Ottoline, 55–56
Morris, Charles, 281
Morris, Jan, 252
Motor Boating, 19
Moynihan, Daniel Patrick, 151
Mundy-Castle, Alistair, 150
Murdoch, Iris, 48, 256
Murdock, Kenneth, 246
Murphy, Gardner, 77
Murray, Henry, 33–36, 63, 91, 246
Muselier, Émile, 42
Musselman, Phyllis, 195

National Academy of Sciences, 62, 181
National Education Association, 184
National Science Foundation, 62, 180,
    194, 197–198
nativist psychology, 59–60, 160, 177
Naturwissenschaft, 36
Neckritz, Mr., 20
Neonatal Assessment Test, 147
Neumann, John Von, 60, 121, 128
New Look, 67–72, 75, 79–86, 90–95,
    103, 145, 237

"New Look at the New Look, A"
    (Erdelyi), 68, 85n
New School for Social Research, 273
newspapers:
  infancy research covered by, 151
  in 1920s, 12, 13
  wartime, 42
New Yorker, 4, 39
New York Sun, 12
New York Times, 13, 23, 151, 196
Nijmegen, Netherlands, research at,
    174–176
1919 (Dos Passos), 108
Ninio, Anat, 171
Nixon, Richard, 196
nous, 94
novels:
  of 1932, *Zeitgeist* in, 108
  views on, 5–6, 13, 35, 48, 136,
    234–235

objectivist psychology, 59–60, 68, 78
Office of Public Opinion Research, 43
Ogden, C. K., 230
Oliver, Douglas, 190
On Knowing: Essays for the Left Hand
    (Bruner), 204, 284
"On Liberty" (Mill), 240
"On Perceptual Readiness" (Bruner),
    101
"Ontogenesis of Speech Acts, The"
    (Bruner), 168
Oppenheimer, Robert, 44, 95, 110,
    120–121, 179, 223, 237–238
Orcutt, Miss, 15
"orienting reflex," 145
Osgood, Charles, 114
Oxford Book of Oxford, The (Morris),
    252–253
Oxford University, 247, 252–272
  Harvard vs., 255, 268–270
  students at, 270–272

Padel, Ruth, 259
Page, David, 183–184
Pais, Bram, 95, 111
Panofsky, Erwin, 111
Papousek, Hanus, 150
Paradise Lost (Milton), 25, 262
Park, Mungo, 188
Parsons, Talcott, 8, 46, 63, 87, 208
Patterson, Franklin, 191, 240
Patton, George S., 56
Paul, Randolph, 50
Pauli, Wolfgang, 61
Pavlov, Ivan Petrovich, 144–145, 161
Pea, Roy, 271

Pearse, A. S., 71
Pêcheur d'Islande (Loti), 25
Peirce, Charles Sanders, 46, 227, 232,
    233, 278, 281
perception, 65–104
    art and, 67, 72, 89–90, 202–203
    "central" vs. "ambient," 150
    "defense" vs. "vigilance" in, 80–81
    defined, 82
    experiments with, 69–70, 75, 85–86,
        87, 93, 99–100, 101, 145, 148–149,
        203
    "gating" of, 99–100
    New Look theory of, 67–72, 75,
        79–86, 90–95, 103, 145, 237
    "social," 91, 276
    of sound, 73–75, 99–100
    study of, 8, 25, 36, 38, 44, 57–58, 61,
        276–277
"Perfectibility of Intellect, The"
    (Bruner), 63, 196, 280
Perry, Ralph Barton, 38
Personal Impressions (Berlin), 256
Personality (Allport), 30, 35
"personality theory," 136, 228
Peter Pan (Barrie), 5
Peterson, Karen, 234, 235
Philosophical Investigations
    (Wittgenstein), 127, 129–130, 159
philosophy, psychology vs., 129–130
Philosophy of "As If," The (Vaihinger),
    44
physicalism, 59–60
Physical Sciences Study Committee,
    178
physics:
    defined, 183
    psychology vs., 95–96
    teaching of, 179–180
Piaget, Jean, 8, 60, 112, 125, 186, 204,
    238, 271
    Bruner and, 136–139, 142, 145–146
    on child development, 133–134, 141,
        163, 169, 170, 181, 183
Piel, Gerard, 197
Pierce, J. T., 210
Pieron, Henri, 49
Pines, Maya, 151
Placzek, Georg, 95
Plato, 134, 243, 292
play, 20, 150, 169
Ploog, Detlev, 174
"Poet and the Daydream, The"
    (Freud), 227
poetry, views on, 18, 26, 204, 232–233,
    292
Popper, Karl, 38, 56, 81, 139

*Portrait of the Artist as a Young Man,
    A* (Joyce), 32, 71, 136, 205, 208
positivism, 72, 165
Posner, Michael, 107, 126
Postman, Leo, 68, 75–81, 85, 88, 98,
    276
Potter, Molly, 103
"Poverty and Childhood" (Bruner), 196
Practical Criticism (Richards and
    Ogden), 230
Prentice, Bill, 37
prerecognition, "covaluant" vs.
    "contravaluant," 81
"President and the Children, The"
    (Bruner and Bronfenbrenner), 196
President's Science Advisory
    Committee, 146, 186
Pribam, Karl, 99
Principia Mathematica (Russell and
    Whitehead), 55, 121
Principles of Gestalt Psychology
    (Koffka), 30, 70–71
Principles of Reflexology (Bechterev),
    32
problem solving, study of, 105–106,
    129, 140, 144
Process of Education, The (Bruner),
    184–186, 284
Project TROY, 210, 219, 238, 251
psychoanalysis, theories of, 6, 79, 213,
    227
Psychological Bulletin, 140
Psychological Warfare Division of
    Supreme Headquarters Allied
    Expeditionary Force Europe
    (PWD-SHAEF), 45
psychology:
    academic origins of, 57–59, 68–69,
        91, 92, 97–98
    anthropology vs., 29, 59, 115, 133,
        134–136, 138, 146
    "applied," 102
    British approach to, 101–102, 264
    controversies in, 24–25, 28–29, 33–34,
        91–92, 122, 134, 227–228, 237
    "experimental," 36, 60
    experiments in, 24–25, 28–29, 59,
        69–70, 75, 85–86, 87, 93, 99–100,
        101, 112, 116–120, 127, 128, 145,
        148–149, 166–167, 203
    industrial, 68
    philosophy vs., 129–130
    physics vs., 95–96
    trends in, 60–64, 67–68, 101–102,
        106–110, 114–115
    see also specific schools and theories
psychophysics, 57–58, 68–69, 91, 92

puberty rituals, 5, 20
Purcell, Edward, 210, 221, 224
Purposive Behavior in Animals and Men (Tolman), 29, 108–109
purposivism, 109–110
Pusey, Nathan Marsh, 228, 247, 248, 249–252

Queen Christina, 23
Quinton, Tony, 255

Rabi, I. I., 179
Radcliffe-Brown, H. R., 110
Rapoport, David, 114
"reafference copies," 100–101
Reagan, Ronald, 194
Rees, Goronwy, 77
referents, 119
reflection (metacognition), 127, 129
Reich, Lee, 143
Relevance of Education, The (Bruner), 196
Remembering (Bartlett), 108–109, 157
Renoir, Pierre Auguste, 202–203
Republic (Plato), 292
Richards, I. A., 125, 230–232, 233, 234, 252, 283
Richards, Martin, 166
Riemann, Georg, 26, 205
Riesman, David, 228, 235
Riley, John, 46
Robbe-Grillet, Alain, 192
Roberta, 23
Roosevelt, Franklin Delano, 19, 40, 42, 43, 50, 268
Roosevelt, Theodore, 12, 187, 238
Rosch, Elly, 120
Rosenblith, Walter, 99
Rosenman, Samuel Irving, 43
Round Manhattan race, 19
Rubin, Edgar, 44
Russell, Lord Bertrand, 4, 55–56, 121, 206, 289
Ryan, Joanna, 166
Ryan, Maire Logan, 170
Ryle, Gilbert, 183, 203–204, 253, 254, 255–256

Sabatini, Raphael, 18
Sagan, Carl, 215
Saltmarsh, Dr., 235–236
Santayana, George, 31, 209
Sartre, Jean-Paul, 4, 48, 49, 228, 244
Saussure, Ferdinand de, 269
Scaife, Michael, 170, 271
Scheler, Max, 280
Schlesinger, Arthur, 246

Schoolmen, 94
Schorske, Carl, 208
Searle, John, 166
Second Signal System, 144–145, 161
Selbstbeobachtung, 92
selective attention, 145
self, concept of, 226–228
Semantics (Lyons), 206
sensationalist psychology, 58–60, 61
"sense datum" theory, 38
Seven Storey Mountain, The (Thomas Merton), 4
Shakespeare, William, 71, 292
Shaloru, Chief, 187–188
Shannon, Claude, 86, 96, 98, 113, 277
Shawnee, 39
Sheldon, Bill, 34
Shotter, John, 166
Shriver, Sargent, 151–152
Signs, Language, and Behavior (Morris), 281
Simon, Herbert, 60, 107, 114, 121
Skinner, B. F., 34, 68, 122, 157, 159
Skinner box, 128
Sloan Foundation, 272
Slobin, Dan, 231
Smithsonian Institution, 63, 280
"Smoke Gets in Your Eyes," 23
Snow, Catherine, 166
Snow, C. P., 247, 262
"socialization process," 19–20
social psychology, 115
Socrates, 181
Solberg, Admiral, 62
Solomon, Dick, 83, 84–85
Sorokin, Pitirim, 46, 63, 249
Sound and Meaning (Jakobson), 233
Sparrow, John, 247, 263
Spence, Kenneth, 27, 182
Spencer, Ted, 283
Spender, Stephen, 25, 283
Stein, Gertrude, 48–49
Stephenson, Hugh, 225–226
Stern, William, 132–133
Stevens, Smitty, 33–34, 73–75, 76, 106, 122
Stimson, Henry, 238, 239
Stoetzel, Jean, 47
Stouffer, Samuel, 63
Stout, G. F., 94
Strachey, Christopher, 247
Stranger, The (Camus), 209
Stratton, Julius "Jay," 222–223, 224, 239
Strawson, Peter, 166, 270
Structure of Appearance, The (Goodman), 90

Structure of Scientific Revolution (Kuhn), 85
Stuart, Logan, 195
Studies in Cognitive Growth (Bruner), 145–146, 161, 231
Study of Thinking, A (Bruner), 65, 115–122, 127–128, 140, 144, 146, 277–278, 284
Study of Values (Allport), 280
sucking reflex, 148–149, 151
Sun Also Rises, The (Hemingway), 39
Supper Club, 219–226, 238
syllogism studies, 106, 112
Syntactic Structures (Chomsky), 121, 159–160

tabula rasa, 92
Tajfel, Henri, 9, 287
Taylor, Charles, 255, 270
Teacher's Word Book (Thorndike and Lorge), 84–85
Teague, Olin, 197
Thatcher, Margaret, 267
Thematic Apperception Test, 35
thinking:
    analytic vs. synthetic, 158–159
    study of, 8, 25, 60, 61, 63–64, 105–108, 112–113, 126–128
    see also cognition, cognitive development
Thomas, D. M , 214
Thorndike, Edward Lee, 24–25, 33, 34, 84
Thought and Language (Vygotsky), 139
thresholds, study of, 78–79
Times Literary Supplement, 259, 265
Timon of Athens (Shakespeare), 292
Tinbergen, Niko, 71, 167–168, 170, 257, 261, 271
Titchener, Edward, 91, 92
Tolman, Edward Chace, 29, 34, 43, 86–87, 91, 95, 105, 128, 202, 238
    purposivism of, 108–111, 149
Tolman, Richard, 43–44, 110, 236
Tolman, Ruth, 43–44, 110, 111, 236–238
Tractatus logico-philosophicus (Wittgenstein), 290
transformational grammar, 161–162
Treatise on the Theory of Sense Perception (Wundt), 92
Trevarthen, Colwyn, 125, 150
Trial, The (Kafka), 68, 208
Triesman, Ann, 264
Trilling, Diana, 285
Trilling, Lionel, 224, 234–235, 285
Truman, Harry, 211

Turquet, Pierre, 45–46
Tversky, Amos, 84–85, 125

Uexküll, Jakob Johann von, 71, 133
Umwelt, 71, 133
universities:
    Jews at, 243–244
    life at, 229–230, 242–273
    "locals" and, 235–236, 247
    see also specific universities
Unpopular Essays (Russell), 289

Vaihinger, Hans, 44
Valentino, Rudolph, 5
Varieties of Human Value (Morris), 281
Verbal Behavior (Skinner), 157, 159
Vercors (Jean Bruller), 227
Villiers, Peter de, 128
vis integretiva, 94
Voir, 49–50
Vonnegut, Kurt, 221
Vorstellung, 92
VTE (Vicarious Trial and Error), 28–29, 105, 202
Vygotsky, Lev Semyonovich, 60, 112, 136–137, 139–140, 141, 143, 145, 146, 158, 161, 181, 204, 216, 271

Wahrenhmung, 92
Wald, George, 78, 246
Wallach, Hans, 87
Wallas, Graham, 105, 113
Wanner, Eric, 288
War Information Office, 45, 47
Warnock, John and Mary, 247
Washburn, Sherwood, 190
Wason, Peter, 162, 287
Weaver, Warren, 86, 96, 113, 277
Webb, James, 210
Weber's Law, 57–58, 68–69
Wechsler, Jacqueline Grennan, 186
Weems, Elizabeth, 160, 284
Weisskopf, Victor, 221, 224
Weisskrantz, Larry, 252
Werner, Heinz, 75
Wertheimer, Max, 106, 113
Wester Till, 232, 285
White, Morton, 76, 191, 240
White, Robert, 33
Whitehead, Alfred North, 55, 121
White Hotel, The (Thomas), 214
Whiting, Johnny, 135
Whorf, Benjamin Lee, 82, 158–159, 163
Wiesel, Thorsten, 88
Wiesner, Jerry, 186
Wilde, Oscar, 262
Wilder, Thornton, 47

William James Lectures, 33, 165, 223
Williams, Shirley, 267
Wilson, Bright, 245, 246
Wilson, Harold, 259, 267
Witkin, Herman, 93
Wittgenstein, Ludwig, 127, 129–130, 159, 163, 206, 219, 223, 234, 269, 290, 293
Wolff, Robert Lee, 154, 210, 220–221, 223, 225
Wolfson, Sir Isaac, 258
women's movement, 151
Wood, David, 166, 171
Woods Hole conference, 182–184
World Three, 56, 139
World War II, 38–40, 42, 45–50
Wunderlich, Dieter, 174

Wundt, Wilhelm, 38, 69, 91, 92, 201
Würzburg School, 105

Yale Cross Cultural Index, 135
Yarbus, A. L., 145
Yeats, William Butler, 68, 204–205, 216, 288
Yerkes, Robert, 30, 31
Young Lonigan (Farrell), 108

Zacharias, Jerrold, 178–182, 188, 192
Zangwill, Oliver, 235, 287
Zeitgeist, 34, 66, 108, 124, 274
Zener, Karl, 24, 30
Zimmerman, Claire, 111
Zuckerman, Lord Solly, 257–258
Zuleika Dobson (Beerbohm), 223

Biog. 153 B   110682

Bruner, Jerome Seymour.

In search of mind

Biog. 153 B   110682

Bruner, Jerome Seymour.

In search of mind

DATE DUE	BORROWER'S NAME
11/1/94	J. Pitta
OCT 12 9	J. Pellegrino
10/28/96	P. Miranda